MW01625918

Numismatic Art in America

Numismatic Art in America

Aesthetics of the United States Coinage

2nd Edition

Cornelius Vermeule

www.whitmanbooks.com

Whitman Publishing, LLC
Atlanta, Georgia

Numismatic Art in America

www.whitmanbooks.com

3101 Clairmont Road · Suite C · Atlanta, GA 30329

Correspondence concerning this book may be directed to the publisher, Attn: Numismatic Art in America, at the address above.

ISBN: 07984822746
Printed in China

Disclaimer: Expert opinion should be sought in any significant numismatic purchase. This book is presented as an aesthetic study. No warranty or representation of any kind is made concerning the completeness of the information presented.

The covers of this book feature several classic designs from America's rich numismatic history.

About the cover: *Center:* The concept of the Libertas Americana medal was proposed by Benjamin Franklin while United States commissioner to France. To Franklin, the infant Hercules symbolized America, strangling two serpents representing the British armies at Saratoga and Yorktown. Minerva, with shield and spear, symbolized France in her role as America's ally, keeping the British lion at bay. *Left:* This gold coin features the Capped Bust portrait of Liberty, sometimes called the Turban Head, as used on some American coinage in the late 1700s and early 1800s. *Right:* The Buffalo design (actually an American bison)—one of the most popular in American coinage—was featured on the nickel five-cent piece from 1913 to 1938.

About the back cover: *Left:* In the Standing Liberty design (used on the quarter dollar from 1916 to 1930), the left arm of Miss Liberty is upraised, holding a shield in the attitude of protection. Her right hand bears the olive branch of peace. In 1917, with war raging in Europe, Liberty's exposed breast was covered with chain mail in another symbol of protection. *Center:* The Indian Head design used on gold $2.50 and $5 coins from 1908 to 1929 was a departure from all precedents in United States coinage. It features no raised edge, and the main elements and legends are incuse—sunk below the surface of the coin. *Right:* The copper-nickel Flying Eagle cent was the first small-sized coin of that denomination; older copper "large cents" were about 50% larger and more than twice as heavy. The Flying Eagle lasted from 1856 to 1858 before being replaced by the so-called Indian Head—actually Miss Liberty in an Indian headdress.

For a compete catalog of numismatic reference books, supplies, and storage products, visit Whitman Publishing online at www.whitmanbooks.com.

William Sumner Appleton
1840–1903

At enim quis noverit haec apte tempora distinguere?
—Eckhel, *Doctrina Numorum*, 1792

Contents

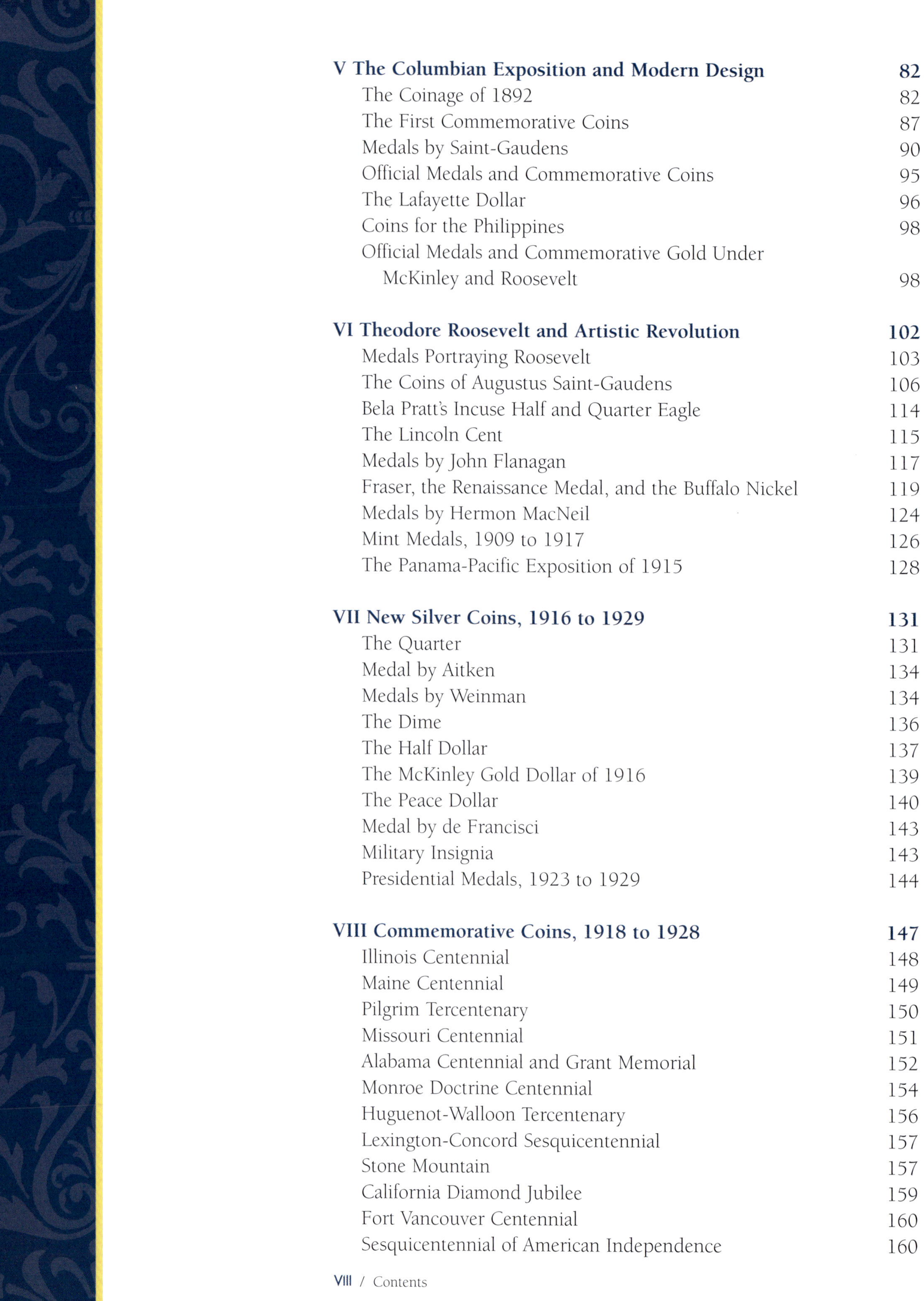

Illustrations

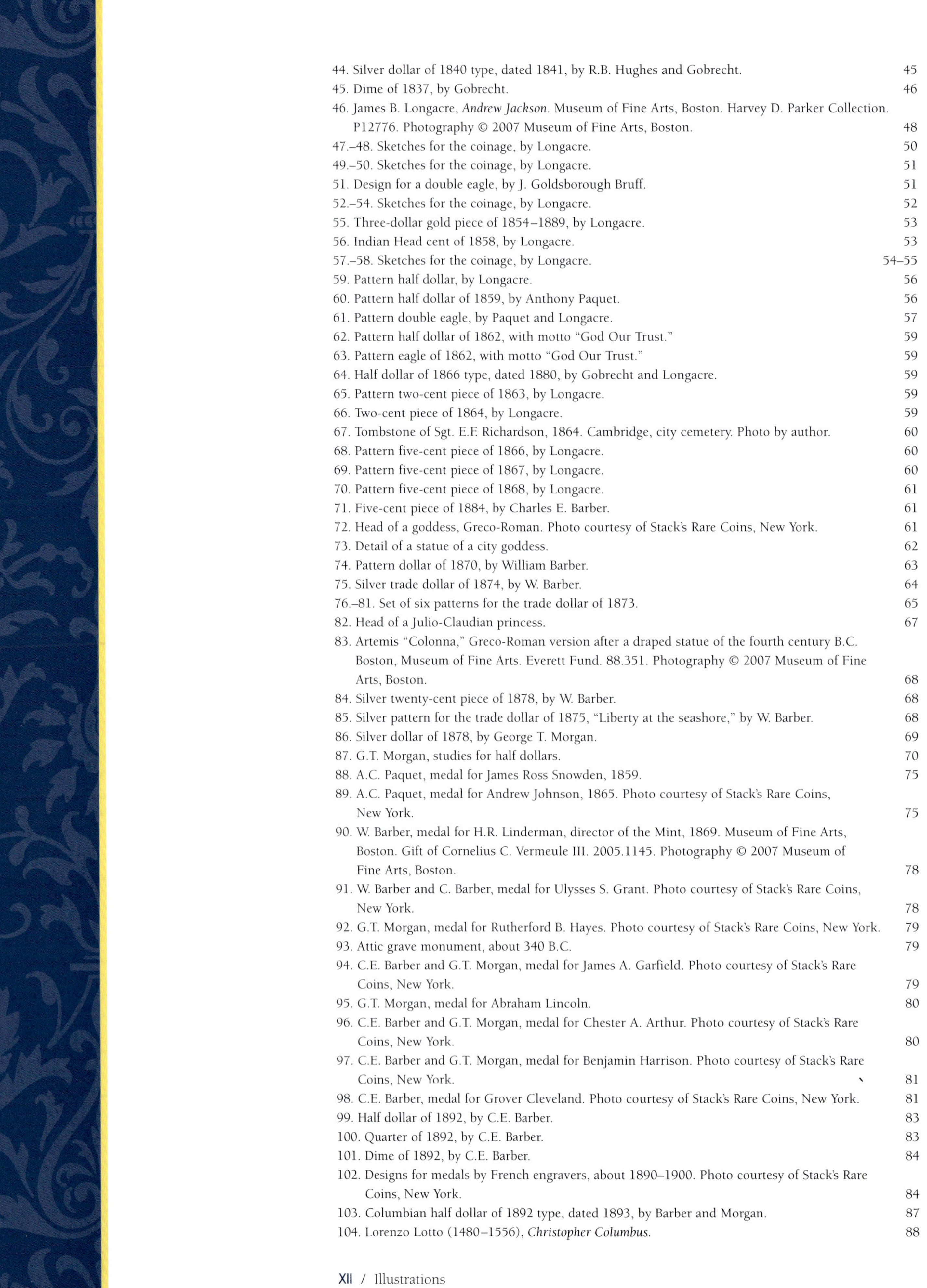

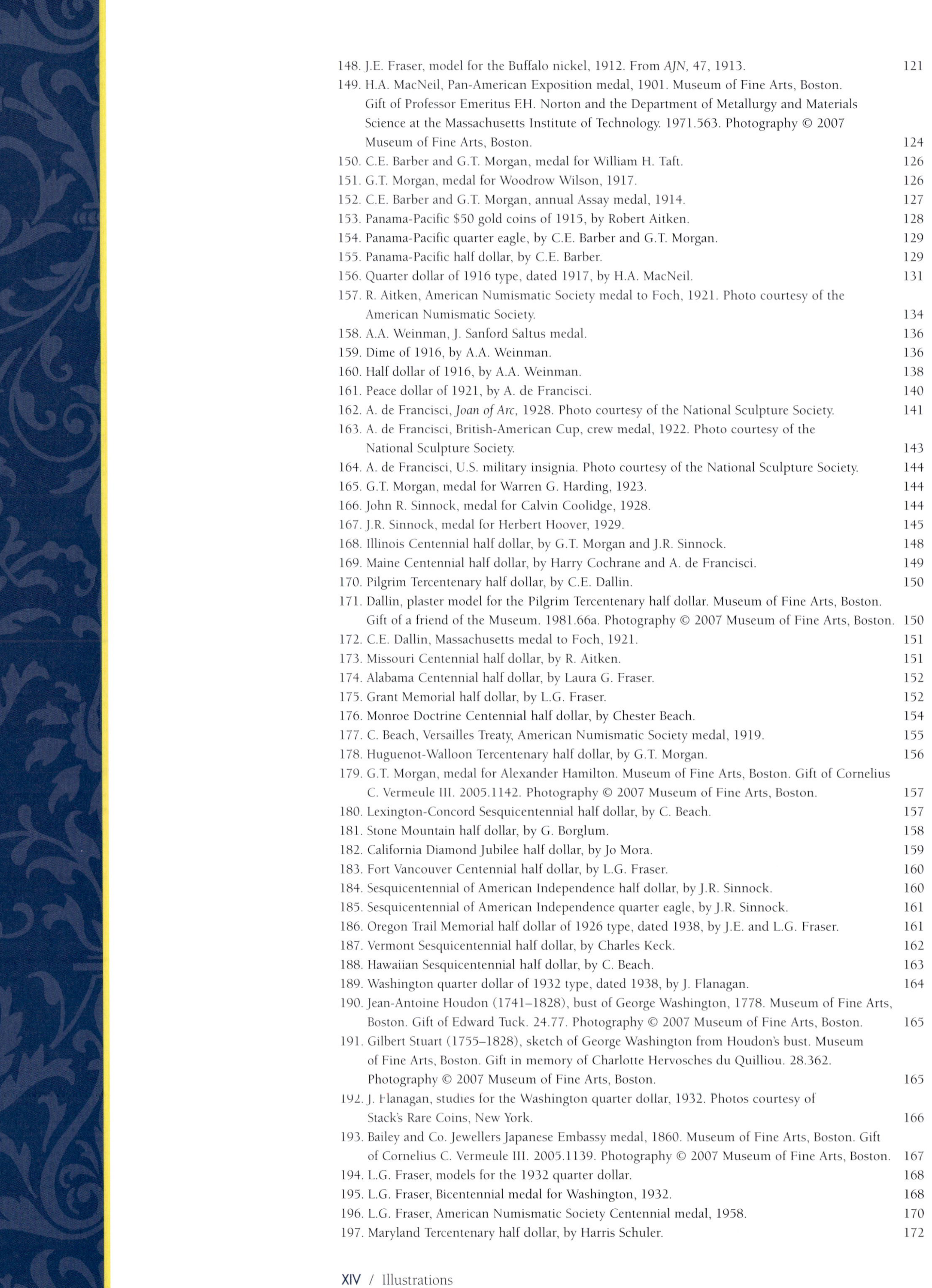

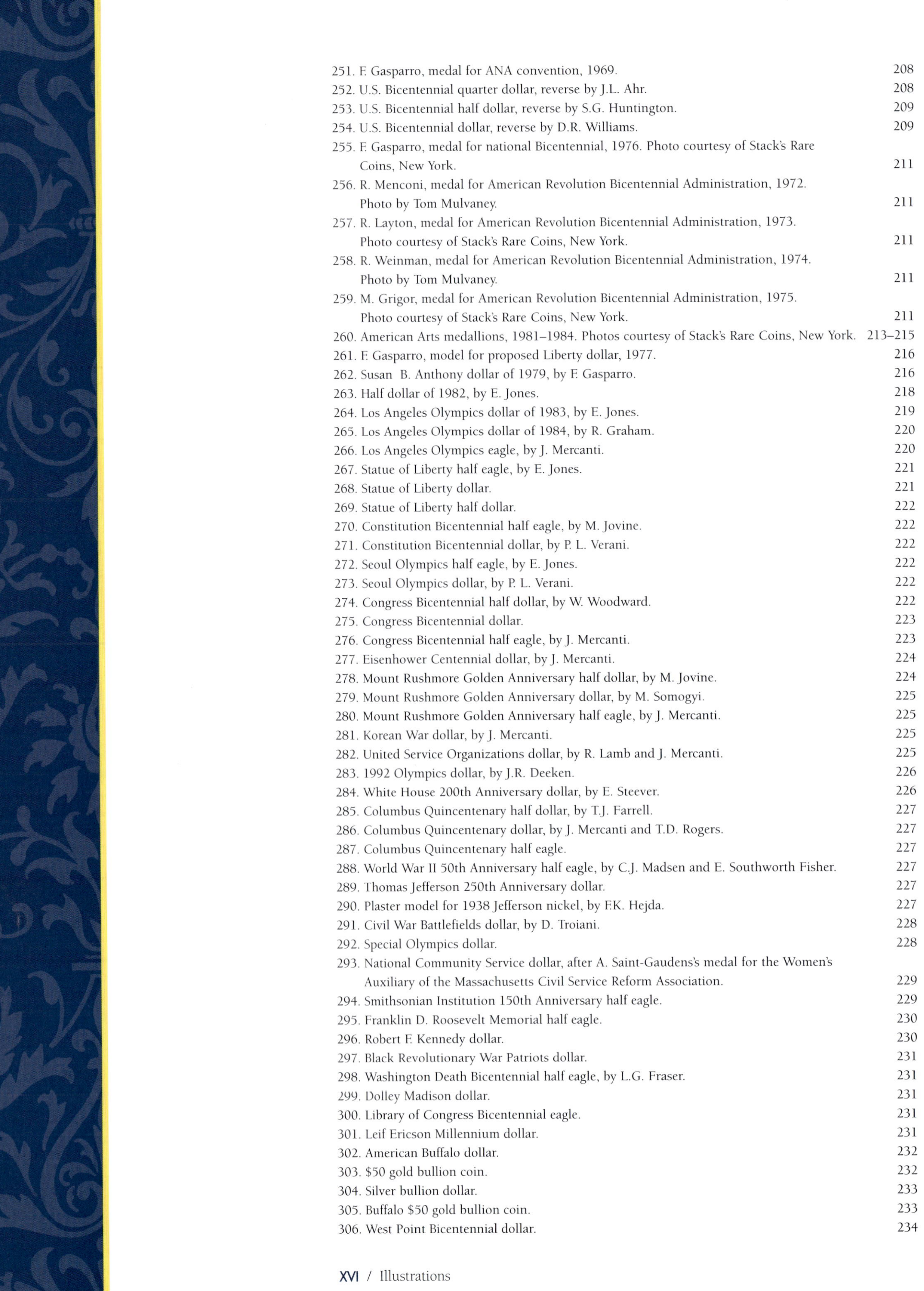

About the Author

Cornelius Vermeule started collecting coins as a boy in 1930s England. He entered Harvard in 1943 but then joined the Army, was sent to the Pacific Theater in World War II, and stayed in Japan after the war as a language expert, rising to the rank of captain. He finally earned his Harvard degree in 1947 and a Ph.D. from the University of London in 1953. He then embarked on an impressive academic and curatorial career. He was twice director of the Museum of Fine Arts, Boston, while serving as curator of classical art; was a lecturer in fine arts at Harvard University; and was professor of both fine arts and classics at Boston College for over 20 years. He authored and edited more than a dozen works on applied numismatics, archaeology, painting, sculpture, and other arts.

Preface

The U.S. coinage represents a great attempt, still in process, to provide democracy with instruments of visual beauty. Disparaging remarks have always been heard about American coins as works of art. This book was written partly to stay such criticisms and redress a balance. Many coins produced by the United States since 1792 rank among the greatest creations in the medallic medium. Coins are the one form of art to which every American is exposed at every moment. They are the only class of sculpture that a large segment of the population ever handles. Beauty does not take comfort in numbers, but knowledge that coins and related medals are a form of official, historical art designed to reach citizens in every epoch of U.S. affairs makes an aesthetic study worthwhile.

This book resulted from a series of lectures given under the auspices of the Lowell Institute in 1966, a seminar at Boston University in the spring of 1967, the Moritz Wormser Memorial Lecture at the American Numismatic Society in April 1967, and others over the years. A grant from the Penrose Fund of the American Philosophical Society and, later, a Guggenheim Fellowship supported research in its final stages. Many numismatists, curators, and professors have helped with advice, training, and photographs. Foremost among these have been the late Vladimir Clain-Stefanelli of the Smithsonian Institution and Harvey Stack of the famous New York firm that bears his family name. My colleagues in the Department of Classical Art at the Museum of Fine Arts, Boston, have been pillars of good sense. John McQuade, Herbert Hamilton, and their fellow photographers labored mightily over the illustrations for the original edition, and additional thanks are due to Jennifer Riley, Greg Heins, and Bob Krajewski for their contributions to this one. Maud Wilcox helped me in ways best understood by her admirers. The burdens of making the manuscript of the first edition literate fell to Ann Louis McLaughlin and to Mary Comstock, Keeper of Coins, whose numismatic forebears were friends of the Bostonian humanist to whom the book is dedicated. For the second edition, in addition to David Alexander, editorial reviewers included Q. David Bowers, Roger Burdette, and Larry Stack. My gratitude is measureless to Patrick McMahon for all of his editorial additions, corrections, and good counsel for this edition.

Cornelius Vermeule
Coolidge Hill, Massachusetts

Numismatic Art in America

Introduction

To the uninitiated a series seemingly devoid of aesthetic merits, on closer study U.S. coins turn out to be perhaps the richest, most varied coinage any nation has issued since the American and French revolutions. Germany is of course an exception, because until 1871 the nation was a collection of separate kingdoms and principalities, and these polities continued their own coinage in one form or another until 1918. Despite the number of colorful rulers and great events connected with her modern history, Great Britain only began creating an artistic coinage well into the reign of Queen Elizabeth II. With the exception of Benedetto Pistrucci's innovative designs for the aged King George III in 1816 to 1818 and some of the early, Gothic issues of Queen Victoria, the vaunted and highly skilled British die engravers behaved all too predictably. It was only with the George V Jubilee crown of 1935 that British artists began to have opportunities to produce sets of Proof coins and commemorative crowns with more imaginative designs. These reached an unfortunate low with the ghastly Winston Churchill memorial crown in 1965, but in more recent years some outstanding portraits and commemorative themes have graced not only British coinage but the issues of such Commonwealth countries as Australia, New Zealand, and smaller territories such as Bermuda and the Bahamas. France in modern times has relied on the revival of traditional designs of the 1800s and even the 1790s. The adoption of the uniform-reverse euro coins of the European Union has further restricted scope for creativity.

American coins have always been loved, longer and with greater emotion than any other modern series. Patriotism and inquiring minds in the young republic led to collecting by dates at a time when anywhere else such pursuits were deemed ludicrous. Ever since the famous Philadelphia pioneer collector Joseph Mickley tried to find a cent of the year of his birth, 1799, and thus quickly realized that a certain date in a series could be extremely rare, Americans have been scrutinizing, classifying, assembling, and publishing their major and minor coins and the deviations therefrom, such as the varied pattern series. To a great extent this enthusiasm was responsible for the first rich series of commemorative coins. The agitation for medals prepared by the government's designers and sculptors is a side product of this enthusiasm. The artistic level of U.S. coins has been varied, but no new issue has appeared since 1793 that was not greeted with articulate popular criticism sitting as judge on the results. These results form a vital calculation in the sum of art in America.

American coins have sometimes been close to and at other times far from the mainstream of American art. At present, the only minor arts that parallel our coins are the medals produced by the U.S. Mint or by private manufacturers. The similarities or relationships in the major art media are confined to a few generally inferior war memorials or ornaments for government centers. Thus, the plaques and national seals displayed in the foyer of the John F. Kennedy government building in Boston are on the same artistic level as the inaugural medals and half dollar reverse designed in 1961 to 1964. Such was not the case when the first U.S. coins appeared. Their creators partook joyously of the iconography of the infant nation, with the same excitement expressed by major decorators of talent, and on the same level. The Sully-Gobrecht Liberty Seated and the Peale-Gobrecht Flying Eagle were creations of major artists working with a gifted die engraver that found their way forthwith into the repertory of patterns and coins.

The extensive Liberty Seated, "Liberty at the seashore," and "defiant eagle" class of patterns by the three Englishmen at the Philadelphia Mint—William Barber, his son Charles, and George T. Morgan—kept the American coinage in step with the art of patriotic festivals and major expositions in the decades after the Civil War. The upheavals generated by Theodore Roosevelt, Augustus Saint-Gaudens, and the latter's medalist students gave the United States one brilliant series of coins that from cent to $50 gold piece had no artistic peers on the face of the earth. These guided efforts in stimulating design carried over into the classic series of commemorative half dollars and thus continued through the 1930s.

The official designers at the Mint, Charles E. Barber and George T. Morgan, came in for considerable outside criticism in the 1900s because their medals were allegedly commercial and conservative artistically. Yet history will surely judge these men masters of design and technique. Their art was different from that of Saint-Gaudens, James Earle Fraser, or Adolph A. Weinman, but they evolved their own formulas of expression that reflected the best in American national art on the loftiest levels of craftsmanship. Their patterns and their sketches reveal a lifetime, two lifetimes, spent thinking how to use the purposes of U.S. coins and reveal the repertory of governmental medals in the fullest degree within the iconographic and technical frameworks fashioned by our national polity. John R. Sinnock carried something of their genius down to the end of the Second World War, but these national crafts and their attendant ideas were by the 1960s strongly in need of stimulus such as that provided by Theodore Roosevelt and the men around him.

The art of U.S. coinage continually has been sacrificed to economic and political pressures little related to efforts at creating a worthy metallic monetary series. For years the silver lobby and its opponents turned on or off the flow of coins, particularly silver dollars. The elimination of the gold standard meant that no coins, even of commemorative nature, appeared in this attractive metal between 1933 and 1984. The political pressures that eliminated commemorative coinage between 1954 and 1982 impoverished the nation's coinage art immeasurably. The century-old law that seems to mandate the appearance of an eagle on all reverses of the highest silver or copper-nickel clad denominations has cramped the autonomy of our designers.

Yet the law that limits changes in circulating coin designs to every 25 years has been cast aside whenever a crisis such as a president's assassination dictates. In addition, insistence on formulaic mottos such as "Liberty," "E Pluribus Unum," and "In God We Trust"—is another persistent obstacle to truly original design, as difficult now as in 1907. In times of stress in earlier eras, American free enterprise was always able to provide private coinage substitutes such as merchants' tokens to supplement scarce national issues. Such issues ended, however, with the Civil War and its aftermath. By the mid-20th century, coinage design had become the subject of much conversation, but the rigid requirements of the machine age allowed less and less variation from the limited roster of circulating coins and less latitude for artistic imagination.

When the first edition of this book appeared, American coinage seemed immobilized in an unyielding web of unvarying monotony. After 1970, as we shall see, the appearance of the Eisenhower dollar, the creation of Bicentennial coinage, the emergence of the American Arts gold medallions, and the startling and wholly unexpected rebirth of commemorative coinage restored unlimited opportunity for creativity after a dry spell that had lasted for decades. How American coinage has responded to this unexpected opportunity is still being revealed!

1

Background of the Federal Coinage

Coins of the United States have long cried for study as works of art. No series, ancient or modern, has been so minutely investigated for die varieties, number of coins issued, condition of surviving specimens, or potential as investments rather than objects of numismatic science or mere hobbyism. Scholars of Greek, Roman, and early medieval coins have traditionally looked down upon those who study modern coins, and no group has less been regarded as scientific than those who have investigated the coins struck by the U.S. government since 1792. The pendulum has swung during recent years and students of U.S. coins are now achieving the recognition they deserve. With this awakening, or perhaps revival, of interest and appreciation of critical standards an aesthetic evaluation of America's federal coinage can be made.

Many persons, including numismatists who specialize in other areas or ages, regard the U.S. series as devoid of artistic interest. Nothing could be further from the truth. One reason this misconception has persisted is that the federal coinage was long dominated by the ideal form of the abstract concept (or "Virtue") Liberty on the obverse and the varyingly naturalistic substance of an eagle on the reverse. But, although the types of American coins seemed to change too seldom, not being affected by external matters such as the death of a ruler, there was always such a wide variety of denominations in all metals as to preclude monotony in the series as a whole. Coins from 1793 through 1836 manifest all the symptoms of a young republic striving to find its iconographic and artistic identity, and, therefore, have always been objects of charm and, at worst, primitive beauty. The neoclassic designs instituted in the years following 1836 gave U.S. coins a dignity and originality worthy of any struck pieces in any age. It is only unfortunate that a mediocre version of these types persisted for too long—more than 50 years—until the eve of the World's Columbian Exposition of 1892. Part of the reason for this was no doubt that the nation was torn apart by civil war from 1861 to 1865.

The artistic upheaval that began in 1892 led to one of the most beautiful regular coinages ever conceived, but it did not become effective until the decade from 1906 to 1916. Those who claim to find the U.S. series dull forget the commemorative coins in gold and silver. They continued the tradition, begun with Augustus Saint-Gaudens and Bela Lyon Pratt in 1907, of entrusting models for obverses and reverses to leading sculptors of the age. They offer every variety of subject that any nation or its sovereign components could devise for a coinage. National and local history, from colonial times to the completion of the Bay Bridge across San Francisco harbor in 1936, marches across the planchets of coinage ranging in value from the $50 gold pieces of 1915 to the magnificent range of half dollars that were interrupted for 28 years by a peevish group of congressmen in 1954. Although commemorative coinage unexpectedly revived in 1982, many U.S. commemorative coins still could be characterized as feeble efforts at works of art. Nonetheless, the classic commemoratives of 1892 to 1954 and the modern series launched in 1982 contain enough stunning masterpieces to make the series as a whole unrivaled in aesthetic richness among modern coinages of the world.

American Mint officials and the artists in their employ strove from the tentative beginnings in a rented house in Philadelphia in 1792 to create a coinage of quality in design and content. Despite long runs of the same type in a single denomination, there was hardly ever a time when the coins were not being altered slightly, refined in various minor ways. A nation rich in precious metals after the westward migrations between 1815 and 1860, the United States could afford a large, diverse coinage from several mints at the same time. Wars increased rather than curtailed issues ranging in size from the $20 gold piece down to the half cent. Particularly in the Golden West, private coinages circulated alongside those of the government, and the stresses of the Civil War called forth a minor coinage of tradesmen's tokens of more than passing interest and artistic imagination.

All this should convince even the most passive critic that an aesthetic investigation of U.S. coins can yield fascinating conclusions not only about the coins themselves but about other arts, major and minor, in the various decades when these coins were struck and circulated. An aesthetic view of U.S. coinage would be incomplete without a study of the medals prepared over the years by engravers at the Mint, the medallic creations of famous sculptors commissioned to design coins, and major statues or reliefs in marble and bronze that relate to compositions and styles of the regular coins. In every era of American history there have also been paintings, drawings, and engravings—including the paper currency—or photographs that influenced numismatic art in America. The grand allegories of Benjamin West at one extreme and a photograph of a bear in a California zoo at the other end of the spectrum have worked their messages into die design.

Artistic Background

A nation fashioned as was the United States needed a coinage as different from the immediate past as the ideals of sovereignty and forms of government with which the country first developed. At the same time, a century and a half of colonial rule could not be wiped from memory by legislative acts, and the tradition that allowed individual colonies or states to import or strike coins could not be cast aside until a federal coinage was instituted. Since so many British, Spanish, French, and other coinages circulated throughout the new nation, there were many technical and artistic examples at hand to show what the federal coinage could be. It is to the credit of the Revolutionary leaders that, from the beginning, they sought designs and styles for the coinage that would be original and expressive of the nation's intellectual aspirations. Ten years were necessary, from 1782 to 1792, to bring a true federal coinage into being. The founding fathers thought and wrote extensively about the symbolism involved in the designs, and they were able to reject nearly all visual reliance on the long-established coinages of major European nations. The problems of a new coinage were iconographic and aesthetic. As a result, sources for obverse and reverse compositions, from figures to lettering and secondary decoration, had to come from contemporary European and American art of all forms. This art could range from sculpture and painting to decorative engraving in miniature.

While institution of a coinage necessitated many tasks and choices for the leaders of the United States, monumental prototypes for the symbolism sought were everywhere available in the paintings of Americans who had mastered and, indeed, come to dominate British aristocratic circles on both sides of the Atlantic. In one such painting can be seen expressions of the quasi-official artistic atmosphere surrounding the instigators and artists of the new coinage.

In 1783 John Adams was in London as one of the American ministers engaged in signing the treaty resulting from America's success in six years of struggle with England. On this occasion he was painted by the Anglo-American portraitist John Singleton Copley, documents in hand and on the rich rug beyond his left hand a prophetic map of the new United States stretching out beyond the Atlantic Ocean in the direction of the future Louisiana Purchase (fig. 1). What concerns us here is not so much the plump little statesman in his sword and finery, or the geographic paraphernalia in front of him, but the classical symbolism that dominates the vista into the landscape at the upper left of the composition. The 13 colonies had been nurtured in material expressions from the Roman Republic, and Copley's contribution to the Peace of Utrecht was no exception. On a Roman cippus or altar stands Pax, holding out her branch of olive and putting her torch into a pile of arms and armor. The motif was a famous one, going back to coins of the emperor Domitian

1. John Adams, *after Copley*

late in the first century A.D., and popular in the complex visual symbolism of the Italian Renaissance.[1] Here the design and the figure of Pax are part of that Roman, neoclassic intellectual heritage adopted by the leaders of the young republic to express freedom, self-identity, and federation in artistic and iconographic terms. Out of this visual tradition the coinage of the United States was to be born in 1792.

Twenty years before John Adams stood to Copley, the Pennsylvania Quaker Benjamin West opened his studio as a portrait painter in London. By the time of his death in 1820, West had risen to become president of the Royal Academy and premier painter to the court of King George III. His fame was equal in Britain and in the land of his birth, three generations of Americans having visited large-scale replicas of his paintings on display in a palatial one-man museum in London. His works not only were studied and admired there but were widely circulated through engravings and catalogs. The canvas *Omnia Vincit Amor,* "Love Conquers

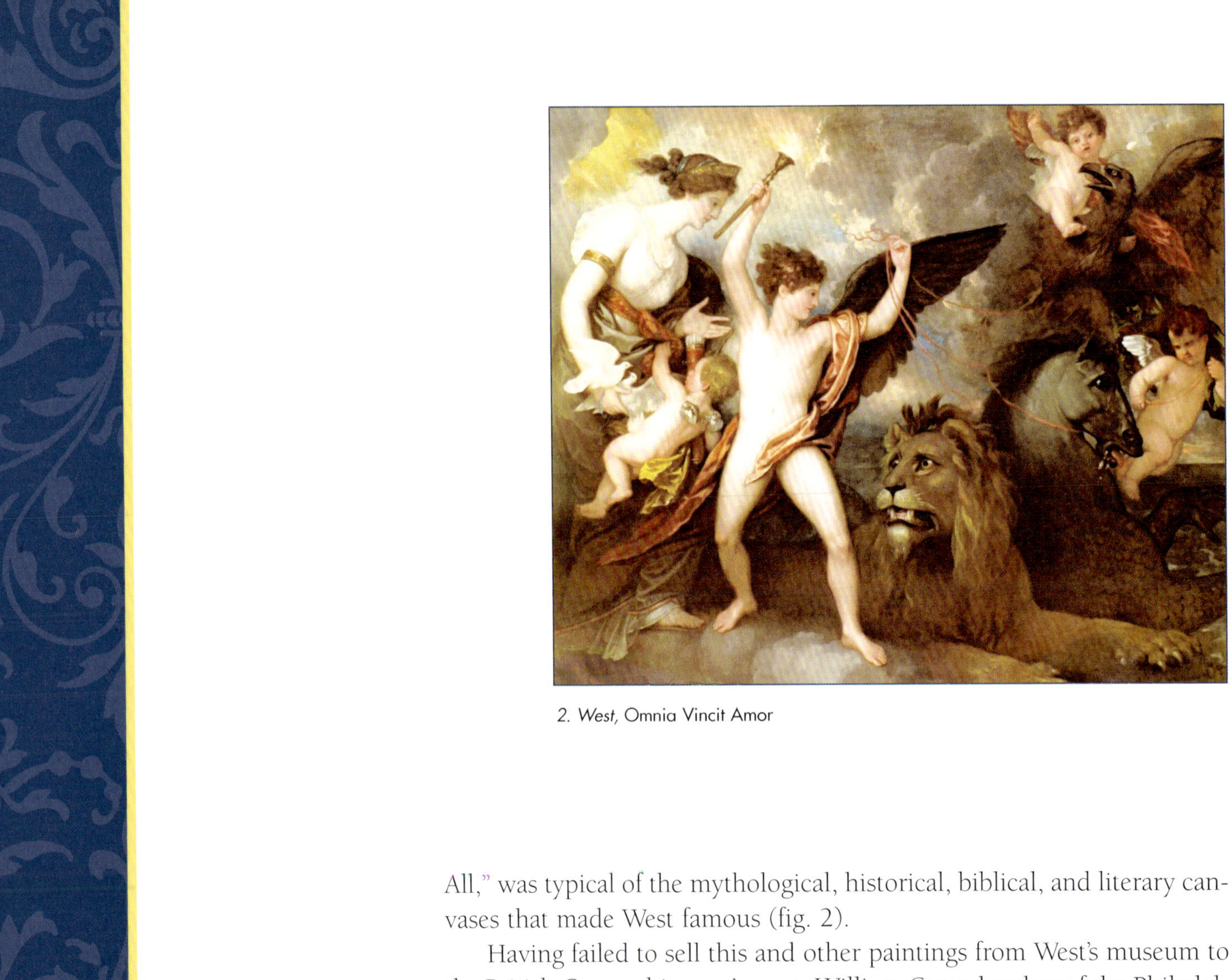

2. *West,* Omnia Vincit Amor

All," was typical of the mythological, historical, biblical, and literary canvases that made West famous (fig. 2).

Having failed to sell this and other paintings from West's museum to the British Crown, his sons' agent, William Carey, brother of the Philadelphia publisher and author Matthew Carey, drafted a letter proposing a massive sale to the U.S. government in 1826. The letter was read in the House of Representatives, and details of the collections were published as a government document, but no action was taken. The collection was gradually dispersed. *Omnia Vincit Amor* reached America in 1839 in the possession of Mr. and Mrs. Arthur Sequin, proprietors of an opera troupe celebrated in their day. The painting was on deposit in the Metropolitan Museum in New York from 1881 to 1923, when that institution purchased this and other paintings of West's legacy.

The theme "Love Conquers All" is obvious. A large, torch-bearing Cupid reins in a troika of lion, horse, and eagle, while lesser Amorini frolic about. Venus at the left amid her doves demands the attention of those studying the Roman and neoclassic origins of Liberty on U.S. coins. Her classic profile, her diademed brow, the golden beads binding her hair, and the bun behind enter the numismatic repertory with the large cent of 1816. Within another generation this aspect of divine Venus as beautiful Liberty was to dominate the obverses of a major segment of American coinage (figs. 39–41).

Benjamin West's eagle with head and open wings in a form of wide, flat profile will appear on the Liberty Head silver dollar of 1878, a design by

3. Eagles, Italian drawing

George T. Morgan that grew out of pattern pieces made by all the engravers at the Philadelphia Mint in the decade following the Civil War (fig. 86). In the other direction Benjamin West's eagle can be shown to derive from studies made by an anonymous Italian artist about 1525 or earlier, at the height of the Renaissance. Benjamin West owned a drawing attributed in his day and for perhaps 200 years before the American Revolution to Giulio Romano (1499–1546). That powerful and impressive decorator finished Raphael's frescoes in the Vatican and went on to decorate the palaces of Mantua. The drawing, now in a private collection in Boston, presents 17 incisive yet impressioned sketches of eagles in various poses (fig. 3). A number of these eagles of the age of Raphael and Michelangelo in Italy and the lands across the Alps turn up on American coins in the 19th and early 20th centuries, as late as Anthony de Francisci's Peace dollar of 1921. An excellent example of this type of eagle is embodied in the painting *Hebe* by H. Rottenhammer (fig. 4).

4. Rottenhammer, Hebe

Since the organizational basis of a coin is iconographic—portrait or personification on one side and emblem or coat of arms on the other—the choosing of an iconography for the coinage of the new republic posed numerous problems. Imbued with Roman Republican virtues and mindful of the neoclassic decorative forces at work in contemporary Europe, the early statesmen strove to find a system of design for the American coinage that would avoid all suggestion of European royal power, especially of kingly Britain, from which the colonies had so recently won their independence.

Iconographic Background

> In the decorative arts, . . . the representational subject-matter is suggested by the chance shape and appearance and purpose of the material to be decorated. In the "pure" arts, such as sculpture and painting when they are producing works which have no other use or purpose than their purely artistic and esthetic aim, the choice of subject-matter is not dependent on the invention of animate analogies.[2]

The United States experienced some minor difficulties in establishing a suitable iconography for its coinage, and the subject has evoked considerable discussion over the nearly two centuries since the Declaration of Independence. Once it was agreed that neither Washington nor any other president should grace the coins of a young republic, there was little question that the goddess or personification of Liberty was an apt theme for the obverse. The eagle, or like subject, on the reverse posed special problems, for there were no emotional precedents for a national coat of arms or excerpts therefrom on the coinage.

Liberty

Liberty or Columbia (from the first they are amply draped females carrying the cap on a pole or branch of peace) grows quite naturally out of the seated Britannia or Hibernia of British coins. In 1785 the "Immune Columbia" cent, identified with the border area of Vermont and New York, carried a matron in windblown drapery, a Liberty cap on a pole, and a pair of scales in her hands. The following year saw cents of Vermont inscribed INDE[PENDENCE] ET LIB[ERTY], a bust imitating that of George III on the obverse and, opposing, the image of the seated Britannia holding out the olive branch in her right hand, staff diagonally in her left, and a small, round shield at her left side. Iconography becomes confused, for the castles of Spain appear as a device on one of the shields, while most of the others display the crosses of Saint George and Saint Andrew superimposed in true British fashion. Coins identified with New York (including issues evidently struck in England as a speculative venture), with Connecticut, and with New Jersey used the same motifs, the goddess standing or seated. They are dated in the years 1785 to 1788. A Pine Tree pattern cent, seemingly made in Massachusetts in 1776, shows Liberty seated on a globe, cap and staff in her grasp. A halfpenny of the same year has a similar Liberty, seated in the opposite direction, and the inscription GODDESS LIBERTY. Thus, it would appear Liberty had been an integral part of American numismatic art from the earliest struggles of the 13 independent colonies and the first union of sovereign states.

The Libertas Americana medals (fig. 5) created by the French artist Augustin Dupré (1748–1833) to commemorate the victories of Saratoga and Yorktown were also a font of subjective and iconographic inspiration, notably in the regular coinage of 1793. The obverse of Dupré's Libertas Americana medal, streaming hair on a Hellenistic bust of Artemis or a maenad, Greek helmet or *pileus* on a small pole, exerted its influence on Philadelphia's first heads of Liberty once the national coinage was commenced, but the reverse of the same medal was more a tribute to France as protector than the infant nation as a cultural entity. Clearly, Dupré had no notion of what was going on across the Atlantic from 1777 to 1781, and so, with promptings from Benjamin Franklin, he resorted

5. Dupré, Libertas Americana medal

to the tried and true old formula of pure classical allegory to express political action. "Not without the gods is the infant courageous," reads the Latin legend. Infant Hercules strangles the snakes in his crib while his perennial protectress Minerva uses her French regal shield to ward off an attacking lion, a beast no doubt symbolic of those on the coat of arms of England. The forms of the pyramidal composition are those of the Italian Baroque, dramatic art in the tradition of the 17th century. Save for the startling, vivid iconography of the obverse, there was nothing in this medal to set it off from a host of other commemorative pieces produced in Europe in the 18th century to celebrate numerous, varied events, and the reverse design of the piece exerted no further influence on American numismatic art.[3]

The Eagle

In January 1791 the secretary of the Treasury, Alexander Hamilton, made a long report to the House of Representatives. "The eagle is not a very expressive or apt appellation for the largest gold piece, but nothing better appears. . . . The devices of the coins are far from being matters of indifference, as they may be made the vehicles of useful impressions. They ought therefore to be emblematical, but without losing sight of simplicity. The fewer sharp points and angles there are, the less will be the loss by wearing."[4] Thus, from the beginnings of the full national coinage, technical problems were deemed on a par with or superior to aesthetic considerations.

In a letter to his daughter, Mary Bache, Benjamin Franklin had opted for the turkey as the most native of our potential national birds. When the eagle was first proposed for the coins, a Southern representative opposed the symbol because the "King of Birds" was too regal for the coinage of a nation created out of colonies that had cast aside their king and his royal governors. Judge Thatcher retorted, "perhaps a goose might satisfy the gentlemen better, as it was humble and republican enough, while the goslings would serve for the subsidiary pieces."[5] More than a century later, at the World's Columbian Exposition of 1892, the eagle was so firmly established as an iconographic necessity as to have developed a martyr and a cult of its own. A description of the exhibit set up by the Philadelphia Mint at the fair states:

> In the centre of the room is a large hexagonal case, made of the same material, and in the same general style [as the coin cases], over which is suspended the old American eagle whose history is so long and closely connected with the Mint. "Old Pete," who had served as a model for the eagle on

several of our National coins, had the freedom of the Mint, but his flying proclivities proved his death, for one day his wing was caught in the machinery, and he had to be killed.[6]

More will be said about Peter the "Mint Bird" presently!

Perhaps the worst fate that had befallen our coin types as regards the eagle is the Coinage Law of 1873, which states that the larger silver and the gold coins must bear "the figure of an eagle or representation thereof."[7] This led to the insertion by Mint engraver Gilroy Roberts of the tiny heraldic eagle to the right of the Liberty Bell on the reverse of the Franklin half dollars of 1948 to 1963 (fig. 232), for fear there would be legal objections if anything but the national bird were used. Both the heraldic and the free-form eagle appeared on the coinage of the states united before 1792. New York's Excelsior cent of 1787 combined a chickenlike eagle on the upper segment of the globe with the eagle of the national coat of arms, backward, on the reverse. On the Indian cent struck for the same state in the same year, a larger version of the free eagle, placidly facing to the front with half-spread wings drooping, stands on a half-globe on the reverse. Cents and half cents of Massachusetts in 1787 were required by direction of the Council to display "a spread eagle" as a reverse device.[8] This took the form of the national emblem again, eagle's head to the left, the arrows either correctly in the bird's right talon or exchanged with the branch of peace. New Jersey seems to have produced other variations of the device on the Immunis Columbia and Washington cents of 1786.

Thus, by 1792 and 1793, when a national coinage became a reality at Philadelphia, there were ample iconographic precedents in the coinage and elsewhere for the naturalistic and the emblematic eagle. Turkeys, geese, and other candidates had been consigned back to the realm of less official decorative arts, from furniture ornament to embroidery.

The design of the heraldic eagle reverse can also be traced back through the coinages of the newly independent states to Dupré's medal commemorating the Declaration of American Independence, which was struck in Paris shortly after the Revolution (fig. 6). This creation was termed the Diplomatic medal, since it was conceived of as a work of art suitable in the precious metals for the presentation to foreign statesmen who had aided the colonies in their struggle for freedom. On the obverse appears:

6. Dupré, Diplomatic medal

> THE UNITED STATES OF AMERICA; an eagle displayed, on his breast a shield,—Argent, six pales Gules, a chief Azure,—in his right claw an olive branch, in his left thirteen arrows, in his mouth a ribbon inscribed E PLURIBUS UNUM; above a sun of thirteen stars, from which issue rays, passing through a circle of clouds, and extending below the wings of the eagle.

The reverse comprises:

> TO PEACE AND COMMERCE.; in exergue, IV JUL. MDCCLXXVI; to right, DUPRÉ. F.; at the left an Indian Queen, personifying America, is seated, holding in her left hand a horn containing fruits and grains; by her side are bales, a barrel and an anchor, to which she points with her right hand; at the right Mercury just alighted extends toward her his right hand; behind him is the ocean, on which at the extreme right is the forepart of a ship, and beyond this is land.[9]

In these two designs, especially in the shield on eagle, can be seen the genesis of much of America's numismatic iconography.

Thomas Jefferson wrote to William Short in Paris, suggesting the basic elements of this design, "but having little confidence in our own ideas in an art not familiar here, they are only suggested to you, to be altered, or altogether postponed to such better device as you may approve, on consulting with those who are in the habit and study of medals. Duvivier and Dupré seem to be the best workmen; perhaps the last is the best of the two."[10] Since the first specimens of the medal were intended as presents to friends of the United States, particularly those who had assisted the colonies in gaining their freedom, the medal came to be called the Diplomatic medal. This name could have been applied with equal justice to the Libertas Americana medal or to a number of other, less important, commemorative efforts on behalf of the new nation.

There is a certain interesting continuity in this Franco-American medal of peace, commerce, and independence by Dupré, for the future chief engraver Charles Barber made a copy that was struck at the Philadelphia Mint and circulated in commemoration of the centennial of 1876. The replica is quite faithful to the style of the original, and, since iconography is the main concern of this book, illustration of Barber's tribute to Dupré (fig. 7) alongside a version of the original shows how much the medal dated 1776, but prepared between 1790 and 1792, contributed to the vocabulary of American coins.[11] The "Indian Queen" is that curious mixture of noble savage and seated Artemis which the French Rococo could concoct out of a nymph by François Boucher (1703–1770) and a vague understanding of what went on among the native inhabitants of the New World. Grass skirt and feathered headgear hardly belong with Roman throne, himation, footstool, cornucopia, classical quiver, and the svelte figure of Mercury, god of commerce. The combination of commercial apparatus at the left and a vista of ocean with ship at the right is a medallic motif that would be taken up again in the centennial decade of the 1870s in connection with the seated Liberty of the trade dollar (figs. 75–81). The quaint, un-Indian crown of feathers would be adopted by James B. Longacre in 1854 as the appropriate dress

7. Barber, copy of the Diplomatic medal

for his head of Liberty on the gold dollar and the gold $3 coin (fig. 55). Dupré's pioneer effort was clearly fraught with potentials utilized by engravers in the mint established at Philadelphia in 1792 and by those artists, often one and the same, engaged in engraving bonds and banknotes for the Republic and its components.

Inscriptions

Of the three inscriptions deemed a necessity to U.S. coinage, the word *Liberty* and the federation motto "E Pluribus Unum" were already on the coins, tokens, and medals of the Congress or the states before 1792. The pious aphorism "In God We Trust" was added as a result of pressure by a backwoods divine on the secretary of the Treasury at the beginning of the Civil War. As a result of Theodore Roosevelt's decision to omit the phrase from the splendid Saint-Gaudens $10 and $20 gold coins of 1907, Congress passed an act in 1908 requiring that the words "In God We Trust" appear on all new coins. Since then, with the exception of the Buffalo nickel of 1913 to 1938, where the invocation to God was ignored, no regular issue has dared omit any of the three statutory inscriptions, and only a few commemorative coins made so bold as to ignore one or more of them.

In connection with the new coins of 1916, specifically the dime (fig. 159) by Adolph A. Weinman, curator and critic Howland Wood measured the iconographic chains that have traditionally bound designers of the U.S. coinage.

> Before commenting on any of the new pieces it is but fair to consider the limitations and difficulties that beset the designer. Artistic rendering and a super-abundance of lettering do not go hand in hand towards the best results. Our artists at the start are handicapped by having to place on the coin "United States of America," "E Pluribus Unum," "Liberty," "In God We Trust," the date, and the denomination. In other words, six separate mottoes or legends. Consequently, the artist cannot strive for simplicity, and, despite his best endeavors, one or both sides of the coin are bound to be chopped up with a lot of discordant elements. According to the requirements of a modern utilitarian coinage, the designer is precluded from employing or arriving at the best effects in modeling; for both the upper and lower planes of the relief must be considered. High relief and certain effects cannot be employed, and, despite everything the artist may strive for, a certain mechanical technique must be used.[12]

Iconographic Progress From the 19th to the 20th Century

If there was enthusiasm for the eagle, or for Liberty and her paraphernalia, in the first decade of freedom, the iconographic trappings had grown wearisome by the time the United States embarked on the second century of independence. In 1879 Robert Morris could write:

> There is but little in American coinage, to be sure, that will compare favorably with the wise and instructive symbols seen upon the money of the olden time. Our eagle, stars, arrows, olive-twigs, and women, are pitched on to the coins at random, and cannot be "read" by any rules of heraldry or numismatics. Yet, in reply to the query what is this "stick with a nightcap on it," which the French lady holds on our trade dollar, I answer it is the *rudis* and *pileus*, the "rod of touch," and the "cap of announcement" connected with the ancient forms of freeing a slave. . . . The celebrated *Phrygian cap,* whose name appears so often in the story of the French Revolution, may be recognized as bent back at the lower end. This I suppose is what our Mint engravers have in mind when they sit down to draw designs for American money. They might better study the beautiful coins on the shelves in the show-rooms of the Mint,—those representing Atys, and Iulus, son of Aeneas, for instance, if they would give us more artistic forms, while perpetuating the truths of history.[13]

For better or worse the iconography of American coinage was firmly established between 1836 and 1840 by neoclassic reforms in the early designs. At this time too a strong bid was made to settle the question of heraldic versus naturalistic eagle in favor of the latter, but the emblematic survived with persistence right down to the presidential seal on the Kennedy half dollar of 1964 (fig. 240). Indeed, the bird that mirrored nature lasted on the coinage only through several trial series and one small issue of the silver dollar in the few years after 1836 (fig. 35). It reappeared momentarily as the same flying eagle on the cents of 1856 to 1858, but not until the vision of Theodore Roosevelt teamed with the artistry of Augustus Saint-Gaudens and Bela Lyon Pratt was the American bird to take on aspects of naturalism again (figs. 131 and 136).

Finally, in 1917 the medalist Theodore Spicer-Simson argued, perhaps unwittingly, the case for another extreme, numismatic impressionism, in an article titled "Portrait Reliefs, Medals and Coins in their Relation to Life and Art." His theme was that the art of modern coinage must be grounded in nature but aware of the technical processes involved in coin production.

> As the effigy of an eagle on a coin is obviously infinitely smaller than the living object, any attempt to give an accurate reproduction of the details would be ineffective; since when the feathers are reduced in size they become so microscopic as to be invisible to the naked eye and a seemingly smooth surface results. The strength and ferociousness of the bird of which the proportions give character, the movement and decorative effect become so much more important than the number of feathers, which we leave to the naturalist to numerate. This holds true of the details of a man's figure on a small coin.[14]

It was not until the Isabella quarter dollar of 1893 (fig. 105), a commemorative issue in connection with the World's Columbian Exposition, that the artistic theories of a human figure on a small coin were to be put into practice.

Continental, Early Federal, and Mint Medals

The institution by which the engravers at Philadelphia are permitted to prepare a continuous supply of new designs, most of which are available in perpetuity for sale to the public at normal prices, has been an immeasurable stimulus to the arts. The custom goes back to the early years of the 19th century, and restrikes exist of several famous medals from the dawn of the Republic. The annual Assay Commission medals were the only series that was never struck in quantity nor available for sale through the democratic process of sending a small sum to the superintendent of the Mint.

The medals struck at the Mint have often been related to the regular coinage. At times, especially in the first century of the United States, the connections have been less apparent because both medallic designs and especially the coin types could be relatively simple, repeating standard motifs from decade to decade with little variation. With the advent of commemorative coins after 1892 and, ultimately, the introduction of presidential portraits on the denominations from cent to half dollar, designs tried out by Mint engravers in medallic form came to have a constant importance for the coinage. Thus, aside from their own merits as works of art, the medals of the U.S. Mint command an important place in the aesthetic history of the federal coinage. These Mint medals could be considered separately, but their stylistic or subjective links with coin designs demand that they be discussed at appropriate chronological intervals from the American Revolution to the present.

Just as there was considerable free enterprise in the production of coins between 1776 and 1792, so the first official medals were designed for the founders of the Republic by several independent artists in Europe and America. Once the Philadelphia Mint had been in operation for a number of decades, efforts were made to secure the dies of these earliest medals. When this proved impossible, new dies were prepared from existing specimens, and the continuity of medals furnished by the Mint was extended back to Revolutionary times. Since medals honoring famous men and events had been a part of the British and French colonial tradition in North America, it was natural that the newly independent colonies and then the United States should turn the tradition to the propagandistic efforts of the young nation. It is a tribute again to the developed artistic sensitivities of Thomas Jefferson, Benjamin Franklin, and other statesmen that first-rate artists created designs and executed medals of superior artistic merit.

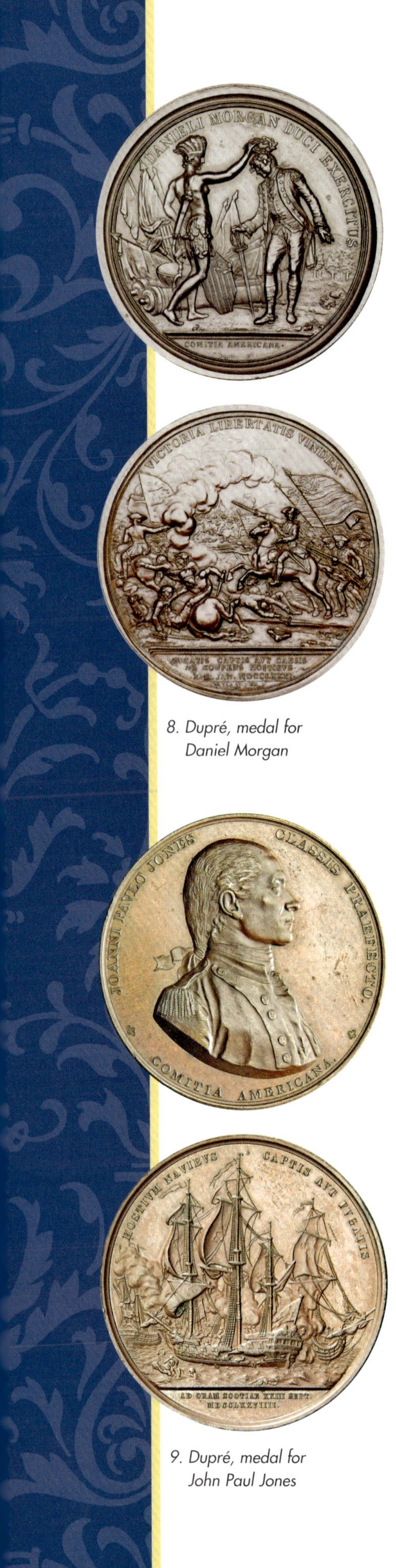

8. Dupré, medal for Daniel Morgan

9. Dupré, medal for John Paul Jones

Two medals by Augustin Dupré, so responsible for the early official artistic efforts of the colonies in revolt, bear the authorization of Congress and, like his Diplomatic medal (fig. 6), were sold to the public as late as the 1980s. Both relate to battles in the war, one on land and one a naval engagement. The medal to Daniel Morgan for his victory at the battle of the Cowpens on January 17, 1781, is a mixture of the noble-savage allegorical obverse found on the Diplomatic medal and a grand vista of battle in the medallic tradition of Louis XIV on the reverse (fig. 8). John Paul Jones's raids off the coast of his native Scotland, particularly the victory of September 23, 1779, in the *Bonhomme Richard* over the *Serapis,* is commemorated in more orthodox fashion (fig. 9). Jean-Antoine Houdon's plaster bust of the hero in naval dress, now in the Museum of Fine Arts at Boston, has provided the source for the obverse, while a naval battle that could have taken place almost anywhere in the middle of the 18th century occupies the reverse.

The Cowpens medal led nowhere in terms of medallic aesthetics. America, Liberty, or Columbia (the last-named not yet established as an American divinity) was clad in a European idea of Indian costume and was shown placing a wreath on Morgan's brow. As the United States matured artistically, the design must have soon seemed quaint and dated. Dupré has created a composition in the classical tradition, updated by the trophy of flags, drum and bugle, and guns seen beyond America's personification as an Indian Queen, whose shield vaguely suggests the arms of the new nation. Fortunately, Daniel Morgan's dress is contemporary, and the stubby trees at the right were no doubt designed to indicate the Southern terrain of the battle. Dupré's attempt to make allegories in terms of a land he saw from afar through engravings was charged with backward mannerisms whenever he tried to introduce local color or personifications derived from his misunderstood America. To do him justice, Augustin Dupré was undoubtedly one of the best medalists of his day, even among his several compatriots who worked for the Continental Congress; his high relief, combined with a crisp style and attention to detail, influenced several other craftsmen who produced this type of commemoration for the Republic during its first 50 years.

One of the important, now almost forgotten, iconographic sources for the development of the national coat of arms was the series of Indian Peace medals prepared during George Washington's administration. Those created between 1789 and 1795 were oval plaques engraved by silversmiths, some of whom, such as Joseph Richardson (1752–1831), were well known.[15] Joseph Richardson, of a long line of New York and Philadelphia silversmiths, was appointed assayer at the Mint in 1795 and held the office until his death. His engraved Peace medal (of a type similar to fig. 10), stamped with his initials at the bottom, shows Washington greeting a pipe-smoking Indian in a setting of rural industry. The Indian, a chief presumably, has already received his oval plaque and wears it suspended from a collar about the neck. The reverse presents an equally animated yet somewhat primitive version of the federal heraldic eagle.

10. Indian Peace medal

From these beginnings, individual creations for the government on the part of the famous silversmiths, the art of the Indian Peace medal came to play an increasing role in the activities of medalists in federal employ. During the first four decades of the 19th century the most notable official medals of the Philadelphia Mint were those struck for presentation to Indian chiefs, often during special expeditions such of that of Lewis and Clark in 1804 to 1806. The first struck medals for George Washington were purchased from a private mint in England, and it was Thomas Jefferson in 1802 who instituted the logical practice of producing Indian Peace medals at the U.S. Mint. The reverse designed for these medals remained standard late into the century. The obverse also set a subjective fashion, presenting a half-figure bust of Jefferson, then the third president. The reverse showed two clasped hands, one in an officer's cuff and the other wearing a broad bracelet enriched with the heraldic American eagle of the silver coinage after 1807 (fig. 11). On the Peace medals of presidents after Jefferson this bracelet was omitted, and the eagle was transferred to the buttons on the officer's cuff. A crossed tomahawk and peace pipe (calumet) appeared above, and the legend was invariably PEACE AND FRIENDSHIP. There was nothing artistic about this medal, the dies of which were credited to John Reich shortly after his arrival from Bavaria as an indentured servant, but the purpose was utilitarian. Like many simple, standard coins, the Indian Peace medal with its changing gallery of current presidents on the obverse enjoyed a longevity far beyond most single, commemorative medallic issues.

11. Reich, Indian Peace medal

Mint Medals and the Regular Coinage

As already mentioned, there has been some interrelation between the designs of Mint medals and regular coins. Mint artists and engravers were able to try out details in medals that later turned up on coins, such as the Barber-Morgan standing figure of Columbia or Liberty with a child at her side. Another classic example is the 1964 half dollar honoring the assassinated President Kennedy (fig. 240). An acceptable coin was produced with admirable dispatch because the portrait on the obverse and the seal on the reverse had been worked out by the chief engraver and his assistant for medals in the presidential series (figs. 238 and 239).

Architecture on U.S. coins can be said to be an innovation on the commemorative gold of the early years of the 20th century. As far back as the years just before the Civil War, however, Anthony C. Paquet designed a medal of James Ross Snowden, superintendent of the Mint, the reverse of which is dominated by a noble vista of the neoclassic Mint building in Philadelphia (fig. 88). If ships enter the repertory of U.S. coins with the "Liberty at the seashore" pattern (fig. 85) or the World's Columbian Exposition half dollar (fig. 103), they have a distinguished earlier history on congressional medals honoring naval heroes (fig. 9). For a century, therefore, official medals alone did what commemorative coins tried to achieve after 1892: they supplied an imaginative repertory of creativity to the art of American numismatics. Official medals continued this practice throughout the era of commemorative coins, and they are the chief vehicles of aesthetic impulses in the current age.[16]

At times when stagnation beset the art of the U.S. coins, Mint medals were all the more necessary as a creative outlet for the government engravers. In the era of Longacre, the Barbers, and Morgan, engravers could give free rein to their ambitions and vent their energies on patterns. The custom of striking pattern examples for proposed circulating designs practically came to a halt at the time of the First World War. Without Mint medals our continuing artistic heritage so far as numismatics are concerned would be impoverished indeed.

Since coins and Mint medals are essentially artistic studies in miniature, or at least on a relatively small scale, the artists designing for the government used or created a host of national motifs that had repercussions in a number of related practical and purely decorative objects. Although these applications of numismatic compositions and details were generally small in scale, there were many exceptions. Because every feature of U.S. coinage can be considered a patriotic design—Liberty, the eagle, the heraldic shield, or even the wreath around the denomination—the public tendency to use numismatic composition in the decorative arts was further stimulated by national pride. Manufacturers found the works of artists employed by the federal government a subsidized source of inspiration for their own private programs of decoration. The process also worked in reverse, for artists of the Mint had often been associated with outside firms before taking up their governmental duties, and were just as susceptible to the styles and fashions of their times as their cohorts in private enterprise.

Early Numismatic Motifs in the Decorative Arts, 1776 to 1876

The relation between the designs on coins and in the minor arts of all varieties was a continuous one. It began with the medals struck in France following the first blows for independence, grew in breadth and imagination with the colonial and early federal coins and tokens, and flowered into a major industry with the establishment of the central Mint in 1792. The happiness with which craftsmen in all media greeted the opportunity to place national emblems on glass, on furniture, in the newspapers, on cookie cutters, in the carved detail on the transoms of ships, as freestanding shop signs, and as flags for patriotic occasions was everywhere in evidence. Coins furnished visual material of most official sort for artists in all quarters. Changes in coin design were echoed in the minor arts, and occasionally these arts influenced variations in numismatic iconography.

The eagle of the various seals of the United States was obviously one of the prime series used for reference. The variations tried on the gold and silver coins all appeared in due course. After the initial iconographic confusion and debates over eagles, turkeys, and goslings, artistic selection of the eagle as a national hieratic emblem was made in 1782. Prominent patriots were involved in details of design as well as in selection. The well-known Philadelphia sculptor William Rush wrote his suggestions to the governmental committee choosing figureheads and, particularly, the subjects for transom carvings on naval vessels. Charles Thomson and William Barton shaped the form of the eagle in the Great Seal of the United States, and their efforts, accepted on the third try, were adopted on June 20, 1782. From the time of George Washington's triumphal tour of the new federation, the bird in emblematic form of some nature was used everywhere in all media.

Since then sculptors with advanced ideas about birds and emblems in art have never tired of seeking sources in the eagle, knowing the bird's ornithological nobility and its emblematic connection with the central government of the United States. In 1893 Augustus Saint-Gaudens made seated eagles of Hellenistic Greek (Ptolemaic) type for the sides of his niche and relief to Colonel Robert Gould Shaw on the common opposite Boston's State House (fig. 133). Years later he and Bela Lyon Pratt were to scale these birds down and transfer them from freestanding marbles to metallic or plaster reliefs for the gold coinage of 1907 and 1908. The various modern eagles on the silver coins of 1916 to 1932 and on the commemorative half dollars of the 1920s and 1930s fall into a similar logical sequential relation to the other arts.

In 1918, for instance, the Philadelphia sculptor Albert Laessle modeled an eagle of victory for casting in bronze.[17] This bird is the Saint-Gaudens or Adolph Weinman eagle in "defiant" pose, seen in the third dimension rather than in relief. The creature has the strongly feathered legs common both to modern numismatic eagles and to the birds of Ptolemaic times. There are excellent freestanding parallels from antiquity, from the first to third centuries of the Roman Empire. They exist in both marble and bronze, ranging up to four feet in height (fig. 12). Often they come from Syria or Asia Minor, areas where the cult of the eagle survived from Hellenistic into Roman imperial times. A question arising from professed or acknowledged modern parallels between Saint-Gaudens, his successors, and classical art is how much or how often 19th-century Mint engravers relied on contact with antiquity. A cogent example is the eagle of the Barber and Morgan patterns of about 1873, the trade dollar reverses, in one of the pediments on the lid of a large Roman sarcophagus of about A.D. 140, in the museum at Heraklion on Crete. The giant coffin in marble was found a generation ago in a tomb chamber under the Early Christian basilica at Marmara, near the site of the Minoan palace at Mallia. Half of a natural type and partly heraldic in nature, the bird appears in full frontal view, head turned up and to the right, amid a decorative scroll of vine and rosettes. Where the eagle on a trade dollar or on a brochure for the 1876 centennial clutches a scroll or fillet bearing a motto, this Roman eagle of the age of Hadrian grasps a snake or a coil of the foliage in his beak (fig. 13). Although this particular eagle was unknown to artists of the 19th century, other similar reliefs have been documented since the Italian Renaissance.

Needlework is hardly the first place to look for designs relating to the coinage, but a heraldic composition of 1806, calling for "Independence," already includes the shield in the center of the eagle. An embroidery of 1825 shows the coat of arms or Great Seal as it appears on coins of 1798 and later. The similarity is strong enough to suggest the anonymous young lady took her homework from a coin rather than from the common source.[18] In the functional field of door knockers, made before and after

12. Eagle on orb, Greco-Roman

1776, a British lion can be contrasted with an American example that presents the eagle on an inverted palmette and holding a scroll between his talons. The early scrolls usually bore the motto E PLURIBUS UNUM.

Furniture and its gilded or metallic fittings provide many examples. The eagle on a globe, forerunner of later and parallel to the earliest patterns, graces a banjo clock fashioned by Simon Willard between 1800 and 1810. The thin, goose-necked eagle of the silver coins from 1795 to 1798 surmounts a Hepplewhite mahogany tambour secretary made

13. End of a Roman sarcophagus

between 1780 and 1800 at Salem, Massachusetts. Gilt convex or straight mirrors exhibit the relationship of the gooselike eagle to the phoenix in the years 1750 to 1780. In Boston about 1800, painted panels and convex mirrors feature the spread eagle and shield. From the shop of John and Simeon Skillin came finials with an eagle on an orb, like the bird of such schematic outline and trussed anatomy on the 1787 to 1788 coppers of Massachusetts. As early as the dawn of independence George Bright of Boston was adding the new national bird to the decoration of secretaries, a practice that he is documented to have kept on to about 1785. In brief, therefore, heraldic eagles, thin eagles, and even eagles in motion both parallel the coinages and were evident in the decorative repertory before the adoption of the national coat of arms.

As the 19th century progressed, patriotism, publicity, and national numismatic motifs were intermixed. News media gave maximum scope to patriotic compositions in the visual arts during the War Between the States. The eagle was seldom omitted from the many hundreds of Union or Northern recruiting posters and advertisements that swept the Northern states. Many motifs involving eagle, mottoes, Liberty and her regalia, or minor details such as wreaths and stars are vignettes of the coin and medal designs. The humble medium of pressed glass bottles and tableware did more than its share. The Sinnock quarter eagle of 1926 and half dollar of 1948 were anticipated by the "Liberty Bell" on a covered dish of 1876. "Chafee's campaign tumbler" of 1861 featured a shield like that of the two-cent pieces struck during the Civil War or of the first series of nickels. All the familiar motifs came together in Thomas G. Cook's designs of November 11, 1873, for a centennial goblet and mug.

The apex of the relationship between pressed glass tableware and U.S. coinage came in the "Silver Age" pattern made by the Central Glass Company. Collectors knew these post–Civil War products as the "Coin" pattern. Legend has it that a certain Albert Mader, who worked for the company, in his travels to the West had seen a barroom floor decorated with silver coins and sensed such an idea would appeal to pressed glass buyers. The place in question is thought to have been the old Silver Dollar Grill at the Davenport Hotel in Spokane, Washington. The molds were expensive to produce, but the design was most successful. Then disaster struck. The U.S. government stepped in and ordered the Central Glass Company to stop making the new line. The authorities claimed that any actual reproduction was counterfeiting, and the molds were destroyed. The custom of such coin designs in pressed glass goes back at least to 1831, for the eagle pattern of that date on a plate is like a half dollar in reverse.

Among miscellaneous items historical flasks were very popular, no doubt for that patriotic swig on the Glorious Fourth. The eagle clutching arrows and olive branch was a standard design. An eagle salt container even circularized the standard 1840 to 1892 or pre-Barber half dollar reverse. In 1866, the year of issue, a wooden fire bucket for some patriotic brigade was painted with the shield obverse of the new nickel. Inn signs form another category of paint on wood. The heraldic eagle of the Barber series in 1892 is anticipated, for instance, on W.P. Witt's "Liberty" sign of 1829. Finally, bread service plates or platters were a popular commemorative item in the circulation of coin designs, present and future. For the Centennial Exposition year, eagles, flags, and mottoes were sought-after motifs. Another combination that caught the public fancy was the oval bread platter known as "Centennial with Eagle," which had an eagle in the center and in the border the phrase "Give us this day Our Daily Bread." Liberty and the eagle share a ribbon with LIBERTY AND FREEDOM, 1776.

Thus, the theme of the first hundred years was one of pride in a straightforward iconography based on designs and motifs used by government and private craftsmen alike in a multitude of media on a variety of scales. Official medals and coins were crucial, and beside them can be ranged the great array of private medals and tokens of all classes.[19] In the best sense of the idea the United States by 1876 had produced a democratic art for a joyously independent society.

The basic ingredients of U.S. coinage have always been relatively simple, despite pressures to make them otherwise. Liberty dominated the obverses of most coins until the 1930s and 1940s, when portraits of presidents or patriots became the accepted standard. The eagle in some form, heraldic or quasi-natural, has been the main reverse element of

gold and silver coins. Inscriptions or legends have become rigidly fixed by custom and legislation. The sources of these iconographic requirements lay in the monumental and decorative arts of neoclassic Europe going back through the Italian Renaissance to Greek and Roman times. Once established on the federal coinage, they came to play an important part in all forms of creativity, from official medals to privately produced works of art of a functional or practical nature.

II

Early Coins and Medals of the United States

The new nation subsisted on a variety of foreign currencies, coppers struck by the states, and federal or unofficial tokens until active men of intellect such as Thomas Jefferson moved the establishment of a national mint in a simple Georgian building in Philadelphia. The very first national coinage in 1792 is said to have been struck from silver plate donated by George and Martha Washington and was, from the artistic point of view, a crude parallel to the Continental paper money that had financed the War of Independence. Dimes or "dismes" and half dimes were struck in silver. Of the former less than half a dozen have survived. Two sizes of cents were designed, but again very few coins were actually prepared, making the pieces essentially patterns. There was also a pattern quarter dollar struck in copper and white metal. The bust of Liberty, labeled "Parent of Science and Industry," is an unflattering cross between Martha Washington and one of the wide-eyed harridans who knitted while heads rolled during the French Revolution. The eagle on the reverse is an ailing barnyard fowl, with undersized wings spread at odd angles, curving neck, and oddly foreshortened body, a creature nowhere better seen than on the small surfaces of the dime and half disme (fig. 14).

14. Half disme of 1792

The Coins of 1793

Given all the conflicting interests and pressures from both sides of the Atlantic at work in the infant republic, it is amazing how rapidly U.S. coinage was elevated to a respectable artistic level. No effort was spared. Within a year, clever immigrant and local coiners, such as Henry Voigt, Adam Eckfeldt, Joseph Wright, and Robert Scot, were creating likenesses of Liberty and simple, balanced reverses after designs once thought to have been laid out by the Swiss medalist Jean-Pierre Droz but probably

15. Chain cent of 1793

16. Wreath cent of 1793

concocted by a talented Philadelphian such as the elder (Charles W.) Peale. Thomas Jefferson tried on several occasions to reach a firm agreement with the temperamental Droz, who worked in both France and England, and other candidates offered their ideas or were considered. The men who cut America's first dies (fig. 15) were German bondsmen, local mechanics and watchmakers (as was Voigt), British craftsmen with similar interests, and amateur scientists—a host of backgrounds as diverse as those of the Revolutionary patriots themselves. It was really not until the arrival of William and Charles Barber and George Morgan from England at the end of the Civil War that the Philadelphia Mint was fully staffed by engravers trained to prepare dies for coins rather than basically unrelated products from watchcases to book illustrations.

The Wreath cent of 1793 (fig. 16) of Eckfeldt or Wright presents a more sophisticated Liberty than the bust on the coins of 1792. It still reflects French influences, from the design created by Dupré for a medal at the time of the War of Independence (fig. 5). The strong profile from brow to neck was a contemporary interpretation of Greco-Roman sculpture in marble or bronze, and the streaming hair was Dupré's expression of excitement stirring in the colonies and among intellectual circles in France as the United States came into being. The fraction beneath the wreath on reverse reminds us that the still relatively limited audience of the federal coinage had to think in terms of decimals and hundredths rather than in pounds, shillings, and pence.[1] In addition, as economic historians like to observe, a distressing variety of coins from several countries in Europe and South America were circulating everywhere during the first half century of the United States.

Along with the later cents of 1793 a half cent with bust of Liberty facing to the left appeared (fig. 17). This unusual coin was not continued in 1794, when the half cent became scarcely more than a reduced version of the large cent. The half cent of 1793 presents a vigorous if rather earthy concept of Liberty, with strong strands of hair overwhelming a tiny cap on pole scarcely showing above the back of the head. The type is hardly beautiful, having something of the rustic qualities of pre-federal coins and tokens. The coin's reverse, however, is elegant in its studied detail, wreath, inscription, and fraction below. From the aesthetic standpoint, the issue can be regarded as transitional to the Liberty Cap cent of 1793 and 1794.

Late in 1793, only days before his death from yellow fever, the gifted Joseph Wright appears to have designed and cut the dies for a copper known as the Liberty Cap cent. His new coin was continued in 1794 and 1795, giving way in 1796 to the Scot-Stuart obverse that will be considered among the designs marking sophistication in the first phase of U.S. numismatic art. A well-preserved cent of 1794, a die by Robert Scot, shows Wright's full, simple obverse and a reverse that has eliminated the fussiness of trailing berries and minor leaves from the wreath (fig. 18). Liberty's face is stronger, the neck thicker, and the bust below the neck deeper and less metallic or less like an engraving in appearance. The whole presentation resembles an 18th-century version of a Greco-Roman marble bust rather than a linear profile copied from some printed broadside of the French Revolution. While still long, the hair has been smoothed down, softened, and made more articulate. The cap on the pole scarcely distracts, and its size is much more in keeping with the ideal power of the head than the like motif on Dupré's famous Libertas Americana medal celebrating the events of 1776 to 1781 (fig. 5). The Wright-Scot obverse lasted so short a time because it was too plain and direct for the increasing commercialism of the federalist age. A more luxurious Liberty was poised to make her debut upon the coins.

17. Half cent of 1793

18. Liberty Cap cent of 1794

Innovations of 1794 and 1795

Before the new bust of Liberty was introduced on the silver dollar late in 1795, the main silver coinage of 1794 and 1795 was prepared and issued. The obverse presented a simple, young Liberty with long tresses, while the reverse design was built around an eagle very much of the early 1790s in concept (fig. 19). This design was continued until new reverses were prepared for the dollar and the dime in 1798; similar new reverses were also used for other coins as they reappeared at various intervals (half dime in 1800, quarter dollar in 1804, and half dollar in 1801). The impact of the silver dollar of 1794 on its potential users is best described by the pen of a contemporary journalist.

> Some of the dollars *now* coining at the Mint of the United States have found their way to this town. A correspondent put one into the editor's hands yesterday. Its weight is equal to that of a Spanish dollar, but the metal appears finer. One side bears a head, with flowing tresses, encircled by *Fifteen Stars,* and has the word "Liberty" at the top, and the date, 1794, at the bottom. On the reverse, is the Bald Eagle, inclosed in an *Olive Branch,* round which are the words "*United States of America.*" The edge is well indented, in which are the words "One Dollar, or Unit. *Hundred Cents.*" The *tout ensemble* has a pleasing effect to a connoisseur; but the touches of the graver are too delicate, and there is a want of that boldness of execution which is necessary to durability and currency.[2]

This criticism of device, style, and execution is one of the earliest surviving impressions of the first monumental coin of the United States.

19. Silver dollar of 1794–1795

20. Silver dollar of 1795

Robert Scot was evidently responsible for this clean-cut coin and for the companion half dollar and half dime. The obverse head of Liberty and accessories, well-spaced-out lettering and six-pointed stars, have a flavor of successful transition between the states' or proto-federal coinages and the more complex silver with the deep, draped bust of Liberty to follow. The young face and the youthful, flowing hair were admirable symbols of the liberty of the young republic. Obverse and reverse were reissued in 1795, and the goose-necked, tubular eagle within a wreath was to continue for three more years in combination with the rich, sensuous bust of Liberty decreed for the dollar and the expanding repertory of fractional silver, the half dollar, the quarter dollar, the dime, and the half dime.

The edges of this and other early coins are impressive, the form of reeding visible outside the inscriptions being derived ultimately from ancient bronzes of the Roman imperial period. Sunk into the actual edge of the silver dollar was an inscription, divided by stars and circles or rectangles, indicating that one dollar equaled a hundred cents. The lettering and the date on the obverse were conceived in an almost-cursive script, while the UNITED STATES OF AMERICA on the reverse seems more solid, like a series of blocked letters. The details of Liberty's face and hair or those of the eagle and wreath with ribbons and berries on the reverse are so subtle that they can only be appreciated from specimens in perfect preservation. Clearly, the early engravers and coiners had not the need or the equipment to begin wrestling with the problems of heavy edges and flattened, incused designs able to withstand the effects of mass circulation. These technical innovations were to come by degrees early in the 19th century, and then more fully with a new Mint, machinery, and coinages in the 1830s.

Sophisticated Designs and Complex Iconography

In 1795 Robert Scot seems to have been responsible for producing a new concept of America's deity or personification, under the inspiration, it is said, of the portraitist Gilbert Stuart. Liberty on the silver dollar (fig. 20) is now a buxom Roman matron, with rich, curling tresses scarcely contained by the ribbon and large bow at the back of her head; her full face has been endowed with a Roman dignity that recalls some massive marble bust of Minerva or Dea Roma, goddess of Rome and her empire, in the second to fourth centuries A.D., the type of antiquity that was just beginning to reach the New World in the form of plaster casts. Two new states are represented by stars, as they had been on the previous dollar, and it is soon to be apparent that a quota of 13 stars is all the coinage could accommodate, regardless of the size of the Union. The eagle in the wreath of the

21. Flying eagle, in pine

reverse is not yet drawn from nature, but he emerges on the coinage out of a tradition, at least a generation in length, of American wood carving, ornaments on doorways, enrichment on the sterns of ships, and shop signs. The curves of his neck and wings are an admirable complement to the wreath and lettering, with milling beyond, and he exhibits decisive talons on his perch of clouds rather than rocks. The wooden eagle, screaming and in flight, that may have been the shop sign of Samuel Williston's button factory in Easthampton, Massachusetts, demonstrates the same rather primitive and almost conceptual elongation, shape of the wings, and airborne scream (fig. 21).

The dollar of 1798 through 1803 (fig. 22) maintains the same obverse, with the canonical set of 13 stars or states, and with a reverse that has abandoned all pretense of faithfulness to ornithology in the eagle. The bird is now part of the Great Seal of the United States, a design that can also be found on medals struck in the first days of the Republic. All the attributes of future coinages are there in big bold form, the motto in the beak, the arrows of war and the branch of peace in the talons, and the shield with bars. The clouds are now above, and the stars occur again amid the heraldic feathers.

22. Silver dollar of 1802

For a space of a few years around the turn of the century, the design came to be used on all silver coins from the dollar to the half dime. The dollar with its broad, flat surfaces and careful execution of subtle interior details was perhaps the finest in type and quality of the federal coins that can be thought of as belonging to the 18th-century and pre-neoclassic phase of numismatic art. It was in every respect a coin most worthy of America's new national aspirations, one that could stand with no apologies beside the crowns, thalers, or other large silver coins of Europe and the East. When reduced for the half dollar, the quarter dollar, the dime, or even the tiny half dime, the obverse and reverse designs suffered in no way, retaining all their monumental qualities. The coiners at the Mint

23. Cent of 1803

24. Half dollar of 1809 type

were extremely careful with these issues, and badly struck, hastily produced coins are rarely found. The coinage gives the impression, from both art and craftsmanship, of being one designed for connoisseurs in a small nation, although early in the century (1806) the half dollar reached a mintage of 839,576 pieces. There were often many minor varieties within each date of a single denomination, testifying to the number of dies that had to be cut for this series.

Consolidation of New Conventions: The Cent, 1796 to 1807

When transferred to a large copper of 1803 (fig. 23), the newly established obverse—that is, the draped bust of Liberty found on silver of the period—seems more simple and, consequently, more at home. Small details make a stronger profile and a less busy, distracting presentation of interior lines and ridges. The hair lies more evenly on the forehead, and the folds of drapery on the bust seem more solid and therefore more cohesive. The reverse is little changed from the Wright-Scot cents of 1793 and 1794, but a slight increase in the thickness of the lettering, smoothing and squaring of dentils on the edge, and removal of some fussy details by strengthening the stems of the wreath have done wonders for the monumentality of the message. When in mint condition with all subtleties of modeling visible, these cents combine the last primitivism of the 18th century with the new machine organization that would dominate the 19th.

Early Italian Neoclassicism

A few years later, when Napoleon was consolidating his power on the continent of Europe, the primitive wave of Italianate influence reached the Philadelphia Mint. A half dollar of 1809 (fig. 24) illustrates this, especially in the Liberty of the obverse. The artist is said to have been E. Lugio or Luigi Persico, of a Neapolitan family of sculptors and medalists; but some other Italian new to government circles was more likely responsible, for the coins appear to predate Persico's arrival in the New World by a half decade. The die cutter was John Reich, a Bavarian immigrant. As in the case of Stuart and Scot, the combination of the pseudo-Persico and Reich demonstrates that a leading artist could initiate coin designs but it took a master craftsman of the Mint to transform them into dies for the coins. The new coin combined a Liberty in a Phrygian cap with a pseudonatural heraldic eagle. The bird was later said by a perceptive government official to defy both nature and art. In commenting on the Liberty, one critic remarked that the artist had put a picture of his fat mistress on the coins. The reverse was to remain on the silver coinage, almost without modification, until 1891.

The form of the "sandwich-board" eagle that persisted for over 80 years on our coins may not have been a new design in 1807, and may not even have been of American origin as far as numismatics are concerned. It graces the Mott token dated 1789, which may have been manufactured in England for the fashionable New York firm of jewelers and importers. The reverse of this early tradesman's token shows a fancy French tabletop clock of a type associated with the neoclassic revival under Louis XV and XVI. The inscriptions around the obverse and reverse speak of the Motts as importers, dealers, and manufacturers of gold and silver wares, specifically watches and jewelry. This is the milieu out of which came the first artists of the U.S. coinage, and it is only natural that at least one of their major numismatic designs should be linked, through trade tokens, with the world of precision craftsmen in precious materials. The first federal die designers and engravers could have produced a cruder coinage, full of the linear qualities found in an engraving—that on the face of a clock, for instance, or that on the Indian Peace medal of 1793 (fig. 10). The talents and instincts of these artists were such that they quickly projected the mechanical aspects of coin design into the realm of creative sculpture in relatively small dimensions.

On the obverse of the 1807 half dollar and other coins redesigned by John Reich, "turbaned" Liberty's little Phrygian cap, like the eagle, was also destined to call forth complaints, whether in connection with these issues or the coins of 1892 to 1916. In Roman historical and funerary art of the late Republican period and Empire, such a cap had been the object bestowed on slaves when they were given their freedom, and no one wished to think of the United States as a nation of bondsmen who had been given their independence by the British or even by the revolutionary patriots now in power. The late-antique heaviness of Liberty's face remained. In sum, this half dollar and its fractions were different from their predecessors, and perhaps a trifle suaver in their details, but as yet the true impact of Italian or French neoclassicism had not been felt in the coinage. The slightly primitive aura remained. It was not until the end of the Napoleonic Wars, the years from 1815 to 1818, that Benedetto Pistrucci's great neoclassic designs appeared on medals, such as the giant medallion prepared to commemorate the Battle of Waterloo (fig. 25), and on the British coinage, most notably with the Saint George and the Dragon (fig. 26) based on the riders of the Parthenon frieze. American die designers thus can be excused the fact that modern Italian neoclassicism did not arrive in Philadelphia until a generation later, with the Christian Gobrecht dies of 1836.[3]

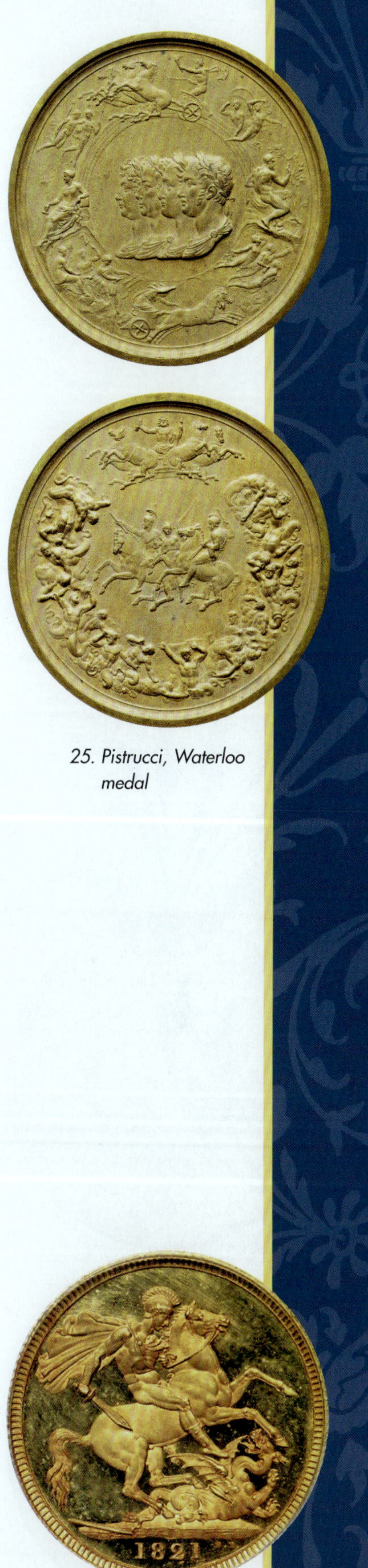

25. Pistrucci, Waterloo medal

26. Pistrucci, St. George and the Dragon

Several technical features of the half dollars coined from 1807 to 1836 can be related to aesthetic consideration of these coins. The reeding or dentils on the obverse and reverse edges were made heavier, even more like ancient coins than the edges of the earlier half dollars, to protect the designs within. The LIBERTY on the obverse and the E PLURIBUS UNUM on the reverse were incised, on the band of Liberty's cap and in a scroll above the eagle on the secondary side. Finally, the details of Liberty's hair and the feathers of the eagle were made bolder and deeper. Since these unusual but essentially handsome coins were among the first federal issues to achieve extensive circulation, and since specimens wore evenly and well with minimal loss of detail, the technical innovations can be viewed as a great success from the artistic point of view. The same can be said for the quarter dollar, dime, and half dime in this series of silver coins.

27. Cent of 1811

28. Cent of 1817

Early Neoclassic Cents

From 1808 to 1814 a succession of cents were issued from dies prepared by the same John Reich. These are also of the so-called Turban Head type, although the inscribed cap has been reduced to a thin band over a mass of unruly locks and curls, which almost seem to poke out on top (fig. 27). The strands over the low forehead and the large eye, a trifle popped like those of George III, do nothing to detract from the "blowsy barmaid" epithets hurled at this concept of Liberty. Lacking the deeper bust and artificial, rubbery drapery of the silver, this is a more straightforward design, better suited to minor coinage. Only the curious coiffure destroys the effect, making Liberty look as if she had just risen from sleep and flung open the window to see what was going on in the streets. The wreath of the reverse is now a more solid, closed, continuous affair, more like a Christmas wreath and less like an ancient Greek gold funerary diadem.

The same designs in reduced form were used in the half cent, lasting with minor variations from 1809 to 1836. From the technical standpoint the cents were less durable than their predecessors, the copper having less alloy and the coins tending to wear badly in short time. This was not the fault of John Reich. Despite Liberty's stylistic idiosyncrasies, her hair was modeled more deeply, and the lettering in the band around her brow stood out strongly in sunken relief. The six-pointed stars, carried over from the earlier gold and silver issues, were also designed in a forceful fashion, and the beading around obverse and reverse edges was given a roughness that echoed the disorder of Liberty's hair.

In 1816 Robert Scot, who was to remain engraver at the Mint until 1824, designed a new obverse (fig. 28) for the cent. This Liberty, wearing an inscribed coronet, is a crude forerunner of the Roman Liberty that emerged on the gold coinage a generation hence and remained until Theodore Roosevelt modernized these coins in the first decade of the

20th century. The basic forms of a Greco-Roman Juno or Venus are present in the new cent, but the face is ill-proportioned, the head is too square, and the early American penchant for long, curling tresses is still manifest. The new disposition of the stars in an unbroken circle around the head hints at the future possibilities in this area of the composition. As yet the stars are inordinately large, and the head is poised in such a fashion as to appear about to tumble on its squashed, pseudoclassical nose.

29. Quarter eagle of 1807

Gold Coins

The industrious Robert Scot seems also to have created the bust of Liberty (fig. 29) that dominated the gold coinage from 1795 until John Reich introduced his turbaned ladies in 1807 and 1808. His source could well have been an idealized, somewhat backward portrait of Martha Washington arrayed for an evening reception—a considerably more suave, tranquil presentation than that identified with the half disme of 1792 (fig. 14). The Liberty cap is a great tumultuous affair of soft felt that somehow manages to tower amid a large, curled forelock and long, wavy tresses. It is hard to say what is cap and what is hair entwined about it. The face is flat, blunt, and thoroughly bourgeois. The draped bust is a truncated curiosity. Greco-Roman classicism has been misunderstood here, for this is the type of draped neck ordinarily found in ancient art when a marble bust has been created for insertion into the body of a draped statue. The entire presentation makes little sense as an immediate visual experience. Scot surely did not originate this form of classicism in the federalist period; no doubt he adapted the design from some cast after the antique or some contemporary marble by a sculptor of modest talents.

The eagle with wings half spread that first appears on these gold coins, before the adoption of the heraldic reverse, is even more difficult to describe in ornithological terms than the bird first placed on the silver coins. Criticism comes easy, however, and it must not be overlooked that Robert Scot's first gold coinage has a positive character of its own, a healthy individuality and almost rustic charm that conveys the message of a young nation seeking its identity as well as any monumental manifestation of the early arts in America.

The first coins of the United States, and their related medals, were the fortuitous products of distinguished European engravers and their less-trained but equally talented American counterparts. After creating a head of Liberty based on French medallic traditions, the artists of the Mint turned to models in the realm of society portraiture in the major cities of the young republic. Early in the 19th century, heightened neoclassic influences from France, Italy, and England led to revisions that foreshadowed strongly Greco-Roman prototypes for Liberty after 1830. Whether

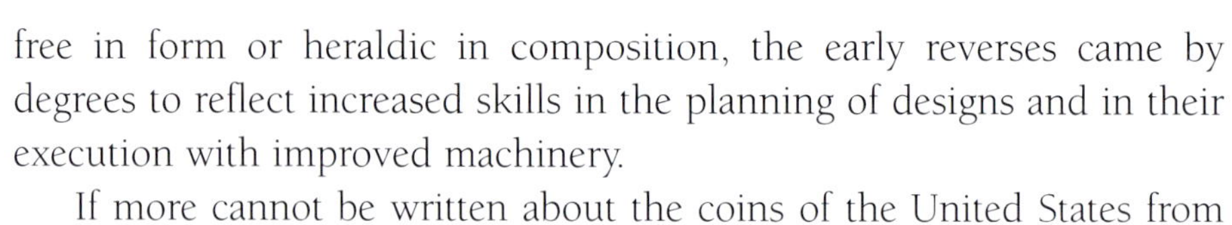

free in form or heraldic in composition, the early reverses came by degrees to reflect increased skills in the planning of designs and in their execution with improved machinery.

If more cannot be written about the coins of the United States from 1792 to the 1830s, it is because they were brief and direct in their artistic messages. The ingredients were simple enough. Variety existed in the various heads or busts of Liberty on the obverse and in the heraldic eagles on the reverse. Otherwise, stars, wreaths, inscriptions, and milling, however varied, cannot allow for and do not demand excessive stylistic criticism. Denominations were few. Most series were not issued each year. The earliest federal coins had charm, style, and creative vigor, but, just as the country itself was small, so these coins were relatively few and simple.

III

America's Classical Coinage

The American republic had been thoroughly conditioned by the tastes of Thomas Jefferson and Napoleonic Europe to appreciate the supposed purity of Greek and Roman sculpture, painting, and the minor arts. The time was perfect to adapt these canons, this iconography, and the purely American interpretations of neoclassic republicanism to the coinage. The stricter neoclassicism of U.S. coinage can be associated with the American artists, especially sculptors, who studied and worked in Italy in the generation after the Napoleonic Wars. Foremost among the sculptors who were to achieve a scientific neoclassicism in coinage was Horatio Greenough. His bust (fig. 30) by Hiram Powers, a younger contemporary in the movement, shows a man of the Regency and early Victorian period in the chilling precision of the portraits perpetuated by Bertel Thorvaldsen (1768–1844) and other, lesser followers of Antonio Canova (1757–1822). This bust provides an excellent visual transition from statuary to the coinage. Statues of Greco-Roman gods or busts of famous men, which seemed to lack sympathy and individual personality in monumental marble, came off perfectly in the precise limits of a coin die designed in the neoclassic idiom.

Horatio Greenough was eminently qualified to give the United States a coinage comparable to what Benedetto Pistrucci (1784–1855) had devised for Great Britain in the last years of George III. He supplied a set of ideas for the improvement of our coinage that would have added immeasurably to its richness and variety—but which never progressed beyond the stage of sketches because they sought to overthrow or change the canonical emblems and inscriptions that lawmakers and other lesser minds deemed a perpetual necessity in our metallic media. His ideas ranged from the removal of Liberty and her inscription to the introduction of figures or objects symbolizing Industry and Plenty, Agriculture and Mechanics. He favored wreaths of native produce, such as Indian corn, designs that actually came onto patterns and the regular coinage a generation later. A marble relief of oval (and therefore medallic) shape, featuring the Dioskouroi of classical mythology passing each other on

30. Powers, Horatio Greenough

31. Greenough, Castor and Pollux

horseback, shows what Greenough had in mind when he expressed Greco-Roman ideas and compositions in tondo form (fig. 31). Castor and Pollux, the heavenly twins, are presented in a synthesis of neo-Attic reliefs from the first century of the Roman Empire and the equestrian compositions of the Parthenon frieze in the Greek fifth century B.C., the source used by Pistrucci for British coinage.

Medal by Gobrecht

While not a product of the Philadelphia Mint, like the majority of medals considered in these chapters, Christian Gobrecht's medal for an industrial exhibition of 1826 (fig. 32) marks a transition to new classicism and new techniques, just as his coins heralded a new age at the American mints. The Napoleonic pictorialism and patriotic fussiness of Reich and Fürst in the first two decades of the 19th century have given way to a grander combination of sculptural relief, spaced lettering, symbolic details, and neutral space. Gobrecht's obverse and reverse were commissioned by the New England Society for Promotion of Manufactures and Mechanic Arts. The bust of Archimedes on the obverse, replete with poet's fillet in the hair, chiton, and himation thrown over his shoulders, is copied from some neoclassic cameo or intaglio allegedly showing the greatest mathematician of antiquity. Archimedes lived throughout most of the third century B.C., dying in 212 at the Roman siege of his native Syracuse, while engaged in constructing all manner of wonderful machines to withstand the ill-fated siege. Although the portrait as rendered by Gobrecht has every aspect of a Hellenistic marble bust, no such likeness of the Sicilian Greek scientist has survived the Roman era. The neoclassic sources that Gobrecht studied derive from a combination of portraits of Homer and Sophocles going back to the Hellenistic period and the fourth century B.C. The precise classicism that Gobrecht was to use in his U.S. coinage of 1836 and later, particularly in the interpretation of Sully's seated Liberty on the obverses of the dollar and lesser silver, has come off with masterful monumentality and precision in this medal. Antiquity lives again at the knowing hand of a modern sculptor, engraver, and machinist.

32. Gobrecht, medal, 1826

The reverse is equally impressive, although the three vignettes within tondi recall banknote designs, and thus something of the quaint pictorialism of the earlier part of the century lives on in this medal. The theme is well suited to the obverse, and the ensemble thus makes a worthy monument to the society responsible for its creation. As the inscription above states, GENIUS, INTELLIGENCE, AND INDUSTRY TRIUMPH. In a burst of clouds and rays, what Longacre would term a "glory," Gobrecht has enshrined the names of socially correct scientists of all ages, a proper mixture of antiquity, the Renaissance, England, and young America. From top to bottom are Archimedes again, Galileo, Newton, Franklin of course, and

33. Sully, study for an obverse

34. Peale, study for a reverse

one of the most modern, Fulton, whose contribution fills the long oval above the unrolled fillet left blank to receive the recipient's name. I take the two machines above to be a loom on the left and a lathe, suspiciously like a device for engraving dies, on the right. Native American foliage and corn, of the type found as filling ornaments on banknotes, complete the well-balanced harmony of the modern sciences and their progenitors. Small wonder, after a medal such as this, that Christian Gobrecht was called to the Philadelphia Mint a decade later.[1]

Coinage of 1836

The initial sketch (fig. 33) for the obverse of the new coinage of 1836 was made by the portraitist Thomas Sully.[2] The flying eagle of the reverse was entrusted to the astute eye of Titian Peale, of the gifted Philadelphia family. He was the ornithological draughtsman who was to prepare for publication studies of birds by Charles Lucien Bonaparte and also possibly some of those by John James Audubon (fig. 34). The dies were made ready and the obverse signed by or for Christian Gobrecht, the Pennsylvanian whose private commissions for banknote plates and medals had earned him a place in the Mint. The seated Liberty owes a great deal to the seated so-called Fates in the east pediment of the Parthenon, carved about 435 B.C., but the eagle flying amid the stars of all the states is the first numismatic bird that could be said to derive from nature rather than from colonial carving or heraldry (fig. 35). Some criticisms were leveled at this new Liberty; Gobrecht had made the area from her neck to her right shoulder too long, and the left elbow seemed to balance without comfort above the long left thigh. Rocks and plinth emphasized the statuesque origins of the ultimate prototype. The signature was considered tasteless for its time; medals made by the artist of the U.S. Mint are usually signed with the engraver's full name, but the most allowed on the coinage is initials or monogram.

35. Dollar of 1836

The identification of Liberty on the half dollar of 1807 to 1836 with a blowsy lady had been the first of a long series of attempts to endow images on our coins with specific names and personalities. The American eagle was perhaps the next. In the early days of the Mint, evidently in its first Philadelphia home, which was used until January 1833, the establishment and its personnel were adopted by a tame eagle named Peter. The bird used to soar over the city and swoop down over the chimney pots, always returning to the Mint in the evening or at odd times during the working day. It was during such a day that Peter met his sad fate, being caught and killed in one of the giant flywheels of the new-style coining presses. Granted visual and historical immortality by being stuffed, Peter was to reign in this form as late as 1892, as the centerpiece of the Mint exhibition at the World's Columbian Exposition in Chicago. Legend has it that Peter posed for Titian Peale's Flying Eagle reverse of 1836. Conservative congressmen and the like must have found the design too daring, for the Flying Eagle went into only brief circulation on the silver dollar. A generation later he made an appearance (fig. 36) on the new, reduced-size cent, the forerunner of our present designs.[3]

36. Cent of 1857

37. Half eagle of 1834

Patterns of 1838

The dies by William Kneass and Christian Gobrecht introduced qualities of machine-designed precision to the regular gold and silver coinage (figs. 37 and 38). Kneass was still a primitive artist of the first wave of Italian neoclassicism in American coinage. He was essentially a craftsman of the period before the influence of Canova or his American imitators such as Greenough was felt in the numismatic arts; and no matter how much Gobrecht reworked his late Roman classicistic "turban-headed" bust of Liberty or his stereotyped version of the "sandwich-board" eagle, he could scarcely be expected to come up with a new and very vital vocabulary for the arts in U.S. coinage. In view of all that was written between 1836 and 1839 about improving the coinage, it is surprising that the authorities could have been so aesthetically blind as to reject the glorious flying eagle in favor of the old convention, half naturalism and half heraldry, on the second side of the larger silver coins.

No more direct contrast exists between old and new than in pattern half dollars dated 1838 and 1839 (fig. 38). The obverse is a large, much-bedecked bust of Liberty identified with a design prepared by William Kneass before he was incapacitated by a stroke late in August 1835. The reverse is Gobrecht's powerful bird in a field devoid of stars. There are only the necessary inscriptions and two metallic rosettes or buttons, like those often seen on bronze plaques with lettering in relief, on the reverse. A unity of details, such as the dentil borders on obverse and reverse, suggest that both the Kneass design or die and the Gobrecht-Peale eagle die were styled in their final form by Gobrecht. Naturally he could not rid the obverse of its awkwardness, tasteless elaboration of accessories, and general flavor of a milkmaid on her way to the fair.

38. Pattern half dollar, 1839

39. Cent of 1839

It is almost impossible to follow the details of this so-called Liberty. A coronet like a riveter's shield is adorned with the solar spray of the ANNO COEPTIS pyramid on Continental and later currency down to recent dollar bills. Behind this it is hard to say what is cap and what is hair, but persistence reveals the word LIBERTY to be written large along a broad band that stars as a headcloth and ends as a band under the tousled mass of loose hair. The drapery of the bust can only be described as timid and unnatural. It resembles a nightgown at the chest and thin armor on the shoulder. By contrast the famous Flying Eagle reverse looks like one of the greatest symphonies of die design and cutting to be performed on any flan at any period in the history of Western civilization. This is cold observation, not mere national pride. Only the most sensitive, most penetrating photograph can bring out the bold yet subtle relief and foreshortening of the bird as he flies across our vision from right front to left rear. Feathers, wingtips, beak, and curled talon are presented with a naturalistic power and precision as advanced in American numismatic art as was Benedetto Pistrucci's 1818 portrait of the aged George III.

With or without a starry background, with or without talons grasping arrows and olive branch, this vision of the national bird on the wing was as magnificent a presentation in depth, detail, and silhouette as the human mind could conceive and the human hand translate into the mechanics of coining processes between 1836 and 1840. Less fortunate in its claims on greatness was another reverse design by Gobrecht for a projected half dollar of 1838, an eagle seen in twisted, frontal view with wings half-spread and drooping, an olive branch in the right claw and four arrows in the left. The bird was too like a reversal of the eagle with shield on its chest, going back to the half dollar designed by John Reich for the coinage of 1807. Naturally this less exciting, more heraldic, and relatively mediocre bird was to find flavor on the coinage to a greater extent than the Peale-Gobrecht eagle soaring off to the left. The drooping eagle reappeared in an interpretation by William Barber on the trade dollars of 1873 through 1885 and on the twenty-cent piece of 1875 through 1878 (figs. 75 and 84). Combined with the Sully-Gobrecht Liberty Seated obverse, either reverse presents a higher level of art than the revised version of John Reich's "sandwich-board" eagle with drooping wings, which was destined to continue on U.S. silver until 1892.

Christian Gobrecht's other contribution to this rich series of pattern half dollars was an obverse bust of Liberty wearing a diadem with her identifying inscription across the surface in prominently incused, mannered capitals. Related to the Liberty on contemporary cents (fig. 39), the bust is also an elaboration of that to be considered in connection with new gold coins of 1838 to 1840. The ropelike hair with extra knots around the bun at the back, the great curls falling down to the shoulder, the corkscrew bangs, and the pseudo-haughty face are a good demonstration of Napoleonic "Empire" styles surviving in Philadelphia a decade past their day abroad. With nose too long, eyes too porcine, jaw too fat, and brows too lowering, this Liberty is the milkmaid bust of William Kneass given supposedly modern, Continental arts. If we can mourn the failure to make better use of the Peale-Gobrecht Flying Eagle reverse on U.S. coins, we can be grateful that this bust of Liberty did not achieve any more currency than on four or five combinations of patterns.

Roman Liberty and Her Sources

In the same period that he produced the Liberty Seated and the Flying Eagle, Gobrecht executed new designs (1838) for the $10 denomination in gold, a coin known as an eagle. The bust of Liberty with an inscribed coronet in her hair that graced the obverse was to remain on the gold coinage until 1908. The reverse differed little from the design in use since 1807 on the $5 gold piece save that the wings of the eagle spread from one edge of the coin to the other (fig. 40). On the $5 gold piece, or half eagle, and even on the last series of large cents, this sober yet young and sympathetic head of Liberty was to vary only in details of tresses on the neck or strands of pearls in the bun on the back of the head (figs. 41 and 39). Perhaps the key to charm in this arrangement is that only the 13 stars and the date occupy the field, making an even simpler, less-active design than the Liberty Seated obverse of the comparable denominations in silver.

The motivation for this Roman head of Liberty stems from vast, varied Roman neoclassicism of the Napoleonic era. Typical of the sources is a small painting, a free study for a larger composition, by Jacques-Louis David's contemporary Pierre Narcisse Guérin, *Pythagoras* or *The Earth Is Round,* painted about 1800 (fig. 42). The mathematician harangues a

40. Eagle of 1847

41. Half eagle of 1840

42. Guérin, Pythagoras

royal couple, evidently the king and queen of Syracuse, amid scribes or students and other hangers-on. It is the diademed or coroneted, white-robed, seated female that should attract our attention, for she is related to the heads of Liberty on our 19th-century gold and copper coinage. The queen is based on some Greco-Roman statue such as the so-called *Agrippina* (A.D. 20)—actually Saint Helena, the mother of Constantine the Great (A.D. 325)—in the Museo Capitolino in Rome. This statue in turn can be traced back to work in Athens about 420 B.C. in the generation after Pheidias and the Parthenon. Engravings of this ancient sculpture and its ancient replicas in Naples or Florence reached America in the late neoclassic era, and the new United States received not only reproductions of paintings such as Guérin's *Pythagoras* but plaster casts of ancient heads comparable to that used in the figure of the queen contemplating the philosopher.

Antonio Canova's statue of Letizia Bonaparte (fig. 43), mother of Napoleon, is a close modification of the same group of statues studied by Guérin for the queen in his painting. The old lady's head, made young again under the sculptor's chisel, parallels quite closely the

43. Canova, Letizia Bonaparte

Roman heads of Livia or Juno that have been restyled by Christian Gobrecht in his dies for the gold coins and cent. Just as Canova's classicism lingered on in monumental sculpture in England and America until late in the Victorian age, so it survived in coins like this until the rise of American sculptors trained after the Civil War in new French ideas of photographic realism.

It should be emphasized that the republicanism of Thomas Jefferson and the artists of the young nation was derived from the world of Augustan or Hadrianic Rome rather than the Athens of the tyrant Peisistratos or the statesman Perikles. Sculptors in Italy, and their imitators in the glyptic arts of the Philadelphia Mint, had only Roman copies of Greek statues, such as the Apollo Belvedere in the Vatican or the diademed Juno then in the Villa Ludovisi at Rome, to measure the majesty of Livy's or Cicero's worlds. When federalist art sought an American eagle, the Flavian relief set over the door of the Church of the Holy Apostles (SS. Apostoli) in Rome was the ultimate source. The delicate calligraphy of Greek vases was known to certain connoisseurs in Italy, and by 1835 the Athenian Acropolis was being probed by Greek and German archaeologists, but the world of pure Pheidian or Praxitelean form was still far removed from the antiquarian yearnings of a Sully, a Ball Hughes, or a Gobrecht; instead the best materials at hand in the museums of Italy were used.

Neoclassicism liked the cold profiles and positive outlines of statues and reliefs in marble; these experiences could be easily excerpted and reduced in sketches, mechanical and otherwise, to the coinage. Unfortunately, as the 19th century progressed, it becomes almost painfully evident that similar sources were consulted both by the engravers of U.S. coins in Philadelphia and by the cutters of tombstones from Maine to Illinois.

The Coinage of 1840

The silver dollar that circulated from 1840 through 1873 (fig. 44) is typical of the Gobrecht-executed designs as they emerged on our major and minor silver coins. The seated Liberty has lost much of her plastic quality, becoming flatter and more like an engraving than a statue on a plinth. A curl of hair on her right shoulder masks the long, awkward line from neck to arm, and extra folds of drapery now buoy the left arm. The reverse is a disappointment: the same old unnatural, unartistic eagle with shield on his stomach, like a baseball umpire's protector, has returned, once again to clutch branch and olives in one foot, arrows of war in the other oversized set of claws.

44. Silver dollar of 1840 type

It seems hard nowadays to realize that this is the design that dominated American silver coinage to the exclusion of all others for over 50 years, starting just before 1840 and continuing until 1891. The only variations, so to speak, were the absence of the eagle on the dime and half

45. Dime of 1837

dime, merely the denomination within a wreath being shown (fig. 45), and, after the Civil War, the introduction of the motto IN GOD WE TRUST on the dollar, half dollar, and quarter dollar. In 1853 a concession to monotony was tried in the form of rays around the eagle on these coins to signal a change in weight; but this detail, a handsome feature, giving depth to the eagle and cohesion to the empty background within the heavy lettering, lasted only one year. In 1860, both dime and half dime saw the national name replace the obverse stars, with a wreath of cereals now surrounding the denomination.

Despite the relationship with Greek and Roman forms, the seated Liberty on the obverse of the silver dollar and its divisions is a thoroughly American creation of the age when artists from the young republic were traveling to Italy in the generation following the Napoleonic Wars.[4] The long nose, the large eye (like that of a baby chicken), the hair combed not back but down across the temples in a loop like that worn by the young Queen Victoria, and the rubbery physique are characteristics of neoclassic heroines in American painting of these decades. Jane McCrea massacred by Indians in upstate New York during the Revolutionary War or merchants' daughters sitting for their portraits are given the same set of features, both the details and the general proto-Victorian aura of plump, wide-eyed youthfulness. Clutching her ridiculous little hat on a pole and the small shield nestling in the drapery at her side, Liberty looks anxiously over her shoulder as if a horde of Indians were sprinting through the starry firmament toward her. The 13 six-pointed stars around Liberty and the whole plan of the reverse predate the adoption of the statuesque seated goddess in 1839, going back through the progressive forms of the obverse (stars) and reverse that appeared on the quarter and half dollar in 1831, 1836, and 1838.

Sully's design for the seated figure of Liberty, as interpreted by Gobrecht in the coinage of 1836, was improved upon by Gobrecht himself in 1839, when drapery was added from the left elbow to the thigh on the half dollar. In 1840 Dr. Robert Maskell Patterson, director of the Mint, engaged Robert Ball Hughes, the Anglo-American sculptor, medalist, and maker of portrait miniatures in relief, to improve the proportions and model the drapery in more naturalistic fashion. These minor changes, keeping close to Sully's design as rendered by Gobrecht, at first affected the silver dollar, the quarter dollar, the dime, and the half dime. The half dollar alone remained closest to the original scheme of details until 1892.

Robert Ball Hughes enlarged Liberty's head and her cap on the pole. He fattened the right arm reaching down to the shield. This object was brought out in slightly higher relief with the word LIBERTY in heavier lettering on a straighter band. The twisted, dishmop effect of the long hair, especially the tresses down the back of the neck, was smoothed out, and a curl was added to bring the disjointed right shoulder closer to the head and neck. A larger, curved series of folds of drapery was introduced from the left elbow to the knee; structurally impossible in classical terms as part of the main garment, this can only be thought of as a cloak or himation over the left arm. Finally, the folds of the main garment or chiton were smoothed out and regrouped in stricter adherence to a Greek model of the time of the Parthenon and the followers of Pheidias. Greater clarity emerged in the proportions of the body beneath. These modifications also eliminated the distressing similarity to a shower curtain in the crinkly folds of vertical drapery derived from the original interpretation of Sully's sketch.

Quaint and dated though the entire ensemble may seem in the light of later coin design, the seated Liberty symbolizes American numismatic art during the generations of westward expansion, the Civil War, the centennial of the young republic, and commercial expansion that was to propel the United States into the role of a worldwide power. Other versions of Liberty in use at this time—the diademed Greco-Roman bust or even the young lady with Indian headdress—have always resembled designs in European or South American coinage. Conceived in the classical tradition, nurtured by a triad of gifted artists, the seated Liberty presided over the coinage of the United States with an individuality matching that of the pioneers, soldiers, merchants, writers, and craftsmen who were making the Republic great.

Pre–Civil War Quaintness and Mediocrity

Christian Gobrecht died in office in 1844, and his successor as chief engraver, the fourth to hold the office, was James Barton Longacre (1794–1869). A native of Delaware County, Pennsylvania, he had achieved a name as an engraver, chiefly as a portraitist. For the epic *National Portrait Gallery of Distinguished Americans,* published in four volumes between 1834 and 1839, he not only prepared plates but drew from life for engravings prepared by others (fig. 46). The two artists most thought of in connection with Longacre's work at the Mint were the German-born Anthony C. Paquet (1814–1882), assistant engraver from 1857 to 1864, and the Englishman William Barber. Barber became fifth chief engraver, from 1869 to 1879, and passed the position on to his son, in a dynasty lasting down to Charles E. Barber's death in 1917. With the exception of several Mint medals (figs. 88 and 89), which prove his qualities as a master of incisive verism or of heroic sentiment in the early Victorian classical tradition, Paquet never had a chance to demonstrate his abilities as an official engraver. He soon left the government coining establishment for other, related work. Until William Barber's eye for quality as

46. Longacre, Andrew Jackson

a preparer of die designs began to manifest itself at the end of Longacre's career, the United States was treated to a series of designs having the common denominator of timidity.

Uniform in their dullness, lack of inspiration, and even quaintness, Longacre's contributions to patterns and regular coinages were a decided step backward from the art of Sully, Peale, Hughes, and Gobrecht. There were routine Greco-Roman heads of Liberty wearing her coronet. The $20 gold piece of 1849 to 1907 was one of these, although the reverse had some commendable points of heraldic imagery. Beauties of several ages in cigar-store Indian bonnets were labeled as Liberty. Mostly there were just plain wreaths and words or numerals of value. Until the Civil War the only evidences of new art in the coinage were random patterns by Paquet, notably a half dollar and a double eagle or $20 gold piece, and the revival of the Peale-Gobrecht Flying Eagle reverse as obverse of the reduced-scale 1856 to 1858 cent.[5] Much has been written about Longacre's inability to prepare master dies. Whatever his previous qualities as an engraver of portraits, he seems not have brought much imagination to his important post at the Philadelphia Mint. Since portraits were not demanded for the coinage, perhaps he was at a loss how to create new designs within the allegorical repertory of American numismatic art. Certainly the coins he did design seem to bear this out. Medals prepared at the Mint should have offered scope for his talents as a portraitist, but Longacre appears to have left this work undone, turning it over to Paquet, or to medalists in private practice.

Longacre's Sketches

A group of about 50 drawings related to the U.S. coinage, now in the collections of the Detroit Institute of Arts,[6] confirms that James B. Longacre thought of die designs as development of themes and motifs worked out initially as engravings. His ideas very seldom depart from flat surfaces. He liked outlines, heads in profile, and eagles flattened into poses of twisted heraldry. He profited from the work of his predecessors, but such three-dimensional qualities as his style possessed were often merely faithful renderings of studies by Titian Peale and others. The one area in which Longacre gave free rein to his imagination was in the matter of fancy headdress for his renderings of Liberty. His caps of feathers, his bonnets of freedom, and his starry diadems are joys to behold.

As engraver in the Mint at the time of the Civil War, one of Longacre's major preoccupations was placing the motto GOD OUR TRUST and, permanently, IN GOD WE TRUST on the coins. This task is reflected throughout the drawings. The double eagle or $20 gold piece was his major coin, and the reverse is like a frontispiece for a patriotic brochure (fig. 47). The same can be said for the Civil War shields and their vegetable produce, which became the first type of the nickel and the only design for the two-cent piece (fig. 48). Longacre loved to design wreaths, and his drawings show how often he turned his eye to their delights.

Two studies give positive evidence of interest in eagles on Greek and Roman coins. It is perhaps typical that 16th-century engravings have been used rather than the coins themselves. A different style results (fig. 49). Various heraldic eagles are obviously essays for the reverse of the gold coinage (fig. 50). J. Goldsborough Bruff, "Designing Artist and Draughtsman," of Washington, Georgia, sent the Mint a carefully planned study for the reverse of the double eagle (fig. 51), which pleased Longacre enough for him to preserve it amid his own sketches.[7]

There are a few novelties among the drawings. The study after the Apollo Belvedere that becomes the half dollar patterns of 1859 is there (fig. 52), and a full page of the Liberty seated with globe and flags, the obverse of the pattern dollars of 1870 and 1871, emphasizes the linear qualities of the design (fig. 53). An awkward little Liberty Seated reverse, dated 1845 (fig. 54), may be one of the first designs made by Longacre after he was appointed to Gobrecht's position.[8]

47

48

47.–48. Sketches by Longacre

49

50

49.–50. Sketches by Longacre

51. Double eagle design by Bruff

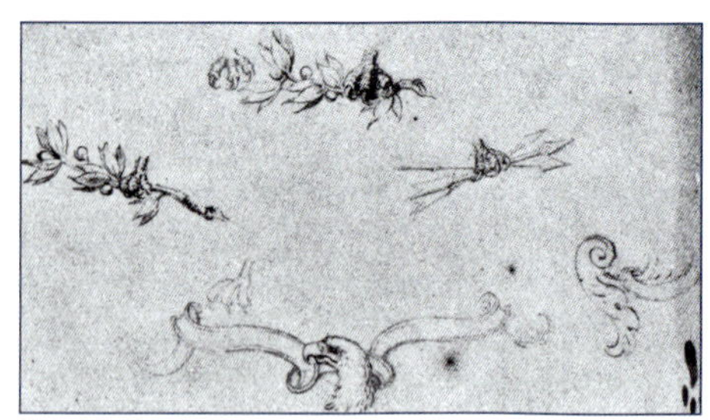

52

53

54

52.–54. Sketches by Longacre

Coinage of the 1850s

Longacre designed the $3 gold piece, which was coined from 1854 to 1889 but never circulated to any appreciable extent (fig. 55). Standard guides to U.S. coins describe this denomination in the following terms: "The head on the obverse represents an Indian princess with hair tightly curling over the neck, head crowned with a circle of feathers, the band of which is inscribed LIBERTY. A wreath of tobacco, wheat, corn, and cotton occupies the field of the reverse."[9] Essentially the same designs were employed by the engraver for the gold dollars of 1854 and 1856 to 1889. The "princess" of the gold coins is a banknote engraver's elegant version of folk art of the 1850s. The plumes or feathers are more like the crest of the Prince of Wales than anything that saw the Western frontiers, save perhaps on a music hall beauty. Iconographically this type of Indian maiden had occurred in American patriotic and "primitive" paintings for many years past. The figureheads of ships and the sculptures before tobacconists' shops sported faces, tresses, and bonnets of this type.

In 1858 Longacre modified the bonnet to create a more seemingly naturalistic headdress, sharpened the features of the Indian girl, changed the flowing hair to a few cascading feathers, and added a necklace. The result emerged in the regular coinage as the famous Indian head, really Liberty with Indian attributes, of the cents from 1859 to 1909 (fig. 56). The oak wreath of the reverse was typical of what Longacre had been producing for most coins since his accession to office 15 years earlier. Wreaths of oak, laurel, grain, corn, cereal, or tobacco all created pretty much the same aesthetic effect, the same plastic yet somewhat heraldic expedient for framing the minimum necessary lettering or numerals. Far from a major creation aesthetically or iconographically, and far less attractive to the eye than the Peale-Gobrecht Flying Eagle and its variants, including the small flying eagle turned more toward the viewer, the Indian Head cent was at least to achieve the blessing of popular appeal. The coin became perhaps the most beloved and typically American of any piece great or small in the American series. Great art the coin was not, but it was one of the first products of the U.S. mints to achieve the common touch and to identify itself with the transitions from frontier to industrial to social expansion during its decades of circulation, from 1860 to 1930.

The democratic aspects of the small cent led to the inevitable legend that the essentially idealized, stereotyped form of the young Liberty in Indian headgear was a specific person and that creation of the coin could be associated with a specific event in a known locale. The Indian Head cent became another one of the early U.S. coins in which the identification myth or cult of personality blossomed forth. The American public was desperate to trade the classical ideal of Liberty for someone of flesh and blood rather than gilt bronze or marble, and the girlish features of Longacre's "goddess" seemed to give them opportunity. The tale is one of the first of

55. Three-dollar gold piece

56. Pattern Indian Head cent

several such legends that clustered around Liberty. They only ceased when portraits of martyred presidents, founding fathers, or a world-recognized symbol of American political maturity pushed Liberty from the coinage in circulation, as late as the dime of 1946 and the half dollar of 1948.

One version of the creation of Longacre's Indian Head cent runs as follows:

> The suggestion of the panache [i.e., the tuft of feathers] is said to have come from a visit of a delegation of Indians from one of the tribes of the North-west, who came to talk with the "Great Father" in Washington; and while in the East they were taken to see the operations of the Mint. At the time, as the story is told, Miss Sarah Longacre, the daughter of the Mint engraver, was present while the chiefs and their followers were going through the building, and attracted the attention of their leader. In a mood of sportiveness he took his crown of feathers from his head and placed it upon hers. She was a child of five or six years of age, and as she stood for a moment wearing the novel head-dress, some one of the company made a sketch of the little maiden and her feathery cap, and in due time the design was engraved and used upon the coins, dies for which were then in preparation. Such is the story as told by a correspondent of a New York newspaper. Whether the tale is a true one the writer is unable to say; but certainly the device is far more appropriate to American coins than the conventional cap, which was originally given to the slave who had been freed by his Roman master, the awkward bonnet on our first coins, or the equally hideous turbans that so long disfigured the matronly heads on the silver pieces in the later years of the first half of the last century.[10]

One drawing now in the Detroit Institute of Arts may be the closest we can come to the first sketch of Longacre's daughter Sarah in the Indian bonnet (fig. 57). A finished drawing for a cent was obviously produced

57. Sketches by Longacre

58. Sketches by Longacre

at the time the "Indian Head" coin was being considered; it shows an eagle on the obverse and a version of the Civil War–era shield on the reverse (fig. 58). The early study for the Indian Head cent, combined with a modern version of the traditional reverse in use until 1857, makes it seem very unlikely a small girl was the ultimate model. The lady involved seems fairly mature and very Victorian, although her unusually long nose was actually a genetic fixture within the Longacre family.

The legend either ignores or grew out of the fact that Longacre had shown a penchant for Indian bonnets on Liberty at least five years before the cent gained currency. Since Liberty in Indian headgear is no anthropological study, it should be remembered that James E. Fraser was the first die designer to represent the Indian with dignified accuracy, on the so-called Buffalo nickel of 1913 (fig. 147). Bela L. Pratt had, however, taken the Native American out of the stage of cigar-store primitivism and American quaintness with the half eagle and quarter eagle of 1908 (fig. 136). Longacre enriched the mythology of American coinage in a pleasant if unpretentious fashion. Given his pattern half dollar designs of 1859 as a yardstick, he could have done worse.

The year 1859 was one of minor changes and potential major activity in the coinage. Unfortunately for the Paquet patterns, but perhaps fortunately for those of Longacre, the suggestions adopted were confined to the silver half dime and dime. Here Longacre's reverses with wreaths of cotton, tobacco, sugar cane, corn, wheat, and oak leaves were introduced, to allow fullest development of relief in the obverse designs. They lasted until the termination of the half dime in 1873 and, with modification by Charles E. Barber, on the dime (fig. 101) until the advent of A.A. Weinman's winged Liberty design in 1916, when the fasces became the principal element of the reverse (fig. 159).

Longacre's set of patterns for the half dollar comprised one obverse with three different versions of HALF DOLLAR, 1/2 DOLLAR, or 50 CENTS in the famous cereal wreath. Of these reverses the first presents the lettering in simple, direct, even fashion. On the second reverse, the

59. Pattern half dollar by Longacre

60. Pattern half dollar by Paquet

word DOLLAR begins to take on the curve of the 1860s Gothic design. The obverse is a horror by any standards of taste in any age. The bust of Liberty is none other than that of the Greco-Roman Apollo Belvedere with a large wreath of oak and vine leaves, an awkward ribbon set at various irregular, jerky angles around the base of the neck being the surface for display of the word LIBERTY. The cereal wreath is florid, pleasing, and only pedantic if someone stops to tell the viewer what its elements contain. The Apollo Belvedere of the Vatican was one of the touchstones of learned America's neoclassic adventures in classical art abroad between the fall of Napoleon and Bull Run, but only a literate engraver of national biography such as Longacre would think to absorb the bust of the statue into the repertory of Americana as the "goddess" Liberty (figs. 52 and 59).

Anthony Paquet's obverse for the projected new half dollar is a kind of Athena goddess of rectitude: Liberty seated stiffly, supporting fasces with the right hand and a shield with the left. Three arrows and an olive branch lie on the rough, metallic mound of rocks and earth on which Liberty must be thought to be sitting. The reverse of wide-winged eagle holding olive branch and arrows is a spirited, brittle yet forceful rendering of the emblem. This wide, angular eagle serves as a stylized but satisfying vehicle for the shield that had been a part of this general composition since 1807. In hitherto unexploited, imaginative fashion, the fillet or ribbon in the bird's mouth crosses the shield and bears the motto on it, partly covering the shield. Paquet was a superior craftsman of master dies. His goddess is plump, strained, and rather earthy, a contrast to the brittle carefulness of the details, especially around the base of the group and in the intelligent spacing of the small stars (fig. 60).

For the double eagle Paquet cleverly produced an obverse that is merely an elaboration of his design for the half dollar. The eagle of the reverse is placed behind the seated Liberty with all her trappings, in the manner in which the draped, semi-Amazon Roma on sestertii of the emperors Nero or Galba about A.D. 64 to 69 received additions of shields, arms, and cuirasses to her basic attributes. The oak wreath of the reverse is a very metallic Roman *corona civica* with precise lettering akin to that of a newspaper just before the Civil War. Perhaps in comparison Longacre's double eagle obverse and reverse were more dignified. Certainly Paquet's offering was in advance of its time, looking ahead to the Barber-Morgan patterns of the 1870s. One of the most satisfying combinations is the Paquet obverse with the Longacre reverse (fig. 61).

From 1830 to the Civil War, U.S. coins and medals reflected the stringent Greco-Romanism of Europe under Napoleon and in the decades from 1815 to 1835. In the 1850s these neoclassic designs were supplemented by those, mostly patterns never put into circulation, in which so-called native motifs displayed an increasing part. Longacre turned Liberty into a classic young Indian girl, and American produce, wheat and corn, replaced the classical oak or laurel in reverse designs. After a brilliant phase of design from 1836 to 1840, artistic levels reflected a more workmanlike approach to the coinage, with few changes in the designs, little outside help from great artists, and no coin—except the short-lived Flying Eagle cent of 1857—that could be called truly venturesome.

61. Pattern double eagle

IV

The Civil War and Its Aftermath

The Victorian Gothic phase in the art of American coinage is reflected in a series of patterns and minor coins struck during and just after the War Between the States. The emotion of the Civil War brought forth an urge to acknowledge God on the coinage, and after experiments with such legends as DEO EST GLORIA and GOD OUR TRUST (figs. 48, 62, and 63) the formula IN GOD WE TRUST was reached (figs. 48 and 64). There have been only a bold few coins since Appomattox that have not borne this mild form of prayer. The coin that is both most Gothic and most expressive of the Civil War is the two-cent piece, especially the pattern of 1863 with GOD OUR TRUST (fig. 65) as opposed to the regular issue of 1864 (fig. 66). The shield, arrows, and wreath of the obverse need only flanking cannon to be the consummate expression of Civil War heraldry. On the reverse, the manner in which the word CENTS curves against the tondo of wreath and legend recalls monumental lettering, like inscriptions on tombstones in the second half of the 19th century. The wreath meets in a form of Gothic arch above the denomination. The same combination of shield in this shape, curve and countercurve of lettering, and pointed arch is found in the standard tombstones provided by the United States for burial of the fallen and veterans of the War Between the States in local cemeteries throughout the North (fig. 67).

The chief engraver at the Mint in Philadelphia at this time, James Barton Longacre, has already been mentioned as an artist better suited to engraving plates for reproductions of portraits of famous men than to the deeper, more strenuous modeling of designs to be reduced into coin dies. That may explain why these two-cent pieces have such a strong calligraphic, nonsculptural appearance, which would be more at home on a banknote or a postage stamp. Patterns for the obverse include an overemphasized, stringy bust of George Washington, a forerunner of future portraiture on U.S. coins that was rightly rejected by James Pollock, director of the Mint, in his proposal to the secretary of the

62. *Pattern half dollar of 1862*

63. *Pattern eagle of 1862*

64. *Half dollar of 1866 type*

65. *Pattern two-cent piece*

66. *Two-cent piece*

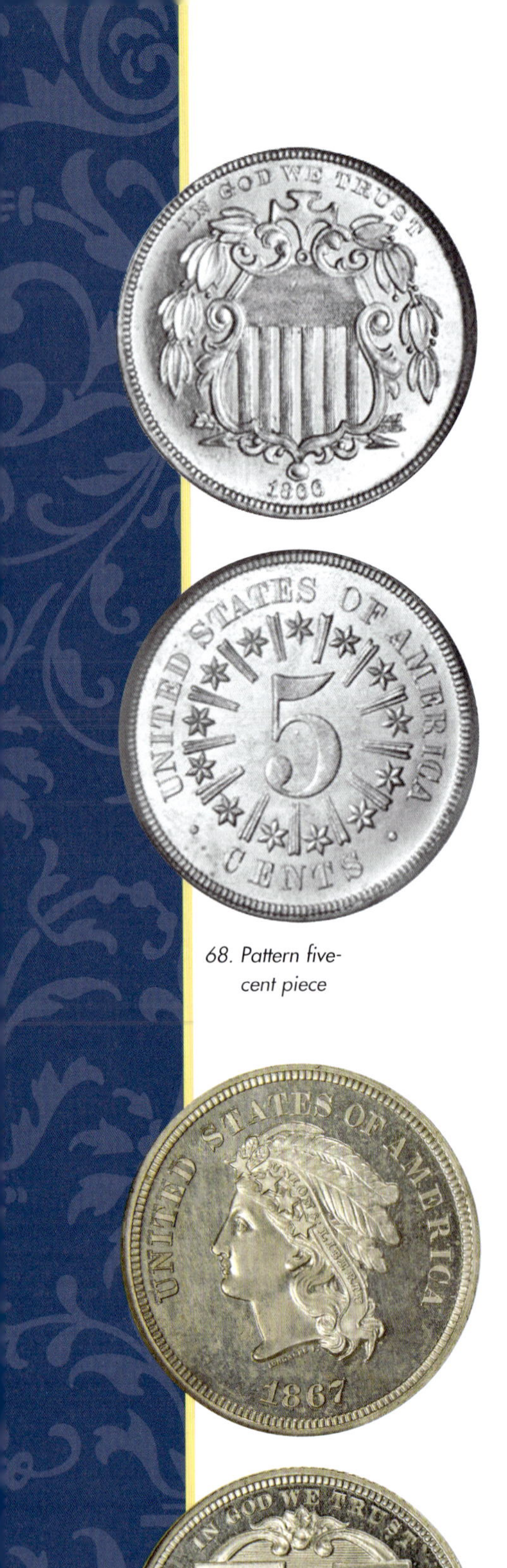

68. Pattern five-cent piece

69. Pattern five-cent piece

67. Tombstone of Sgt. E.F. Richardson

Treasury. An engraving of Andrew Jackson after a portrait by Thomas Sully shows Longacre as his better artistic self (fig. 46). In 1867 and 1868 the engraver made patterns in aluminum and other metals for what was already in circulation as the five-cent piece in nickel. The design of 1866 differed little from the wartime two-cent pieces; even the bold, individual feature of rays on the reverse was eliminated in 1867 (fig. 68). Longacre's signed pattern of 1867 presents perhaps the most unusual head of Liberty in the entire U.S. series. A Greco-Roman goddess wears a band of stars, above which there is a ribbon inscribed UNION & LIBERTY, with over the top of her head a headdress composed of four large feathers, all partly concealing long tresses that hang down to her shoulders (fig. 69). The total effect is a curious parallel to some of the hats created by fashionable milliners a century after Longacre sat down with his pad and pencil. The reverse presents a large roman numeral of denomination set against a shield encased in a Victorian frame, of the type used for mirrors in the hallways and parlors of American homes some hundred years ago.

The 1868 pattern has reverted to the diademed head of Liberty, with only one of the stars remaining above the forehead. The reverse is less opulent also, the large V in a conventional wreath (fig. 70). In 1883, when a variation of this reverse was issued on a nickel designed by Charles E. Barber, the quick-witted plated the coins in gold and passed them into circulation for five dollars in merchandise or change. The word CENTS was quickly added to the die (fig. 71). The diademed and wreathed head of Liberty on the obverse was modeled almost verbatim from a Greco-Roman head of Juno or a major personification such as Concordia, a marble cult statue for some shrine in Rome or the provinces. It so happens that the very head said to have been used as the model for this nickel, which was coined until 1913, is the centerpiece in the entrance salon of the premises of Stack's, the well-known dealers in coins on 57th Street in New York. This Greco-Roman restyling of a Greek head of the fourth century B.C. was on display in the Philadelphia Academy of Art when Charles Barber, George T. Morgan, and other artists of the Mint in the period from the Civil War to the First World War admired it and turned its full, grave, if not heavy profile into designs for the coinage (fig. 72).

70. Pattern five-cent piece

71. Five-cent piece

72. Greco-Roman goddess

The head passed through various private collections in Philadelphia. At one time it belonged to S.H. and H. Chapman, and Barber knew of it through his friendship with the numismatist and antiquarian Henry Chapman. Thus, what modern critics would consider a dull, academic standard of classical divinity in visual form became a keystone in the redesigned denominations of American coinage.

In the mid-20th century an over-life-sized statue of a city goddess with diadem and mural crown was found in western Asia Minor, at the site of a Roman colony in the uplands of Anatolia. The dry, precise carving of the head, work of the early second century A.D. after a model of about 430 B.C., is, like the Chapman head, precisely what designers of U.S. coins looked for in the decades from 1860 to 1890 (fig. 73). Even the piling up of attributes in the hair and the sharply defined curls

73. Detail of a city goddess

cascading on the shoulders are what American artists sought as they endeavored to create a classical iconography for the idealistic expressions of the United States. Academic revivalism of the second century A.D. found its champions in the United States as the centennial approached. These Roman canons of ideal sculpture not only inspired the creations of die designers in Philadelphia but determined types of monumental statues and reliefs for public buildings and elaborate tombs throughout the land. Although this specific statue was unavailable to engravers in Victorian-era America, comparable Greco-Roman sculptures were known in Philadelphia through the media of plaster casts and engravings or even photographs. The city goddess illustrated here, however, is everything the Barbers or Morgan could have desired in an ancient prototype had the statue been above ground when they worked.

Except for the examples noted, the patterns of the Civil War years and the years thereafter are mainly dull and of dubious artistry, until William Barber, who had become chief engraver upon Longacre's death in 1869, launched "standard" reverses for silver coins of all denominations in 1870. These new reverses were combined with some of the obverses of 1869, busts of Liberty with "firemen's" caps and massive diadems or starry coronets, but they also engendered new types of Liberty Seated that heralded the wealth of patterns associated with the 1870s. William Barber produced a seated Pheidian goddess draped in a long, girt chiton and himation cascading down over the rocks on which she presumably sits. She holds a medieval shield with accolade of LIBERTY on a thick band with large knots, and her Phrygian or Liberty cap seems to balance miraculously on a rapier beyond her right arm. The faults with the design lie in the limp left arm and olive branch at her left side. All of this is lost in a confusing mass of drapery, lumps, and crisscross folds that are too much when set off against the simple Greco-Roman head with its plain ribbon. The obverse comes not only with the "standard" reverses but also with the regular reverse dies for the dollar through the half dime (fig. 74). The seated Liberty really looks best when shown with the large, simple, yet rich "Standard 1 Dollar." Here the curved lettering so characteristic of Victorian Gothic is set off by a wreath of cotton and corn, a late and vigorous reminiscence of Horatio Greenough's strictures to Mint director Robert M. Patterson in 1842 that native products such as corn, "one of the few fruits which form a staple from Maine to Georgia," grace the coinage.[1]

The late Longacre's influence on this new series of obverses was confined in 1870 solely to the silver dollar, but in 1871 it blossoms forth on all the silver coins both with and without the surrounding stars (fig. 53). These coins include the regular issues, the Standard Silver, and in the instance of the silver dollar something called the "commercial dollar," which was a forerunner of the pattern trade dollars of 1872 and the regular issue of 1873. The idea of Liberty seated is splendid, but the iconographic details are overwhelming. Liberty wears one of those unfortunate

74. Pattern dollar of 1870

cigar-store Indian headdresses that Longacre loved so much. She sits on a rock, and her right hand holds the cap on the pole with firmness and obviousness not found in the Barber design. The left hand rests on one of those giant LIBERTY-girt globes so distressingly like a gymnasium medicine ball. Twin flags, one clearly showing 22 stars, serve as props for the complex drapery and overly curved form of the goddess.

The ideas for enriching the iconographic complexity of America's standard numismatic figure in the 1870s were most laudable after the stilted Roman busts of the 1860s, and even after the crude Washingtons and Lincolns that were considered for the nickel five-cent piece in 1866. Their chief fault is that the artists could not avoid the frilly complexity of the high Victorian era. Barber's Liberty was plainer and therefore stronger, but the lower part of the figure was too fussy for the upper. Longacre's Liberty swayed forward like a ship's figurehead, and was accompanied by an inordinate mountain of paraphernalia. The years immediately to follow would bring a happy simplification of these experiments.

Trade Dollars and Their Patterns

75. Trade dollar of 1874

From 1873 until 1885, merely as collectors' items in the last seven years, the mints at Philadelphia, Carson City (Nevada), and San Francisco struck a series of trade dollars in a high grade of silver for circulation among the hard monies of the Far East. The design is a kind of glorification of all neo-Roman symbolism popular on U.S. coins in the 19th century (fig. 75). In the year these silver dollars appeared, a numismatic reporter described the seated Liberty on the obverse, a figure based on the Roma or Italia of Julio-Claudian to Antonine sestertii, in the no-nonsense terms of post–Civil War commercialism: "A female figure [is] seated on bales of merchandise, holding in her left hand a scroll bearing the word 'Liberty.' At her back is a sheaf of wheat, expressing, with the bales of goods, the commercial character of the coin: her right hand extended holds the olive branch."[2] Peace and commerce are dispatched from the United States of America over the seas, for this Juno sits on a grassy plinth, inscribed with IN GOD WE TRUST and set beside the waves. A particularly satisfying eagle graces the reverse, small yet bold and a happy compromise between heraldry and concessions to feathery nature. The plethora of titles, mottoes, and inscribed statistics somehow does not seem out of place on either obverse or reverse.

In the process of creating the trade dollar of 1873, the chief engraver, William Barber, and his colleagues executed a series of six

76.–81. Set of six patterns for the trade dollar

pattern trade dollars that were sold in limited sets to those interested. These dollars said just about all the idiom of neo-Romanism could express with seated Liberty, the head of Liberty, eagles posed with shields, and the standard set of inscriptions necessary to this coin of commerce. They form a handsome group, one salient quality being the uniformity of effect and detail that characterizes the designs (figs. 76–81). The eagles wave ribbons with E PLURIBUS UNUM in their beaks; or they scream while grasping arrows, the olive branch, or a shield draped with the ribbon of IN GOD WE TRUST. One reverse is all wreath and inscriptions. The most unusual presents a defiant eagle, head lowered in fighting pose, wings half spread, and claws planted firmly on olive branch, arrows, and shield, the last serving as a plinth for the whole ensemble. Lettering is of a similar, careful, printer's Victorian quality; the tondo fields are framed by Roman dentils; the stars have a uniform height and shape; and the motif of twin stars below, flanking the eagle, occurs on six of the eight reverses.

One Liberty Seated differs only in slight details from the design used on the coins put into circulation. The other three examples of ornate Roman classicism are about as unusual as any animal, bird, human, or personification on the U.S. coinage. The debt to the figure of Italia on brass sestertii of the emperor Antoninus Pius in the second century A.D. is quite direct. The Roman orb of universal domination now looks like a large medicine ball inscribed LIBERTY. The Greco-Roman turreted crown in one instance has become a feathered bonnet, like those worn by wooden cigar-store Indians. Flags, Phrygian caps on poles, a plow, bales of King Cotton, and sheaves of wheat complete the picture of American peace, freedom, and prosperity. The preoccupation with sheaves of wheat is a truly Victorian one, with its parallel in freestanding sculpture on a type of tombstone mass-produced in the generations from 1850 to 1890. A novelty of short duration on the coinage, these complex figures of Liberty or America or Columbia were to have a longer life; they exist still, as the vignettes of stock or bond certificates and banknotes.

The two heads of Liberty in this series of patterns for the trade dollar are stringent in their Roman classicism (figs. 80 and 81). The wreathed head has a pouting, compressed face, prominent lips, and a full, forceful line of the chin taken verbatim from a Greco-Roman head of the first century A.D. that may be an idealized portrait of Julia, daughter of Augustus, in the guise of a goddess such as Artemis (fig. 82). The Roman head in marble demonstrates the source for the rough, moplike hair and the combing of heavy strands into the bun at the back. The diademed head in the series of patterns for the trade dollar is very Victorian in its pretty interpretation of Roman classicism, but it too can be related to several common Greco-Roman marbles, ancient copies after originals of the fifth and fourth centuries B.C. For the length of the neck,

82. Julio-Claudian princess

shape of the chin, lips, line of the forehead, and what can be compared of the nose, and the wavy undercutting of the hair, whether below a diadem or a thin band, I have chosen a good Hellenistic or Roman copy of the fourth-century statue known as the Artemis Colonna (fig. 83). Both these heads seem to have arrived in America in the 1880s, but they represent the type of antiquities first collected in the original or as plaster casts for libraries, athenaeums, historical societies, and academies of art in the United States before the scientific acquisition of classical art at the end of the 19th century.

As a coin intended for circulation in a special market, the trade dollar was in many respects like a commemorative issue. At least these handsome coins afforded the designers in the Mint an opportunity to break away from the usual seated Liberty of the silver coinage and the diademed head of that divine creature that graced the gold, or the Liberty in Indian bonnet that had become a part of the bronze "penny" or cent.

84. Twenty-cent piece

85. Pattern trade dollar

83. Artemis

Patterns of 1875

The years before and after the centennial were among the most productive of designs for the coinage in America's two centuries of independence. In 1875 William Barber prepared an extensive series of patterns for the twenty-cent piece (fig. 84). The coin was issued over a brief span of four years, with only the 1875 mintages at San Francisco and Carson City being produced in sufficient quantity to make the denomination more than an unwanted curiosity. Nothing unusual characterizes the design selected, which is a pleasing synthesis of traditional elements. The only new departure was the introduction of the awkward eagle on the reverse that William Barber had used on the trade dollar of 1873 and a number of patterns in various denominations and metals. The bird is a fatter version of the one that appeared on the silver coinage of 1796.

One of the complex symbols of American iconography produced on pattern twenty-cent pieces and silver dollars of the year 1875 was the obverse showing "Liberty seated at the seashore." The debt to Britannia on British coppers is obvious and natural, considering that the three engravers of the Philadelphia Mint—William Barber, his son Charles, and George T. Morgan—were native-born Englishmen. "Liberty seated at the seashore" (fig. 85) is reminiscent of some monumental statue in front of a building in Fairmount Park, Philadelphia, at the Exposition of 1876. The seashore was a logical escape away from patterns at the beginning of the decade, in which the extremely statuesque Liberty is shown seated on a rockwork plinth like that used for Roman statues of personifications. A glimpse of the sea creeps into the left rear corner of three obverses in the 1873 series of patterns for the trade dollar. On the regular, adopted obverse die for the trade dollar of 1873 through 1885 a generous portion of sea fills the left rear, and a speck of water seems to have flooded around behind the sheaves of wheat to complete the plinth at the right front corner (fig. 75).

"Liberty at the seashore" presents little that is not part of other complex representations of the patron personification or "virtue" in these years. The vista opening to the left, however, is refreshing if not dramatic. The sea suggests unlimited depth in a medallic surface, and the ship is as dated a document as the whole concept of Liberty amid the fruits of farm and field. Appropriately enough, the vessel is powered by steam and shows sails set, like the Cunard liners that plied the North Atlantic sea lanes in the restless, prosperous decade after the Civil War. The hand plow found on certain other designs where the sea is barely visible preserves the "Cincinnatus" motif of hardy pioneers prepared to drop farming tools and seize rifle in defense of liberties. Liberty at the expansive seascape, like other less exciting variations, exhibits two flags where the plow should be. Together with the olive branch, this suggests a nation reunited after the strife of the previous decade. Wheat and cotton speak of the golden West and the repossessed South, an iconographic totality as overwhelming as that of the goddess Roma on coins of the Roman emperors Nero or Galba in the first century A.D.[3]

86. Dollar of 1878

The Liberty Head Dollar

In the instance of the famous Liberty Head or Bland-Allison silver dollar of 1878, designed by George T. Morgan in his capacity as assistant to Chief Engraver William Barber, we have a direct conflict between the artist's own word that a Greco-Roman head provided the model and the apocryphal, romantic legend that a certain young woman was the model for the head of Liberty (fig. 86). Morgan wrote the director of the Mint

87. Morgan, studies for half dollars

November 1, 1876, about his studies for patterns that appeared in 1877, of half dollar size (fig. 87), but from sketches he enclosed as well as from the letter it is clear that Morgan had in mind the head of Liberty that was to be used on the "Morgan" dollar of 1878. He wrote:

> I have your letter of yesterday in which you say I may proceed with the models according to my own judgment. I fully realize the responsibility and assure you they shall have my earnest attention.
>
> I have taken one to the mint today for reduction—I have entered as a student at the Academy of Fine Arts—where I am making a profile study from a Greek figure which I feel will be useful in finishing the head of Liberty. I shall endeavor to get studies in nature for the Eagle—I have been considering the wreath on the reverse of the Dime—although it could be improved by being more sharply & clearly defined, I have come to the conclusion myself that the wreath is too elaborate & complicated in so small a coin—I have therefore prepared a design of a wreath much simpler—but I think it without novelty.[4]

In a later letter, early in 1877, Morgan describes how he has been working on the head of Liberty, "making more of the cap and less of the hair."[5] In addition to his study of ancient sculptures, he indicates he has been looking at coins of other countries, including no doubt E.A. Oudine's ideal head instituted for the French coinage of the Second Republic in 1848 and recently revived with the Third Republic in 1870.

As a contrast to all this, a newspaper article about the Liberty Head dollar of 1878 to 1921 was reprinted in *The Numismatist* in May 1896, under the title "To Marry a Goddess." "Every man, woman, or child who has a silver dollar carries the handsome profile of the Philadelphia schoolteacher, Miss Anna W. Williams. Her classic features have been stamped upon millions of the silver disks. . . . Mr. Morgan was so enthusiastic that he declared Miss Williams' profile was the most perfect he had seen in England or America." Twenty years later, on the eve of her marriage, the *New York Mail and Express* continued, "Miss Williams is a decidedly modest young woman. She resides on Spring Garden Street, not far from the school in which for years she has been employed as an instructor in philosophy and methods in the kindergarten department. She is slightly below the average height, is rather plump, and is fair. She carries her figure with a stateliness rarely seen and the pose of the head is exactly as seen on the silver dollar. The features of Miss Williams are reproduced as faithfully as in a good photograph."[6] The whole psychology of the story of the girl as Miss Liberty is just like the tale of Phryne, mistress of Praxiteles, posing for the Knidian Aphrodite, a contemporary or later attempt to give specific personality to an ideal creation. It is amusing to note that the public press derived satisfaction in attributing "all-American" virtues of modesty and milkmaid physique to the girl allegedly the model for the American goddess.

The tale of Anna Williams, as told in 1896, goes back to a report in the Philadelphia *Sunday Republic* early in 1878:

> The head of Liberty is chaste and beautiful, and, in an artistic sense, is considered the best executed head that has ever appeared upon United States coin. It is so well distributed as to be susceptible of easy work under the die, and altogether will certainly reflect credit upon both the designer and the Government. Like its predecessor of 1808, it was taken from life, and is a fair type of beauty of one of our Philadelphia ladies, the model having been a young lady who is a teacher in one of the public schools in the Fifteenth Section, and who naturally objects to having her name published.

The *American Journal of Numismatics* for April 1878,[7] in recording this and other opinions about the coin and about William Barber's design that was not adopted, states, "The head of the Morgan eagle is very poor, and the wings are badly managed. The Barber design shows the eagle with wings as if just unfolding for flight. . . . In our judgment the Barber dollar is far superior to the one adopted."[8]

The Philadelphia *Record* elaborates:

> Mr. Barber's eagle looks as if it was just recovering from a severe spell of sickness, or that it had been disturbed in its meditations by some unruly schoolboys. Mr. Morgan has a good idea of America's proud bird of freedom, and his original design showed an eagle with wings that nearly enveloped the whole coin. Its wings were so large that Dr. Linderman, no doubt, feared it might get loose and fly off,

> so he ordered its wings clipped. In this position it will appear to the public. In its talons is a dart, containing only one feather at the tip of the barb. The director ordered more feathers, so that the barb would present a ship-shape appearance, and not be liable to fly off lop-sided.[9]

It can also be noted from the snatches of correspondence quoted above that George T. Morgan was unsatisfied with the tradition of Peter, the then-stuffed eagle at the Philadelphia Mint. The "studies in nature" that he would seem to have procured for the eagle, however, must have had little effect on his oeuvre, for the bird on the reverse of the 1878 silver dollar is much more removed from reality than the creatures on some of the patterns for trade dollars in 1873. Some details, to be sure, like the broad tail, betray ornithological research, but in total substance the eagle with wings spread is as heraldic as his early 19th-century counterparts with the shields on their stomachs. Clearly, Morgan's dollar was a refreshing step away from the standard Gobrecht-styled seated Liberty and "sandwich-board" eagle, but the decisive moment of revolution in American numismatic art had not yet arrived.

The head on the obverse of the new dollar looms large, making almost too much sculptured or sculptural surface for the area involved. This was doubtless part of the reaction to decades of seated Liberties with their small heads. Lettering and stars, the latter six-pointed as was the tradition, offer nothing unusual, save perhaps that the motto is spaced out in handsome fashion around the head. This was a visual innovation of Barber and Morgan patterns in the 1870s. The borders on obverse and reverse are taken from Roman dentils, as had been the case with trade dollars earlier in the decade. On the reverse, the very open, relatively slender wreath is a successful bit of innovation, and the Victorian temper of the times is mirrored in the Gothic lettering used for the motto.

Public Dissatisfaction With Coins

The June 1876 issue of the *Galaxy* made a long and vehement attack on the obverses of our silver coinage. Strangely enough, the ghost of Peter lingered on, for the reverse was condemned for being too natural, too unheraldic. Suggestions for portraits were offered in 1876 that had to wait until 1932 (Washington) and 1948 (Franklin) to be incorporated on the regular coinage.

> Why is it that we have the ugliest money of all civilized nations? For such undoubtedly our silver coinage is. The

design is poor, commonplace, tasteless, characterless, and the execution is like thereunto. Our silver coins do not even look like money. They have rather the appearance of tokens or mean medals. One reason of this is that the design is so inartistic and so insignificant. The young woman sitting on nothing in particular, wearing nothing to speak of, looking over her shoulder at nothing imaginable, and bearing in her left hand something that looks like a broomstick with a woolen nightcap on it—what is she doing there? what is the meaning of her? She is Liberty, we are told, and there is a label to that effect across a shield at her right, her need of which is not in any way manifest. But she might as well be anything else as Liberty; and at the first glance she looks much more like a spinster in her smock, with a distaff in her hand. Such a figure has no proper place upon a coin. On the reverse the eagle has the contrary fault of being too natural, too much like a real eagle. In numismatic art animals have conventional forms, which are far more pleasing and effective than the most careful and exact imitation of nature can be. Compare one of our silver coins with those of Great Britain, France, or Germany, and see how mean, slight, flimsy, inartistic and unmoneylike it looks. Our coins of forty or fifty years ago were much better in every respect, and looked much more like money, the reason being that they bore a head of Liberty which was bold, clear, and well defined in comparison with the weak thing that the Mint has given us for the last thirty years or so. The eagle, too, although erring on the side of naturalness, was more suited in design to coinage. But still better were the coins struck at the end of the last century and the beginning of this one. The eagle was a real heraldic eagle, the head of Liberty had more character, and the whole work was bolder and better in every way. But even they had the great defect of being without significance in design. What is a head of Liberty? What distinctive character can be given to a head upon a coin which will make it more like Liberty than anything else? . . . The coins of the French republic bear a head supposed to typify the Republic. It has in its features and in its decorations some character and significance, and it is bold and stands out in good relief, as it should. But we can do better than to use such mere abstractions, no matter how bold the designs, how high the relief, or how fine the workmanship. . . . From this utterly unmeaning and uninteresting condition our coin might be lifted by the substitution, in place of this so-called Liberty, of two heads, the appropriateness of which upon our coins—and indeed almost their

> right to be there—would be felt by every American, and not only so, but recognized by the whole world. It is hardly necessary to say that the heads we mean are those of Washington and Franklin. . . . And fortune, nature, Providence—what you will—so ordered it that neither if them left descendants of their own name to be elevated by the appearance of their ancestors' head upon a nation's coinage. There are no Washingtons, no Franklins to say, "This is the image and superscription of the head of our family." All democratic fear of the elevation and glorification of individuals or families is therefore to be set aside at once as having no occasion. It so happens also that these two men represent the two elements of our population, the two great divisions of our country. One was a Virginia planter; the other, a Philadelphia printer, born in Boston, grew from a printer into a philosopher and a statesman. The proper place for Washington's head would be upon the gold pieces; for no one would dispute the appropriateness of placing that of the author of "Poor Richard's Almanac," and of the adage, "A penny saved is a penny earned," upon the silver coins representing fractional parts of a dollar, and upon the cents. Thus our gold and silver coins would be distinguished from each other in design, not as they now are by the mere difference between a meaningless head and a meaningless sitting figure, but by two noble portrait busts of which an American might be prouder than any European ever was of the effigy of king or kaiser. With this change and with a return to the old breadth of piece, and the heraldic eagle used in the beginning of this century (the two examples now before us are dated 1803 and 1805), we should have a coinage which instead of being as now the meanest in appearance and most insignificant of all that is known, would be the most beautiful and the most fraught with associations of historic interest and national pride. We commend the subject to the attention of the House, and hope that some member may be found who will take it up and bring it before the people.[10]

Amateur and professional aestheticians continued to take a long look at the U.S. coinage, especially the silver issues, which had hardly changed since 1836, in the case of the obverses, and 1807 for the reverses. In 1887 a critic summed up the situation in an essay in *The Century* magazine:

> [W]ith a few exceptions, the coinage of the modern world is unnecessarily inartistic. And none will gainsay Mr. Stillman that, among all, the products of the United States Mint are

the most barbarous, the most contemptible in the weakly grotesque design of their eagles, in their illdrawn and commonplace Libertys, and in the vulgarly staring lettering of their legends.

Modern coinage must, of course, always conform to modern conditions of evenness and regularity. But living art—and to see that art is not yet dead, we need look no further than to the work of French sculptors, and to that of some we have among ourselves—makes light of such restrictions. The Parthenon frieze proclaims for all time what can be done within fixed lines, and in the extreme of low relief. It rests simply with the Treasury department to consign to oblivion when it will, our gawky fowls and disjointed goddesses, and to set an example to the world by the issue of a series of coins bearing for each denomination independent designs—the most meritorious obtainable. Such series, renewed at fitting intervals, and presenting, within the possible range, the best contemporary conceptions of personified civic virtues and the best portraits of our great men, would surely exert a potent educating influence upon the eyes and thought of our people, and would emulate even from afar, the interest of the ancient coinages as an enduring record of history and art. The administration which is the first to adopt this reform, will win for itself high and deserved honor, and will at the same time give to the medallists' art an impetus greater than it has enjoyed since the day of its generous patrons of the Renaissance.[11]

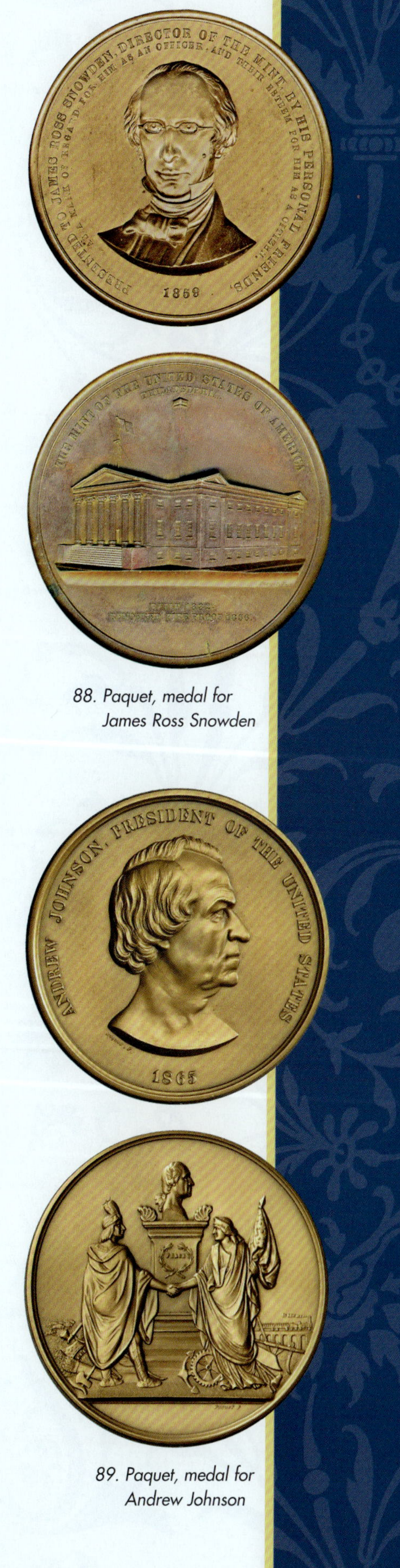

88. Paquet, medal for James Ross Snowden

89. Paquet, medal for Andrew Johnson

Official Medals by Anthony Paquet

Medallic art of the prosperous decades after the Civil War cannot be understood without studying certain crucial forerunners, especially the official medals by Anthony C. Paquet. Paquet has been criticized for having been a mediocre engraver, but study of his coins and patterns reveals he never really had an opportunity to unleash his talents on the coinage because Longacre, the chief engraver, did all the work himself. Patterns have suggested Paquet's potential. Four medals can be singled out from among the limited number of existing examples that amply confirm his skill. The first was executed in 1859 to honor James Ross Snowden's career as director of the Mint (fig. 88). The second belongs to the presidential series, is dated 1865, and portrays Lincoln's controversial successor, Andrew Johnson (fig. 89). The two other medals discussed in detail were commissioned by Congress and awarded for bravery to the rescuers of the wrecked steamship *San Francisco* and to the man who protected Secretary of State Seward from an assassin.

The medal for Snowden presents two novelties, departures from the heroics of the early 19th century and the Greco-Roman classicism of the Civil War era. A brutally naturalistic facing portrait on the obverse is coupled with a magnificent, factual rendering of an architectural complex on the reverse. Both are far out of pace for their times. James Ross Snowden is shown with hexagonal spectacles, a wart on his cheek, and contemporary dress. The relief is high and sharp, a circumscribed contrast to the two sizes of low, rectangular lettering that run like a halo around the field within a high, molded rim. On the reverse is the second Philadelphia Mint, built, as the inscription states, in 1832, and rendered fireproof in 1856. The latter statement is borne out by the slender chimney rising in the background. Again high relief is used to emphasize outline and volume, almost making the severe, neoclassic, Greek Revival building seem like a freestanding miniature rather than a mere medallic relief. Bold, severe, detailed yet comprehensive, the Mint at the hand of Paquet has become one of the most successful architectural vistas on any example of numismatic art. Successor to the *architectura numismatica* of imperial Rome, Paquet's Mint makes an unforgettable transition to the delicate renderings of the Capitol by George T. Morgan on presidential medals of the early 20th century (figs. 150 and 151).

As the traditions of the series dictated, Paquet's single presidential medal is less novel than his monument to Snowden but no less imaginative and interesting. Andrew Johnson's portrait is a strong likeness in the German neoclassic tradition. The wrinkles of the face and the turn of the neck are well articulated. The reverse, vistas of the United States, prairie and industry, divided by allegory, is the prototype for Frank Gasparro's reverse of the medal for Eisenhower's first term, Freedom dividing sweeps of rural and urban America (fig. 236). Perhaps because there was little to say about Andrew Johnson himself or perhaps because Civil War themes might have been too abrasive in 1865, "peace" is symbolized by thoughts that go back to the peace medals of the earlier part of the century given as tokens of friendship to Native American chiefs in alliance with the United States.

Before a bust of George Washington on a Roman altar, Liberty and a thoroughly Roman Indian shake hands. The latter holds his pipe of peace, and his tools of war or the chase are at his feet. Buffalo and an Indian on horseback gallop across the plains at the left. Gears, anchors, forging tools, and the inevitable plow lie at the Greco-Roman Liberty's feet. The train speeding across a viaduct at the right rear complements the scene of galloping bison on the opposite side of the apotheosis of Washington. The Indian and Liberty clutching her flag are set on a podium that leads to the steps of the Washington Memorial, as if the whole ensemble were a monumental marble relief or a painted signboard. After Paquet and until McKinley in the early 20th century, presidential medals were considerably less varied, less exciting or amusing, as works of art; and reverses became mere wreaths and inscriptions. This in itself is a major measure of Anthony C. Paquet as a designer of official medals.[12]

U.S. Mint List numbers 525 and 634, both of heroic proportions, show the truly Victorian grandeur of Paquet as a medalist of events deemed noble enough to be commemorated by congressional resolutions. The first, authorized July 26, 1866, was presented "To the Rescuers of the Passengers Officers and Men of Steamship San Francisco Wrecked Dec. 1853. Testimonial of National Gratitude for his Gallant Conduct," with an appropriate place being left for addition of the recipient's name. The second, awarded March 1, 1871, was "To George F. Robinson . . . for his Heroic Conduct on the 14. Day of April 1865, In Saving the Life of the Honorable Wm. H. Seward Then Secretary of State of the United States." Seward was attacked on his sickbed by one of the assassins in the plot that took Abraham Lincoln's life.

On one side of the first medal a distressed man and woman await the rescuers from a wave-tossed raft, the former gesturing in anticipation as the ship rises over the horizon, while the latter slumbers in classic-romantic exhaustion. The opposite side, that bearing the struck and engraved inscriptions, shows America, Liberty, or Columbia crowning a kneeling navigator amid Capitol, eagle on fasces and shield, and the ship again at the left rear. All is fused with the lofty sentiment that marked press dispatches about such events and would have attended their commemoration in theatrical representations or tableaux at patriotic parades. The obverse of the Seward-Robinson medal gives a civilian bust of the latter, twin wreaths (of the Senate and the House presumably) above. The reverse, sketched by G.Y. Coffin, presents the scene in the sickroom in the same theatrical terms that *Harper's* and the *Illustrated London News* showed John Wilkes Booth's attack on the president. Paquet's genius as a medalist, however dated, has transcribed and compressed both events into the limits of his medium with no loss of dramatic appeal, no crowding of figures and inscriptions, and full understanding of the dimensions of sculptural relief.[13]

Official Medals by the Barbers and Morgan

James R. Snowden's immediate successors as director of the Mint, James Pollock and Henry R. Linderman, were both modeled by William Barber, his two works in this subdivision of the federal medallic series. The portrait of that vigorous bureaucrat Linderman, under whom the general direction moved from Philadelphia to Washington with the Mint Act of 1873, is as arresting a portrayal as appears on any medal from the Philadelphia Mint. Lofty forehead, leonine hair, hooked nose, and outthrust beard are caught with amazing strength, in high relief against an empty tondo. The reverse, as befits a medal of 1869, sets the inscription in a series of Gothic curves and counter-curves within the traditional wreath of laurel and oak (fig. 90).

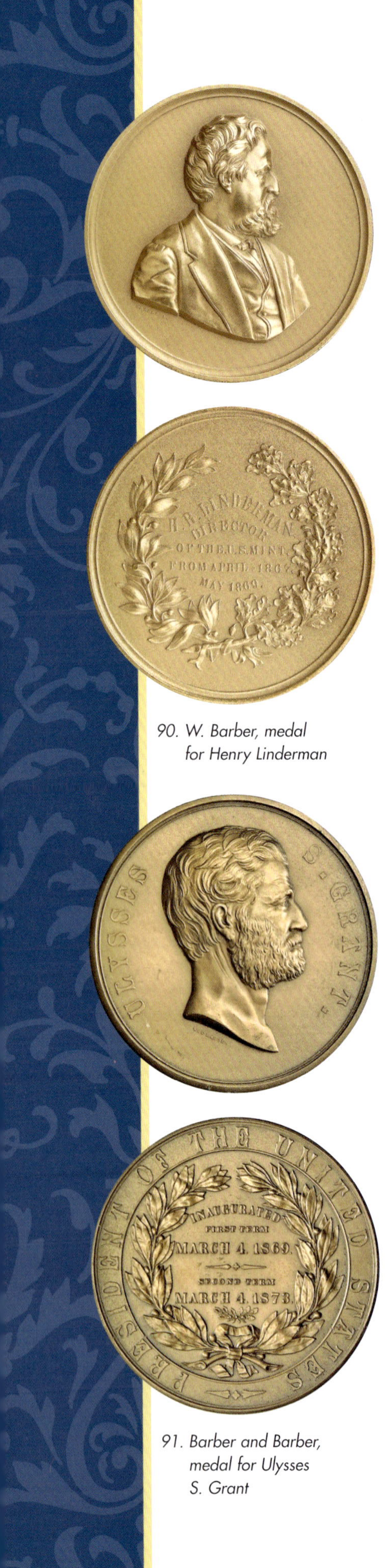

90. W. Barber, medal for Henry Linderman

91. Barber and Barber, medal for Ulysses S. Grant

The medal for Ulysses S. Grant is the only contribution to the presidential series by William Barber, and, like Morgan's medal for Abraham Lincoln, it is a disappointment as a work of portraiture and art in general (fig. 91). The signature beneath the truncated bust is "W. & C. Barber," indicating that the father was responsible for the ungainly Roman likeness on the obverse and the son for the commonplace mélange of foliage and lettering that constitutes the reverse. The only thing that can be said in the latter's favor is that a certain relief from monotony is derived by the planes or steps of rim and molding that separate the elements of the design. Paquet's straightforward lettering in the Johnson medal has been replaced by pseudo-Gothic forms, like the titles of newspapers in the middle to late Victorian era. Grant as a Civil War general or as a civilian president was a definite personality, but Grant as a Greek of 350 B.C. or a Roman of the Hadrianic era is no comprehensible factor in American history. William Barber has even made him resemble Aristotle, who lived in the fourth century B.C.

If a passion for the Greek has distorted the official image of Grant, it has done worse for the portrait of Rutherford B. Hayes on the obverse of a medal by Morgan (fig. 92). The simple president of the United States has become a veritable Socrates or, worse, Antisthenes, the unkempt philosopher of the early Hellenistic period. The bearded elders of Greek grave reliefs of about 340 B.C. offer similar heads, comparisons that transcend the realm of coincidence (fig. 93). The reverse is the routine wreath and inscriptions. Most of the mannerisms of lettering have been removed, but were to return, most immediately on C.E. Barber's obverse of the medal of 1881 for the martyred James A. Garfield (fig. 94).

This medal is the first of six, extending to William H. Taft in 1910, that mark the collaboration between Charles Barber and George Morgan. The portrait is no less Roman, but it is more forcefully natural and, fortunately, more like the subject. Americans of the post–Civil War era certainly wore their hair like Romans, but the human element was never lacking, never distilled into cold marble. Barber was to develop into a great portraitist, and his gifts are very evident here. For the wreath of the reverse, Morgan went back to the civic crowns of imperial Rome, producing a combination of tightly bound oak and laurel worthy of the golden crowns borne in procession in the small frieze on the Arch of Trajan at Beneventum, a triumphal monument of the early second

93. *Attic grave monument*

92. *Morgan, medal for Rutherford B. Hayes*

94. *Barber and Morgan, medal for James A. Garfield*

century A.D. He used the same reverse for his medal to Abraham Lincoln (fig. 95). The lettering on the medal to Garfield is beautifully planned, as to form, size, and spacing. On the Lincoln medal it is overwhelmed by the wreath and the foliage at the bottom.

The medal for Chester A. Arthur at first glance differs little from the others in this series of latter-day Greco-Roman creations, save that Morgan's reverse reverts to the type chosen for Grant and Hayes (fig. 96). Arthur's homey face and large, mutton-chop sideburns are impossible to confuse with the notables of Greece or Rome, and the portrait marks another step toward modernization of the presidential image. The refined incisiveness of hair, profile, and planes of relief again confirms the younger Barber as a master of the official likeness, adequately natural, yet slightly generalized and thus elevated to the level of rulers throughout all ages.

For Benjamin Harrison, president between the first and second Cleveland administrations, Barber and Morgan executed a medal in 1889 that combines a bust in the highest relief possible with the pseudo-Gothic lettering encountered previously in the medals to Grant and Garfield. Harrison's medal (fig. 97) also displays a heavy, beaded border derived from Roman imperial sestertii or their cinquecento imitations by the Italian medalist Giovanni Cavino of Padua (1499–1570). The other noteworthy innovation is the revival of civilian dress in the place of the Greco-Roman heroic nudity. Barber alone designed the medal for Grover Cleveland in 1893, and as an integrated work of art it sums up the tradition of bust and mere name on the obverse, full statistics in a wreath on the reverse (fig. 98). This wreath, enframing a plaque, is the Roman *corona civica* of oak leaves and acorns, one which in simpler form had graced obverses of bronze and copper coins struck under the emperor Augustus (27 B.C.–A.D. 14), who made the motif popular. The bust of Cleveland is not as high as that of Harrison, and the beading of the borders has been reduced to a sensible modern size. All in all, the fat face of Grover Cleveland looks out from a very successful medal in the most conservative tradition.

This series of presidential and other official medals is evidence that Barber and Morgan had no objections to work in high relief, provided it did not interfere with processes necessary for mass production of coins. Years later, in 1907, when Henry Hering was having his conferences at the Philadelphia Mint about producing the Saint-Gaudens gold coins, Barber was painted as a villain. He is said to have used technical pretexts that high relief was impossible only to mask his jealousy because commissions for new designs were given to outside artists when they should have been the work of himself or Morgan. This is partly true, but Barber was a consummate craftsman as well as a gifted portraitist, and his sense of what was necessary for the coinage did not cloud creation of a series of medals that satisfied all the demands of art. He could foresee that the dates would wear off Fraser's nickel of 1913 and MacNeil's quarter dollar of 1916, and I cannot believe it is a fault to be as concerned with the purpose of a work of art as with its beauty. In modern, machine-made coins and medals the two must march together. A great die designer can make aesthetics and function move in unison within the combination of obverse and reverse of a tondo or a rectangular plaque.

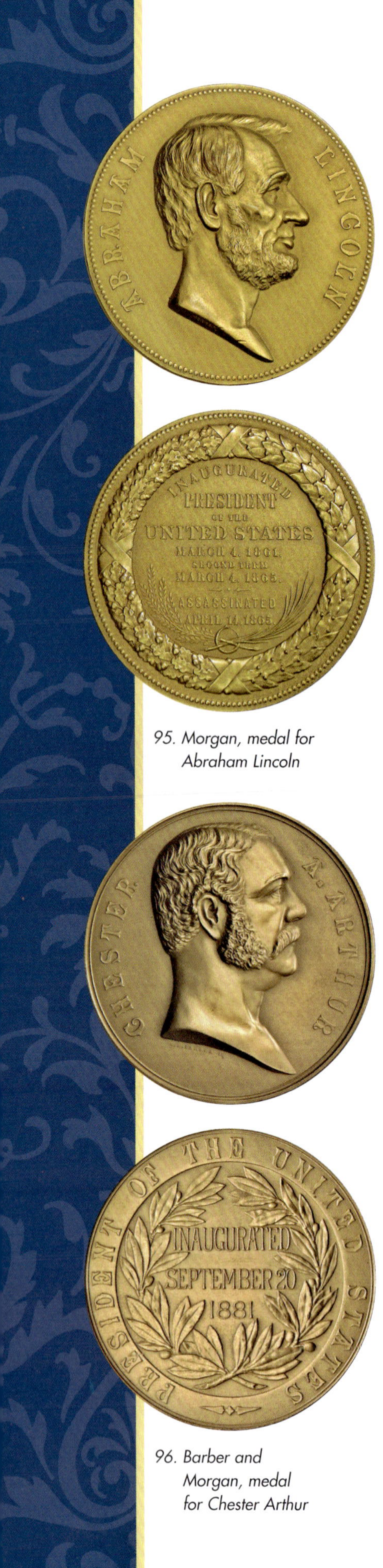

95. Morgan, medal for Abraham Lincoln

96. Barber and Morgan, medal for Chester Arthur

The economic demands of the Civil War and westward expansion thereafter produced some new coins, like the two-cent piece and the nickel, and some new designs, like the silver dollar of 1878. A host of patterns and medals reflected the expanded artistic activity of engravers at the Mint. In addition to a restudy of Greco-Roman prototypes, often in favor of an antiquarianism based on single works of art at hand, there was a taste for Gothic designs and forms of lettering. This romanticism was paralleled in other expressions of American art from tombstones to banknotes or newspapers.

97. Barber and Morgan, medal for Benjamin Harrison

98. Barber, medal for Grover Cleveland

V

The Columbian Exposition and Modern Design

The year 1892 could have been the moment of numismatic decision for the United States. The World's Columbian Exposition, held in Chicago to commemorate the 400 years of the Americas' modern existence, rallied painters, sculptors, and decorators, including artists accustomed to working with metal dies, in the service of major and minor creations that were both temporary and permanent. Among them were several sculptors capable of designing significant modern coins, and the team of Charles E. Barber and George T. Morgan at the Philadelphia Mint was at the height of its creative powers. All elements favorable to an extensive improvement in the gold, silver, and copper denominations were present.

The Coinage of 1892

Officials of the U.S. Treasury and Mint decided to redesign the dime, the quarter dollar, and the half dollar for the issues of 1892. Although it was not stated explicitly, the tradition of making all their obverses and the two larger reverses alike was to be maintained. A competition for the best designs was opened, but the rewards were minimal, and few artists outside the Mint expressed any interest in undertaking the effort of making drawings or models in plaster. For the first time since 1840 artists other than those employed at the Mint were to be involved, and the customary friction between the entrenched craftsmen in government service and artists who fancied they knew how to prepare designs that could meet the demands of machine coinage came quickly to the fore. The so-called contest was a complete failure, and the new designs for the issues of 1892 were all produced in the Mint by the chief engraver, Charles Barber. Many public and private critics felt keenly disappointed when these new silver pieces appeared, but the last word as to their aesthetic merits has yet to be written. Little admired or collected for more than three generations after their appearance, these essentially conservative but most dignified coins suddenly became extremely popular with collectors, as symbols of America coming to maturity and the hard-money era of transition from the post–Civil War era to the period between the two world wars (figs. 99–101).

The failure of the government's competition and the triumph of academic designs from the studio of the Mint is best told in the words of an editor of the *American Journal of Numismatics,* writing during the summer of 1891. Despite the somewhat emotional flavor of the disputes, the editor was obviously trying to keep an open mind regarding the virtues of work by outside artists and those in the Mint. At the time of writing he had not seen the designs to be adopted in 1892, although all manner of patterns for this series were prepared by Barber and Morgan in 1891. As finally issued, the obverses showed a staid, heavy-featured head of Liberty derived from both 19th-century French coins and medals (fig. 102) and sketches made years earlier after Greco-Roman marbles copying Pheidian originals of the fifth century B.C. The larger reverses reverted to the purely heraldic eagle of the Great Seal, the bird introduced on the silver between 1796 and 1798 and reworked by Barber in 1876 when he copied Dupré's Diplomatic medal of 1790 to 1792 (fig. 7). The coins are a combination of delicacy, surface busyness, and harmonious balance, such devices as the wing tips of the eagle overlapping the letters or the incised letters in the ribbons on obverse and reverse combating the problems of maximum message in relief low enough to serve modern machinery. Potentials of great numismatic art were scarcely realized, but a useful triad of coins emerged.

The initial comment on the new coinage concerned the novelty of a contest, its failure, and the inevitable result that the commission would go, as always, to the chief engraver and his staff. The practical views of trained coiners took precedence over the kind of aesthetic adulation later accorded the work of Saint-Gaudens.

> It was publicly stated, when these proposals appeared, that the inducements offered by the Government were not sufficient to elicit suggestions of value, much less complete designs for the purpose. Artists who might have given thought to the matter, complained that their time would be wasted, as they would receive nothing for their labor unless their models were accepted; and the result seems to have been, as was anticipated, a complete failure to produce anything that would unite beauty with utility and the practical necessities involved. When the Director of the Mint suggested to the engraver at Philadelphia that he get some one

99. Half dollar of 1892 type

100. Quarter dollar of 1892 type

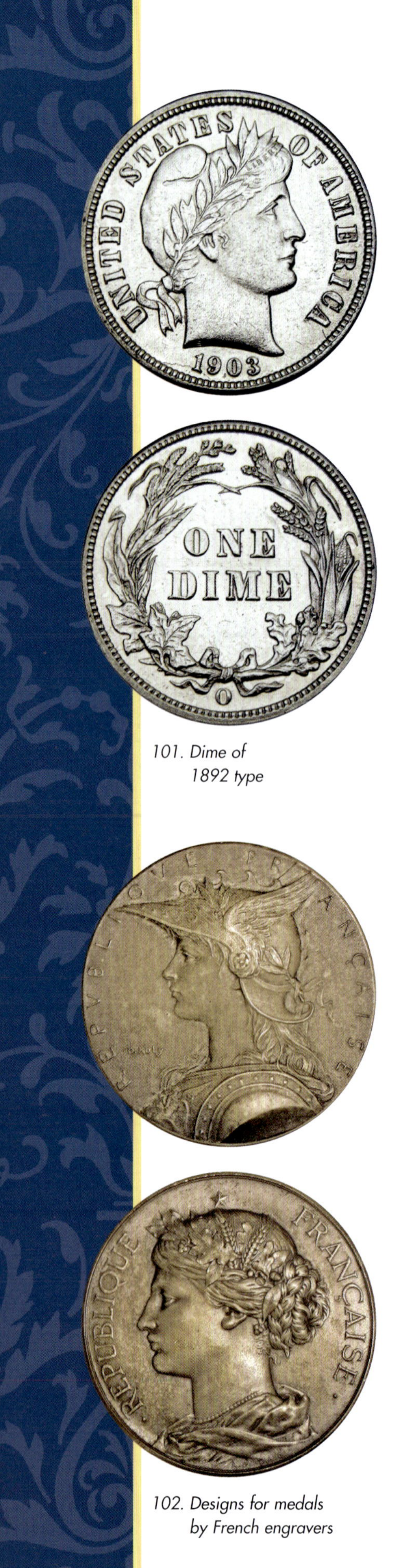

101. Dime of 1892 type

102. Designs for medals by French engravers

to assist him in some special work that was under way, he replied that he did not know of any one in the United States who was competent to assist in this work. During the recent competition the celebrated sculptor, Augustus St. Gaudens, who was one of the judges in the contest, told Mr. Leech that he knew of only four artists who were competent to do this class of designing, and that three of them were in France and he was the fourth. He could say this without egotism, for he made a special study of this subject before he attained celebrity as a sculptor. Admitting most willingly the pre-eminent genius of Mr. St. Gaudens as a sculptor, we fear that he can hardly be said to have shown equal talent for producing designs adapted to the coinage.

We understand that the design favored by the latter gentleman was something after the rude but beautiful coinage of the Greeks. But these designs it would be impossible to follow, and Mr. Barber said in a recent interview, that there was no machinery in existence to coin such pieces as cheaply and as quickly as was necessary. Doubtless American ingenuity could overcome this difficulty, but there are others which cannot be overcome. No three coins could be piled with stability; the third would inevitably fall; their high relief would not sustain the constant wear of circulation without soon being defaced, the protecting rim on our present coins not being compatible with such devices; their irregularity, and that is one of the chief features advocated by those whose suggestions seem to have been sought, would prevent their use, and at the same time make an easy field for counterfeiters.

A correspondent of the *Boston Transcript* writes (July 31): "'It is not likely that another competition will ever be tried for the production of designs for United States coins,' said Mr. Leech, the Director of the Mint, yesterday. 'The one just ended was too wretched a failure. Doubtless it was the first contest of the sort ever opened by any Government to the public at large. The result is not very flattering to the boasted artistic development of this country, inasmuch as only two of the three hundred suggestions submitted were good enough to receive honorable mention. . . . Anticipating a severe popular criticism, the chief engraver will do his utmost to render the five cameo pictures called for, as unexceptionable as possible, aesthetically speaking. No alteration is to be made in the gold coins, because they are really exquisite now and could hardly be improved upon. It is realized that the money of a nation is expressive of its art culture. [!] Therefore, lest posterity imagine the present generation to have been barbarous, it is desirable that our silver pieces should be as handsome as may be.'"

"I have told our engraver," said Mr. Leech to another reporter a few days ago, "to prepare me a set of designs for the subsidiary coins to be submitted to Secretary Foster. I shall not do anything about the dollar for some time. There is no hurry about it, and the weather is too warm for us to worry ourselves about anything which does not require immediate attention. Our engraver at Philadelphia is the only competent person to prepare these designs, but it does not follow from the action I have taken that his work will be final. Of course, he receives no additional compensation for this. It is part of his regular work. I do not see any prospect of getting designs elsewhere in this country. We might get them in France. The French coin work is of the most artistic description. But the people of the United States would never forgive us if we went outside this country for our designs. To be sure, our designer is of an English family, but he is regularly in the employ of the Mint." [He came at an early age we believe, to Philadelphia, with his father, and upon the death of the latter was appointed to succeed him.]

The fact seems to be proved from this attempt, that there are no American artists, outside the Mint, who are competent to furnish designs which it would be possible to follow. Whether the Mint officials can supply an acceptable device, under the limitations provided by statute, remains to be proved. We understand that Mr. Leech is glad that he tried the experiment of inviting outside assistance, notwithstanding his regret at the failure of his efforts.

The final decision in such matters, too often rests in the hands of those whose taste has not been numismatically educated, and it would therefore not be surprising if a design of much greater artistic merit than that which shall finally be adopted, should be rejected, possibly on the ground of utility, as has been the case heretofore. . . . Even a Cabinet officer, with his multifarious talents, is not necessarily endowed with that discriminating taste in the choice of "the fairest" and most beautiful, so happily possessed by the son of Priam. "The judgment of Paris" in awarding the apple of discord received the approval of mortals, though Olympus frowned: in like manner, the Secretary's ultimate decision, whatever it may be, will no doubt give popular satisfaction and incur the wrath of those who reign in the realm of art.[1]

After the new coins appeared, W.T.R. Marvin was moved to write in the *American Journal of Numismatics* for 1892:

> The general effect is pleasing; of the three the Dime is to many the most attractive piece. The head of Liberty is dignified, but although the silly story has been started that the profile is that of a "reigning belle" of New York, she can hardly be called a beauty; there is a suggestion, difficult to define, yet perceptible, of the classic heads on some of the Roman coins, and a much stronger suggestion of the head on the French Francs of 1871 and onward; but there is a fullness in the upper lip, which detracts from the expression, and a slight swelling on the back of the neck, that led one irreverent critic to remark "she is going to have a boil," and another to say "the throat is that of a gladiator"! The eagle is a compromise between the buzzard on the Dollar, and the heraldic eagle on the gold coinage: the wings are not so erect, and are more widely expanded, and their tips extend nearly to the rim: it has not the slender neck and body of the conventional eagles on the German coins, nor their serrated pinions, but the legs and talons are wide-spread, and decidedly heraldic in their treatment; the head is spirited and well drawn.
>
> From this description it may be fairly inferred that in many respects these coins are an advance on what has hitherto been accomplished, but there is yet a long distance between them and the ideal National coin. . . . [C]oins of the highest type of art will be struck for popular use about the same day that the quadrature of the circle shall be exactly accomplished.[2]

The designs of Barber's coins were more attuned to the times than even he perhaps realized. The plumpish, matronly gravitas of Liberty had come to America seven years earlier in the person of Frédéric Bartholdi's giant statue on Bedloe's Island in New York Harbor. Such sculptures, whether called Liberty or Columbia or The Republic or a personification of intellect, were dominant themes of the Chicago World's Fair, the World's Columbian Exposition of 1892, termed by Saint-Gaudens "the greatest meeting of artists since the 15th century."[3] Chief among these statues was Daniel Chester French's colossal *Republic*, a Pheidian matron holding aloft an eagle on an orb in one hand and a Liberty cap on an emblem in the other. The heavy profile, solemn eyes, thick jaw, and massive neck of the statue were absolutely in harmony with what Charles Barber had created for the coinage in the year of the fair's opening.

Of all American coins long in circulation, no series has stood the wearing demands of modern coinage so well as the half dollar, quarter dollar, and dime developed by the chief engraver at Philadelphia. Liberty's cap, incised diadem, and wreath of laurel were designed to echo all the depth and volume of her Olympian countenance. These classical substances are offset, almost literally, by the sharply rectangular dentils of the raised rim and by the strength of 13 six-pointed stars. On the reverses of the two larger coins, an equal constellation of stars has five points and is clustered above the eagle's shaggy, craggy profile. On both sides the simple dignity of motto, legend, and denomination binds the pictorialism into a cohesive tondo. The wealth of irregular surfaces and sharp angles is an almost electrifying aesthetic experience. The wreath of the dime's reverse carries the plasticity of the eagle's feathers into miniature dimensions and entwines the less complicated inscription in forthright fashion. This wreath also exhibits its own freshness and sculptural activity: leaves, berries, and stems are alive with a carefully controlled sense of nature. Even when these coins have been worn nearly smooth, their outlines suggest the harmony of interior detail in careful planes of relief that make Uncirculated specimens a pleasure to contemplate. The sculptor was unsurpassed in the mechanics of creating a durable design of monumental validity.

The First Commemorative Coins

The epic year 1892 also marked the appearance of the first commemorative coin, the half dollar issued to celebrate the World's Columbian Exposition of 1892 and 1893 at Chicago. The designs were overt products of the medallic academicism fostered by the officials of the Mint in Philadelphia, the obverse being the work of Charles Barber (portrait design by J.Q.A. Ward) and the reverse the creation of George Morgan. The total effect was one of dignity and, considering what had appeared for so long on the gold and silver coinage up to 1892, novelty of types. From the start controversy raged about the alleged portrait of Columbus on the obverse, and the reverse stirred considerable emotion, for the *Santa Maria* appears to be gliding on the two hemispheres as if they were giant tires (fig. 103). Arlie Slabaugh has written with his customary wit, "The design received considerable criticism from the public, some suggesting that the portrait was not Columbus but Daniel Webster or Henry Ward Beecher. . . . [Y]ou can take the portrait on any coin and someone will resemble it. Just as movie stars have 'doubles.' The only solution is to stop using people on coins."[4] At least it was a giant step forward to have produced a regular coin with someone other than Liberty on it, however controversial the portrait of the Admiral of the Ocean Seas might have been.

103. Columbian half dollar of 1892 type

Sources for the Columbus have been given variously as the medal struck in Madrid to commemorate the same 400th anniversary, a statue in that same city, and Lorenzo Lotto's painting of a learned man identified as the Navigator. Complaining about the low relief of the coin, a critic wrote in the 1893 *American Journal of Numismatics:* "As a work of art it is certainly a great disappointment. . . . The beardless face serves to show which side of the discussion concerning his whiskers the Mint authorities have taken, and they are evidently free from the uncertainty which has pervaded the Post Office Department, and evoked so much amusing comment on the special issue of Postage stamps."[5] Three issues later the same journal seems to have settled the problem in its own mind by stating about the painting signed by Lorenzo Lotto: "This portrait served as the model for the face of Columbus upon the souvenir Half Dollars, and was awarded a silver medal at the Columbian Historical Exposition at Madrid, as being the most authentic likeness of the Discoverer."[6] Both this likeness of 1512 (fig. 104) and the plumper one painted by Sebastiano del Piombo are thought to be copied after the sketch of an artist working in Rome about 1500.

To complement the Columbian half dollar the government succumbed to a petition of the Board of Lady Managers of the Chicago exposition and authorized a smaller coin, a quarter dollar, for the year 1893. Charles E. Barber was again the designer, and women were acclaimed throughout (fig. 105). The crowned head and richly clothed bust of Queen Isabella

104. Lotto, Christopher Columbus

on the obverse follow Gilbert Scott's Victorian Gothic tradition of photographic classicism, best summed up by the groups of continents and the reliefs of famous persons on the Albert Memorial in London. The kneeling woman with distaff and spindle on the reverse, from the point of chronology, could in 1893 owe pose and some details of drapery to a figure of a servant girl from the east pediment of the temple of Zeus at Olympia, work of about 460 B.C. with additions and revisions in the first or second century A.D. Nowadays the coin seems charming for its quaintness and its Victorian flavor, a mixture of cold Hellenism and Renaissance romance. Perhaps one of its greatest joys is that none of the customary inscriptions, mottoes and such, appear on it.

105. Columbian quarter dollar

The invaluable contemporary source, the *American Journal of Numismatics,* however, viewed the twenty-five-cent piece of Bertha Palmer's board pessimistically.

> Of its artistic merit, as of the harmony which is reported to have prevailed at the meetings of those Managers, perhaps the less said the better; we do not know who designed it; but in this instance, as in the Half Dollar, the contrast between the examples of the numismatic art of the nation, as displayed on the Columbian coins, on the one hand, and the spirited and admirable work of the architects of the buildings, for instance, on the other, is painful. If these two coins really represent the highest achievements of our medallists and our mints, under the inspiration of an opportunity without restrictions, the like of which has never been presented hitherto in the history of our national coinage, we might as well despair of its future, and should be forced to believe that the merely mechanical side of the art of coining was all that was thought worthy of attention. We are not ready to admit this to be true. Not to speak of Saint-Gaudens, and La Farge among the living, and Hunt and Richardson among the dead, artists confessedly at the head of the various departments of the fine arts to which they have devoted themselves, the architecture of the Exposition buildings, as we have remarked above, and the skill and taste with which the grounds and waterside have been laid out . . . prove that there does exist in America an artistic instinct, . . . an appreciation of beauty as well as of utility, a genius to design and an ability to execute works not less eminent in the world of art than (achievements of engineers, inventors, mechanics). . . . [W]e shall search in vain in our national coinage for evidence to sustain our confidence.
>
> The figure on the reverse is mournfully suggestive of the old anti-slavery token, "Am I not a woman and a sister."[7]

Medals by Saint-Gaudens

In 1892 a star blazed into the numismatic firmament of America in the person of Augustus Saint-Gaudens. Son of a French artisan and an Irish mother, brought from his birthplace in Dublin as an infant, his career as an artist began as a cutter of cameos. Thus, while his fame rested in the creation of monumental sculptures in bronze, his predilection for medallic forms stemmed from early connections with a process akin to the cutting of dies. When an official medal was needed for the World's Columbian Exposition, Saint-Gaudens was the leading choice for designer. Bertha Palmer is reputed to have offered the sculptor the princely sum of $5,000 to execute the designs. He refused twice before accepting, perhaps conscious of the furor his composition would create.

The obverse of the medal for the World's Columbian Exposition is dominated by a transfigured Columbus, arms extended from his sides and palms turned outward. The Navigator has been caught at the moment when he first stumbled ashore on a rise of ground in the New World. A standard-bearer, whose face and hood recall the aged Michelangelo, struggles along behind, and the bow of a small barge protrudes behind their legs. An officer and possibly a crewman, evidently still in the boat, fill the lower right. A version of the arms of Spain is above the inscription, and Saint-Gaudens signed in full on the ground on at the bottom. The sculptor has intended all the details to center around the powerful emotions of Columbus; for this reason the other participants are kept away from the center, only the swirl of the banner counteracting the upturned, youthful head of the discoverer, so like ideal portraits of Alexander the Great. As an entity the composition breathes mastery of the human figure over a limited area made interesting by variations in surface planes (fig. 106).

106. Saint-Gaudens and Barber, Columbian Exposition medal

Not everyone shared the general admiration for the Saint-Gaudens obverse. An editor wrote in the *American Journal of Numismatics* of 1896: "an inspection . . . shows that the object supposed to be a sword, near the left leg of the principal figure, is really the staff of the banner held by the man behind Columbus; the leg which shows, is however so far to the left, that even on the medal the first thought is that it pertains to some one else beside the standard bearer."[8]

The final reverse of the medal was the work of Charles E. Barber, chief engraver at the Mint in Philadelphia. (Saint-Gaudens's proposed models, having been several months late, were rejected.) The design, really a vehicle for the inscription plate, has much in common with Morgan's reverse of the Columbian half dollar. The *Santa Maria* sails over Greek waves in the background, and crouching Nikai record triumph over the globe, by voice and by the pen. This motif of classical crouchers is one beloved by the Mint medalists, and it will be seen again, notably on Morgan's reverse for the Assay Commission medal of 1910 (fig. 117). The remainder of the Barber reverse of the World's Columbian Exposition medal is prosaic in the extreme, the torches with fillets and the layers of inscription. Still, the total design was not so hideous as to call forth the condemnation that accompanied rejection of the Saint-Gaudens reverse for reasons beyond the control or business of the Mint officials.

The reverse designed by Saint-Gaudens, as we know it from one of the studies, shows a nude youth of Praxitelean or Lysippic proportions holding a group of wreaths in his left hand, a torch in his extended right. His face recalls the vigorous ideal of young men in memorials carved after the First World War. The lad leans on a large classical shield enriched with the standard numismatic motto E PLURIBUS UNUM and an eagle that will reappear on the $10 gold piece of 1907, signs that Saint-Gaudens still had the coinage of 1892 in mind. The inscription necessary to the medal, the raised area for the recipient's name, and a young oak tree fill the background in most unobtrusive fashion (fig. 107). To the aestheticians of the time there is no doubt that this composition surpassed that of Charles Barber, if only because it was less obviously like a medal and more like an essay in patriotic idealism in a relatively unencumbered setting. Of the two, the Saint-Gaudens design is superior because it subordinates the lettering to the figure. The eye is not bothered by a mass of details. The message of art is realized at a glance.

Homer Saint-Gaudens, the sculptor's son, described the failure of the reverse as the result of Victorian naughtiness and prudery. The Page Belting Company "improperly obtained a copy and printed a caricature of it so villainous that the boy, who on the original stood as a bit of artistic idealism, appeared in all the vulgar indecency that can be conveyed by the worst connotation of the word *nakedness*." National morality is said to have produced an interminable hue and cry, with the result that the medal emerged with a reverse "an invention from the hands of Mr. Charles E. Barber, the 'commercial medallist' of the mint."[9]

107. Saint-Gaudens, reverse design for Columbian medal

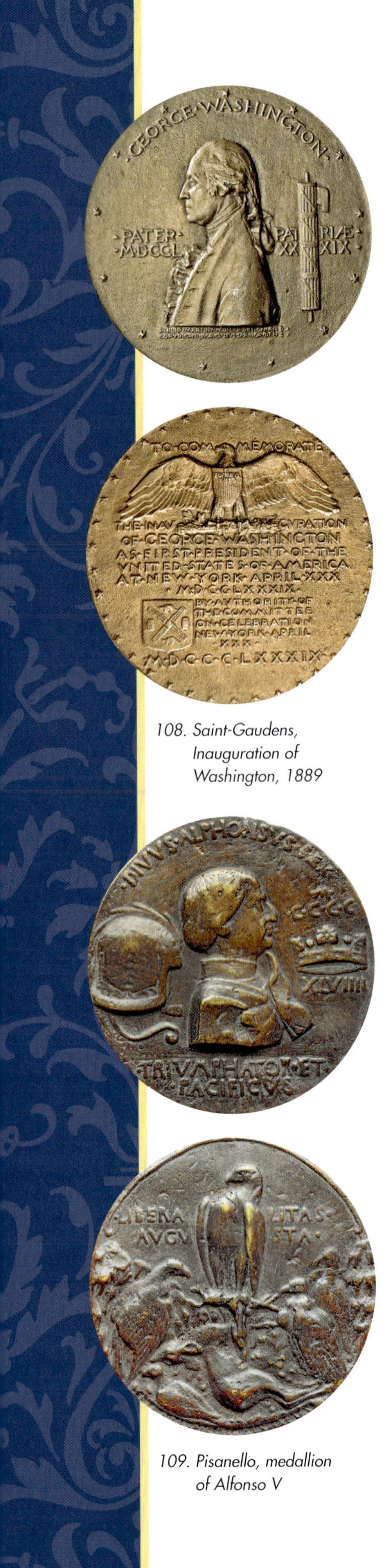

108. Saint-Gaudens, Inauguration of Washington, 1889

109. Pisanello, medallion of Alfonso V

This family version of why the reverse was rejected is at variance with one reported in the *American Journal of Numismatics* for 1894:

> The Columbian Exposition Medal to be presented by the authority of Government to the exhibitors who are to be honored, and the design of which, by St. Gaudens, was first approved and then rejected, as has been so frequently stated in the daily press, is still unfinished. The situation would be amusing were it not rather pathetic. If we may believe the reporters, the artist at first introduced a ribbon which floated before the youthful figure, but failed to please those who objected to his previous model; a shield was then proposed, evidently with no better success, for early in the present month it was stated that Secretary Carlisle had rejected both the amended designs.[10]

This excursion into official medallic design, marred by a comic controversy, ended Saint-Gaudens's connections with U.S. coins and medals for another 15 years. When he was to return to the subject, at the very end of his career, it was to be in a blaze of glory and amid more friction with Barber and the Mint.

The projected medal for the World's Columbian Exposition was by no means the famous sculptor's first semiofficial work of this nature. In 1889 he had prepared a bronze medal in low relief to commemorate the inauguration of George Washington as first president of the United States. The commission came from the Committee on the Celebration of the State of New York, and the piece bore the dates of the centennial in New York City, April 30, 1789 to 1889. A number of characteristics manifest in the later medallic work by Saint-Gaudens are present. The reverse is given over to an American eagle, with wings spread, bearing the arrows, olive branch, and shield with E PLURIBUS UNUM. The coat of arms of New York State is also introduced at the lower left, and the 38 stars of the Union form the border. The obverse is much less pedantic in traditional terms and thus much more thrilling (fig. 108). Saint-Gaudens's admiration for the 15th-century medallions of Pisanello and Sperandio is mentioned over and over again in his correspondence and in critical essays on his sculpture (fig. 109). The Washington medal of 1889 definitely established the Early Renaissance format in the sculptor's medallic work, and this organization of obverse is present in medals and coins by his pupils and their students for two generations to come.

The bust of Washington, after a statue or half-figure *modello* by Philip Martiny, a contemporary of Saint-Gaudens, differs refreshingly from the countless medallic portraits in the tradition of Houdon and Duvivier or Dupré. Almost a half-figure and in "Continental costume," or coat, neckband, and lace shirt, the strongly defined profile in high relief brings to mind busts of nobles and men of intellect in the Italian quattrocento. The spacing of large letters is fully in keeping with the tradition of Pisanello (1395–1455), and the signatures in two lines of small, slightly rough letters beneath the bust is a format found on a number of medals by Sperandio (about 1431–1504). Latin is used partly but not boringly, since PATER PATRIAE is really much happier on a surface such as this than "Father of His Country." Perfect symmetry is broken in fine, forceful fashion by the fasces at the right. The Roman bundle of lictors' staves with an axe in their midst is perhaps a concession to the iconography of modern war memorials. For the next two generations in the United States this motif would appeal in its vertical balance to a number of sculptors in relief, notably A.A. Weinman and the dime of 1916. The 13 small stars around the outside of the tondo make the medal seem all the larger by their unobtrusiveness.

If, finally, the formula for greatness in this medal can be summed up in words, it is the feeling for texture and surfaces that recalls medals of the Renaissance. The Washington Centennial medal of Augustus Saint-Gaudens is a notable contrast to the machined pieces of several previous generations of American medalists. Not only in America but in Europe also Saint-Gaudens could be singled out as the man who found the perfect formula for modern medallic monumentality in terms of the best that the Italian Renaissance had created out of Roman imperial antiquity. He not only mastered the small cameo or medal but was a master of larger marble or metal plaques, usually monuments to the successful, the learned, the beautiful, or the artistic of his day. His likenesses of children in relief were fully worthy of the Italian Renaissance or of the anonymous Roman die cutters who gave us the infant features of Marcus Aurelius's son Annius Verus or of the emperor Caracalla.

The mental processes by which Saint-Gaudens arrived at his formula for modern patriotic medals and coins in the Renaissance Greco-Roman idiom can be probed or explored through a pseudo-Roman, pseudo-Hellenistic bronze medal of 1880. The subject, appropriately enough, was John Singer Sargent, the Bostonian who was everything to society in painting that Saint-Gaudens was in sculpture (fig. 110). The inscription reads MY FRIEND JOHN SARGENT, PARIS, JULY MDCCCLXXX, BRUTTO RITRATO. Between this pseudo–Roman Republican combination of English, Latin, and Italian is the word FECE and a Greek-form monogram of the medalist.

110. *Saint-Gaudens, model for Sargent medal, 1880*

The key to the great sculptor's concept of the great painter lies in the words "brutto ritrato." On the surface this phrase, "bad portrait," would be a modest little joke between sculptor and subject. In a deeper sense these words convey the key to the style and inspiration of both the medal and its portrait. A Roman Republican coin of the famous types with portraits of Caesar's assassin Marcus Junius Brutus on the obverse and the daggers of the Ides of March on the reverse has given Saint-Gaudens his aesthetic point of departure. The word *brutto* means more than merely "bad" in the sense of poor in quality. It means brutal, vigorous, forceful, and consequently veristic. This is just what the Roman Republican portraits of the famous Brutus are, and this is just what the bearded John Singer Sargent appears to be, in the strongly plastic modeling of a gifted sculptor in the era when the art of Auguste Rodin (1840–1917) was achieving its fullest development.

Since the Roman Republican denarii or aurei of Brutus are silver or gold, Saint-Gaudens looked elsewhere in antiquity for his surfaces in bronze. He found them in some of the earlier Roman Republican issues, the later stages of the bronze aes of about 222 to 187 B.C. Other bronze coins, of the Greek cities of southern Italy or Sicily, contributed their stylistic share to the surfaces and balance of the portrait. Quite by coincidence, but perhaps by scrutiny of some Hellenistic portrait series—that of Macedonia or as far afield as Cappadocia—Sargent's lock of hair above the forehead and his curly beard give him a strong resemblance to T. Quinctius Flamininus on the gold staters struck after the victory of Philip V of Macedonia at Cynocephalae in 197 B.C. Prusias I of Bithynia in northwest Asia Minor, king in the years 228 to 180 B.C., offers another source for the hair, the beard, and especially the angle of the neck. In the Seleucid series, silver tetradrachms of Antiochos IX Philopator minted at Tarsus in Cilicia about 105 B.C. carry these parallels farther afield. Augustus Saint-Gaudens thus presents the picture of a maker of medals and, ultimately, coins to whom antiquity and the Renaissance were not mere abstract ideals for verbal adulation. They were living, vital, studied forces in his program of development.

As befitted a great sculptor, Saint-Gaudens could project ideas suitable for a medallion onto a larger surface, or he could take a monumental design, such as one of his eagles, and adapt it to the size and format of numismatic composition. His control over the medallic tondo, whether on a broad scale or in reduction, can be summed up in his bronze relief of Mildred Howells, dated 1898. Posed in simple but heroic profile at a simple table, the elegant and intelligent daughter of the great American writer and critic William Dean Howells is a study in its roughness of dress and smoothness of face and uncluttered background. The epitome of the aristocratic young lady in American society at the time of the Spanish-American War, Mildred Howells has been given the same nobility in sculpture that John Singer Sargent bestowed on his sitters in painting. A sculptor who could say so much for a subject in a circle more than a foot in diameter could not fail to produce monumental elements when designing an official medal or a coin. Saint-Gaudens planned the wooden frame for his tondo of Mildred Howells, and it is perhaps an index of his thoughts that the wooden border close to the bronze has beading similar to that found on many coins (fig. 111). From such essays in American social portraiture Saint-Gaudens

111. Saint-Gaudens, Mildred Howells, *1898*

found no difficulty in turning to the patriotic themes of U.S. coinage. In his studies of patriots from colonial times to the Civil War, he had already taken steps to combine the two.

Official Medals and Commemorative Coins

During the years following 1892, Barber, Morgan, and the craftsmen of the Mint were not idle. They produced numerous medals, a commemorative silver dollar, and patterns for the gold coinage, restyling of which was long out of date. Barber designed William McKinley's Presidential Inaugural medal of 1897, with a civilian bust of the president facing to the left and wearing his Grand Army button. The reverse recalls the least exciting features of the World's Columbian Exposition medal, with torches flanking the inscription plate. An olive wreath encircles the inscription and surmounts a large fasces, a motif that anticipated the reverse of the Weinman dime of 1916.

The Lafayette Dollar

America's second commemorative series consisted of the 1900 silver dollar struck in connection with a statue of General Lafayette paid for in part by the youth of the United States and set up in Paris at the time of the French International Exposition. Barber was again the artist of this novel document of coinage that, unfortunately, emerged as a pedestrian design (fig. 112). The jugate busts on the obverse were an innovation on American coinage, although European nations had shown kings and queens in this fashion, and a grand numismatic tradition of classical antiquity was followed in that the reverse was copied from a statue. Like the Column of Trajan on bronzes of that emperor, the statue used by Barber was not the finished work of art but one of the artist's studies displayed before completion of the commission. It has been demonstrated that the source for the jugate busts of Washington and Lafayette was the obverse of the Yorktown Centennial medal of 1881, the period when Barber was just beginning his career as chief engraver in the Philadelphia Mint. Behind this 1881 combination lie Jean-Antoine Houdon's bust of Washington, made in 1785 and now at Mount Vernon, and a French medal of Lafayette by François-Augustin Caunois, dated 1824. Thus, the first appearance of an American citizen on our coinage, appropriately enough our first president, is connected with the series of busts in plaster or marble by Houdon. By 1932 this tradition had come to have the force of law, and John Flanagan was required to model his Washington after the bust at Mount Vernon for the quarter dollar instituted on the bicentennial of our Founding Father's birth.

112. Lafayette dollar of 1900

The statue of Lafayette was the work of an expatriate American sculptor, Paul Wayland Bartlett (1865–1925), who also executed a richly composed pedimental group for the House wing of the Capitol. The bronze Lafayette on horseback was to be placed in the Place du Carrousel within the court of the Tuileries palace, where thousands would see it from the windows of the Louvre (fig. 113). Bartlett described it thus:

> Lafayette is represented in the statue as a fact and a symbol, offering his sword and services to the American colonists in the cause of liberty. He is shown sitting firmly on his horse, which he holds vigorously. . . . Lafayette's youthful face is turned toward the west, his sheathed sword being slightly uplifted and delicately offered. He appears as the emblem of the aristocratic and enthusiastic sympathy shown by France to our forefathers. His youth, his distinction, his noble bearing, the richness of his costume and of the trappings of his horse—everything serves to emphasize the difference of his race and his education.[11]

113. Bartlett, statue of Lafayette

Lorado Taft explained why the figure on the silver dollar, struck on December 14, 1899, differs in some details from the finished bronze.

> The statue was desired for the 4th of July, 1900, but the order was given so tardily that it was impossible to have the bronze ready. Indeed, the one-third size model was completed but six weeks before the date of unveiling. A colossal plaster model was therefore prepared and used upon the occasion. That even this could be accomplished in six weeks is remarkable, but the French are at home in such problems. The "working model" was sawed into pieces and distributed in several establishments in Paris; thus the horse and rider developed in various parts of the city at the same time. . . . These scattered fragments were brought together only a day or two before the ceremony but fitted perfectly.[12]

The Lafayette dollar lacks the quaint, dated appeal of the Isabella quarter dollar or the amusing originality of the Columbian half dollar. Despite the necessity for low relief, the jugate busts are too linear. The reverse suffers from too much lettering of uniform size. The words PARIS 1900 might have been enough; at most, the addition of "From the Youth of the United States" would have conveyed the message.

114. Peso of the Philippines

Coins for the Philippines

An attractive and pleasant interlude in the formal, academic quality of U.S. coinage occurs in the issues struck for the Philippines from 1903 on. The artist was a native, Melecio Figueroa, who had studied in Madrid and Rome. The reverses were uniformly in the American tradition, bearing an eagle perched on the shield with stars and stripes; still, the treatment has a freshness and simplicity about the spacing. The obverse of the larger denominations brought forth the original design of a windblown Filipino woman in Greek dress standing at an anvil, while Mayon Volcano smokes in the background (fig. 114). On the minor coins a breechclouted Filipino sits beside an anvil and looks to the right, where again the volcano is seen in the distance (fig. 115). Modern and satisfying, these coins are far superior to the design not adopted: a head of Liberty appearing as a native Philippine girl. Such variations on the American emblem, although perfectly admissible from a historical or ethnic point of view, cannot be related to the classical Greek idiom, which did not allow non-Greek humans in ideal guises. On these coins a Filipino Liberty would have been as unsuited to the recognized classical tradition as the ideal heads then in circulation on the coins of Haiti. A new reverse was designed for the Commonwealth of the Philippines in 1937, but the obverses remained substantially the same. The Filipino woman was made larger, her head crowding into the legend. These designs of Figueroa were as exciting when last struck, in 1945, as they were in the days of Theodore Roosevelt.

115. Centavo of the Philippines

Official Medals and Commemorative Gold Under McKinley and Roosevelt

Meanwhile, in 1903 at the Philadelphia Mint, the team of Barber and Morgan was producing designs that were conservative and academic in flavor for medals and coins that emerged as masterpieces of routine craftsmanship. A good illustration is the McKinley medal, issued by the Mint to commemorate his two elections and his untimely death in 1901. Another "very successful" profile bust by Charles Barber graced the obverse, and George Morgan was credited with the secondary side, a standing Columbia who touches a shield that displays the American eagle and contemplates a wreath at her feet. A palm extends upward beside a long inscription (fig. 116). Barber and Morgan seemed to like this concept of Columbia standing in various poses, but the journalistic rumblings of the decade suggest that the aesthetically critical public, or at least its officials and certain influential artists, demanded something bolder than a weak, updated Victorianism in its numismatic art.

A pattern double eagle or $20 gold piece made by Charles E. Barber in 1906 may have been a response to the summoning of Saint-Gaudens by Theodore Roosevelt to revitalize the coinage. The style is the soft, slightly blurred "modern" of the early 1900s, and the source of influence was the French medallic school.[13] Barber had used the figure on the reverse, Columbia standing, as the obverse of a pattern half dollar in 1891. The McKinley medal was another manifestation. Between 1891 and 1906 the chief engraver had learned much about poising the human figure in a medallic tondo, making a more relaxed Columbia, and removing the lumps of stars and letters behind the rays. In the new pattern thin, delicate letters were designed to give the compositions their modern look. The draped bust of Liberty on the obverse is the patroness of France rather than the United States, famous French die designers having shown the way with a host of new personifications of the French Republic in the generation immediately preceding (fig. 102).

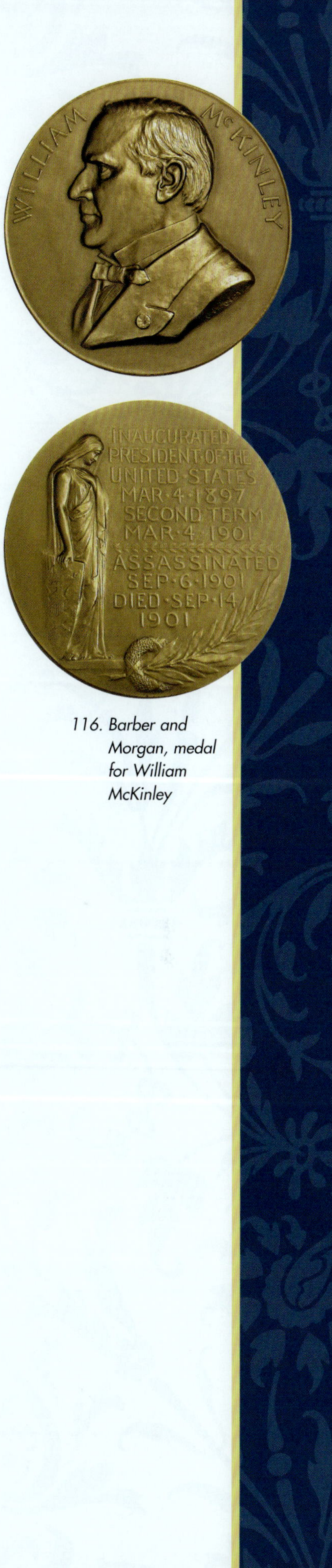

116. Barber and Morgan, medal for William McKinley

The annual Assay Commission medals, although generally mediocre in terms of artistry, occasionally point to designs to be adopted at a later date on the coins. In their final decades these medals served as one of the few continuing outlets for creativity on the part of Mint engravers stifled by the lack of change in the regular issues and by the curtailment of commemorative half dollars. Morgan designed the medal for 1903, with the usual bust of Theodore Roosevelt on the obverse and an "aged workman" or "assayer" on the reverse. The influence of his own Liberty Head dollar and the fractional silver by Barber is manifest, for the workman was "erroneously described in 1901 as wearing a cap, due to the arrangement of the hair."[14] The same reverse had been used not only in 1901 but, on a smaller scale, in 1891. The medals for 1904 and 1905 were also by Morgan, having the "defiant" eagle on the reverse, and thereby recalling patterns for half dollars, regular dollars, and smaller silver struck in the 1870s. These were Morgan's formative years as a young engraver under William Barber in the Philadelphia Mint.

The 1906 medal, designed by Charles Barber, presented a new obverse, with fatter features for the president. The seal of the Treasury graces the reverse, and it was suggested that this should be the standard design henceforth for Assay Commission medals. In later years, when pressed for ideas or time to create original reverses, the engravers of the Mint on more than one occasion fell back on the convenient expedient of using the Great Seal. The 1964 half dollar in memory of John F. Kennedy is an outstanding illustration.[15]

The group of commemorative dollars struck in gold in 1903 and 1904 to 1905 were all designed by Charles Barber, and in terms of later commemoratives all are singularly dull. The Louisiana Purchase Exhibition dollars presented two obverses, one of Jefferson and the other of McKinley, with a common reverse. On the reverse a series of inscriptions is relieved only by an olive branch that runs across the field from lower right to middle left. An unusual feature was introduced in the 1904 and 1905 dollars for the Lewis and Clark Exposition. A bust of the aging Lewis graces the obverse, above the date, and a corresponding likeness of Clark occupies the reverse. The lack of spark in these coins, as in so many designs by Barber or Morgan, stems from the fact that the faces, hair, and drapery are flat and the lettering is small, crowded, and even. The later commemorative gold dollars, most notably the Panama-Pacific Exposition issue of 1915 by Charles Keck, demonstrate that the failings in the Barber gold dollars do not come from the minute size of the flan. Even when Barber and Morgan collaborated—one doing the obverse and the other doing the reverse of a coin of this type—the results were almost oppressive. The McKinley Memorial dollars of 1916 and 1917 bear witness to these stylistic judgments, with the unclothed bust on the obverse looking tastelessly Roman and the classical, colonnaded memorial building placed across a reverse further constricted by too much, too-large lettering.

Still, the 1903 to 1905 commemorative dollars had features pleasing to some. "These coins indicate a popular desire for a new departure from the somewhat monotonous types of Liberty which have characterized our money, as compared with the changes which appear on foreign coins when a new ruler comes to the throne. Early historic events or personages who have had a marked influence on our national affairs—Columbus, Queen Isabella, Lafayette—seem to be preferred. If this tendency could make itself felt on the regular coinage, it would give a new zeal to collectors."[16] Prophetic in terms of the Lincoln cent of 1909 and the changes beginning with the Washington quarter in 1932, the statement appears to belittle modern collectors, who needed not zeal but encouragement or cooperation from the government.

In 1910 Barber and Morgan again collaborated, on the annual Assay Commission medal. (The 1913 medal would repeat their design; see fig. 117.) Barber's obverse presents a bust of President Taft, which is an unquestioned success because of the size and strength of the sitter. The lettering is in Barber's new, thin, "modern" style but is tolerable because of its relatively unobtrusive spacing on either side of the massive head. The reverse is almost comic. Morgan tried to capture the Pasitelean classicism of the early 20th century in his ideal nudes. No critic would wish to deny him what had been refused Augustus Saint-Gaudens on the

World's Columbian Exposition medal in 1892, but these hunched-over nudes with their modest draperies and their giant ingot inscribed with the year are illogical distortions in the circle within the circle of a medallic reverse. When their saccharine heads with Greek transitional–style filleted hair and modern faces bob up beneath the spreading wings of a Saint-Gaudens eagle, the results are ludicrous.

So they seemed to W.T.R. Marvin, distinguished editor of the *American Journal of Numismatics,* writing in 1910.

> The reverse is very disappointing. The attitude of the figures is anything but graceful; they are bending forward, as if the weight of the ingot taxed their strength; their backs are curved to conform somewhat to the outline of the planchet, and one is in doubt whether they are endeavoring to get their heads under the protecting wings of the eagle, or crouching to avoid a threatened blow. The lower part of the legs of the figure on the left are concealed by its impossible attitude, and this gives to the thighs the suggestion of two meal bags. The contrast between these and some of the graceful figures on recent medals of private workmanship can not be regarded as particularly creditable to American art. If this is the best achievement of which the Mint is capable, it would have been better to have continued the arms of the Treasury Department and the laurel branch on the medals of the last year or two.[17]

117. Barber and Morgan, Assay medal

In the years between 1892 and 1907 America became a strong power in economic, military, and, not the least, artistic realms. The creative impetus of international exhibitions was answered by painters and sculptors able to hold their own alongside their European teachers. Augustus Saint-Gaudens was foremost among the sculptors, and his training as a medalist led him to take an active interest in improving the coinage. His genius shone in contrast to the prosaic yet necessary artistry of engravers at the Mint. The institution of commemorative coins gave artists, at first only those employed by the Mint, opportunities to carry out types of numismatic design heretofore reserved only for medals. The disappointing artistic level of the silver coins of 1892 resulted in clamor, in and out of the government, for the participation of famous independent artists in official numismatic design.

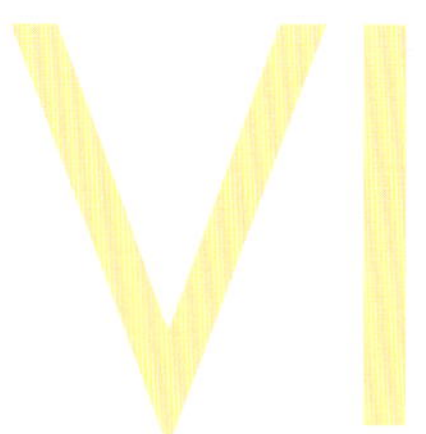

Theodore Roosevelt and Artistic Revolution

Neither before nor since the generation following 1907 were efforts to achieve a better coinage in the United States placed in the hands of a more distinguished group of monumental sculptors and medalists. For this, credit must be given to enlightened government officials, chiefly President Theodore Roosevelt. Among the sculptors, Augustus Saint-Gaudens was the leader in this movement; the younger men involved—Fraser, Weinman, Flanagan, and others—were his pupils. American sculpture was just beginning to move away from the French influences that had succeeded the Italian and to find its national identity. Commissions from the new mercantile barons and the spate of memorials resulting from the Civil War had given two generations of sculptors an opportunity to develop a new, American vocabulary.

Writing in the 1920s, an American historian of art whose own career had developed with the generation that followed Saint-Gaudens, Chandler Rathfon Post of Harvard University, could comment in summation:

> The most distinctive qualities of American sculpture are its moderation and seriousness of purpose. Despite our dependence upon France, the somewhat melodramatic agitation of French postures and compositions has been largely tabooed. Little patronage has been afforded to ideal sculpture as an end in itself, that is, ideal sculpture not designed for decoration of monuments, except in the case of "exposition sculpture"; and even the greater part of this has been done by foreign craftsmen. . . . A large number of our sculptors have occasionally gravitated to Indian subjects, and a few almost exclusively, in the desire to be truly American; but only one or two of them have succeeded in doing more than bestow an Indian head upon a classical or Parisian body.[1]

Although usually identified with Indians, Rough Riders, and the strenuous life, Theodore Roosevelt had art—national imagery, that is—

very much on his mind from the moment he entered the White House as president.[2] He inaugurated the National Arts Commission, and it was not long after he became chief executive in his own right that his aspirations for a better national image in the arts turned to the coinage. "It will be remembered that the American Numismatic Society appointed a Committee on New Coinage last year, who had an interview with President Roosevelt, by whom they were cordially received, and whose influence has been given towards carrying out the suggestions made by them."[3] Within the year following, 1907–1908, the society suggested that the sum of $10,000 be appropriated for each coin model: $1,000 each to the best six designs, and an additional $4,000 to the winner.

118. Barber and Morgan, medal for Theodore Roosevelt

119. Saint-Gaudens and Weinman, medal for Roosevelt

Medals Portraying Roosevelt

Two medals of Theodore Roosevelt point up the contrasts between official art at the Philadelphia Mint and the ideas evolved by the president and Saint-Gaudens for the new coinage. Both medals were designed and struck in connection with the second inauguration, of March 4, 1905. The first, perhaps naturally, is the official presidential medal designed by Charles E. Barber and George T. Morgan and produced at the Philadelphia Mint (fig. 118). The second is the inaugural medal sketched out by Saint-Gaudens and executed by his pupil Adolph A. Weinman (fig. 119). The story of its creation will be told in connection with Weinman's career and the coinage of 1916. This is the medal that the president admired so thoroughly and that Weinman was so eager to model. Most important, it is the work of art that Saint-Gaudens held up to the president and posterity as the antithesis of the commercial mediocrity of Barber and his school. Posterity is now in a better position to judge whether the Barber-Morgan medal was so hideous and the Saint-Gaudens–Weinman creation such a superior example of medallic taste and beauty.

Barber's obverse is a combination of head in profile and bust in three-quarters view that was used on a number of medals during Roosevelt's terms of office. A fuller view of substantially the same portrait turns up on the obverse of the 1907 plaque commemorating the departure of the Atlantic Fleet from Hampton Roads, Virginia, on its flag-showing cruise around the world (fig. 120). The strong, square Dutch face with aggressive, almost truculent outline, emphasized by the pince-nez, and the rough coat with high-buttoned waistcoat are all caught with an attention to generalities and detail that perfectly, incisively characterize the president whose watchword was action. Roosevelt may not have been pleased with Barber's portrait, but the likeness is posterity's perfect vision of the hero of San Juan Hill. The Hampton Roads medal of 1907 suggests that Roosevelt has aged a bit, but the tilt of his head is slightly back, the jaw is more determined, and it is clear that six years in office have only strengthened those qualities characteristic of the soldier-statesman and

120. Barber and Morgan, Hampton Roads medal

121. Pisanello, medallion of Leonello d'Este

our memories of him. Barber's portraits are a combination of photographic naturalism and medallic modeling. They are strong, competent, and most effective. A medalist could hardly be asked to do more.

Morgan's reverse for the official medal of 1905 could well have irritated Roosevelt and Saint-Gaudens because of its derivation from the facile, feminine classicism of French medalists from 1880 to 1900. It contains too many clichés, and lacks the emotional unity, inner strength, and physical containment of figure found in the reverse that Morgan created for the official medal commemorating William McKinley's term of office and his martyrdom (fig. 116). At first glance the reverse of the Roosevelt medal presents an awkwardly poised, plump-armed Liberty or Columbia trying to blank out the Capitol with a tiny scroll that looks like a shade-roller. In reality, the total composition has elements of dignity and even grandeur. "Liberty," in her French cap and Grecian garb, stands beside a cippus surmounted by an urn like a Cycladic or early Greek marble bowl and bearing national emblems on its surface. What the scroll actually symbolizes, save "History Writ Large," is hard to say. A wreath or eagle on the upward palm might have made more sense, or at least balance in the composition. The Capitol in the upper background is a masterpiece of how to pose a giant architectural monument on a medallic surface. The low relief combines accuracy with a faint suggestion of atmospheric impressionism. Since most presidential medals of the 19th century merely comprised lettering in wreath for the obverse, the reverse little deserved the condemnation heaped upon it by the president and his friends in artistic circles.

The virtues of the Barber-Morgan medal for Theodore Roosevelt's presidency become all the more apparent when the piece is viewed alongside the Presidential Inaugural medal designed by Saint-Gaudens, executed by Weinman, and praised by Roosevelt. The debt of this second medal to the Italian Renaissance is painfully obvious. The size, form, and position of the lettering on the obverse are found in a number of medals by Pisanello, Sperandio, and other artists of the 15th century praised by Saint-Gaudens and imitated in his medals and those of his followers. Even the position of the spade-shaped stops between the words derives from quattrocento medals such as the creation by Pisanello in 1444 for the marriage of Leonello d'Este with Maria of Aragon (fig. 121). The portrait, bereft of pince-nez, waistcoat, and everything else, is meant to exhibit Renaissance clarity, but it is really quite out of character since Pisanello and Sperandio invariably showed their sitters in contemporary costume. Even Roman emperors were given drapery or a cuirass in the 15th century, and the neck is too truncated to relate to heads on Roman medallions or coins. The crowning indignity to posterity lies in the fact that the portrait does not resemble Theodore Roosevelt, but looks like some relative of the German Kaiser. The planes of the head have been squared off; the curves have been flattened to create a Prussian neck and skull; there is an unnatural squint to the eyes; the moustache is too small, and the whole cast of the lips and chin above which it is perched is not the face of Roosevelt. Of course, it is a well-known principle of art today that quality should not be equated with photographic accuracy, and as a work of art this obverse evidently pleased a number of persons. As a medallic commemoration of President Roosevelt's second inauguration, however, the piece falls far short of the standards set by Charles Barber.

The reverse foreshadows the Saint-Gaudens designs for the gold coinage, on which he was working at the time Weinman carried out the inaugural medal. The similarity of the eagle to the bird first considered for the $20 coin and adopted for the $10 piece is readily apparent (figs. 126, 127, and 130). In that Weinman's reverse for the medal eschews the dated iconography of vague Franco-American classical allegories, it can be considered more successful than Morgan's design for the medal struck at the Mint. Simplicity is usually better suited to a medal than the concept of large females before architectural complexes. Weinman's reverse, however, really has little to do with the theme of inauguration and is much more the design for a coin than a medal. Because he created a composition to commemorate the event, Morgan's "Liberty before the Capitol" is a much more courageous theme than merely a bold eagle on a rock amid a conventional motto and a mixture of Latin and English in a Renaissance framework. Each medal has its merits. It is sad that the creation of Saint-Gaudens and Weinman had to be evolved amid so many disparaging remarks about the equally valid, perhaps more suitable, artistic contribution of Barber and Morgan.

Another member of the Saint-Gaudens circle was to provide an intimate medallic vision of Theodore Roosevelt. A year after the death of the rough and ready president in 1919, James E. Fraser executed a medal of honor for the Roosevelt Memorial Association (fig. 122). Fraser, whose medallic and other achievements are part of the saga of his Buffalo nickel in 1912, was the supreme portraitist of Theodore Roosevelt. His mighty equestrian group, portraying Roosevelt as explorer and hunter, leader of the Rough Riders, dominates the triumphal arch in memory of the hero of San Juan Hill. This monument stands next to the Museum of Natural History on Central Park West in New York City. On the memorial medal, a rough-textured bust faces to the right, head thrust slightly forward in the characteristic aggressive squint. Ribbon on the glasses, necktie, shirt, and suit are all stirred up into an impression of tweedy activity. The lettering follows Renaissance organization, size, and form. Only perhaps the size of Fraser's signature might be said to disturb this obverse, but Pisanello was never bashful about spreading name and occupation over his creations. Fraser's name and the date do provide a small point of focus behind Roosevelt's shoulders.

122. J.E. Fraser, Roosevelt Memorial medal

A flaming sword and a few classic lines justifying U.S. forcefulness in the era of "Big Stick" diplomacy make an unusual reverse. Balance, size, interlinking, and superimposition of lettering turn a potentially dull composition into a strong statement of modern medallic art in the Renaissance manner. Fraser's medals are never dull, and, as might be expected, they differ from each other as well as from the mediocre average. This medal, created just after Roosevelt's death, was a great artist's tribute to the man who had done so much to revitalize U.S. coinage.

The Coins of Augustus Saint-Gaudens

The first redesigned coins in the era of new endeavors for the arts were the eagle or $10 gold piece and its multiple the double eagle, both first issued in 1907 (figs. 123–132) and both modified within the year to bring the artistry of Saint-Gaudens in line with the mechanical practices of the Mint. Barber and Morgan would have been the logical artists to redesign these coins, unaltered in essence since 1838 and 1849 respectively, but Roosevelt had been convinced by Saint-Gaudens and others that the artists who were responsible for the academic creations of 1892, the regular coinage and the World's Columbian Exposition coins and medallic reverse, could by no means be expected

123. Saint-Gaudens, models for double eagle

124. *Saint-Gaudens, model for double eagle*

125. *Saint-Gaudens, model for double eagle*

126. *Eagle of 1907*

127. *Saint-Gaudens, model for double eagle*

128. *Saint-Gaudens, model for the coinage, Liberty as a Pergamene Nike*

129. *Liberty in an Indian bonnet*

130. Saint-Gaudens, models for double eagle

132. Saint-Gaudens, model for double eagle

131. Double eagle of 1907

to produce coins (a numismatic art) that would rival those (that) of classical Greece.

The eagle with its head of Liberty in an Indian bonnet and a standing eagle recalling the bird of Ptolemaic missed being a great coin because Roosevelt interfered in the choice of the headdress (or no headdress) for Liberty. The preliminary studies for the coin avoided this nonsensical bit of Americana, one that recalls the fancy feathers worn by Liberty standing on a plinth inscribed E PLURIBUS UNUM atop the dome of the Capitol. The double eagle is perhaps the most majestic coin ever to bear our national imprint. The Liberty striding forward is as grand in miniature as the Hellenistic Victory of Samothrace on a heroic scale.[4] The eagle in flight against the sun on the reverse achieves complete domination of motion and expanding vista over the confines of a tiny tondo. Although the authorities at the Mint flattened the relief to facilitate striking and handling, this coin has remained a forceful demonstration that modern, mechanical coinage need in no way be pedestrian. Even the required additions of IN GOD WE TRUST to these two issues in gold could not ruin the sculptor's relief, spacing, and arrangement of figures vis-à-vis lettering. Both coins seem as modern a century after they were conceived as any issues, American or otherwise, produced in the past generation; and compared with what had been tolerated heretofore in the United States, both burst as artistic skyrockets in the horizons of our academic creativity.

Saint-Gaudens was as good a teller of tales as he was a sculptor, and this Gaelic gift of wit and acumen passed to his son, appropriately named Homer, who set down the events of his father's life in the form of a partial biography. The story of the creation of new coinage for the United States has never been told more vividly than in the words of father and son.

> The scheme for the United States coins—the cent, the eagle, and the double eagle—also originated about this time at a dinner with President Roosevelt in the winter of 1905.

There they both grew enthusiastic over the old high-relief Greek coins, until the President declared that he would have the mint stamp a modern version of such coins in spite of itself if my father would design them, adding with his customary vehemence, "You know, Saint-Gaudens, this is my pet crime." . . .

November 11, 1905

Dear Mr. President:

You have hit the nail on the head with regard to the coinage. Of course the great coins (and you might almost say the only coins) are the Greek ones you speak of, just as the great medals are those of the fifteenth century by Pisanello and Sperandio. Nothing would please me more than to make the attempt in the direction of the heads of Alexander, but the authorities on modern monetary requirements would, I fear, "throw fits," to speak emphatically, if the thing was done now. It would be great if it could be accomplished and I do not see what the objection would be if the edges were high enough to prevent the rubbing. Perhaps an inquiry from you would not receive the antagonistic reply that would certainly be made to me from those who have the "say" in such matters.

Up to the present I have done no work on the actual models for the coins, but have made sketches, and the matter is constantly in my mind. I have about determined on the composition of one side, which would contain an eagle very much like the one I placed on your medal, with an advantageous modification. On the other side would be some kind of a (possibly winged) figure of liberty striding energetically forward as if on a mountain top, holding aloft on one arm a shield bearing the stars and stripes with the word "Liberty" marked across the field, in the other hand perhaps a flaming torch; the drapery would be flowing in the breeze [figs. 123, 124, and 125]. My idea is to make it a living thing and typical of progress. . . .

[My father] first proposed to model the cent with a flying eagle, the formal lettering treated in a new fashion, and to execute for the gold coins a full-length figure of Liberty mounting a rock, with a shield in her left hand and a lighted torch in her right, backed by a semi-conventional eagle, with wings half-closed. For one reason and another, however, the scheme proved impracticable. So, after months of confusion, he settled that the one cent should exhibit a profile head and the lettering; that the ten-dollar

133. Eagles on monument to Robert G. Shaw

gold piece should carry the same head, with the inscriptions shifted, and the standing eagle [figs. 126–130]; and that the twenty-dollar gold piece should exhibit the full-length figure of Liberty, without wings or shield, and the flying eagle [figs. 131, 125, and 132].

To accomplish this result, my father altered and realtered the coins for a year and a half. The suggestion for the flying eagle he developed from the bird on the 1857 "White Cent" [fig. 36]. The conception of the standing eagle he drew from a design he had often used on such work as the Shaw Memorial [fig. 133], the medal struck to commemorate the inauguration of President Roosevelt [fig. 119], and the shield of the monument to President Garfield in Fairmount Park, Philadelphia. In all, he created seventy models of this bird, and often stood twenty-five of them in a row for visitors to number according to preference [fig. 130].

The profile head he modeled in relief from the favorite, but superseded bust of the Sherman "Victory" [figs. 128, 134, and 135], adding the feathers only upon the President's emphatic suggestion [fig. 129]. Many persons regarded it

134. Saint-Gaudens, head of Nike

135. "Beautiful Head" from Pergamon

with disfavor at the time because it was thought to have been posed for by an Irish maid, Mary Cunningham, when none but a "pure American" should have served for a model for our natural coin.[5] As a matter of fact, the features of the Irish girl appear only at the size of a pin-head upon the full-length Liberty, the body of which was posed for by a Swede, while the profile head, to which exception was taken, was modeled from a woman supposed to have negro blood in her veins. Who, other than an Indian, may be a "pure American" is undetermined. In reality here, as in all examples of my father's ideal sculpture, little or no resemblance can be traced to any model; since he was always quick to reject the least taint of what he called "personality" in such instances.

Finally he attacked the difficult problem of the inscriptions by placing upon the previously milled edge of the coin, in one case, the forty-six stars and, in the other, the thirteen stars with the "E Pluribus Unum." The motto "In God We Trust," as an inartistic intrusion not required by law, he wholly discarded and thereby drew down upon himself the lightning of public comment. It is interesting to discover in regard to this that Secretary Salmon P. Chase received quite as severe a censure for placing the words upon this coin as was aroused by their removal.

> Upon the striking of the coins it seemed impossible to reach a satisfactory understanding with the Mint authorities, who, shortly after my father's death, began issuing the Eagles with extremely poor results. In vain his assistant, Mr. Henry Hering, who had personally carried on the alterations protested to the authorities. They replied that they were forced to lessen further the proportional depths of relief, and that in the process details were lost. Mr. Hering promptly exhibited three grades of relief reduced abroad to the same extent from the same original by the same machine that the mint employed. The details stood out quite as vividly in the low relief as in the high. At last, however, Mr. Frank A. Leach, the new Director of the Mint, took a hand in the turmoil and brought the matter before the President, with the consequence that the designs remained for a time somewhat as my father planned them, though what with the lowered relief and most careless reproduction, especially of the profile head, the results appeared far from those he would have allowed had he been alive.[6]

The tale about a woman of African heritage serving as ultimate source for the head of Liberty on the $10 coin may be correct in that artists had constant recourse to living models, but there is a clear line of classical progression from the so-called Beautiful Head made at Pergamon about 165 B.C. to the Nike of the Sherman Monument and thence to the coins (figs. 135, 134, 128, and 129). The sculptures at Pergamon had been excavated in the previous generation, and they were artistic sensations of the decades when Saint-Gaudens was at the height of his fame and creativity. The Berlin Museum, recipient of these sculptures from western Asia Minor, sold casts in abundance, and the "Beautiful Head" was one of the works most accessible to a perceptive sculptor in America.[7]

The obverse of the double eagle also shows degrees of alteration and development, none of them related immediately to any human model. In the first finished study (fig. 124), a form of feathery headdress seems to have been inserted discreetly behind the windswept hair of the winged Liberty. The whole surface is unified by removal of the wings and increased emphasis in the sun's rays thrusting out from the disc just visible behind the Capitol (fig. 125). Greek sources for Liberty's costume have been strengthened in the second three-dimensional design, where heavier folds and lines of drapery were gathered together and then flattened out to reveal fleshy contours in a fashion practiced to the same full degree at Pergamon or on Rhodes after 200 B.C. Almost overt in their dependence on Hellenistic antiquity, the $10 and $20 gold coins designed by Saint-Gaudens still managed to emerge as perhaps the greatest statements of Americanism in the official minor arts.

Bela Pratt's Incuse Half and Quarter Eagle

136. Half eagle of 1908 type

After the new eagle and double eagle by Saint-Gaudens had been put into circulation, the two coins most in need of redesigning in 1908 were the half eagle or $5 gold piece and the quarter eagle or $2.50 coin. The larger denomination had been little changed from Gobrecht's design of 1839, and the smaller coin dated back to 1840. Since a noted sculptor had been summoned to do the largest gold coins, the eagle and the double eagle, it was logical to commission the remaining gold coins from a younger contemporary of established reputation. Bela Lyon Pratt of Boston (1867–1917) presented a novel coin, the same designs for each size,[8] which was adopted amid some protest (fig. 136). An Indian brave in war bonnet adorns the obverse, and the same Ptolemaic eagle with wings closed walks along on the reverse. Pratt was aware of the type of eagle favored by Saint-Gaudens on his war memorials, such as the relief of Robert Gould Shaw leading his African American regiment off to the Civil War opposite the State House on Boston Common (fig. 133); on his medals, such as the rejected reverse for the World's Columbian Exposition, where the shield beside the "ideal youth" bore an example (fig. 107); and on the large gold coins being designed or just issued.

The innovation in these coins was one of technique as much as design. Instead of being modeled in relief within a protecting rim, the Indian, the eagle, and the lettering were sunken in incuse or engraved in the uniformly flat plane of the coin. Noted coin dealer S.H. Chapman of Philadelphia wrote Theodore Roosevelt on seeing the new coins that the Indian was emaciated, the eagle was the European golden eagle rather than an American variety, and the sunken design failed on several points. It looked like an engraving and was therefore easy to counterfeit. It would convey dirt and disease. As summation of his condemnation, Chapman wrote that the new issues lacked beauty, were easy to counterfeit, were unhygienic because contagious dirt would stick in the incuse relief, and—the age-old cry against numismatic artistry—the pieces would not stack in equal piles.[9]

Boston's collector of Far Eastern art, the learned William Sturgis Bigelow, seems to have been the mediator with Theodore Roosevelt between Pratt the sculptor and Chapman the critic. Bigelow also appears to have originated the notion of incuse relief in modern coinage, having in mind the Egyptian reliefs in Boston's Museum of Fine Arts. Since he had convinced Roosevelt of the potentials of Pratt's models, he replied to Chapman's attack that the sunken relief was taken from a glorious tradition in Egyptian art and the Indian developed out of a photograph of the genuine native,[10] as opposed to the less characteristic type of Indian sometimes fattened by inactivity or oil royalties on a reservation. He sent a photograph from a plaster *modello* by Pratt to prove the relevant vitality of the subject. Chapman's rebuttal centered around an inept, irrelevant judgment: "Egyptian art, unlike the Greek, remained frozen in conventionalism and did not progress to the full free rendering to the round."[11]

The Native American is far from emaciated, and the coins show more imagination and daring of design than almost any other issue in American history. Pratt deserves to be admired for his medals and coins, but he was not as highly regarded as a sculptor of large figures. Morey wrote that he "endeavored to add a greater robustness to the idealism of the old school, and found the synthesis beyond his powers. Perhaps the very confusion of his ideals accounts for his popularity. People like the imprecise since it imposes no touch of definition. . . . His most successful works were minor decorative themes involving forms of immaturity."[12] In 1907, it is interesting to note by way of coincidence, Bela Lyon Pratt designed the Yale Bicentennial medal—as Chief Engraver John R. Sinnock was to do for Princeton in 1946, the year of his Roosevelt dime (fig. 234).

The vogue for real Indians, rather than merely little girls or Pergamene heads in Indian bonnets, had reached the coinage. These gold fractions of the eagle were not the Native American's last appearance. The Buffalo nickel was to follow in 1913, and there were to be Indians on the commemorative half dollars. Chandler Post was correct when he observed in his various writings on American sculpture how few sculptors could capture an Indian with naturalistic accuracy. Still, new ideas in numismatic design were afoot under the bullying of Theodore Roosevelt. Saint-Gaudens had produced classical perfection in modern die design. Pratt's work marked a transition, in the "emaciated" Indian at least, to naturalism. The Lincoln cent of Victor D. Brenner and the Buffalo nickel of James E. Fraser were to proclaim the arrival of photographic naturalism in American coinage.

The Lincoln Cent

The year 1909 was to Lincoln what the year of 1932 was to be to Washington, an anniversary of birth. The "copper" cent with the head of Liberty in an Indian bonnet had been in circulation since 1864, the design going back to 1859. It seems natural, therefore, that the smallest denomination should be redesigned, and that a portrait of the Great Emancipator should ornament the coin. Nevertheless, it took the dynamism of Theodore Roosevelt to break with tradition and make the "penny" the first regular issue to bear a recognized portrait. At first, a commemorative coin with Lincoln's portrait was proposed for the centennial of his

137. Brenner, Abraham Lincoln

138. Cent of 1909

139. Lincoln Memorial reverse of 1959 type

birth. Meanwhile, the president had befriended the young Lithuanian-born Victor D. Brenner while sitting to him for the portrait to be used on the Panama medal. Brenner showed him the model for a bronze plaquette marking Lincoln's centennial, and Roosevelt recommended to MacVeagh (who would become secretary of the Treasury during the Taft administration) that the design be placed on a coin (fig. 137). The cent of 1909 emerged, an obverse that has been in use ever since.

Brenner, a pupil of Louis-Oscar Roty (1846–1911) in Paris, had instructed at the coin- and medal-designing and die-cutting class in 1901–1902 that opened at the National Academy under the direction of the Academy of Design and the American Numismatic Society. Morey wrote that there was a "rare combination of qualities of good relief in miniature in Brenner's work, namely, clear contours that nevertheless coax the light and shade, and an economy of forms with sufficient area left to the unworked field."[13] These characteristics are visible in the tiny tondo of the cent, a durable coin because Brenner cleverly made the surfaces slightly convex within a raised rim. He succeeded in conveying the feeling that a photograph of Lincoln has been turned into a three-dimensional experience in metal. An aura of impressionism hovers about the hair and beard, and presentation of subject in everyday dress seems natural enough. Photographic naturalism is in itself a major numismatic advance, but when it is taken in connection with a famous person in everyday clothing a giant stride has been made away from the Greco-Roman or neo-Pheidian French Libertys of the earlier coinage. Brenner's reverse, simple lettering flanked by ears of grain, took much thought on the part of the artist, as his correspondence reveals, and this modest design served well until the 150th anniversary of Lincoln's birth, when it was replaced by Frank Gasparro's reverse showing the mausoleum-like Lincoln Memorial in full, frontal view (figs. 138 and 139). Ten years later, in 1969, Brenner's obverse underwent certain modifications, designed to bring Lincoln's bust back to the sharpness of the original issues and their immediate successors. By 1968 the master die was producing a blurry image, with lettering intruding into the rim. On the new master die, the highest wave of Lincoln's hair was centered under the W of WE (TRUST), the details of the beard were restored, and the bow tie has took on something of its pristine vigor. The word LIBERTY was made shorter, with narrower, taller letters, and a greater swing to the tail of the R. The results are eminently successful, a reminder that the clarity and precision of a restyled older masterpiece can easily surpass timid new designs in modern coinage.[14]

140. Brenner, medal for Hay

Brenner's formula for the slightly impressionistic, photographic presentation of a bearded man of note in profile was applied with equal success elsewhere. In 1908 he had exhibited his medal of Collis P. Huntington, in modeling and profile anticipating the reliefs of Lincoln. His portraits of John Hay in 1912 and of Samuel Putnam Avery on a medal from "his friends and the architects of New York" in 1914 were to achieve the same sense of faithful naturalism and plastic surfaces (fig. 140). It is amusing to note that Brenner himself wore a beard like Lincoln's and looked every inch the model for his own preferences in medallic portraiture.[15]

Officials and artists next turned their attention to the five-cent piece, commonly called the nickel. Brenner had considered this denomination as a candidate for his Lincoln, but it was decided that the cent needed redesigning first. In 1909, no doubt mindful that changes would be made, the artists of the Mint produced a series of patterns for the five-cent piece of three-quarters copper and one-quarter nickel. The obverses displayed almost half-figure busts of Washington to the left or right in military frock coat and epaulets; the usual combination of "5" and lettering comprised the reverses. The design was ruined by the pseudonaturalism of Washington, who after all lived before the photograph and is best remembered from noble paintings in the British courtly tradition or the neoclassic busts by Houdon. Otherwise, this essay for a new nickel was pedestrian, demonstrating that fresh ideas from the outside were also required for this coin.

Medals by John Flanagan

In 1912 a friend and pupil of Augustus Saint-Gaudens, John Flanagan from Newark, New Jersey (1865–1952), designed a medal that combined the styles of Pisanello or Sperandio with the powerful idiom of Michelangelo in portraying a contemporary event in the age of steam.

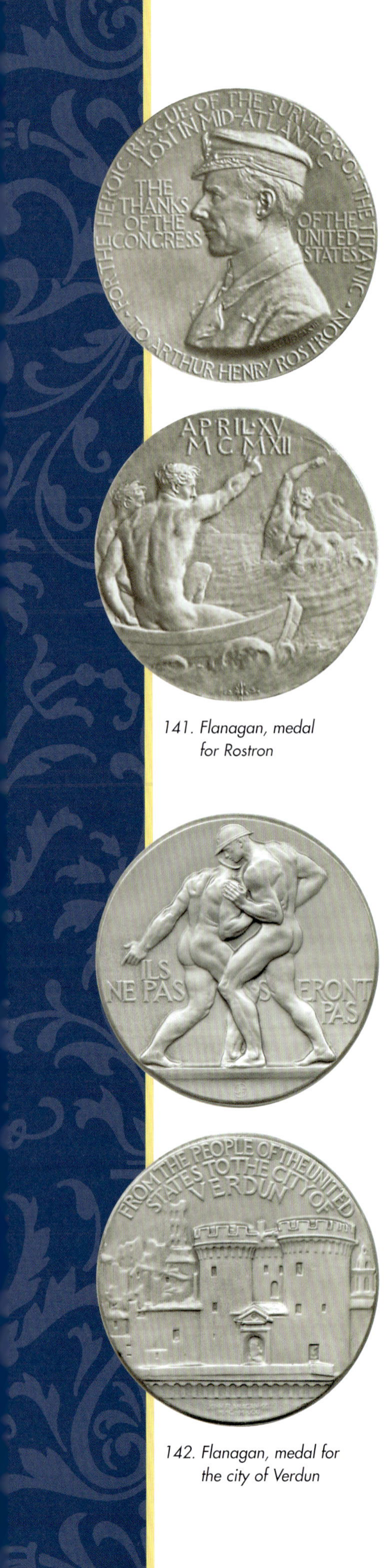

141. Flanagan, medal for Rostron

142. Flanagan, medal for the city of Verdun

The analogy is closer, for Flanagan was to go on to create a new coin, the Washington quarter dollar of 1932. April 15, 1912, is remembered as the day the *Titanic* hit an iceberg and sank in the North Atlantic amid great loss of life and heroic deeds. One of the heroes was the British captain Arthur Henry Rostron, whose crew rescued a number of survivors. The gold medal voted him by the Congress of the United States was designed by Flanagan (fig. 141).

Its obverse follows the tradition of quattrocento medalists, a stern profile of the captain in his "brass" cap and coat with ribbon above the heart; the lettering, like that of Fraser's medal of 1901 in honor of Saint-Gaudens (fig. 146), is divided between the edge of the field and the area either side of the bust. As happens so often, there is too much lettering; the words "for the" or "lost in Mid-Atlantic" and perhaps "the thanks of" could have been omitted without curtailing the message. The artistic impact would have been greater, for unlike Fraser's Saint-Gaudens, Flanagan's heroic merchant captain is somewhat lost in epigraphy. He almost pokes his sharp nose into the THANKS OF THE CONGRESS.

Michelangelo's gigantic nudes symbolize the struggle for survival in the icy seas. My first reaction was one of unpleasant surprise that figures from the Sistine Chapel ceiling could represent a tragedy that was in everyone's mind while Flanagan was working. Such a dramatic occasion might best have been handled in contemporary terms, to match the naturalism of the obverse. On reflection, I feel the sculptor has utilized the medallic tondo to its fullest by adhering to a completely ideal concept. The alternatives of a lifeboat full of women and children or the sinking four-stacker would have been too much for the medium. An impressionistic ship might have been successful, but photographic naturalism would have led to excessive detail in a subject where no good photographs existed and where much of the nocturnal horror existed only in the minds of those not directly concerned. Even among the survivors, few could have reconstructed the disaster with the graphic drama of an artist for the *Illustrated London News.*

In 1921 John Flanagan produced another medal in the mixed styles of the 15th and 16th centuries (fig. 142). It was titled "From the people of the United States to the City of Verdun." As in the case of his medal to Captain Rostron for heroic rescue of *Titanic* survivors, Flanagan could not resist mixing the struggling male nudes of Michelangelo or Vasari with a format based on the work of Pisanello. On the obverse the famous order attributed to Pétain forms a background for two well-muscled nudes locked in combat. The reverse is modeled after Matteo de'Pasti's classic medal of 1446 with the bust of Sigismondo Pandolfo Malatesta on the obverse and on the opposite side a view of the "Rocca Malatestiana." This was the great castle at Rimini with its rectangular, crenelated keep, its massive wall and lofty towers, and its gates and outer fortifications (fig. 143). The bastions of Verdun could be treated with equal roughness of stone and earthworks on the medallic surface. The style of the Renaissance medalist lent itself admirably to the heroic, wasteful siege that saved the Western Front from collapse in the spring of 1916.

Flanagan's gentler, more poetic side in medals is demonstrated in his George Robert White medal of honor for the Massachusetts Horticultural Society, dated 1909 (fig. 144). His typically simple, rectangular, thin lettering dominates obverse and reverse. The idealized young horticulturist kneels to plant his tiny tree in a great English 18th-century park or on the lawn of a large American estate in the 1890s. The great round greenhouse or gazebo in the background, with its marble urns, statuary, and baroque architectural details, is just what one would find on a Long Island estate landscaped by James Renwick to suit the architecture of McKim, Mead, and White. The sense of mission, of repose, and of manicured nature in this vista is perfectly in keeping with the spirit of the medal and the tastes of those who sponsored it.

On the reverse the weight of the inscription is framed, appropriately, by the Hellenistic swath of flowers and garden or orchard produce forming a crescent at the left. The little palmette motif in the lower center is a secondary signature of the artist, for John Flanagan also used it on his congressional medal for Arthur Henry Rostron.

143. Matteo de'Pasti, medallion of Malatesta

144. Flanagan, Massachusetts Horticultural Society medal

Fraser, the Renaissance Medal, and the Buffalo Nickel

The man who furnished fresh ideas for the nickel was James Earle Fraser. This versatile sculptor of memorable themes was born in 1876 at Winona, Minnesota, and died in 1953 at Westport, Connecticut. He studied at the Art Institute in Chicago and worked for Saint-Gaudens in Paris and in the United States, on the equestrian statue of General Sherman at the southeast corner of Central Park. It was a rejected study for the head of Victory leading the general's charger that became the inspiration for the head of Liberty on the gold eagle of 1907. Morey termed Fraser "the ablest of the many pupils of Saint-Gaudens . . . a universal craftsman, equally able in the medal, the portrait and the monumental."[16] In the memoirs of Saint-Gaudens there is an amusing caricature of the studio assistant Fraser by the master, which suggests that, despite all that has been written about Native Americans posing for the nickel, the pupil may have looked in the mirror to find his profile for the ideal Indian! Fraser's most famous monumental sculpture was another noble

145. Fraser, The End of the Trail

savage, *The End of the Trail,* termed by Lorado Taft "that poignantly expressive climax of the Panama-Pacific Exposition."[17] The bronze shows an aged Indian on an aged pony, both bowed by a lashing blizzard and both patently facing death on a lonely prairie (fig. 145). Fraser's work of this nature places him among the few American sculptors who could begin to understand the Indian. His statue of Meriwether Lewis, of Lewis and Clark fame, was equally forceful, with a slenderness of profile and freedom of modeling that recalled Rodin's *Burghers of Calais.* (His ideal male creation called *Primitive Power* and based on Rodin's *Thinker* was less successful.)

James E. Fraser had already won acclaim as a medalist before he ventured out amid the Indians and buffalo of the five-cent piece. The key to his style as a designer of medals lies in the lines by Saint-Gaudens to Theodore Roosevelt: "the great medals are those of the fifteenth century by Pisanello and Sperandio."[18] The special medal of honor created for Augustus Saint-Gaudens in 1901 on the occasion of the Pan American Exposition at Buffalo bears Fraser's signature in full beneath the Greco-Roman herm-bust of the master in profile. Arrangement and type of lettering, especially the balance of either side of the full-profiled portrait, are designed to recall work by the masterful medalists of the quattrocento (fig. 146). In 1914, two years after designing the new nickel, Fraser was still playing the role of a modern Pisanello. His Edward H. Harriman

146. Fraser, medal for Saint-Gaudens

Memorial medal, an American Museum of Safety award to the Southern Pacific Railroad Company, follows the Renaissance in spacing of bust and lettering on the obverse. On the opposite side, the ideal brakeman walks the tracks, a powerful vista that uses full surfaces without any borders, only the tracks speeding off at an angle. Such work is the application of photographic naturalism to a world governed for nearly 500 years by a classic aesthetic organization.

Like Flanagan, Fraser had achieved a perfect synthesis of the ideal, the real, and the traditional in medallic design. It was Fraser who first related these principles to designs for the U.S. coinage, and he was the more successful of the two men in applying them.

The so-called Buffalo nickel, designed in 1912 and placed in circulation in 1913, is the ultimate homage to our native or Indian-prairie tradition. The small coin is overwhelmed by the mighty plasticity of the Indian's rugged head and the majestic buffalo on his plot of prairie (fig. 147). In the model dated 1912 (fig. 148) and the first issue of 1913 the bit of earth was like a mound, but the words FIVE CENTS, having been placed on the raised surface of the mound, were in danger of wearing away too quickly. The solution, which was evident on coins minted beginning in May 1913, was to remove all of the mound except the part on which the animal actually stood, so that the denomination would rest in the flat field of the coin. Despite the rough naturalness of modeling and the true flavor of the man and beast, it is an amusing commentary on Fraser's sources of photographic faithfulness that the three models used for the Native American were probably all performers on the Wild West show or sideshow circuit, one having been snatched from performances at Coney Island. Some numismatists have questioned the traditional account that the buffalo (or technically bison) had been "captured" by the artist in a New York zoo, but modern research shows that this was probably the case.

The impending appearance of the coin elicited the following from Franklin MacVeagh, secretary of the Treasury, in January 1913:

147. Nickel of 1913

148. Fraser, model for Buffalo nickel

> A new five cent piece will shortly be issued with designs that will again assist the art students of our coinage. Coins have always aimed to be works of art, both in ancient and modern times. We do not hope, under present conditions, to equal the coins of the great ancient periods. The artists then had a far greater opportunity because the coins did not have to be stacked. Notwithstanding our practical limitations, however, modern coins can still be immensely interesting and beautiful; and the designs for the new nickel will give this coin a place with the best modern work.[19]

It is interesting to see the desire to serve students of art and the level of numismatic art in general in MacVeagh's statement. It is also significant that Roosevelt's aim, expressed to Saint-Gaudens at dinner in 1905, to make modern coins worthy of their classical Greek or Roman predecessors has not been forgotten. Fraser's new five-cent piece could not have emerged under more favorable auspices.

When the coin appeared in 1913, a startling contrast to the old Greco-Roman diademed head of Liberty and large roman numeral, cautious praise came from T.L. Comparette, curator of the collection at the Philadelphia Mint, in his annual review of numismatic and medallic activity in the United States. "It may not have been wise to place a type on each side of the small piece, a simpler reverse might have been better; the Indian head and the buffalo may be too softly modeled for coin types; perhaps inscriptions have been sacrificed to the types, so that the former are too small and the latter too large for the size of the field; but with all the faults that may be alleged against the new piece, one outstanding truth remains, that Mr. Fraser's designs are works of art, powerfully modelled, and strong."[20] Comparette leveled the obvious criticisms about the largeness of the Indian and bison as opposed to the letters, but this is one of the basic ingredients in the greatness of the coin. The date on the Buffalo nickel is too close to the highest surface, causing it to wear off after a number of years in circulation. This fault is a minor one, however, and has been more of a joy to collectors of nickels by date than a concern to those interested in the coin for its artistic or functional qualities.

As is known to most readers of the popular press, especially the periodicals devoted to coins, the Indian or Indians who posed for the head on this obverse have been discussed at length. The legends about models for Liberty and about the influence of photographic naturalism on the new design make it of interest to pursue this figure further. The bison is easily disposed of. The model was an aged beast named Black Diamond. At age 20 in 1915 he was sold for $700. "He weighed 1,550 pounds and dressed to 750 pounds of usable meat. His hide, 13' × 13', was made into a robe, and his head, a magnificent one, was mounted, but where preserved your deponent knows not."[21] So much for the vanishing bison.

Black Diamond's head was rediscovered in the 1980s and was a star exhibit at the 1985 American Numismatic Association convention in Baltimore, Maryland.

The key to the Indian's origin lies in Fraser's letter to the Indian Office after his design became widely known. He stated that his model was a composite portrait of three different men: a Sioux chief named Iron Tail, a Cheyenne chief called Two Moons, and another Native American whose name he had forgotten at the time of writing. Obviously, if any legends were going to arise, they would revolve around the man whose name had been forgotten. This seems to have been just what happened. In another account Iron Trail (not Tail) is called a Cheyenne, and the nationality of Two Moons is not specified. In 1913, a certain W.H. De Shon added to the confusion by writing, "On the obverse is a most artistically executed head of a Comanche Indian. . . . The head dress presents no suggestion of the war bonnet of the Sioux, which the Buffalo Bill show has led the public to believe is typical of the garb of all American Indians."[22] He goes on to say that the face of the buffalo is very suggestive of a human being! This statement, which recalls the old man-headed bull on coins of Gela and other Greek cities of the fifth century B.C. and later, is the ultimate in reading personality into an artistic document of the new photographic naturalism.

The forgotten Indian, the one Fraser could not remember, reappeared in the *Numismatic News* for April 25, 1966, under the headline "Chief John Big Tree, the man on the Buffalo nickel,[23] highlights 1966 Texas Numismatic Association convention":

> The limelight of the convention was shared by . . . Chief John Big Tree, one of the three Indians who posed for the Indian Head nickel. Clearly, the spry, witty, old chief stole the show.
>
> Chief John Big Tree who posed as a model for the original buffalo nickel was commissioned by Falstaff Brewing Corporation of Galveston, Texas to appear at the convention of the Texas Numismatic Association.
>
> Chief John Big Tree, who claims to be 104 years old, is a full-blooded Iroquois who now lives with his wife on the Onondaga Reservation near Syracuse, New York. He was one of three Indians selected to pose for design of the buffalo nickel in 1912.
>
> According to the Chief, he was used as the model for the nose and forehead of the Indian nickel while a Sioux modeled for the cheek and chin of the likeness and a Cheyenne for the hair and headdress.
>
> Chief Big Tree says he was working in a Coney Island show when he was chosen to pose, "because of his classic facial features."[24]

He also posed for *The End of the Trail*, "in the mornings and the coin in the afternoons."

Clearly at the age of 104 (some accounts say 103), this third chief has all his facts correct, and the bit about posing for the emaciated old Indian on horseback in a howling blizzard adds credibility to the tale. Pictures taken in 1966 of the aged Iroquois chief holding up an enlarged nickel bear out the likeness, but a picture of Chief Iron Trail (or Tail) of the Cheyennes in the August 1913 *Numismatist* has been termed a "remarkable resemblance."[25] This revival of interest in Chief John Big Tree resulted in a party given by the Chase Manhattan Bank in New York to honor James B. Longacre's Shield nickel, a design typical of the governmental art engendered by the Civil War, and the predecessor of the Liberty and Buffalo nickels.[26] As a *Boston Globe* caption expressed it: "The Chief's 103; the Nickel's 100."[27]

Medals by Hermon MacNeil

With the vogue for Indian subjects early in the 20th century, it is easy to trace the spiritual genesis of Fraser's design to the work of his older contemporary, Hermon A. MacNeil (1866–1947). An assistant in the decorations for the World's Columbian Exposition of 1892, MacNeil went on to have a major hand in the sculpture for the Pan-American Exposition in Buffalo in 1901, the Saint Louis Exposition of 1904, and the San Francisco Exposition of 1915. He was famed for his Indian subjects and for his monumental memorials. The formal, modern neoclassic east pediment of the Supreme Court building in Washington, DC, belongs in the latter category. Among his medals of Native Americans, that most often mentioned is the example for the Pan-American Exposition of 1901. Not only does the naturalism anticipate Fraser, but the geographic allegory looks ahead to a host of designs for the commemorative half dollars of the 1920s and 1930s. MacNeil's impact on the coinage was to be more direct, for it was he who designed the silver quarter dollar of 1916 to 1932.

149. MacNeil, Pan-American Exposition medal

On the obverse of the Pan-American Exposition medal, a nude female with thick legs, presumably Liberty, wearing her French version of the Phrygian bonnet, parades to the right. A winged globe attached to a long cape is on her raised right hand. The famous buffalo Black Diamond, garlanded as if for his 1915 sacrifice, is butting beside her (fig. 149). The composition comes directly from Greco-Roman and French neoclassical sources. As a single figure the "Liberty" can be traced back through Jacques-Louis David's painting *Leonidas at Thermopylae* (1814) to Roman Amazon and battle sarcophagi of the second and early third centuries A.D. The female with butting animal is a composition lifted verbatim from neo-Attic reliefs and thus from the figures of Nikai conducting bovines to sacrifice on the balustrade of the temple of Athena on the southwest bastion of the Acropolis in Athens late in the fifth century B.C.

On the reverse, two Indians share a peace pipe (the bonneted one will later appear on Fraser's nickel). They are geographical personifications of America before Columbus, it would seem, for maps of South and North America grace their shields (fig. 149). The composition recalls a bronze mirror of the fourth century B.C. in the British Museum, where Pan is hunched over, playing a game of knucklebones with Aphrodite. In 1916 Lorado Taft used the same general grouping of two figures for the reverse of his medal to James Whitcomb Riley, the "Poet of Hope and Cheer. Lover and Friend of Mankind." On this medal a farmer and his child face a seated Pan.

Qualities of wholesomeness and all-Americanism seem to have been evoked by MacNeil's medals. They were also seen in the obverse design of his quarter dollar, to be considered presently. W.T.R. Marvin wrote of the Amazon (Liberty or Columbia) leading the buffalo on the Pan-American Exposition medal of 1901 (fig. 149) that this obverse intended to "show a group testifying the dominion of intellect over force."[28] In many respects this composition is an aesthetic and stylistic forerunner of the 1916 quarter. Marvin's editorial of 1901 was prophetic.

> A youthful female figure, without drapery, wearing only the Phrygian cap,—rather, we should say, a helmet of somewhat similar shape,—is advancing to the observer's right; her right hand, uplifted, holds a festoon of oak leaves and a large piece of drapery, which floats away behind her; this is partially caught again by her left hand, the left arm, bent upward at the elbow, being slightly extended backward, and behind her left side. The pose, while not ungraceful, is masculine rather than maidenly; the face is partly turned to the observer, and the figure, typifying Intellect, seems to be virile and Amazonian rather than delicately feminine in character,—"a strong-minded woman," and perhaps not improperly so, if she would maintain her dominion undisputed over Force; there is nothing *spirituelle* about her; she is striding forward like a young athlete returning victorious from a contest, rather than like a graceful, intellectual girl; and she has a fearless, almost a triumphant air, as she bends her head and shoulders slightly back. Yet it is more than probable that when the reduction to the medal size is completed, we shall discover, in the creation of the artist's fancy, a typical American girl, self-reliant, and confident of her power, very different from the "composite beauty" of an earlier Exposition medal, but as charming as her sisters beyond the Atlantic; not helpless, but a "help-meet," and ready to bear her part, as duty calls.[29]

Mint Medals, 1909 to 1917

The Barber-Morgan tradition in medals marking each succeeding presidency was continued in 1909 with the obverse portrait honoring William H. Taft and a reverse giving the usual statistics enframed by allegory, architectural vista, and foliage with an inscribed fillet (fig. 150). Barber's bust of the rotund chief executive is the same likeness discussed in connection with the Assay Commission medal of 1910 (fig. 117). It is as forcefully characteristic of Taft as Barber's inaugural portrait of 1905 was the very official summation of Theodore Roosevelt (fig. 118). At this stage, near the end of his long career, Barber was as capable as ever of presenting a noble likeness in incisive academic terms of the leader of the Republic, a profile that gave as much personality as necessary within the dignified, impersonal limits of the state medal.

The reverse is a variation on a theme played by Morgan for Roosevelt, Taft, and, in 1917, Woodrow Wilson. The constant element is the Capitol in the upper background, seen from slightly below and set at an angle. Small on the Roosevelt medal, the building grows larger under Taft and reaches heroic proportions on the medal for Wilson, one of Morgan's first major solo efforts as chief engraver following the death of Barber (fig. 151). On the Roosevelt medal Morgan had filled the left foreground with that standing Liberty or Columbia found elsewhere in his and Barber's creations, a figure related to French academic designs in the generations of the great Paris expositions. On the presidential medal for Taft the borrowings are more direct and obvious. Morgan has blocked out most of the right front of the Capitol with a rendering in relief of Michelangelo's *Delphic Sibyl*, part of the frescoes carried out between 1508 and 1512 on the ceiling and adjoining walls of the Sistine Chapel in the Vatican.

The idea involved in invoking the Delphic Sibyl at the outset of Taft's administration is no doubt wisdom and farsightedness in government. The Roosevelt medal, however, showed that Morgan had a penchant for figures holding scrolls (fig. 118). Since Michelangelo's Sibyl was thus equipped, she was a self-evident, natural borrowing for a medalist desiring to incorporate this motif in his design. The remainder of the reverse—a branch with berries and a ribbon with the motto E PLURIBUS UNUM—needs little comment. Why this motto had to appear is not clear; perhaps Morgan had been influenced by the dominance of the eagle reverse designed by Saint-Gaudens and executed by Weinman for the unofficial inaugural medal of 1905 (fig. 119).

Again, as in the case of the Barber-Morgan inaugural medal for Theodore Roosevelt, it is easy to complain that the commemoration of Taft's administration lacks the thrilling power of pseudoquattrocento medals by Saint-Gaudens and his followers. The engravers at the Philadelphia Mint, however, were called upon to fashion official medals annually, if not more often. They evolved a vocabulary for their work, in which each

WILLIAM H·TAFT

INAUGURATED PRESIDENT·OF·THE UNITED·STATES MARCH·4· 1909

150. Barber and Morgan, medal for Taft

WOODROW WILSON

INAUGURATED PRESIDENT·OF·THE UNITED·STATES MAR.4.1913 SECOND·TERM MAR.5.1917

151. Morgan, medal for Wilson

medal in a series bore some relation to those going before and those to follow. This was a conservative art on a high technical level. It was a pleasing, dignified art, not marred by tasteless experiment. To my mind they deserve praise for having made the medal as noble an instrument of government as it had been in the Italian Renaissance. Modern medalists, official and otherwise, have much to learn from the men who worked in Philadelphia between the Civil War and the First World War.

Charles E. Barber teamed with his old assistant, George T. Morgan, to design the Assay Commission medal for 1914 (fig. 152). As President Wilson refused to take the time to pose for Barber, however, the latter was forced to work from photographs. He complained that this was not the way to get a good portrait, but the president was not interested. Barber's deep bust of Woodrow Wilson is an old man's portrait of an aging man. Wilson seems more shrunken and worried than he actually was this early in his presidency. Morgan's reverse is dominated by his standard pointed-wing eagle, the bird that goes back to his dollar of 1878, above a series of curved bands and volutes for the lettering. Scales are recognizable below, and foliage fills the background. All this, the bushy wreath especially, has created a very busy pseudomodern swirl of checks and balances within the medallion's tondo. It is evident that the two engravers have made a heroic effort to bring their styles up to date in the French manner, that is, according to the school of Roty at the outset of the century. All that comes through is a sense of medallic craftsmanship and cleanly cut dies. Artistic vitality is lacking. It is small wonder, therefore, that commissions for the new silver fractional coinage—the half dollar, the quarter dollar, and the dime—would be carried out in 1916 by medalists of stature from the outside, A.A. Weinman and H.A. MacNeil.

152. Barber and Morgan, Assay medal

The Indian still reigned supreme in the medallic art of 1914. Cyrus Edwin Dallin, who will appear as designer of the half dollar marking the tercentennial of the arrival of the *Mayflower* and the Pilgrims at Plymouth Plantation (fig. 170), designed the award medal for the National Archery Association (Merion Cricket Club) in 1914. The principle figure is, naturally enough, an Indian discharging his bow. These years can be said to mark the high point of romantic Indian naturalism in American sculpture.

After Charles Barber's death in 1917, George Morgan had to continue the spirit of their collaboration in medallic commemorations of Woodrow Wilson, doing both the portrait on the obverse and the symbolism on the reverse. Morgan's presidential medal of 1917 (fig. 151) is a far more effective work of art than the joint Assay Commission medal of 1914. A vigorous new portrait on the obverse is matched by a continuity of motifs on the reverse. Barber's thin-necked, angular-faced, round-shouldered portrait of the 1914 Assay medal has been replaced by a fuller, more relaxed likeness, with the characteristic glasses and line of the nose and a more accurate shape of the back of the head. The head and shoulders are not so tilted and distorted, producing a satisfying full profile, with the bust in three-quarters view. Altogether this portrayal of Woodrow Wilson artfully blends nobility and humanity to a degree worthy of the best in official medals.

The reverse is less thrilling and hardly novel, but the composition as an entity achieves its purpose effectively. The traditional Morgan eagle, so recently seen on the Assay medal of 1914 and shown also on the Panama-Pacific half dollar of 1915, stands on twin branches, pointed wings spread in front of the largest view of the Capitol to grace any of the inaugural medals. Such use of elements found so often on medals and coins is saved from triteness by the boldness of the eagle, above the subtlety of the Capitol, and over well-balanced, simple lettering. Only an engraver with decades of careful work to his credit would have dared to make something so conventional seem so original.

153. Panama-Pacific $50 gold coins

The Panama-Pacific Exposition of 1915

The World's Columbian Exposition had been commemorated by two silver coins, the work of the two designers in the Mint. The exposition held at San Francisco in 1915 was the only occasion in the history of the United States where a group of coins were issued in one year in different denominations designed by artists of the Mint and by outside sculptors of established reputation. Charles E. Barber's gold quarter eagle (the reverse by George T. Morgan) and his silver half dollar are classic symphonies of old designs, motifs that trace back to the eagles and shields of Longacre and William Barber in the 1860s and 1870s revised into modern form. Charles Keck's gold dollar is a novel, daring use of the limited area afforded by such a small, thin coin. Compared with the earlier gold dollars, the coin is a work of art. It is not the sculptor's fault that the head of a man in a cap, symbolizing a laborer on the Panama Canal, was jokingly mistaken for a baseball player. Americans have been given to poking fun at the creative arts in all ages of our history.

The numismatic sensations of the Panama-Pacific Exposition were the two $50 gold coins, one round and the other octagonal (fig. 153). Robert Aitken tried to create modern, pseudo-Athenian coins, in an idiom of archaeological classicism popular among many American sculptors trained partly at the American Academy in Rome before and after the First World War. His ideas were laudable. There were a minimum of inscriptions, a classic Greco-Egyptian profile of Athena in full panoply, the date in roman numerals, and a naturalistic owl in a mass of Western pine cones. Dolphins fill the corners of the octagonals. Since they also appear on Keck's reverse for the dollar, in a form borrowed from coins of ancient Zankle-Messana or Syracuse, and since no modern ships, locks, bridges, or tollhouses grace the series, Arlie Slabaugh was moved to remark in jest about "the Canal apparently being built for the use of dolphins."[30] In an overall view, the arresting feature of the giant gold coins is their archaistic treatment of details in relief. Athena's crest, wreath, curls, and aegis imitate the work of an ancient bronze. The bead and reel between the outside rims comes from Greek architecture, and the form of the lettering around the rim recalls Roman sestertii of the Empire or Papal medallions of the cinquecento. These coins were a tour de force, dated to be sure, but unusual enough in all respects to be worthy of what American numismatic art could achieve when creativity and mint technique worked in unison.

Barber's obverse for the quarter eagle was, like the dolphins, symbolic of commerce through the canal and dependent on ancient Greek designs. In this instance the source was the Nereid, perhaps Thetis, who bears the shield of Achilles astride a hippocamp on the reverse of a silver didrachm of Pyrrhus, king of Epirus in the third century R.C. Barber has reinterpreted this motif, so popular also on Greek mirror cases, in mosaics, and in jewelry, using some of the crisp prettiness of French medallic art in the 1890s or early 1900s. "Columbia seated on the mythical Sea Horse. Columbia with the Caduceus, the emblem of trade and commerce, inviting the nations of the world to use the new way from Ocean to Ocean."[31] Since the Greek design was disseminated in the age of fourth-century to Hellenistic rococo sculpture and painting—that is, between 330 and 100 B.C.—something of the light, decorative quality just mentioned is taken directly from those phases of the antique. This coin, this obverse, may be Barber's answer to Theodore Roosevelt's and Augustus Saint-Gaudens's clamor for modern coins in the Greek manner. If so, the composition has the volume and balance of its classical prototype. The reverse (fig. 154) is spirited but by no means new, for the old "defiant eagle" of the late 1870s has reappeared, now standing on a platform and pole, a vehicle for E PLURIBUS UNUM that resembles the support for a Roman *aquila* or eagle!

The silver half dollar combines Barber's favorite half-figure of Columbia on the obverse with Morgan's eagle, the characteristic shield, and the usual branches in conservative modernization of traditional elements on the reverse.[32] The obverse is a halfway point between the designs on French silver coins early in the new century and A.A. Weinman's Liberty Walking for the half dollar that appeared in 1916. Liberty or Columbia—both have been specified, and it matters little from an iconographic standpoint—wears her Franco-Phrygian cap and ancient Greek (Doric) chiton and billowy himation in the modern manner. She has a fat posterior, heavy upper arms, and thus an unpleasantly stiff, dumpy manner. The child or putto beside her, holding up the cornucopia filled with flowers, is a feature of Barber's studies after French designs (fig. 155). The same group, almost in mirror reversal, had waved the fleet off at Hampton Roads on the reverse of the medal commemorating the departure of the U.S. Atlantic Fleet on its cruise around the world, December 16,

154. Panama-Pacific quarter eagle

155. Panama-Pacific half dollar

1907—a plaquette with a deep bust of Theodore Roosevelt on the obverse (fig. 120). There is just such a Greco-Roman group of Aphrodite and Eros in the Musée du Louvre in Paris. Waves, land, and the setting sun connote the Golden Gate. The inspiration again is French, from the background of Roty's famous sowing Marianne on fractional silver of 1897 to 1920.

French regular issues of these years offer both general stylistic prototypes for the products of the U.S. mints and specific details used by Barber, Morgan, and A.A. Weinman. On the 25-centime piece of 1904 a draped bust of Marianne in the popular wreathed cap of Libertas is matched with a reverse composed of an axe in a bundle of Roman lictors' staves, the fasces with full magistral powers, amid foliage. This combination of reverse elements formed the design of Weinman's new dime in 1916.

Some of America's greatest coins were produced by artists outside the Mint in the decade between 1907 and 1916. These designers were established leaders in a visual renovation first brought about by the active concern of President Theodore Roosevelt. New designs were created for coins as common as the cent or nickel and as unusual as the $50 piece in gold. Alongside these innovations, the engravers of the Mint turned out traditional but tolerable commemorative coins and a series of governmental medals that did considerable credit to the traditions of their office. Liberty, the eagle, and the conventional legends remained where necessary, but real Indians, a buffalo, and President Abraham Lincoln offered new scope for expression as subjects on the regular coinage.

VII

New Silver Coins, 1916 to 1929

With the three new silver coins of 1916—quarter dollar, half dollar, and dime—designs for the regular issues of American gold, silver, and bronze had been placed almost completely in the hands of artists outside the Mint. The only exception remained the silver dollar by George Morgan, but in 1921 this coin would be replaced by the creation of an independent medalist. Such a state of affairs had never existed in the earlier U.S. coinage. The official designers need not have felt that their past efforts were eclipsed, for coins by Longacre, Charles Barber, and Morgan circulated in vast numbers until the abolition of the gold standard in 1933 and the normal attrition of minor coinage in the 1930s. Silver dollars by Morgan were in common use until 1964.

The Quarter

Hermon Atkins MacNeil has already been introduced in connection with his influential Pan-American Exposition medal of 1901. His new designs for the quarter dollar, therefore, merit description ahead of A.A. Weinman's new half dollar and dime, all works of the year 1916.

Commonplace though it may appear now after so many years, the quarter dollar of 1916 was as revolutionary in concept as the double eagle of 1907. Saint-Gaudens had shown American die designers what could be done, and MacNeil was equipped to grasp the message of his standing or advancing Liberty and his eagle in flight. MacNeil's Liberty is presented as the Athena of the Parthenon pediments, a powerful woman striding forward, with her head and arms conveying a strong sideways motion. The first issue of 1916 showed the chest uncovered, but this design was immediately replaced by a similar Liberty clad in a cuirass of chain or scaled mail,[1] a modern version of the old aegis of Athena. The shield is emblazoned with the stars and stripes of the United States, in the heraldic form of the Great Seal, but everything else about this Amazon

156. Quarter dollar of 1916 type

calls to mind Greek sculpture of the period from Pheidias to Praxiteles, 450 to 350 B.C. (fig. 156).

MacNeil's concept of the armed Liberty, uncovering her shield and holding an olive branch like the writing Victory of Roman triumphal reliefs such as the Columns of Trajan or Marcus Aurelius and imperial coins from Vitellius (A.D. 69) to Caracalla (A.D. 215), would have been a splendid tribute to the sentiment of the time had the artist not chosen to place her at the entrance to a star-studded dado or enclosure, resembling the walls of a private cemetery. This Liberty of 1916 was "intended to express the awakening of the country to the need of preparedness,"[2] and in this connection it was felt appropriate that she step through a gateway enriched with the religious motto, the stars of the 13 colonies, and vaguely suggested panels of relief. As in so many other instances on our coins, the sculptor had already worked out the motif of a monumental figure set against a wall in a freestanding composition of considerable size. The majestic *America* in bronze for the soldiers' and sailors' memorial in Washington Park, Albany, dedicated in 1912, is backed by a large, rectangular block of stone, which is filled with a frieze of marching soldiers. The concept of a statue or statuesque figure related to low architectural surroundings was developed with success in a number of statues or groups by Saint-Gaudens—his Admiral Farragut in New York being an early example. Daniel Chester French, MacNeil's immediate stylistic forebear, carried out this form of grouping with equal success.[3]

The reverse, a small eagle in full flight, is in a sense the old Titian Peale–Gobrecht bird of 1836 seen in reversed direction, flying toward us from left to right instead of away from us from right to left. The reverse at first suffered from crowding of the modern five-pointed stars between the legends, but correction and deepening of the bird in flight, now raised a bit in the field of the tondo, improved the design at the same time that Liberty's bosom was covered with a cuirass of mail. This was the last time until the Sacagawea dollar that a naturalistic eagle adorned a regular U.S. coin, save for Weinman's half dollar of the same year and the silver dollar of 1921, which completed the redesigning of the Morgan-Barber silver coins. When the fractional silver was changed again, in 1932 and 1948, the heraldic bird reasserted itself in the repertory, certainly to the detriment of superior artistry. Perhaps, after MacNeil liberated the eagle to soar within a coin's confines and Weinman presented the bird on the ground as a breathtaking passage of powerful relief, few if any sculptors dared let the natural bird loose on a coin's reverse. The heraldic types were a convenient resort. The Kennedy half dollar of 1964 shows this all too well.

The symbolism of this armed Liberty at the garden gate has attracted writers ever since the coin appeared. It was an expression of the years when the United States was increasingly concerned with international affairs in a world of conflict: "the design symbolized the nation's awareness and preparedness for battle and its equal readiness to proffer peace."[4] In 1913 Hermon MacNeil described the medallic style of the great Frenchman Louis-Oscar Roty: "He, of course, was very eminent, and in most of his works as a medalist expressed very much the style that France has produced in sculpture during the last ten years. I mean that clean, fluent, aesthetic quality, that has considerable femininity in its makeup, as opposed to the more vigorously constructed medal of the Renaissance. . . . The above quality is particularly charming; much of it is due, however, to his rare taste in placing or spacing his design within the medal or plaque."[5] MacNeil went on to say that the sowing Marianne of the French silver coinage was certainly one of his best works. In all, MacNeil's analysis of Roty's medallic art could well be applied to the quarter dollar of 1916, and it was, of course, the Sower that was to influence Weinman in his design for the walking figure of Liberty of the half dollar in the same year.

The identity legend plagued MacNeil's twenty-five-cent piece, in a form that matched all too well what critics had sought in his figures of Liberty, Columbia, or America. In May 1917 a characterization of the artist's model was published in *The Numismatist:*

> From a recent newspaper article by Marguerite Norse we extract the following facts regarding Miss Dora Doscher, who posed for Mr. Hermon A. MacNeil while designing the female figure that appears on our new quarter dollar, and who is now referred to by her friends as "the Girl on the Quarter":
>
> Miss Doscher is 22 years of age, and is 5 feet 4 1/2 inches in height. Through her own efforts she has developed from a half invalid child to a most perfect type of American womanhood. Her days are spent in artistic and intellectual pursuits. She is a lecturer, scenario writer and trained nurse. At the first intimation of war she enrolled in the Red Cross service and stood from that day ready for a moment's call. She presents an attractive appearance in the Red Cross uniform.
>
> Mr. MacNeil's "Liberty" on the new quarter is indeed a beautiful piece of work. The idea conceived by the artist is highly expressive of national sentiment. The figure comes down a flight of steps in an attitude of welcome to the world. In one extended hand she holds a laurel branch of peace, on the left arm she carries a shield. Though she offers peace first she is prepared to defend her honor and her rights. The design suggests a step forward in civilization, protection and defence with peace as the ultimate goal.
>
> As for the coin girl, her pride is just what you would expect to find in a wholesome, ambitious young woman upon whom this honor had been placed.[6]

157. Aitken, medal for Foch

Medal by Aitken

In 1921 the vision of Dora or Doris Doscher (later Baum) was undimmed by the First World War and its immediate aftermath. As a commission for the American Numismatic Society, Robert I. Aitken, designer of the $50 gold coins of 1915, created a medal commemorating the visit of Marshal Foch to the United States (fig. 157). The obverse has the bold plasticity of modern works that recall certain Renaissance medals, with the facing bust that is forceful here but so distasteful in the machine-made medals of Gilroy Roberts, Frank Gasparro, and other modern die designers in and out of Mint circles. The reverse presents a winged Dora Doscher between the shields of France and the United States. As an allegorical symbol like that of the MacNeil quarter dollar brought up to date, she carries the U.S. First World War discharge button on the shield over her left arm. The winged frontality of the Saint-Gaudens double eagle is now frozen and mannered. The light touch imparted by such figures to the coinage of 1907 or 1916 has turned into an overpowering mass of feathers, drapery, and iconography. Even the radiate crown of the Statue of Liberty in New York Harbor, a motif Saint-Gaudens contemplated for the coinage, has become a concentration of heavy, conical spikes.

Medals by Weinman

Adolph Alexander Weinman (1870–1952) studied under Saint-Gaudens and worked with Charles Niehaus, Olin Warner, and Daniel Chester French. In 1913 he executed what was tantamount to a ticket of admission to the best American sculptural circles, a statue of Abraham Lincoln for the Lincoln Monument in Frankfort, Kentucky. "The making of commemorative medals and plaquettes occupies some of our ablest modern sculptors. Most of them are also excellent in portraiture, as would be expected, and some in larger sculptures. Such is the case with Adolph A. Weinmann [*sic*], perhaps our foremost medalist. . . . An artist of powerful line, Weinmann carries the unhesitating precision evinced in his medals into monumental sculpture. The virile movement of his silhouettes has significance as well as authoritative beauty."[7]

As had happened with so many of Weinman's contemporaries, the Indian afforded one of his early sculptural triumphs. Weinman's first opportunity for individual work in a commission for a large group was "The Destiny of the Red Man" at the Saint Louis World's Fair of 1904. His statue of Alexander Johnson Cassatt, which once stood in New York's Pennsylvania Station, is one of the truly striking official portraits of the 20th century. The monumental bronze of the railroad's great president looking out over the waiting room is worthy of the Farnese Hercules and other ancient marble statues designed for the Roman imperial prototype of the station, the Baths of Caracalla on the edge of the Eternal City.

"Architectural sculpture, with the restraint which it imposes and the opportunity which it offers for rhythmic treatment of mass and line, has found one of its strongest exponents in Adolph Alexander Weinman." B.G. Proske went on to observe: "The display of European medals at the Columbian Exposition and his work on the Library of Congress doors stimulated his interest in medallic art and led him to begin a series of portraits in relief . . . and official medals [that were] Greek in their purity of design."[8] He was characterized in his monumental sculpture, in his statues and reliefs (as in his Liberty Walking of the 1916 half dollar), by a feeling for flowing line. "The winged figures of *The Rising Sun* and *The Descending Night* for the Panama-Pacific Exposition (1915), most popular among his works, arc composed in upward soaring and downward curving lines eloquent of morning and evening moods."[9] His monumental sculptures could range from the ghastly, dated, Saint-Gaudens–inspired Sphinx of Power for the Scottish Rite Temple in Washington, DC, an Egyptian eclectic creation, to the section of frieze with struggling, marching nudes straight off Roman sarcophagi of about A.D. 150 for the Elks National Memorial Building in Chicago.

Weinman's medals leave no room for doubt that he was an exceptionally talented sculptor. His feeling for subtleties of relief on a small scale, in the framework of a medallic tondo, was most perceptive. In 1919 he designed a commemorative war medal for the staff of Mt. Sinai Hospital in New York. A splendidly lettered reverse sets off an allegorical obverse that borrows from various sources, chiefly Greco-Roman. The "Dora Doscher" concept of Amazonian American womanhood dominates the scene; she wears the habit of Athena, with the Medical Corps emblem on her aegis instead of the Gorgoneion. The Mars or Ares at the left is equally eclectic, being derived from a well-known, oft-reproduced gem that may be Roman but is best known from several neoclassic, 18th-century versions in various European and American collections. This frontal, helmeted god of war has invaded many books on mythology and art, particularly works of the 19th century and the first generation of the 20th. The young, wounded "soldier" at the right is the Diadumenos or fillet binder of Polykleitos (435 B.C.), seized with a sudden illness. Weinman was able to carry out these diverse forays into modernized antiquity with success. Unlike the winged Athena on the reverse of Robert Aitken's medal to Marshal Foch, his Athena, Ares, and athlete of about 440 B.C. are at home on the smooth flan of a medal. They blend and are not merely separate statues in high relief, plastered on a medallic surface.

Equally well thought-out in classical medallic terms is the J. Sanford Saltus Award for Medallic Art, designed for the American Numismatic Society. The medal was first awarded in 1919, to James Earle Fraser, and, appropriately enough, Weinman himself was the recipient in 1920. The next three winners were all medalists of stature who designed regular issues of the coinage: John Flanagan, Victor D. Brenner, and Hermon A. MacNeil. On the obverse, a young female in the nude, wearing only the traditional Liberty cap of Charles Barber's coins, holds a medallic plaster in the left hand and a stylus in the right, as she kneels in the pose of a thoughtful artist. The old Roman convention of a tree fills the design to an appropriate degree at the right and top. On the reverse Pegasus flies upward, in a classic pose that would become all too familiar from the sign used by the Standard Oil Company of New York, with the sun rising and with waves at the lower left.[10] The foliage at left and right is kept at a tasteful minimum (fig. 158). The motif of the rising or setting sun, so popular in French and American coin designs from the beginning of the 20th century, would be seen as a feature of Weinman's obverse for the half dollar.

158. Weinman, Saltus medal

159. Dime of 1916

The Dime

Against this background of selective Greco-Roman classicism in Weinman's medals the dime of 1916 takes its place as the first individual and imaginative design for this small denomination in American numismatic art (fig. 159). The head of Liberty in her traditional cap with a wreath of tight curls over the forehead looks classical but is modern because no stereotype is involved. The wing (or wings implied) has led to comparison with Roman Republican denarii, but this is a banal, superficial observation. Weinman himself wrote that they or it symbolized "liberty of thought."[11] I suspect one reason the wing is there is that Weinman, in the true Saint-Gaudens tradition, liked the effect of feathers in relief on his coins and medals. The large, full-feathered wings of his eagle on the half dollar bear this out. The eagle had, of course, ceased to ornament the reverse of the dime since the advent of the Gobrecht-Sully Liberty Seated of 1837.

The word LIBERTY is beautifully spaced on the dime and the half dollar, a type of simple yet ornamental Roman lettering that is encountered on war memorials and funerary monuments from the era of Saint-Gaudens into the upsurge of commemorative activity engendered by the First World War. Mottoes on obverse and reverse are made as discreet as possible. The dime must always stand or fall, so far as its reverse is concerned, on foliage and lettering. Here the fasces of war and justice are set off by the olive branch of peace, the whole experience being carried out in a bold and lifelike, yet detailed, plasticity. Stars and lettering make the total effect the equivalent in miniature of the best secondary enrichment on war memorials of the 1920s and 1930s. A good strong fillet of a rim and the convex surface have guaranteed long life to this coin. When it was replaced after 30 years of production, the creation of Chief Engraver John R. Sinnock was of moment because it bore the head of Franklin Roosevelt and the torch of freedom, but as a work of art it offered nothing that Weinman had not devised in 1916.

In December 1916 the opinions of leading numismatists about the new dime were published. Excerpts from the observations of Thomas L. Elder of New York City on "the handsomest American coin" are still worth quoting.

> The winged head of Liberty is a real portrait of great beauty and finish. Our American girl in this instance is youthful, refined, and of gentle expression. The addition of wings to the head is taken from ancient art of Greece and Rome. . . . The head is not unlike those of Roty and Chaplain shown on so many modern French coins and medals. The obverse lettering is beautifully simple. The spacing of the letters is not a new idea, and was used on a number of dies rejected by the United States. [About the reverse] . . . Anthony Pacquet [*sic*] designed some pattern half dollars in 1859 with the figure of Liberty sitting by a shield, holding a fasces in her hand, so this is not a new idea in United States coins. . . . [W]e have here a coin which is second to none we have issued, and it will compare favorably with any in Europe, which is saying much.[12]

As so often proves to be true in the American coinage, a living model has been claimed for the head of Liberty. Early in August 1909 the poet Wallace Stevens rented an apartment at 441 West 21st Street in New York. His landlord was Adolph Alexander Weinman, and Stevens lived there until 1916. About 1913 Weinman did a bronze bust of the poet's wife, Elsie Kachel Stevens, who was a classic beauty. "The design he made, using her head, won the competition for a design for the new dime and half dollar issued by the U.S. Treasury Department in 1916."[13] It is in the tradition of Saint-Gaudens to use a plaster or bronze bust as intermediary between a living or ancient Greek model and the ideal Liberty of a coin. Elsie Kachel Stevens as interpreted by Weinman and the dime of 1916 have enough points in common to make this connection convincing. (Convincing, but not proven—similar Liberty images predate what has been presumed to be a portrait of Stevens.) Liberty's mass of hair beneath the cap and wings, her unusually decisive lips, and her strong yet sensitive chin can be traced to the fragile, angular features of Elsie Kachel Stevens.

The Half Dollar

Further insight into Weinman's qualifications to execute two of the new coins of 1916 comes from his master, Augustus Saint-Gaudens. A letter to Theodore Roosevelt on January 20, 1905, concerns the inauguration medal. "I cannot do it," writes Saint-Gaudens, "but I have arranged with the man best fitted to execute it in this country (Mr. Adolph Weinman). He has a most artistic nature, extremely diffident. He would do an admirable thing. He is also supple and takes suggestion intelligently. He has made one of the great Indian groups at St. Louis that would have interested you if brought to your attention. He is so interested that he begged me to fix a price. I named two hundred and fifty dollars."

On a slightly later date Saint-Gaudens also wrote to President Roosevelt:

> General Wilson showed me the inauguration medal, which is so deadly that I had Weinman go down to Philadelphia [fig. 118]. The man there who has charge of the bulk of the ordinary medals already contracted for cannot possibly do an artistic work. He [Charles E. Barber] is a commercial medallist with neither the means nor the power to rise above such an average. Mr. Weinman writes to General Wilson tonight that our reliefs must be put into other hands and this is to beg you to insist that the work be entrusted to Messrs. Tiffany or Gorham. Otherwise I would not answer for its not being botched. . . . I made studies on the train on my way up from Washington and I have struck a composition which I hope will come out well. Mr. Weinman is enthusiastic about it and I am certain would execute it admirably. You know that the disposition of the design on the medal is nine-tenths of the battle [fig. 119].
>
> The simplicity of inscription greatly aids the dignity of the arrangement; but if you believe that more is needed, I will add it with pleasure.[14]

160. Half dollar of 1916 type

The Liberty Walking half dollar, the Standing Liberty quarter dollar, the Mercury dime, the Buffalo nickel, and perhaps the Lincoln cent, more than any U.S. coins before or since, really treat the obverse and reverse as a surface sculptural ensemble. The Liberty Walking design particularly gives the true feeling for breadth and sculptural surfaces on the scale of a coin (fig. 160). These surfaces are formal, like a well-carved marble or precisely cast bronze relief for a war memorial. They are not free and plastic, like Fraser's nickel, which conveys the impression of its clay model turned into metal. The spacing of the word LIBERTY parallels the success of the dime, and the rising sun amid landscape anchors the motion of Liberty, her olive branch, and her starry cloak. On the reverse, the eagle standing on rocks with a gnarled tree at the left dominates but does not overwhelm the design. The working of the feathers is a miraculous *coup de force*, already cited as a hallmark of Saint-Gaudens and his pupils. The bird, indeed, takes some inspiration from one of the sketches or models by Saint-Gaudens for his $20 gold piece, the *modello* at the left in the lower row of the famous studio photograph being a good illustration (fig. 130).

The debt to Roty's Sower is obvious, but the Liberty Walking is an original creation, not a slavish copy. This half dollar, one of the greatest coins of the United States—if not of the world—is as modern as official sculpture can ever be. It has the combination of naturalism, classicism, and dignified inner balance, a generally suave figure style in the midst of traditional poses, costumes, and attributes, cited in connection with Weinman's dime as paralleling the highest level of commemorative art engendered by the First World War. Weinman's creation was governmental art, like a memorial at Arlington or the facade of a post office, but new vitality permeated traditional elements with a power worthy of the exquisite timelessness of the Greek engraver Euainetos at the end of the fifth century B.C.

The McKinley Gold Dollar of 1916

Against the triumph of the MacNeil quarter dollar, the Weinman dime, and the Weinman half dollar, must unfortunately be set the last joint production of Charles E. Barber and George T. Morgan. The obverse of the McKinley Memorial gold dollar is a Roman bust bearing faint resemblance to the subject and perhaps intended to connote his apotheosis. Barber's earlier obverses for inauguration and Assay medals were far more significant, and correct from the standpoint of portraiture. No one wishes to deny an artist in or out of the Mint the privilege of imitating the neoclassicism of Houdon or Pistrucci, but such designs must be Greco-Roman throughout. A silver dollar, such as the Washington-Lafayette coin of 1900 (fig. 112), affords ample room for displaying a classical bust. The constricted surface of a gold dollar does not. The Houdonesque bust of Washington on Flanagan's quarter of 1932 (fig. 189) or even the simple, truncated bust of Kennedy on the half dollar of 1964 carries off the heroic ideal intended in the commemorative coin of 1916 (fig. 240).

In a way the reverse of this gold dollar, showing a view of the memorial building at Niles, Ohio, anticipates the dull frontality of the Jefferson Monticello in 1938 or the Lincoln Memorial in 1959. There are too many columns and too much lettering for the size of the coin. Neo-Roman dullness permeates the design, but this is partly because the architecture is that way when seen in miniature. Buildings like those put up in Washington in the 1920s or 1930s are designed to overwhelm with the functional majesty of government. Only the bravest, boldest artist can translate full views of such Tuscan colonnades and marble pediments to our smaller coins. It is sad that the great heritage of Barber and Morgan had to terminate with a coin such as this in a year of so much splendid numismatic creativity.

The Peace Dollar

161. Dollar of 1921

The Peace dollar of 1921 completed the remodeling of the regular coinage begun in 1907. The slick modern aura, a soft and worn look to the obverse even before the coin had circulated, paved the way for many similar effects in the commemorative coinage between the two world wars. Dependence on ideas worked out by Saint-Gaudens 15 years earlier saved the coin from artistic mediocrity, for enough of the master's style has filtered through in his familiar iconographic types of Liberty and the eagle to ensure an interesting if not a great coin. Anthony de Francisci (1887–1965) was a pupil of James E. Fraser at the Art Students League in New York. He also worked for MacNeil and Weinman. It is interesting to note that, as with the coins of Saint-Gaudens, Fraser, and MacNeil, the relief of the first Peace dollar was too bold and had to be modified slightly in 1922 to suit the mechanics of production at the mints.

Liberty's head on the obverse is certainly based on the widely publicized model or *bozzetto* by Saint-Gaudens for the $10 gold piece or eagle of 1907, and therefore ultimately on the so-called Beautiful Head from the altar of Zeus Soter of about 165 B.C. at Pergamon (figs. 134 and 135). The eagle on the mountain peak also recalls without hesitation the birds of Saint-Gaudens and Bela Pratt for the redesigned gold coinage (figs. 126 and 136). Rays of sun streaming up at the right are likewise a pioneering feature of both sides of the Saint-Gaudens double eagle. The obverse is weak, because an element of prettiness permeates the head of Liberty—an emptiness of face, an elaborateness of hair, and an overall glossiness that adds up to nothing beyond the thick rays, the meaningless locks out behind, and a vapid lower jaw (fig. 161). Spacing and position of the lettering are satisfying enough, and in 1964 became the source for similar features of the Kennedy half dollar. Perhaps as a reaction to the lettering of Weinman's two coins in 1916 the mottoes on obverse and reverse are enlarged out of proportion to their importance, but they do not affect the general design. (This device was used less successfully on commemorative half dollars in the 1920s and 1930s.)

Morey wrote of the sculptor, "A garden sculptor of the Italian marble cutter school, de Francisci's medals are far superior to his statues. They lack the sharp definition with which Weinmann [*sic*] exacts full value for every contour, but avoid the sketchiness whereby many sculptors confuse medallic art with low relief. His power lies in a justly balanced composition and a nice sense of the part to be assigned to the vacant field."[15] Among de Francisci's sculptures, nothing could be more unappealing, more slick and sentimental in the worst traditions of religious art, than the bust of Joan of Arc exhibited at the great traveling exposition of the National Sculpture Society in 1929 (fig. 162). The Maid of Orleans is transformed into a Mater Dolorosa that applies vapid modern sculptural

162. De Francisci, Joan of Arc

technique to an iconographic lapse of the painter Guido Reni in the middle of the 17th century, at the height of the Italian baroque phase of Counter-Reformation art.

What T.L. Comparette wrote in eulogy of Roty in 1913 could be applicable to the ideas embodied in the Peace dollar. On Roty's Chilean peso, "a large Andesean [*sic*] condor just lighting upon a lofty crag, is a powerful piece of work. It is not hard, in looking at a brilliant new specimen, to fancy that one is peering through a small circular glass out at the actual scene, so well is the notion of largeness and loftiness conveyed by the design."[16]

There was no lack of fatuous comment in the press when the Peace Dollar appeared. A Philadelphia newspaper reportedly produced the following:

> Liberty is growing younger. Take it from the new "Peace Dollar" put in circulation yesterday. The young woman who has been adorning silver currency for many years never looked better than in the "cartwheel" which the Philadelphia Mint has just started to turn out. The young

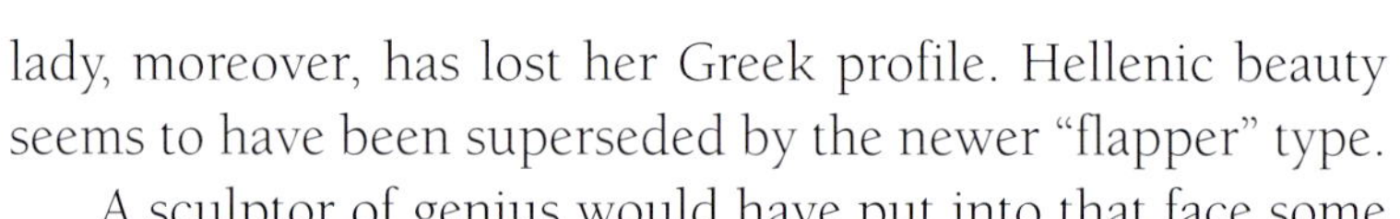

> lady, moreover, has lost her Greek profile. Hellenic beauty seems to have been superseded by the newer "flapper" type.
>
> A sculptor of genius would have put into that face some quality of divinity. He would have suggested divine wisdom, courage, ardor and severe confidence in the triumph of freedom.
>
> Looked at in this way, the head on the new coin is merely that of a fairly attractive girl of 17, . . . whose immature chin and half-open mouth merely suggest the expression of her kind. If words were issuing from her lips they would hardly take the elegant languor of "Line's bizzay!" They would more probably be "Say, lissen!"[17]

The writer was, it would seem, as much impressed by the invention of Alexander Graham Bell as by the artistry of Anthony de Francisci.

De Francisci has stated and his wife has confirmed that she was the model for the head of Liberty. Such evidence as the sculptor's description of opening the studio window to let the wind blow on her hair is difficult to question, even given the ideal purposes of the design. Against this stands the visual fact that de Francisci's Liberty derives from the later study for the head of Victory in the Saint-Gaudens Sherman Monument, the bronze *bozzetto* that came in its patriotic American form onto the $10 gold piece (figs. 128, 129, 134, and 135). The key to this relationship, and thus ultimate derivation from the Pergamene altar of Zeus Soter in the second century B.C., lies in the little-noticed fact that Saint-Gaudens dedicated his study of "Nike-Eirene" to James Earle Fraser. And in December 1921 Fraser wrote, "I have given the Saint-Gaudens head to de Francisci as an example of what we consider a beautiful type."[18]

Whatever the relation to real life, however flattering to Teresa Cafarelli de Francisci, the fact remains that what her husband probably had in his mind as he worked was the unsuppressible vividness and excitement of a classic creation by Saint-Gaudens. It is easy to see where de Francisci deviated from the master's prototype and what elements his wife could have contributed to the design. Windblown hair, naturalism in the bun on the back, reduction of the area around the small eyes, and a mouth like a quattrocento marble child by Desiderio or Mino da Fiesole are all touches that mollify the grandeur of the Sherman Victory. Whether the graceful profile of Teresa de Francisci or, indeed, any pretty young woman's face was needed to create the proper sculptural mood is a point that will always remain open to speculation. As the coin emerged in the regular issues of 1922, it may have lacked the high relief that all outside sculptors have demanded from engravers at the Philadelphia Mint, but the coin was a true expression of the facile, eclectic artistic personality of its creator.[19]

Medal by de Francisci

At the time he was working on the Peace dollar, de Francisci did design a medal that, although cold and academic, is not without certain amusing charm. This was the 1922 crew medal for the British-American Cup Races, a creation exhibited at the National Sculpture Society in 1923 (fig. 163). On the principal side, the Amazon Liberty and Britannia are seated with the British lion recumbent at their feet. A pair of yachts are set against the disc of the sun in the background. Britannia is given the Tyche crown and the aegis without Gorgon mask. Both she and Liberty wear furry or woolly Greek costumes, and both have fierce classic profiles that are a kind of Pre-Raphaelite legacy to the early 20th century. It takes a moment's study to realize that a Saint-Gaudens eagle is perched behind Liberty's shoulder, probably on the fleecy slope out of which grows a gnarled treelet similar to that on Weinman's half dollar of 1916. As it should be, the frame is a rope!

163. De Francisci, British-American Cup medal

Dolphins, seashells, and stylized Greek waves enframe the emblem and the donor's dedication. Much imagination has gone into the balance of elements, using the idea of dolphins around a star found on bronze coins of Syracuse in the fourth century B.C. The elongated bodies of the mammals are seen partly from above, all creating a finished depth and volume. This optic distortion adds up to a thorough command of planes of relief, without resort to a conventional wire or beaded edge and without repeating the element of the rope used with imagination enough on the obverse. One of de Francisci's strong points is lettering, in a style reflecting the Saltus medal of Weinman and the portrait tondi or rectangular plaques of Victor D. Brenner. Medallic work such as this has been much imitated since the Second World War, particularly by the engravers of the Mint. Few recent creations capture the life and imagery of the medallic movement after the First World War.

Military Insignia

Designing military insignia for the U.S. armed forces has much in common with preparing models for medals from the Mint or for coins. Subjects are similar, and methods of attacking the degree of relief or surfaces offer comparable challenges. Anthony de Francisci executed studies for military badges, and his compositions in this sphere were well balanced and brought out in bold, decisive relief (fig. 164). As usual the eagle is the centerpiece of all major insignia, appearing as the Great Seal on cap badges for officers and enlisted men. Stars and leaves play their parts, and regimental insignia offer the same latitude in heraldic design once afforded by commemorative half dollars for various states. There is a

165. Morgan, medal for Harding

166. Sinnock, medal for Coolidge

164. De Francisci, military insignia

certain unity in this form of national art. de Francisci's study of a heraldic eagle surmounted by crossed lictors' rods with axes could exist in any scale. In brass it would be at home on a soldier's lapels. In silver it would have made a bold reverse for a dollar or quarter dollar, in preference perhaps to the design of 1932. Enlarged in marble, this eagle with fasces is a familiar design on the walls of countless public buildings and war memorials throughout the United States.

Presidential Medals, 1923 to 1929

The medals honoring Warren G. Harding, Calvin Coolidge, and Herbert Hoover carry the presidential series of the Philadelphia Mint into the era of contemporary U.S. coinage. The medal of 1923, marking Harding's inauguration in 1921 and his death on August 2, 1923, was the last sculpture of this group by George T. Morgan (fig. 165). In 1928 Morgan's successor, John R. Sinnock, designed the piece commemorating Coolidge's inaugurations of 1923 and 1925 (fig. 166). A year later he was able to prepare a medal for the inauguration of Herbert Hoover (fig. 167). The medal for Harding looks back to early 20th-century traditions, while the designs for Coolidge and Hoover reflect the seemingly archaeological, pseudo–Greek archaic and transitional styles popular in the work of Paul Manship and a number of Italian sculptors after the First World War.

Harding's portrait by Morgan is full, vigorous, and accurately modeled in the best tradition of 50 years' work in the Philadelphia Mint. The relief is varied, not too high and not too delicate, catching light and textures in a most satisfying manner. An engraver might do differently, but he could scarcely do better in accurate perpetuation of a statesman's likeness. Because Harding died in office, motifs of grief dominate the reverse. For the position of the standing figure in Greek dress, for the wreath encircling a palm at her feet, and for the organization of lettering,

Morgan went back to his medal of 1901 to 1903, on the death of William McKinley (fig. 116). Columbia on the McKinley medal was encumbered by patriotic paraphernalia, the coat of arms from the Great Seal appearing on the Renaissance-style V-shaped shield in her lowered right hand. Pure classicism reigns on the medal for Harding, the lady being accompanied by a baldachin of drapery and a columned portico as she adds a small branch to the floral tribute. The heraldic eagle is isolated in a wreath at the upper right. Morgan's youthful fascination with Greek sculptures, mentioned in his letters of the 1870s, has stood him in good stead for this statuesque figure in her several layers of drapery. The archaeological classicism of the 1920s shines forth in the ogee molding across the center of the field and the meander pattern in the exergue. The McKinley design is somewhat updated, but Morgan ended his career as medalist of the Presidential Inaugural series with a full demonstration of that combination of naturalism and Greco-Roman art that he and Charles Barber had so frequently, and in general successfully, adapted to the medallic tondo.

167. Sinnock, medal for Hoover

Coolidge's portrait by Sinnock is the logical extension of his design for the Sesquicentennial half dollar of 1926 (fig. 184). Here the president inaugurated in 1923 and 1925 is not obscured by George Washington, and the extremely low, tentative relief with thin lettering has been for the most part abandoned. Something of Sinnock's penchant for precise delicacy remains, and the portrait, though competent and accurate, lacks the textures of relief seen in Morgan's portrayal of Warren G. Harding. The reverse carries a love of early Greek sculpture and its setting far beyond the traditions of the 19th century summed up in Morgan's memorial for Coolidge's predecessor. The principal elements of the design are surrounded by a heavy ogee base molding, as if the tondo were a Greek mirror. It is the seated Columbia or Liberty—a stern, masculine specimen of womanhood—that evokes surprise, for she is like nothing encountered heretofore in the numismatic art of the United States. Clutching her huge fasces on her marble throne, she wears her hair in a style straight out of Greek art of about 440 to 410 B.C.; her clothing is derived from the Greek transitional period, that is, from 485 to 460 B.C. The ensemble is like one of those great stone monuments in public areas of Mussolini's Italy, some allegory in the Foro Italico or in front of a government building in Rome. Eagle on shield, cornucopia, and paucity of lettering either relieve the ponderousness of the seated divinity or increase the shock at seeing such a female enter the repertory of American symbolism. Sinnock's little eagle is an augury of the future, for this is the bird that Gilroy Roberts placed on the right of the Liberty Bell on Sinnock's Franklin half dollar of 1948, to allay fears that omission of the national bird might violate the spirit of the Mint Act of 1873 (fig. 232). In sum, Sinnock's first presidential medal blazed new aesthetic trails. Pseudoclassical designs of this nature may seem slightly conventional today, but in 1928 the effort was novel enough. A cautious craftsman, who quietly modernized the

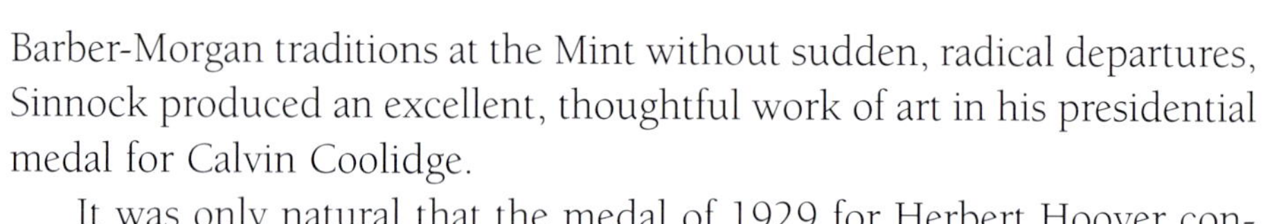

Barber-Morgan traditions at the Mint without sudden, radical departures, Sinnock produced an excellent, thoughtful work of art in his presidential medal for Calvin Coolidge.

It was only natural that the medal of 1929 for Herbert Hoover continued along similar paths. The bust is set away from the edge of the tondo, and a concession to the current vogue for arranging the lettering in the tradition of Pisanello and Sperandio has crept into organization of the obverse. Hoover's head is turned more to full profile, but the likeness is as characteristic as a clear but casual photograph. The reverse is less successful. The goddess, in her Greek transitional–style high-girt chiton with billowy overfold and mantle resembling a peplos, now stands frontally in bolder relief and grips two giant fasces as if they were the columns of the temple of Zeus at Olympia. If this is indeed Hoover the engineer who is honored, as the inscription indicates, then Sinnock has performed a feat of construction for the occasion by erecting this allegory, posed stiffly on tiny feet like an archaic maiden of about 525 B.C. from the Athenian Acropolis and flanked by the staves and axes balanced on points of poles at their bottoms. The figure is again difficult to identify with certainty. Both Liberty and Columbia wear the Phrygian cap, and here the top of such a headgear seems to be peeking straight out at us above her formal curls. Compared with the reverse of the medal to Coolidge, it is clear that Sinnock's medal to Hoover makes too much of a good thing: the early arts of Greece projected into American iconography of the 20th century.

Richness and diversity characterized the coins and medals issued between 1916 and 1929. The impetus toward new designs by major sculptors, instituted by Theodore Roosevelt, continued until all regular coins had been completely remade. The half dollar, quarter dollar, and dime were executed by two leading pupils of Saint-Gaudens in 1916, and the silver dollar was issued as a coin symbolic of peace in 1921. The half dollar also became the standard denomination for commemorative coinage, and the splendid series of designs was the work of independent sculptors and those employed at the Mint. The official medals by Morgan and Sinnock contained both traditional elements and new ideas developed in the excitement of America's artistic maturity before and after the First World War.

VIII

Commemorative Coins, 1918 to 1928

The triad of new types in 1916 completed the redesigning of the common coins in circulation. Addition of the silver dollar in 1921 left no further avenues for activity in the regular issues until the bicentennial of Washington's birth in 1932 brought forth the new quarter dollar by John Flanagan. The tradition of commemorative coins was well established, and there was patently ample room for expression in this direction. A variety of denominations had been included, from the quarter and half dollar of 1892 to the gold multiples of 1915. The most popular or, at least, the most used coins seem to have been the half dollar and the gold dollar. The latter had proved too small for artistry. The former was to become the natural vehicle for special issues. Two more gold commemorative coins were to appear, the Grant dollar in 1922 and the Philadelphia Sesquicentennial quarter eagle in 1926. The former was merely a reduction of the dies for the half dollar of the same year. The latter was America's last attempt at artistry in gold, for October 1929 and the economic policies of Franklin D. Roosevelt were to end our adventures with the king of metals.[1]

Charles E. Barber had died in 1917 at the age of 78, and George T. Morgan, then 72, reigned as chief engraver at the Mint. That same year a young Pennsylvanian named John R. Sinnock was appointed assistant engraver. He was to succeed Morgan when the latter died in harness in 1925 at the age of 79. With Morgan's death the rule of Englishmen as chief engravers in Philadelphia came to an end, a dynasty that had started when James B. Longacre hired William Barber as an assistant in 1865 and continued when the latter ascended the vacant primacy on Longacre's death in 1869.

George Morgan at age 73 and 30-year-old John Sinnock collaborated on one coin, a linking of traditions that extended back to the rich decade of the 1870s and forward to the new dime and half dollars of 1946 and 1948. The Illinois Centennial half dollar of 1918 resulted from conservative tendencies in American die design, and Sinnock was to perpetuate this art down to the present time. His posthumous half dollar of 1948 has a small, heraldic eagle added on the reverse by Gilroy Roberts, his successor as chief engraver or sculptor (fig. 232). Roberts was succeeded in turn in 1965 by Frank Gasparro, designer of the 1959 reverse for the Lincoln cent (fig. 139); the monument of their collaboration is the extremely traditional, conservative Kennedy half dollar of 1964 (fig. 240).

168. Illinois Centennial half dollar

Illinois Centennial

Morgan did the bust of Lincoln on the obverse of the 1918 Illinois Centennial commemorative, and Sinnock modeled the defiant eagle and attendant heraldry of the reverse (fig. 168). The even lettering favored by Barber and Morgan is present, and a classical bead and reel sets off the high wire edge around the low relief. Morgan's bust of Lincoln was copied from a statue by Andrew O'Connor Jr. that was unveiled at Springfield, Illinois, in August 1918, another instance of the interrelation between statues and coins. The Lincoln portrayed is the young lawyer, on the eve of his political career and as yet without his beard.

O'Connor (1874–1941), whose early training was as a carver of tombstones in his father's shop in Worcester, Massachusetts, eventually assisted Daniel Chester French in his studio, having also studied with John Singer Sargent in London and Auguste Rodin in Paris. He made a number of these Lincolns, one variant being cut in stone in 1916 from a model created as early as 1915. Morgan did not need to translate the statue into a bust himself, for O'Connor also prepared versions in this form. There are examples in the Metropolitan Museum and the Whitney Museum in New York, the Royal Exchange in London, and the Art Institute in Chicago. Of the statue Morey wrote: "he is the author . . . of an original Lincoln . . ., whose active pose is what one would expect from O'Connor's restless fingers."[2] Morgan's interpretation has captured the restless plasticity of this bust, yet another indication of the benefits for coin design of good monumental models in sculpture.

O'Connor's authorship of an equestrian statue of Lafayette in Baltimore links his work with Paul Bartlett's equestrian Lafayette in Paris and thus with the commemorative silver dollar of 1900. The repertory of official monuments in American sculpture is really quite limited, and it is not surprising to find the same relationships between statues of Revolutionary War or Civil War heroes and die designs occurring again and again in the commemorative coins struck from 1900 to the Second World War.

Sinnock's reverse, in the low relief that he must have learned from Morgan and that became characteristic of his art, is a version of the seal of the state of Illinois. By design or by coincidence one sees in the eagle a visual survival of heraldry worked out on the trade dollar and half dollar patterns of the two Barbers and Morgan in the 1870s. The little burst of sun at the right is almost a bow to the Roty–Saint-Gaudens–Weinman developments outside the Philadelphia Mint in American numismatic taste and iconography in the generation following 1900. Sinnock's composition can be called conventional, but the entire aura of the coin reflects American art after the Civil War, and this is perhaps truly appropriate for the only commemorative coin to date to honor Abraham Lincoln. A comparison, pointing up Sinnock's success in blending with Morgan's traditionalism and producing a dignified, self-sustaining reverse to a certain specification, lies in the extremely inept reverse of an Adlai Stevenson medal released at the beginning of 1966 by Presidential Art Medals, Inc. The same seal of Illinois has provided the inspiration, but the results are distorted, lumpy, and disagreeable, in finish as well as proportions.

Maine Centennial

The year 1919 witnessed no new designs in the American coinage, a respite after so much activity from 1915 to 1918. If I were considering the art of U.S. coins on a strict chronological basis, Anthony de Francisci's half dollar of 1920 for the 100th anniversary of Maine's admission to the union would have been discussed ahead of his Peace dollar of 1921. The coin was modeled by the sculptor according to required specifications and is therefore not considered typical of his art, or indeed of any art.[3] It looks just like a prize medal for a county fair or school athletic day. The all too common combination of state seal on the obverse and inscription in a symbolic wreath on the reverse is initiated in the series of commemorative coins and medals (fig. 169). Lettering was considered as a characteristic of the sculptor De Francisci. Here the work is light, timid, and pseudomodern, having far less character than the ornamental capitals of the Illinois Centennial coin.

It is no tribute to the sculptor that he consented to abide by the allegedly artistic limitations that produced such a vapid coin. Most artists in history have been able to achieve more when they have chosen to exert their personalities with greater force. The farmer or the fisherman flanking the state coat of arms alone would have made a more forceful and characteristic figure, like the miner panning for gold on the California Diamond Jubilee coin of 1925 (fig. 182). One would not have wished a large potato as principal element of the reverse, and commemorative coins came to have too many ships in their repertory, but an animal characteristic of Maine's northern woods, such as the moose of the state shield, would have created a more arresting design. De Francisci was supposedly one of America's better medalists, winning the Saltus medal in 1927, but the Maine Centennial was not his shining moment. A "commercial medalist" of the most pedestrian sort could have done as well.

169. Maine Centennial half dollar

Pilgrim Tercentenary

170. Pilgrim Tercentenary half dollar

If he is remembered at all, Cyrus E. Dallin is remembered as a teacher and as a sculptor of Indian and colonial themes, the two often related. Morey wrote, "His groups are metallic and lack invention."[4] His 1909 equestrian bronze, *Appeal to the Great Spirit,* depicting an Indian praying to the skies in front of Boston's Museum of Fine Arts, is surely his most popular work. At the time he was commissioned to do the Pilgrim Tercentenary half dollar of 1920 and 1921 he was turning out a triad of related statues or monumental reliefs. There was the *Massasoit* at Plymouth, Massachusetts. At Provincetown he executed a memorial, the *Signing of the Compact,* in 1922, and his *Anne Hutchinson* of the same year in front of the State House on Beacon Hill in Boston is a suave tribute in bronze to religious freedom by way of a Salem martyr. Although Dallin worked from designs supplied to him by a commission, his Pilgrim Tercentenary half dollar is a masterpiece in the conservative tradition (fig. 170). An innovation exists in that this is the first of a number of commemoratives in which the sculptor has left the background or field slightly rough to indicate a modeled surface, rather than smoothing it down to mirror plane in the usual manner of a coin.

In studying Dallin's coin, we are fortunate that the original plaster model, purchased from his home in Arlington, Massachusetts, has survived. It shows certain differences, including the signature C.E.D. rather than the confusing D. of the finished coin (fig. 171). The idealized

171. Plaster models for Pilgrim Tercentenary half dollar

portrait of Governor William Bradford is a clever, fortuitous use of the half-figure bust, necessary to convey the essence of the devoted man in a moment of meditation. The *Mayflower,* sailing to the left rear and thus into the distance, is well conceived in the concave surface of the flan. Thus, the high edge, reminiscent of Saint-Gaudens, provides at least one solution to the problem of design, perhaps one permissible here and not in the regular coinage.

Save for the half-figure bust of Bradford, the design is quite conservative, showing a little less of the "coin" lettering of the Illinois Centennial half dollar. Fifteen years after Saint-Gaudens experimented with the coinage, the great sculptor's influence is evident on Dallin's half dollar in the relationship between the Pilgrim governor on the coin and the statue *The Puritan* in Springfield, Massachusetts; Philadelphia; Brookgreen Gardens, South Carolina; and various indoor collections. The *Mayflower,* more forceful and certainly more imaginative than the *Santa Maria* on the Columbian half dollar of 1892, foreshadows all the ships, five at least, on commemorative half dollars in the 1930s. Seen from the stern on the waves, the Pilgrims' ship is impressive.

In 1920 Cyrus Dallin also rivaled Robert Aitken in designing a medallic homage to Marshal Foch. Aitken's creation had been commissioned by the American Numismatic Society (fig. 157). The state of Massachusetts paid for Dallin's effort in conventional classicism. On the reverse, Liberty, in a hideous Amazon cap, and Massachusetts, with her Indian on her shield, support a wreath with FOCH between. The whole affair, especially the poising of the figures, is weak, vapid, and rather frozen. It can even be called insipid (fig. 172).

172. Dallin, medal for Foch

173. Missouri Centennial half dollar

Missouri Centennial

When Robert Aitken (1878–1949) turned his hand to the first of the two commemorative half dollars issued in 1921, he became the first American medalist to apply the principles of Renaissance medallic design to a coin of the United States and the first such artist to make a frontiersman look like a Medici prince (fig. 173). If we consider the pseudo-Periklean qualities of Aitken's Panama-Pacific Exposition $50 gold coins of 1915 (fig. 153), Morey was correct in labeling him an eclectic. He was also a sculptor of war memorials, and his monumental contribution to the exposition of 1915 was a "Fountain of the Earth." The reverse of his Missouri Centennial half dollar is no less reminiscent, an Indian and a frontiersman standing like Roman soldiers in an Antonine relief on the Arch of Constantine or Renaissance condottieri in a large fresco of court ceremonials. The relief is deep and well modeled, on a concave field with a plain, heavy edge. The lettering on the obverse follows the forms and system of Pisanello, and the coin as a whole is a work of art rather than just another way to market a silver fifty-cent piece because all three of the

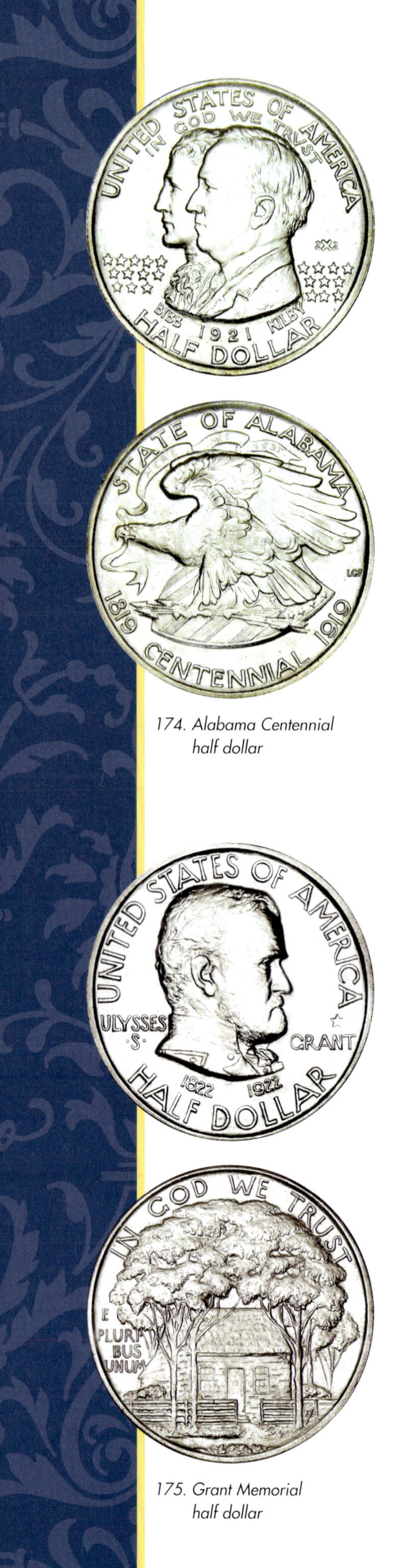

174. Alabama Centennial half dollar

175. Grant Memorial half dollar

mottoes that usually burden and constrict America's attempts at numismatic art are omitted. A final pleasing touch: the name of the Missouri town where the coins were first issued, SEDALIA, is incused in the exergue, a masterful detail.

During the months that designs for the Missouri half dollar were being considered, Aitken made a series of sketches for both the obverse and reverse. These tightly handled, well-shaded pencil sketches were close in composition and details to the ultimately adopted designs of a bust resembling Daniel Boone on one side and a frontiersman (again suggesting Boone) with a Native American on the reverse. The seal of the state formed the most convenient or conventional reverse, and a statuesque, pseudoclassical group of Columbia or Liberty receiving the personification of Missouri dominated one of the suggested obverses. The most heroic obverse provided a dramatic prototype for the star-studded reverse that was finally adopted. A standing frontiersman (Boone) pointed westward over the horizon of the Missouri River toward the setting sun or the star of empire. An Indian crouched at his feet, looking toward the vanishing frontiers. One version viewed the frontiersman in half profile from the front, while the other used the old Roman trick, also in the final design, of showing him in profile, seen from the back. All the tentative compositions were marked by the same grandeur of conception and clarity of detail that characterized the accepted dies.[5]

Aitken's first contribution to the series of commemorative half dollars was a splendid manifestation of Renaissance numismatics in modern guise. His half dollar of 1935 for the California-Pacific International Exposition, which blended designs from America's new repertory, contained a governmental sculptural group and a geographic or scenographic relief, of the type recalling New Deal post office sculpture, reduced to the surface of a conventional coin (fig. 205). Here success was equally evident. Aitken may have been labeled an eclectic, but his imagination in selecting from the past to rephrase the present worked very well in the U.S. commemorative coinage.

Alabama Centennial and Grant Memorial

The Alabama Centennial half dollar of 1921 and the Ulysses S. Grant Centenary half dollar and gold dollar of 1922 were the work of Laura Gardin Fraser (figs. 174 and 175). Born in 1889 in Chicago, she is remembered not only as a skillful medalist in her own right but as the wife of James Earle Fraser, discussed in connection with the Buffalo nickel of 1913. In 1925 she designed the Fort Vancouver Centennial half dollar, and the following year the Frasers, husband and wife, collaborated on the Oregon Trail Memorial fifty-cent piece, a coin struck intermittently until 1939 (figs. 183 and 186). As a maker of medals, Laura Gardin Fraser began her career in the shadow of her husband, doing such traditionally feminine subjects as a Better Babies medal in 1913, filled with the sentiment found in monuments in fashionable Episcopal churches of the pre–World War I era. She graduated early in the following decade to a very Renaissance, very Pisanello-like medal for the Irish Setter Club of America, with a most humanistic dog on the reverse. Her commemorative coins projected her firmly onto the national stage, and the culmination of a distinguished career was reached in 1958 when she executed the Centennial medal for the American Numismatic Society (fig. 196).

The coin celebrating Alabama's century in the union (including the years spent as a Confederate state) is a good example of the trite motifs, partly real and partly symbolic, that go into one of these statehood commemorations (fig. 174). The organization of the portraits, stars and lettering on the obverse is again that of the Renaissance medal,[6] and the reverse, said to present the Great Seal of Alabama, resembles the reverse of the Illinois Centennial half dollar of 1918, also based on the arms of the state. This creates a kind of triple flavor: the Renaissance, the seal and die engraving of the period 1810 to 1870 (especially the decade of the 1870s), and the numismatic art of the 1920s. The jugate busts, one of the then governor and the other of his first predecessor, recall that this classical device was revived in American coinage on the Washington-Lafayette silver dollar of 1900. Fraser was required to exhibit only the religious motto, and the remaining epigraphy is reasonably minimal. Vigorous lettering has saved uninteresting portraits from weakening the obverse, and the defiant eagle of the reverse is handled in a spirit worthy of Saint-Gaudens or the best patterns for silver of the national centennial era.

The obverse of the half dollar marking the centenary of Grant's birth confirmed the canonical obverse of a bust flanked by secondary lettering, with the major inscriptions above and below. The debt to Pisanello is now scarcely recognizable. The motif of the fenced cottage beneath the umbrella of trees that idealizes the Ohio birthplace of the general makes a pleasant contrast with the marble memorial of his fellow Ohio president, McKinley, on the gold dollars of 1916 and 1917 (fig. 175). Fraser has given the surfaces of obverse and reverse a slight roughening, a trick used less forcefully by Cyrus Dallin in 1920 and evidently adapted for the Grant centenary coin from techniques pioneered by James E. Fraser in making models for the Buffalo nickel a decade earlier (fig. 148). Her trees, her little wooden house, and her rail fence are modeled and carved with a gem cutter's precision. The texture of the leaves is one of the most subtle yet lively experiences on any surface of an American coin. Grant is his gruff self, and in sum it can be said that a superlative beginning was made to the iconography of the Civil War in U.S. commemorative coinage. The only possible criticism of the design, that the larger lettering is too large, fades when the curvatures of actual flans are studied. What seems potentially large and flat in photographs falls into harmonious beauty in actuality.

176. *Monroe Doctrine Centennial half dollar*

Monroe Doctrine Centennial

Chester Beach (1881–1956) was born in San Francisco, trained in Paris, and resided in New York City. Of his talents Charles R. Morey wrote, "Wholly modern if not yet entirely personal and consistent is the plastic vocabulary of Chester Beach. . . . A versatile artist, known as a medalist as well as a worker in various stones, bronze and ivory, he displays in each field the power of making his medium expressive by its mere texture."[7] Beach designed the Monroe Doctrine Centennial half dollar coined early in 1923 (fig. 176). The piece is not attractive; but if it can be called ugly, it must also be termed imaginative. Jugate busts of Monroe and John Quincy Adams fill the obverse, while women personifying North and South America, ocean currents, and the scroll and quill pen of the document take up the reverse. The low, flat relief with an attempt at a feeling for modeling rather than carving makes the busts and the females poised to imitate the outline of the continents seem like mounted cut-outs. They can even be said to resemble daubs of clay on a board, or relief outlines in glass.

Adams, with his staring eye, is scarcely a portrait, and Monroe would not be recognized even by an expert. The triple-lined rim is unnecessary. The way the females are contorted to achieve their appearance of continents is a clever tour de force of calligraphic relief but an aesthetic monstrosity, a bad pun in art. North America holds an olive branch and South America half conceals a cornucopia in order to fill out their shorelines. Perhaps the crowning touch is that the northern continent's right hand reaches down to form Central America. This coin was not the first use of the anthropomorphic Western Hemisphere in the die cutter's art. In 1901 Ralph Beck had designed a similar obverse for a medal honoring the Pan-American Exposition at Buffalo, and complained bitterly of Beach's adaptation of his design for the 1923 commemorative.[8] Nor did Beach confine this concept to coins and medals, for monuments exhibited under the auspices of the National Sculpture Society in 1929 adapt versions of the same personagraphic trick to major sculpture and relief. One of these is titled *The Rivers*. The second, for the American Telephone and Telegraph building in New York, is appropriately titled *Service to the Nation in Peace and War*. The figural complements to geography are "Peace" and "War" wrapped beside a telephonic map of the United States. The pose and setting of the central figure, it might be noted, are like those of Dora Doscher on the 1916 quarter dollar of Hermon MacNeil (fig. 156). Beach enjoyed reworking a successful theme, and the telephonic subject "Peace and War" was to appear on his contribution to the Society of Medalists series for 1937.

In 1923 Chester Beach exhibited two medals that give further insight into his methods and techniques in creating modern, mannered, seemingly personal low relief with a neo-Roman element. The first, dated 1917, was for the School Art League. A woman of the Roman Venus Genetrix type, with stylus and tablet, stands on stylized waves, presumably the East River, in front of New York's skyline. The police badge of the City of New York floats at the left. All the characteristics of Beach's art are here: the low-relief planes, the female personification so much a hallmark of the era in commemorative sculpture, the love of geography and vistas, and the use of waves as background or filling ornament. No less symptomatic of his style but far more pretentious is the Peace of Versailles medal of 1919, commissioned by the American Numismatic Society. Various pseudoclassical figures can be culled from the obverse. Mercury in his World War I tin hat recalls the statuette that used to surmount the lampposts on Fifth Avenue. The messenger god leads the Roman commander, lifted out of the French neoclassic painter J.A.D. Ingres's *Martyrdom of St. Symphorian* in Autun Cathedral, while a flapper with a wreath and more drapery of the type associated with Venus Genetrix stands at the right. A body beneath can only symbolize war (fig. 177). The Mercury is labeled JUSTICE, and the female, PEACE. The hero on horseback is really astride Pegasus. The reverse, inscribed PEACE OF VERSAILLES, gives a full, wide-angle view of the palace beneath a sun of Japanese quality, all within a wreath. This emerges as a pedestrian vista; the subject that should have been carried out as a detail or as a single, smaller building seen on diagonal perspective. Form and precision are both lost in and overwhelmed by the wreath. In short, a sketchy view of the palace at Versailles makes no sense, for such rational architecture should be shown closer to the picture plane or not at all.

177. Beach, Versailles Treaty medal

The brochure accompanying the medal describes it with the lofty idealism of the era that gave birth to the League of Nations.

> On the obverse Peace is shown with the palm branch and wreath of victory—a beautiful womanly embodiment. On the other side of the winged horse, there is the manly form of Justice—a figure of Right Triumphant. The helmet of conflict is still upon his head, but the sheathed sword shows that the battle has been won. At the side, the wreathed scales appear. Justice and Peace advance together. Above the longing for peace and justice, however, the treaty of 1919 is distinguished beyond all others by the earnest desire that in the future, war may be eliminated. The powerful figure mounted on Pegasus expresses the idea of the League of Nations incorporated in this treaty. The clasped book of the law and the dynamic outstretched arm need no interpreting—the forcefulness of the

type and its virility suggest that henceforth the principles of righteousness will be in control. This thought is further emphasized in the fallen figure of destruction, whose torch is being trampled beneath the foot of Justice. In its lines, in its planes and in the composition this is a monumental design.

On the reverse is shown the palace of Versailles where the treaty was signed. The sun is bursting through the clouds of war and its rays light up the facade.[9]

As a designer of commemorative half dollars, Chester Beach was to produce the Lexington-Concord Sesquicentennial coin of 1925, more conservative than the Monroe Doctrine Centennial half dollar but a sounder piece of numismatic art. Fuller consideration will demonstrate that the art as such is inherent in the design of the statue on the obverse and the view of the building on the reverse. The former was the creation of Daniel Chester French. The latter was the work of an anonymous colonial architect or village builder (fig. 180).

Huguenot-Walloon Tercentenary

178. Huguenot-Walloon Tercentenary half dollar

The jugate bust and the ship now emerge as standard combinations on obverse and reverse, particularly where early explorers or patriots, their successors, and their vehicles are concerned (fig. 178). This coin, authorized early in 1923 and dated 1924, must be one of the last creations by George T. Morgan. The standard lettering of medals from the Mint and early commemoratives comes through here as a straightforward design containing nothing thrilling or distasteful. The Huguenot-Walloon Tercentenary half dollar is a worthy conclusion to Morgan's long career of distinguished and rich production, marked by imagination within the conservative framework and by a generally high level of appeal. This appeal transcends the fact that all 19th-century issues are now admired because they are dated in iconography and style. Morgan's coin recalls too that the die engravers trained in and around the Mint did have the ability to combine clear-cut designs with considerable detail.

The ship *New Netherland* (or *Nieuw Nederland*) sails away from the viewer, to the left rear, like Cyrus Dallin's *Mayflower* (fig. 170). It is set on a panel of waves that look like jumping dolphins, a convention also found in the silver dollars designed at the Philadelphia Mint with portraits of Sun Yat-sen for the young Republic of China.

When George T. Morgan died at the age of 79 in 1925, he was modeling a series of medals honoring the secretaries of the Treasury from Alexander Hamilton to his own time. The Alexander Hamilton medal presents its subject as a full bust facing three-quarters left, modeled in a creamy impressionism that was no doubt intended to be modern but which departed from portraits of Hamilton's era and Morgan's own style sufficiently to be slick, weak, and consequently rather unpleasant (fig. 179). Morgan also helped adapt his designs of various kinds to postage stamps of all denominations. Conservative in his art, he was equally so in his taste for outdoor sport. Having been born in Birmingham, England, and resident in Philadelphia, he remained an enthusiastic cricket player all his life.

179. Morgan, medal for Hamilton

180. Lexington-Concord Sesquicentennial half dollar

Lexington-Concord Sesquicentennial

The year 1925 was a banner year for commemorative half dollars. Four were issued, all by major sculptors. Chester Beach's Lexington-Concord Sesquicentennial coin was the apogee of photographic naturalism, showing the Concord *Minute Man*, executed by Daniel Chester French (1850–1931) when he was 19, in juxtaposition with the Old Belfry at Lexington (fig. 180). This coin, a true descendant of the Roman imperial products with statues and buildings on them, is almost reduced to the artistic level of a photograph, for little is left that is original on the part of Beach. Since the materials for design are so wretched, artistically speaking, Beach can be forgiven for the excess of inscriptions. They were probably dictated to him. Nothing is more out of place than the religious motto. This was a commemorative half dollar that ought to have been designed by a novice in the Mint. Although less irritating than his half dollar for the Monroe Doctrine centennial, this coin does no credit to Beach's stature as a first-class artist. What the coin exudes in patriotism, it lacks in art.[10]

French was also a medalist, with examples made in 1917 and 1918 commemorating specific events in connection with the Great War. He is, of course, best remembered for his massive seated Lincoln, the overwhelming cult image of the Lincoln Memorial in Washington. This statue later appeared in true Roman *architectura numismatica* fashion on the reverse of the 1959 Lincoln cent, seen between the columns of the Lincoln Memorial as depicted by Frank Gasparro and hardly visible considering the monumental scale of the original (fig. 139).

Stone Mountain

If the relation between monumental sculpture and specific setting was a disappointment on the Lexington-Concord Sesquicentennial half dollar,

181. Stone Mountain half dollar

it was a smashing success in connection with the Stone Mountain half dollar of 1925. The obverse shows a version of Gutzon Borglum's giant group to be carved on the side of the mountain in north Georgia. The reverse presents an eagle, in the tradition of Saint-Gaudens, seated atop the dome of granite, a symbol of the participation of the United States in a "Memorial to the Valor of the Soldier of the South" (fig. 181). Borglum was both the sculptor of the mountain monument and the designer of the coin, a rare combination in U.S. coinage, although a *bozzetto* or *modello* for the Saint-Gaudens Victory of the Sherman Monument in New York became the head of Liberty on his gold eagle of 1907.

So far as the grandeur of the mountainside project is concerned, there was a good precedent in the age when Greek coin types were becoming more specific. About 330 B.C. someone conceived the notion of carving an image of Alexander the Great on the flank of Mount Athos. Borglum's outdoor exercise in commemoration was doomed to failure by its expense and the stormy temperament of the sculptor, but the commemorative half dollar survives as his memorial to the grand ideal.

Considered by Chandler Post "America's gifted exponent of Rodin,"[11] Gutzon Borglum (1867–1941) trained and practiced as a painter. His equestrian monument to General Philip Sheridan is one of the few Civil War bronzes in the capital that catches the fire of a stormy general and his battles. Charles Morey wrote: "The numerous artistic controversies associated with the name of Gutzon Borglum should not obscure his position as a sculptor of power and originality. He has a streak of titanism which assorts none too harmoniously with his generally realistic outlook. He aspired to carve Stone Mountain as Ghirlandaio longed to fresco the walls of Florence. . . . More versatile than his brother Solon, Gutzon Borglum is also a painter, and carries the pictorial impressionism common to both beyond the ordinary rules of plastic form."[12] Pathos in this medium is cited in the familiar subject of a colossal head of Lincoln.

The half dollar and its precursor of 1924, a medal designed for sale to children of Confederate families, are among the few examples of a sculptor using his own die designs as the *bozzetto* or advance propaganda for his major carving. Another such instance is the design of the Column of Trajan on Roman bronze sestertii, showing it topped by the eagle rather than the statue of Trajan. Evidently the record of Trajan's Dacian wars of 104 to 110 was turned into a monument of glorification of the emperor and ultimately into the resting place for his ashes. The obverse of the children's medal by Borglum is really a better design than the half dollar, for President Jefferson Davis appears at the right and General Jackson's hand is not outstretched. Borglum is one of the few artists who by roughened surfaces can convey impressionism on a medal.

In his original models for the commemorative coin, Borglum tried to create a vignette from his mountainside memorial within the confines of a tondo. The purpose was to parallel the glimpse of the monument on the children's medal, the area encompassed on the model for the coin being somewhat to the left of that viewed on the medal. Marching soldiers were shown at the left rear and behind Jackson's arm, which was in the outstretched position. These soldiers conveyed a sense of unseen activity in depth, much as they appear in the triumphal procession on the Arch of Titus in Rome (A.D. 81) or, more immediately, as Augustus Saint-Gaudens used them to fill out his memorial to Colonel Robert Gould Shaw on Boston Common. The sense of movement to the left was balanced by the head and neck of Jefferson Davis's horse intruding into the composition in the right foreground. To my mind, the results would have made a magnificent coin, an unusual compression of monumentality and power into a limited and unorthodox historical space. The Commission of Fine Arts, chiefly James E. Fraser, expressed strong disapproval at this radical tailoring of a longer frieze to the surface of a half dollar, and, amid the sculptor's objections, everything was removed save the two Confederate generals on horseback.[13]

The debacle of the Stone Mountain carving has been told in numerous works on American sculpture. Borglum completed the head of Lee and the figure of Jefferson Davis. He abandoned the project in 1925, and his models were destroyed. Augustus Lukeman succeeded Borglum and had the head of Lee blasted away, making a new one in its place. Work was halted in 1928 for lack of money. If Lukeman's *Soldiers' Memorial* at Elizabethtown, Pennsylvania, is typical of his monumental marbles and bronzes, then he was a sculptor of the heavy, draped neo-Roman creations associated with the art of America's international expositions and of government buildings. Perhaps it is well that the coin remains the most finished souvenir of the project as it was first carried out. The colossal reliefs were at long last brought to completion after the Civil War centennial under the direction of the sculptor Walker Hancock, and a dedication ceremony for the revised monument was finally held in May 1970.

California Diamond Jubilee

Jo Mora's combination of a miner panning for gold and a grizzly bear walking on a statuesque slab for the California half dollar of 1925 is one of America's greatest works of numismatic art (fig. 182). The design is bold and effective. The types are large, simple, and worked out with folds of cloth for the miner's shirt and trousers, felt for his hat, and leather for his boots. Muscles, bones, and tufts of fur express the massive determination of the bear. Within the limits of modern machine design, compositions such as this are about as much as can be expected of a die designer. To add to the boldness of the miner and the ursine companion, the field is unpolished—that is, it is left roughened as it appeared in the sculptor's model. Lettering is effective too, because large and very small sizes are used. Placing is so skillfully handled that it seems hard to realize that all three required aphorisms, the statutory inscriptions, are included.

182. California Diamond Jubilee half dollar

183. Fort Vancouver Centennial half dollar

Fort Vancouver Centennial

The artist of the Fort Vancouver Centennial coin of 1925 was Laura Gardin Fraser, already tested by two ventures into the game of designing commemorative half dollars. The bust on the obverse is labeled Dr. John McLoughlin. Within a circumscribed tondo on the reverse, a frontiersman dominates the picture plane, with the fort and a mountain beyond (fig. 183). The obverse tries Pisanello's spacing of the lettering and circumscribed roughness of the bust, while the reverse has too much scenery in the background, surrounded by too much lettering. This and the Hawaiian Sesquicentennial coin of 1928 (fig. 188) prove that background scenery or geography ought to be omitted from commemorative half dollars. As these coins go, Fraser's is a most acceptable one. Perhaps only because the events commemorated were relatively unimportant and because there had already been too much "frontier" on these coins does the Fort Vancouver Centennial contribution fail to arouse aesthetic emotions.

Sesquicentennial of American Independence

184. Sesquicentennial of American Independence half dollar

The fact that this coin, the silver half dollar commemorating the sesquicentennial of American independence in 1926, is in such low relief was the response of officialdom—not the innocent designer—to the experiments of Augustus Saint-Gaudens and Henry Hering. The edge is relatively high and the flan curves up to meet it, but there are scarcely any surfaces on the compressed bust of Washington and the austere Calvin Coolidge beyond him (fig. 184). Although it is fashionable to cite this as the first time a living president appeared on U.S. coinage, the point is unimportant, for likenesses of current presidents had graced official medals from the Mint for many years. John R. Sinnock, who became first engraver at the Mint in 1925—the year in which Morgan died and the coin commemorating the sesquicentennial was authorized—had enjoyed nearly a decade of producing such government medals under Morgan.

The stepped rim on the outer part of the reverse breaks the potential monotony of delicate lettering. The bell and its inscriptions are jewels of precision. Rosettes on either side of the LIBERTY on the obverse are an unnecessary reminder that monumental bronze relief often guides a coin design, for they are similar to ornaments on the corners of countless war memorials and other commemorations involving lists of names or epigraphy of sorts. If it had been a coin in the regular series, the precise, extremely sensitive work could not have taken the punishment of constant use, but as a commemorative piece that would not circulate it is arresting as a total concept in its difference from the 50-odd other such half dollars that would comprise the "classic" series.

The gold quarter eagle for the sesquicentennial of 1926, also by Sinnock, reverts in part to the allegorical iconography of the 19th century. Liberty stands on a globe and holds both the torch of freedom and a scroll, presumably the Declaration of Independence (fig. 185). The view of Independence Hall falls into the category of straightforward illustrations of buildings on American coins, Monticello in 1938 and the Lincoln Memorial in 1959 being the common examples. Liberty is statuesque and pseudo-Attic, in that classical drapery reveals human form in the manner of the Venus Genetrix on coins of Hadrian or its monumental source in the sculpture of Athens during the Peloponnesian Wars. The upper part of the garment has been made into a Doric chiton with loose, zigzag overfold, a type of Greek transitional or pre-Parthenon classicism. This style would also preoccupy the Mint's new chief engraver in the reverses of his presidential medals for Calvin Coolidge and Herbert Hoover. Despite these Grecian details, Liberty's total impression is thoroughly dated; she looks like a flapper of the 1920s. Her cloth cap accentuates this resemblance, and her position as she steps forward, head in profile, recalls the obverse of Hermon MacNeil's quarter dollar of 1916 to 1931.

Considering the size of the coin, John Sinnock has produced a good design that has the lettering of Weinman's 1916 dime and the obverse monumentality of the same sculptor's 1916 half dollar (figs. 159 and 160). The torch of freedom and scroll together are perhaps too bookishly symbolic and too little like Liberty. One of the traditional attributes of the 1870s, the shield or an eagle beside Liberty, would have been no less symbolic and much less abstract. It was not until 1946 that the "torch of freedom" found its true home in Sinnock's repertory, when it was used on the reverse of the Roosevelt dime (fig. 230).[14]

185. Sesquicentennial of American Independence quarter eagle

186. Oregon Trail Memorial half dollar of 1926 type

Oregon Trail Memorial

By 1926 the two Frasers, James Earle and Laura Gardin, had learned that the raised edge and curved flan of a coin protect the relief most effectively. In their designs for the Oregon Trail Memorial half dollar, an Indian makes a gesture of peace before a map of the United States, and settlers drive their covered wagon toward the setting sun (fig. 186). The actions are explicit, and the design has taken very comfortably to the surfaces of the coin, including Hudson Bay at the upper right of the obverse to delineate Canada as well as the United States. The relief is bold and simple, making everything readily comprehensible. There is no fussiness, and the lettering is expressively thick without being overwhelming. Certainly no one could handle Indian subjects better than James Fraser, but it is too bad the noble savage had to be garbed or robed so that he resembles a Greek athlete of the Augustan period, a late Hellenistic or early Roman imperial restyling of a bronze of about 430 to 400 B.C.

187. Vermont Sesquicentennial half dollar

Vermont and Hawaiian Sesquicentennials

The last two commemorative coins struck before 1934 are half dollars, the first the work of Charles Keck and the second by Chester Beach after the design by artist Juliette Mae Fraser of Honolulu. The Vermont coin of 1927 is spoiled by an excess of lettering on both sides (fig. 187). Morey wrote of Keck: "His monuments, while often lacking content, carry their scale better than much of our sculpture of colossal size. Practice as architectural decorator has taught him to combine weight with fitness; the craftsman is evident in [his] refusal to allow the lovely figures [of his *Chandelier*] to be obvious at the expense of design."[15] Portrait and walking catamount are rugged enough and carry their content well, but part of the legend is merely a recording of history and has no bearing on the designs. It seems superfluous to have to state on the obverse that Ira Allen was "Founder of Vermont."

There was considerable trouble in securing a satisfactory design for the Vermont Sesquicentennial coin. Sculptor Sherry Fry produced models, a dull obverse in the Renaissance tradition of portrait busts in strict profile, and on the reverse a view of the Bennington Monument, an obelisk like the Washington Monument, rising starkly amid balanced lettering. Then Charles Keck tried a series of an obverse and three reverses before the adopted combinations were achieved. His three reverses—the local landmark Fay's Tavern in a Roman *corona civica* with names of prominent Green Mountain boys; a trophy of Revolutionary War flags, swords, rifles, a drum, and a powder horn; and a catamount crouching on a ledge with the same 15 heroes of the battle incised on the rock—were mighty demonstrations of how the circle of a half dollar could best be used. In this sense as well as from the legends forced on the designer, the coin as issued became something of a disappointment. The scene of the catamount defending the ledge of heroes at least made the beast's presence meaningful from the standpoint of historical symbolism as well as of pure art.[16]

The coin honoring Hawaii in 1928 is no more a credit to Chester Beach than was the Lexington-Concord coin, although it is unusual if only in the different iconography of the Pacific Islands as opposed to the pioneer West or the 13 colonies. The symbolic obverse—the bust of Captain James Cook, copied from a Wedgwood medallion, and the eight volcanoes of the islands below—is too crowded, despite the large, flat, clothed bust.

The reverse is difficult to follow (fig. 188). A Hawaiian warrior chief in full regalia, a panorama of Waikiki Beach, and Diamond Head in the distance are all too much for one small coin—especially since the chief is "gaining the summit of a hill, and representing Hawaii arising from obscurity." The same description continues, "The chief's right hand is held out in welcome. The coconut tree behind him denotes romance."[17]

188. Hawaiian Sesquicentennial half dollar

It was time to give the production of commemorative coins a rest and turn back to the regular series. The bicentennial of Washington's birth afforded the opportunity, or the excuse, but the era of commemorative half dollars was far from terminated, even by the Depression. Recovery under Roosevelt was to bring renewed demand for more such coins.

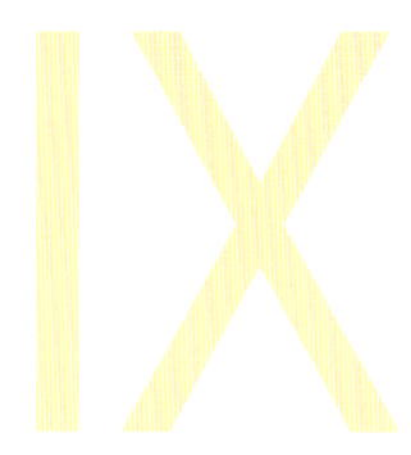

Washington's Bicentennial and Commemorative Half Dollars, 1932 to 1938

189. Washington quarter dollar of 1932 type

The bicentennial of Washington's birth demanded some form of commemoration, although the Depression had halted the production of new commemorative half dollars. First it was decided to issue a commemorative quarter dollar, but from the beginning there was little doubt that Hermon MacNeil's warlike Liberty of 1916 no longer suited the spirit of peace, patriotism, national recovery, and remembrance of the actual heroes of the American cosmos. Victor Brenner's Lincoln cent and the various patriotic commemorative coins of the 1920s had set the tone for introduction of the portrait in American numismatic art. Washington had appeared on Lafayette's dollar of 1900, and on the Sesquicentennial of American Independence half dollar of 1926, which paired his bust with that of the living president, Calvin Coolidge. Patterns of 1909 by the Mint engravers had almost placed a bust of Washington in his dress uniform on the nickel. Only James Fraser's Indian and bison had ridden in off the plains—or out of the sideshows and zoo—to save the day for ideal types on our regular coinage.

The Washington Quarter

Thus, in 1932 everything collaborated to produce a new silver twenty-five-cent piece with a portrait of Washington on the obverse and a revised form of the usual eagle on the reverse (fig. 189). The artist again came from outside the Mint. He was John Flanagan, encountered earlier in the 20th century as a medalist in the modern traditions of the Renaissance and cinquecento. His medal presented by the Congress of the United States to a captain who had picked up survivors of the *Titanic* disaster in 1912 has been demonstrated to be a classic of early Italian and Michelangelesque forms fused in the telling of an epic tragedy in a few images on a relatively small scale (fig. 141). A pupil of Augustus Saint-Gaudens, Flanagan produced a bronze head of his master that was a classic of forceful, impressionistic forms, recalling the elongation of Late Antique Greek philosophers and the plastic vividness of Rodin. He had assisted Frederick MacMonnies in the Columbia Fountain for the Chicago Exposition of 1892, and MacMonnies—the sculptor of marble, a master of writhing, emotional form on a large scale—considered Flanagan the leading medalist of America.

Whether or not he approved, Flanagan's portrait of Washington was a symptom of the frozen, conservative classic naturalism that affected U.S. governmental sculpture in the generation from 1932 to 1950. Officialdom was enamored with the cold, clear, precise, and easily understandable white marble or white plaster busts of Washington by the French sculptor Jean-Antoine Houdon. In 1785 Houdon was commissioned by the legislature of Virginia to sculpt the likeness of the infant republic's first citizen. Benjamin Franklin had been the intermediary. The Frenchman crossed the ocean and made studies at Mount Vernon between October 6 and 12, 1785. A clay bust at Washington's home is souvenir of this visit and was the source of Flanagan's profile for the quarter dollar of 1932. Back in Paris, Houdon produced draped and undraped versions of the portrait, in marble and in plaster, which was often painted white to simulate marble (fig. 190). From 1788 to 1792 he prepared the marble statue in contemporary uniform for the state capitol in Richmond. A version in

190. Houdon, George Washington

191. Drawing by Stuart after Houdon

192. Flanagan, studies for the Washington quarter dollar

bronze stands outside the National Gallery in London. In keeping with his rejection of regal trappings and his portrait on coins struck in his lifetime, Washington is said to have preferred the Houdon portraits in modern rather than Greco-Roman dress, or the heroic nude.

Flanagan's bicentennial quarter was tied to the Houdon ideal by legislation. One of the stipulations of the act breaking the ground for the coin was that the obverse had to be modeled after Houdon's "celebrated bust." Since a perceptive critic has termed the busts, particularly the undraped version in the Boston Athenaeum from the collection of Thomas Jefferson, "unquestionably the finest portrayal of Washington in existence,"[1] a die designer could do little wrong in having Houdon's neoclassic image as his prototype. A sculptor of Flanagan's stature had no difficulty in conforming to these requirements (figs. 189–191).[2] Still, it might be asked whether it was fair to force an ideal portrait of Washington made in 1785 on an artist working in 1932. There is something cold and lifeless about the results. A step backward had been taken from the level of numismatic art reached by A.A. Weinman and H.A. MacNeil in 1916.

Like other artists competing for the commission, Flanagan made a number of experiments in the design. Large plaster or terra-cotta *modelli* in the collection of Stack's show that he considered a right-facing bust, variations on the heraldic eagle of the final design, and other details not part of the coin as struck in 1932 (fig. 192).

The medallic concept of Washington based on the Houdon bust was firmly established in American numismatic art by 1932. A number of semiofficial and private medals of the 19th century had perpetuated the tradition in varying degrees of accuracy, artistry, or individuality. In Washington's lifetime the uniformed bust had predominated, but there had been exceptions, such as the Roman Head cent of 1792, which is neither based on Houdon's bust nor an accurate likeness in its curly-headed, large-nosed nudity. Typical of the classical Roman medals of the middle 19th century exhibiting a variation of Houdon's bust in forceful, personal terms—a hawk-nosed, snap-jawed profile—is the Lovett's of Philadelphia medal "To the Japanese Embassy from Bailey and Co., Jewellers, Philadelphia, 1860" (fig. 193). The high-relief, heavily modeled bust on the obverse, surrounded appropriately enough by a lengthy Latin inscription to GEORGIUS WASHINGTON, is a startling contrast to the routine reverse, an inscription in a wreath. This reverse has been influenced by the comparable arrangement of elements on Longacre's Flying Eagle design of 1856, the reverse then coming into general circulation on the Indian Head cents of 1859 and later (figs. 36 and 56). The curve and counter-curve of the lettering anticipate the Gothic reverse of the two-cent piece, first coined in 1864 (figs. 65 and 66).

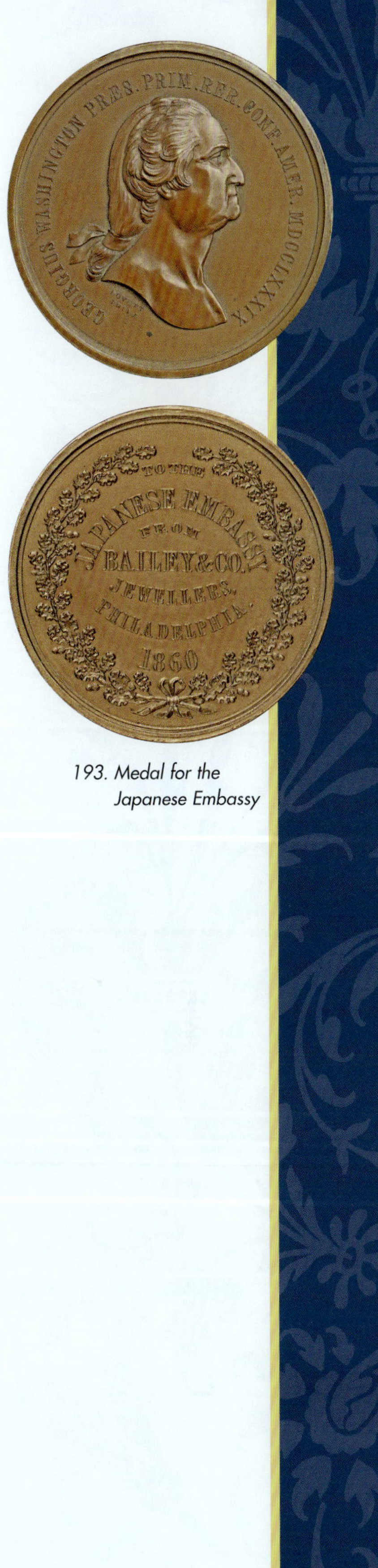

193. Medal for the Japanese Embassy

In connection with a medal for the centennial of Washington's inauguration, April 30, 1789, it was reported in the *American Journal of Numismatics:* "The portrait is by the late C.C. Wright, and though never before published, it is said to be his finest work, and the best reproduction on a medal of the original bust by Houdon."[3] The official Centennial Anniversary medal was designed by George T. Morgan, and the obverse, showing the unclothed bust by Houdon, was employed again in 1897 to commemorate the new Washington Monument in Fairmount Park, Philadelphia.

Flanagan's Houdonesque obverse started a trend in likenesses of the founding fathers on U.S. regular coinage. Houdon's bust of Thomas Jefferson in modern dress was to form the basis for the obverse of Felix Schlag's nickel, which was first coined in 1938 (figs. 227 and 228). John R. Sinnock, chief engraver of the Mint, did not live to see his half dollar go into circulation in 1948, but the clean-cut Romanism of the obverse, with its heavy lettering and neutral space, centers around Houdon's bust of Benjamin Franklin in modern costume (figs. 231 and 232). Flanagan had introduced this form of obverse on his quarter dollar.

All this comment about relationships with Houdon busts might suggest disappointment in the designs put into circulation in 1932, 1938, and 1948. This is partly true. Flanagan's coin had the virtue of novelty, and Houdon's sculptures fit seductively well in the framework of a coin. In the quarter, and indeed in the nickel and half dollar, the disappointment lies in the reverse. Flanagan's bird is a stiff bit of heraldry amid too large a wreath and too much or too large lettering. Given the way the bird's wings droop in a heavy, openwork M, it is hard to see how else he could have arranged the composition. Therefore, it is perhaps passable as a document of official art on the eve of the Roosevelt era. The coin remained in production until 1998 (with the exception of 1975 and 1976, when the Bicentennial reverse was used), far longer than its quality merited, especially weighed against the short span of the MacNeil Standing Liberty quarter dollar. Seen in quantity, arranged in rows by date and mintmark, these quarters are among the

194. L.G. Fraser, models for the 1932 quarter dollar

dullest U.S. coins. A more vibrant work of art could have been expected from a sculptor who had been a pupil of Saint-Gaudens and whose medals were so stimulating. Judged by the level of numismatic art in the generation following 1946, however, Flanagan's Washington quarter was a pioneering success.

Laura Gardin Fraser

195. L.G. Fraser, Bicentennial medal for Washington

The disappointment of the Washington quarter results from the fact that nearly everyone except Secretary of the Treasury Andrew Mellon preferred the designs and models submitted by Laura Gardin Fraser. Through her commemorative half dollars Fraser had already earned her place beside her husband as a leading designer of coins. She was clearly the winner of the competition for the medal, and the Commission of Fine Arts was firm in its repeated selection of her finished plastic models for the quarter dollar (fig. 194). Flanagan's similar models appear to have been chosen solely by Andrew Mellon and confirmed by his successor, Ogden L. Mills.[4]

Laura Gardin Fraser's models combine the firm-jawed vigor of Houdon's head and truncated neck with an eagle marked by many overlapping planes of rough feathers. Proud and pleasing in profile and texture, the Fraser eagle contrasts mightily with the flaccid grace of Flanagan's bird. The traditional branch and arrows in the claws are novel in the way they support the mighty, almost scaly legs. The feathers on the outsides or ends of the wings are spaced apart and curved like many gloved fingers. The effect pleases. On the medal selected for the Washington bicentennial this detail is made too regular, the prodding digits turning into the ratchets of a flywheel (fig. 195). One of the main objections to Flanagan's obverse was the distortion of Houdon's hair into fussy whirlpools around the ears. Combined with a weak modeling of bone and muscle, this reduces the strong facial character of the first president to a glossy, metallic image. The Fraser portrait brings out areas of simple strength in the hair. The slight upward, tilted view of the head heightens the power of the jaw. In short, the essence of Washington is comprehensible at a glance.

Inferior to both Fraser's creation and Flanagan's accepted design is a pair of models now in the possession of Stack's (fig. 192). Whether the work of Flanagan, as supposed, or of an also-ran in the quarter design contest (which included over 100 models from some 98 competitors), this obverse and reverse are weaker than Fraser's conception and more cluttered than the design adopted. A large, truncated head has been used, but hair and modeling are indecisive, and the lettering, especially of the date, is too large. What the eagle on the reverse has in the way of boldness is negated by the overemphasis on spread wings, large lettering, and the motto in a starry circle. There is no question that these models have less to offer than the work of either Laura Gardin Fraser or John Flanagan, as judged by the models chosen. They have neither the unusual dramatic strength of the former nor the calm, if somewhat timid and pedestrian, clarity of the latter.

Perhaps as compensation for having been denied the commission for the Washington Bicentennial coin, Fraser was confirmed in the award of the medal authorized by Congress for the same occasion, which was long one of the list medals sold at the Philadelphia Mint (fig. 195). Although reflecting the sleek machine processes in this department of the Mint, the obverse recalls the Renaissance organization and style of the Martiny and Saint-Gaudens medal commemorating the centennial of Washington's inauguration (fig. 108). The half-figure bust seems to be taken from Houdon's full statue for the Virginia legislature, a refreshing contrast to the truncated heads proposed for the quarter dollar. Washington's coat of arms, often asserted on 19th-century Washington medals as being the basis for the American flag, is set below a signature imitated from the Saint-Gaudens medal of 1889. The reverse anticipates the smooth classicism of war memorials and official medals in the 1930s, a slick, bland, forceless manner and technique seen on presidential medals for Truman, Kennedy, Johnson, and Eisenhower, especially on the reverse of the medal for the latter's first term (fig. 236). Fraser's is one of the strongest of these compositions. All the traditional iconographic props are there. The eagle, a modern bird with feathers like the gears of a large machine, stands on the bundle of lictors' rods. These fasces serve as a columnar setting for Liberty with her spiked crown, torch, and sheathed sword.

The tradition established by Hermon MacNeil's armed Liberty on the 1916 quarter dollar survives here. Laura Gardin Fraser's goddess wears the aegis of Athena, and a large shield, like those carried by medieval knights rather than Greek heroes, hangs across her back. No strap, no means of support, is visible. Like the Hellenistic Victory of Samothrace in the Louvre, Liberty appears to stand on the foredeck of a galley, the prow curving in high relief outward toward the viewer. A firmament of 13 stars tops the giant V of the ensemble. The inscription, with its lettering of modern and Renaissance sizes, comes from the Liberty Bell and will be seen again in 1948, in miniature, on the reverse of the Franklin half dollar (fig. 232).

196. L.G. Fraser, American Numismatic Society Centennial medal

In 1958 Laura Gardin Fraser added new dimensions to her distinguished career by designing the centennial medal of the American Numismatic Society (fig. 196). The subject seems to be coin production in ancient Greece, on Aegina or in Cyzicus (obverse) and at Corinth (reverse). Visual understanding and creative intention often differ, however, and perhaps the message of this medal is best left to the artist's own words as recorded in the brochure accompanying the issue.

> The Science of Numismatics engages the imagination of the artist who creates a design in sculptured form, and the artisan who reproduces that model in permanent metal.
>
> When Nature petrified the first forms of animal and plant life, Nature made the first dies. The obverse of the American Numismatic Society Centennial Medal shows the potential archaeologist, who, having broken a stone asunder, discovers a petrified animal form in one half and in the other a perfect impression of it, or the die.
>
> Since tablets, coins and medals constitute the authority for historical data and our earliest civilizations expressed themselves in terms of their particular mythologies, on the reverse of the medal I used the Pegasus as a symbol of the arts, to indicate as in a vision, that numismatics was a science from the era of the Pegasus to the geo-physical year of the harnessing of the atom.
>
> To the fore of this vision are the artisans who are in the act of forging a medal, using such tools as are the basis of modern medal making.[5]

The "potential archaeologist" is an ill-proportioned, square-faced brute with little else besides a stone-headed mallet and a pair of excellent Hellenistic Greek or Roman sandals. His discovery of petrified form seems to lead to the twin mountains of muscle bending over their great anvil and huge casting-type dies on the reverse. The fire in the foreground looks like a little clump of acanthus shrubbery. Pegasus is rather splendid, and, since the artist has explained his presence, there is no need to protract the misapprehension about the sea or land turtles of Aegina or the tunnies of Cyzicus on the obverse and the staters of the Isthmian emporium on the side opposite.

Too much has been tried on this medal. The men are too anatomical, and the symbolism too obscure. Laura Gardin Fraser was more successful producing simple themes or patriotic designs, new variations of the standard U.S. iconographic repertory. Her ill-fated quarter dollar of 1932 showed the heights to which she could rise. In 1999, her quarter design was finally struck, as a commemorative $5 gold piece marking the bicentennial of Washington's death (see chap. XI).

Commemorative Half Dollars, 1934 to 1938

Once the minting of commemorative coins was resumed, no less than 27 different types were produced over a span of five years. The artists were as varied as those who designed such coins before the Depression, although no engravers connected with the Mint participated to the extent of signing any of the dies. In general the level of participation was lower than in the 1920s, most of the leading medalists having already designed either a regular issue or a commemorative coin. There are more amateur designs among the products of the Roosevelt administration, coins sketched out by members of historical societies or graduate students in local art schools and finished by sculptors or medalists of no exceptional fame. Still, some of the old names such as Robert Aitken and Chester Beach appear, and sculptors of prime stature, such as Augustus Lukeman, turn their hands to the medium of die plaster and tempered steel.

The worst coins look like badges for local societies; the best rise to the traditions of Augustus Saint-Gaudens. In the former category is the York County, Maine, Tercentenary half dollar; in the latter, the Connecticut Tercentenary half dollar with a splendid eagle on the obverse and a view of the Charter Oak on the reverse. The gamut of types is predictable. Several critics have commented on the run of pioneers, ships, animals, maps, excerpts from local seals, and views of buildings or limited areas. Paintings and statues are adapted to these coins. Imaginary figures denote ideals or specific classes of people, such as soldiers of the Union and Confederate armies. Living senators appear, continuing the precedent set by having President Calvin Coolidge grace the 1926 coin commemorating the sesquicentennial of independence. Stephen Foster, writer of songs, and P.T. Barnum, apostle of showmanship, occupy the obverses of coins honoring the cities with which they were associated. A cow's head in full frontal view forms one obverse—because no portrait of the Spanish explorer Cabeza de Vaca could be found!

Since these half dollars are as available as their predecessors in the general literature on U.S. and commemorative coins, a few remarks on the artistry of each should suffice. The potential of the series in the decade before the Second World War was undoubtedly realized as fully as possible, given modern coining techniques and requirements, given the national and local iconographic demands of each coin, and given the general taste of many groups involved in all aspects of producing these contributions to America's official numismatic art. The commemorative half dollars of the Roosevelt era form an impressive series, and they confirm that the aesthetic tragedy of U.S. coinage lies in lack of varied designs rather than the types of coins produced. It is easy to criticize but hard to rival. As was once said about Greek art, it is possible to do differently, not better.

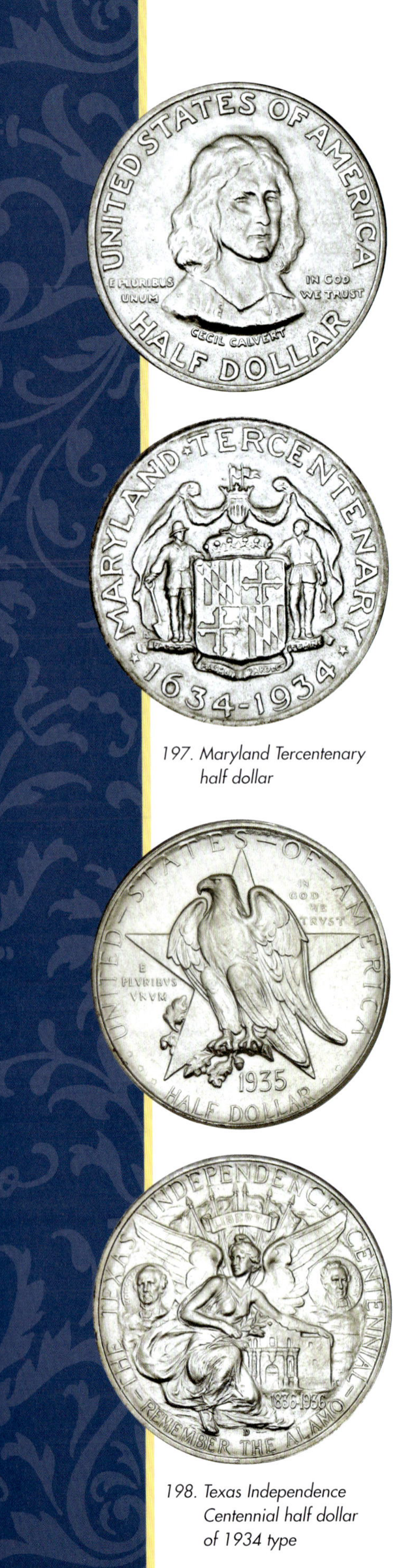

197. Maryland Tercentenary half dollar

198. Texas Independence Centennial half dollar of 1934 type

Maryland Tercentenary

Cecil Calvert's three-quarters-facing bust and the arms of Maryland on the Maryland Tercentenary coin of 1934 add up to a dull design, which looks more like an advertising medal than a commemorative half dollar. Hans Schuler's bust of Lord Baltimore is a conventional rendering of a man of Charles I's reign, and the state's coat of arms on the reverse is standard fare in so many numismatic, and related, efforts (fig. 197). The traditional Renaissance format is maintained on the obverse, save for the facing bust, which was so often taken for good design by mediocre medalists in the next two decades. The reverse could almost be a policeman's badge set to the appropriate tondo and lettering.

Texas Independence Centennial

Pompeo Coppini, the designer of the Texas Independence Centennial half dollar of 1934 (fig. 198), was born in Italy in 1870 and achieved distinction as the sculptor of a number of public monuments in Texas. His Texas War Memorial, a standing soldier with tin helmet, belted breechclout, giant sword, and scaly or feathery shield, is probably as low as one can sink on the index of monumental sculptures that fuse contemporary iconography with Hellenistic Greek sculptural proportions and uncertain allegory (fig. 199). On the other hand, Coppini's commemorative half dollar is the classic triumph of how much can be successfully crowded onto a coin. The eagle is imaginative and majestic against the lone star. Victory, wearing the conventional cap of Liberty and crouching with the Alamo amid inscribed tondo busts of Sam Houston and Stephen Austin, is a tour de force of motion, drapery, and attributes worthy of the masterful silver denarii of the last decades of the Roman Republic. The modeling, spacing, and lettering are clear and lively, while maintaining all the minute precision necessary to fit everything onto the field. This coin has one of the greatest of the designs in the commemorative series, by an artist not otherwise widely associated with coins or even medals.

199. Coppini, Texas War Memorial

Daniel Boone Bicentennial

A sculptor of pediments and Civil War memorials, Henry Augustus Lukeman, born in 1872, was a specialist in equestrian monuments who left the horses to others to carry out. F.G.R. Roth was one of his collaborators, and together they created the Washington on horseback that stands in front of the general's headquarters at Morristown, New Jersey. Lukeman was the sculptor who succeeded Gutzon Borglum at the ill-fated, controversial Stone Mountain memorial in Georgia. According to

200. Daniel Boone Bicentennial half dollar of 1934 type

201. Connecticut Tercentenary half dollar

Morey, "His merit lies in [an] ability to give mass and form to drapery and to keep his faces and realistic allusions sufficiently out of focus. He has a monumental instinct, but an insufficient mastery of technique makes the handling of detail troublesome to him."[6]

Daniel Boone had enjoyed a tenuous connection with American numismatic art long before the appearance of the 1934 Boone Bicentennial half dollars. In 1834 James B. Longacre published in his *National Portrait Gallery* an engraving of Boone after Chester Harding's portrait. This contributed to the iconography of the great frontiersman, but Lukeman's bold portrayal owes as much to Italian Renaissance heads of Julius Caesar as it does to life. The large, broad head and too-muscular neck would have better served a Roman emperor such as Galba or Domitian than the man whose name is associated with frontier warfare and development in Kentucky. In a sense this is a strong, valid obverse, for the head dominates the lettering, and there is no resort to secondary inscriptions on either side for balance (the Pisanello formula). The reverse presents the usual frontier confrontation of buckskinned pioneer and Indian chief, but the figures are large and stand out well in their landscape setting (fig. 200). Because of its broad, bold concept of figures, this coin ranks as one of America's best artistic endeavors. Lukeman should have pursued his career as a designer of dies.

Connecticut Tercentenary

The Wadsworth Atheneum in Hartford exhibits a painting, *The Charter Oak,* created by Charles De Wolf Brownell (1822–1901) in 1857. When Henry G. Kreis designed the commemorative half dollar for the Connecticut tercentenary of 1935 as part of the Public Works Administration program for the arts, he used the great oak (which was blown down in 1856) as a most effective composition on the obverse, and a massive eagle, thrusting like a rocket, on the reverse (fig. 201). Pleased no doubt with the novelty of this mighty bird, the following year Kreis reversed it and tilted the head upward and the tips of the wings down to create the eagle on the reverse of Bridgeport's centennial half dollar in 1936 (fig. 213). All elements of the Connecticut Tercentenary coin blend superbly, the mottoes and aphorisms disappearing amid the leafy clusters on the obverse and the balance of the opposite side as successful as the eagle of 1907. Kreis inherited Saint-Gaudens's feeling for relief, space, lettering, surfaces, and edging. He was to continue the sharp, elongated, angular style of his eagles into the next decade, when he produced a startling medal of the Five Wise and Five Foolish Virgins for the 36th issue of the Society of Medalists.

Arkansas Centennial

202. Arkansas Centennial half dollar of 1935 type

203. Arkansas Centennial half dollar, Robinson obverse

The vapid, dated, and confused coin that marked the Arkansas centennial in 1935 is an unfortunate example in the commemorative series of collaboration between an artist who knew little if anything about die design and an amateur full of notions about local patriotism and local lore (fig. 202). The sculptor was Edward Everett Burr of Chicago, and the model was prepared by Emily Bates of Arkansas. Other such combinations of local artistic or antiquarian zeal and quasi-professional modeling or finishing will be shown to have been even more unfortunate, in the instances of the half dollars for the Old Spanish Trail and the Wisconsin territorial centennial (figs. 206 and 209).

The Arkansas Centennial coin is one of the last examples to use the time-honored motifs of Liberty and a Native American in combination. In addition, with two exceptions in the commemorative series, this coin marks a farewell to the artistic concepts of the Indian and Liberty on U.S. coins. (A head of an Indian appears on the obverse of the coin for the Long Island tercentenary, and a standing Liberty is the centerpiece of the fifty-cent piece for the Lynchburg, Virginia, sesquicentennial.) On the Arkansas coin the Indian's head is jugate to the left with that of Liberty. Liberty resembles a chinless society girl of the 1920s, and the Indian is either a weak death mask or a man in a trance. This combination and its formless, pseudomodern style are flaccid and senseless, and Liberty looks like a contemporary department store model. The obverse is a jumble of spikes, lines, and curves; the state symbolism is so obscure as to be pointless. The rising sun motif forms the excuse for a background. Adolph A. Weinman, following Roty, had demonstrated all that needed to be done with this technique of filling the composition, on his regular-issue half dollar of 1916 (fig. 160).

As in the Boone half dollar, a thick rim affords a valid transition between edge and field. Otherwise, in the Arkansas Centennial half dollar the only decent feature of obverse or reverse is the eagle facing with head lowered. This bird rises to the level of some of the carved heraldry of the 19th century.

In 1936 a new design was prepared to replace the jugate busts of Liberty and the Indian, and this new face was termed the obverse (fig. 203). The designer of this new set of dies was Henry G. Kreis, whose success with the half dollar for the Connecticut tercentenary has been discussed and who was also in this year to produce a visually memorable commemorative coin for the Bridgeport centennial. It is of small matter whether or not Joseph T. Robinson, Senate majority leader, was well known beyond his native Arkansas. The large bust in business dress is a masterpiece of photographic naturalism such as has seldom been seen before or since on any modern coin. This is the very summation of the modern senator, and this businesslike apotheosis of a local hero turned what had been an artistically miserable coin into a passable aesthetic commodity.

204. Hudson Sesquicentennial half dollar

Hudson, New York, Sesquicentennial

Chester Beach, encountered early in the 1920s as both a medalist and a designer of coins, reappears as an artist in the series of commemorative half dollars. In the Hudson Sesquicentennial piece of 1935 he has combined the lettering of his Monroe Doctrine Centennial coin with the plasticity of his Lexington-Concord half dollar. The ship motif occurs again, logically, as the *Half Moon* of Henry Hudson sails toward the right front, across the obverse. The ship, its full set of sails, and the visual pun of a half moon are well enough spaced out in the field, with considerable success, but the word HUDSON squashed beneath the waves is unnecessary since the full title, CITY OF HUDSON, dominates the reverse. This reverse is taken up with the city's unusual seal: Neptune rides backward on a spouting whale, and a mermaid blows a conch shell (fig. 204). While the ship is straightforward fare for commemorative half dollars, the composition on the opposite side is a charming throwback to colonial days and, in American numismatics, to the quasi-federal and state coins of the period 1780 to 1792. One of the most pleasing features of this reverse design is the motto that crosses as upper enframement of the composition, to form a baroque ribbon.

As a total statement, although scarcely novel or exciting, this coin avoids some of the mannerisms of Chester Beach's medallic and numismatic art of the 1920s, flat and busy pseudoclassical figures expressing empty allegory. The Hudson Sesquicentennial half dollar is one of the coins in this series that confers a pan-American dignity on a subject really of moment only to a limited audience. Few of the commemorative coins in the group honoring cities or local organizations were both so unpretentious and so full of historical atmosphere, without resorting to clichés such as the eagle, the Indian, or Liberty and obscurities, such as local animals amid local trees. The baroque motto above Neptune and his group makes it evident that this subject, appealing and amusing in itself, appears here because it is the singular characteristic of the City of Hudson on the river of the same name.

Perhaps underrated in discussions of commemorative coins in the 1910s, Chester Beach did receive the accolade of B.G. Proske. Referring to the sculpture for Brookgreen Gardens in South Carolina, this distinguished scholar of the Hispanic Society called Beach "[o]ne of the few American sculptors to adopt Rodin's vibrating surfaces throughout his work."[7] He is known for a very famous motif, seen in one form or another by almost every American. In his work for the American Telephone and Telegraph Company, Beach not only designed *Service to the Nation,* described by Proske as "a powerful male figure with coils of wire behind the head, and above it a globe supported by personifications of War and Peace,"[8] but also created the *Flying Mercury* in coils of cable that stood atop the telephone building in New York and which for years, together with the bell, was the symbol of the telephone empire. Beach was, therefore, a versatile sculptor who could fashion a large-scale group of lasting import, but could also turn his hand with almost equal skill to the exacting demands of modern, machine-made coins.

205. California-Pacific half dollar

California-Pacific International Exposition

After an absence of 14 years, Robert I. Aitken returned to the field of U.S. coins to design one of the most powerful uses of the facing figure in American numismatic art. Aitken, whom Morey had termed an eclectic and "a sculptor of accomplished technique, but subject to the model or manner of the moment,"[9] had spent the intervening years producing monumental geographic personifications, war memorials, and pediments, perhaps the grandest being that for the stringently Roman classical Supreme Court Building in Washington. All this work suited Aitken well in his conversion of the seated Minerva on the seal of the state of California into the obverse of the half dollar dated 1936 (fig. 205). Comparable to this figure but on a monumental scale is his *Zeus* at Brookgreen Gardens, a composition having the withdrawn dignity and gravitas of a great Roman pedimental figure.

On the coin the principal characters of the state seal are shown in frontal view instead of in profile. Minerva (Athena), iconographically closer to the Roman type of Dea Roma, is seated with a spear in her raised right hand, a shield in her lowered left. The latter bears the cry that only someone versed in the classics could have mouthed, EUREKA, as well as a gorgoneion modeled after the Rondanini Medusa in the collection of ancient sculpture at Munich. A bear and an overflowing cornucopia flank the goddess. The background is unobtrusive but interesting, with its ship, miner, and mountains. The seated goddess is not overly heavy, despite the display of armor and attributes. The required lettering confirms the strength and balance of the total visual experience. Some have termed the peculiarly monogrammatic form of the artist's signature "stylish"; Gilroy Roberts borrowed the idea for the obverse of the Kennedy half dollar in 1964 (fig. 240).

The reverse of the California-Pacific half dollar, with its vista of buildings connected with the exposition, is good enough for what it pretends to show, having the relieving feature of a Gothic or Spanish colonial frame behind and the tower rising atop the lettering. On both sides the use of a heavy rim balances the subtle, imaginative, and clearly defined planes of modeling. The goddess of the obverse, it might be remembered, has a long, worthy history in monumental sculpture and numismatic art, going back to the seated figures of Dea Roma or Roma Aeterna on Roman imperial coinage from the reign of Nero (54–68) through the house of Constantine in the fourth century A.D. An immediate major parallel, of the late 19th century, is the seated Italia by Zanetti on the monument to the Italian statesman Cavour in the square of the same name in Rome.

206. Old Spanish Trail half dollar

Old Spanish Trail

The half dollar of 1935 known as the Old Spanish Trail can safely be designated the ugliest commemorative coin ever produced by a U.S. mint. It may be the strongest contestant for the title of least attractive American coin manufactured under official auspices between 1793 and the mid-20th century. (A potential rival might be the $3 gold piece of the middle 19th century or the silver three-cent piece, but the latter has the redeeming feature of delicate workmanship, and the former is touched by quaintness, like a ship's figurehead or a cigar-store Indian.) The designer of the Old Spanish Trail half dollar was L.W. Hoffecker, the numismatist who conceived and promoted the issue. The workmanship—the composition, that is—certainly smacks of such amateurishness. Technically the coin is passable but dull, because Hoffecker's ideas were translated into plaster models by El Paso sculptor Edmund J. Senn.

On the obverse, the use of a cow's head to represent a man of that name (Álvar Núñez Cabeza de Vaca) is like using a field of roses in place of a portrait of Roosevelt on the dime. The reverse, with its blooming yucca tree on a map of one explorer's wandering, is neither attractive nor readily understandable (fig. 206). Suitable enough for a private medal, the design is too obscure for a U.S. coin. In all fairness, it has had its champions. Arlie Slabaugh has written: "While the design is somewhat unorthodox compared to most commemoratives, it does what it was intended to do: tells the story and then stops, leaving a generally pleasing and uncluttered design."[10] The question is whether the story is worth telling on a U.S. half dollar.

Providence, Rhode Island, Tercentenary

This coin is a classic of the group that relies on state or city badges to convey their messages. Struck in 1936, it commemorated the 300th anniversary of Roger Williams's arrival. The obverse copies the arms of the city of Providence, while the reverse is based on the emblem of the state of Rhode Island (fig. 207). "Roger Williams in his canoe looks like Elpenor amid the bulrushes on a Greek vase of about 440 B.C. with a scene of the dialogue of Odysseus in the underworld."[11] The Indian and Williams are blocked out with a childlike charm of conceptualism. The coat of arms is so simple as to defy analysis, or even comment. Both central designs are overwhelmed by the bands of thick, square lettering.

The artists involved were John Howard Benson and Abraham Graham Carey. Slabaugh has noted with his usual perspicacity: "The design appears to resemble stone carving which is not surprising when we consider that the designers were partners in a stone-cutting firm in Newport, Rhode Island."[12] He goes on to point out that Benson was an instructor in lettering at the Rhode Island School of Design and that Carey was a silversmith before joining Benson in the stonecutting firm. Compared with the half dollar for the Old Spanish Trail, this coin rivals it in simplicity but provides a paragon of stylistic unity and meaningful message to those versed in the iconography of Rhode Island. Far from the sophistication of the commemorative half dollars of the 1920s, it can be admired as an amateur production that is to the series what the paintings of Grandma Moses are to the canvases of Andrew Wyeth.

207. Providence Tercentenary half dollar

208. Cleveland half dollar

Cleveland Centennial / Great Lakes Exposition

The half dollar of 1936 that commemorates the centennial of Cleveland, Ohio, manages to combine most of the faults found in the better designs of the 1920s and 1930s. The relief is flat, having the effect of work with a cookie cutter on the obverse and corrosive acid on the reverse. There is too much lettering on both sides. The reverse is almost impossible to fathom at first glance. The bust of Moses Cleaveland can only be described as commonplace, and the view of the Great Lakes, bisected by a large compass, is nothing short of incomprehensible. As in other commemorative half dollars of the day, stars are used as symbols, in this instance for cities bordering on the lakes. Needless to add, though difficult to visualize, the largest star, pierced by the long needle of the compass, is the centennial city (fig. 208).

Maps in outline or in relief do not as a rule make readable, much less artistic, reverses, for they are too small and too diffused. This map of the Great Lakes can be compared with the view of Greece and the islands on the reverse of the silver crown or 30-drachma piece struck in 1963 to honor the five kings of the Glucksborg dynasty in Greece. But the Greek coin states its message with more clarity. Amid stars and compass, the incused areas of the Great Lakes are more spotty than even their topography warrants and are, basically, meaningless combinations of relief planes.

Brenda Putnam, the creator of the Cleveland half dollar, studied at the Museum of Fine Arts School in Boston under Bela L. Pratt and at the Art Students League in New York under James E. Fraser. Thus she was well equipped to design dies for coins, and the orthodox, slightly retrospective quality—the 1920s look—of her coin is explained by the tastes and eras of her teachers. In the early 1920s Brenda Putnam had specialized in statues or busts of children, in the pretty, smiling manner of Renaissance sculptors such as Desiderio and Mino da Fiesole. In 1927, dissatisfied with this sculptural fare, she went off to Florence—hardly the city for one seeking to escape from the trite forms of the middle or late quattrocento. "The result of this interlude is seen in a greater tendency to simplify the composition and the details, although there is no skimping or distorting of natural forms."[13]

Simplification may be a characteristic of the bust of Moses Cleaveland, and skimpy distortion does not enter into the problems of the Great Lakes and their cities. Omission of one or more of the standard mottoes would have given the bust, lakes, compass, and stars greater emphasis and cohesion. Putnam probably did the best she could to suit the required symbolism and texts to the area of a half dollar. The results, however, suggest that she should have studied the contemporary Italian numismatic art of Aurelio Mistruzzi (1880–1960) or Luigi Raffaele Giorgi (1848–1912) and the Roman die designers rather than the simple compositions of the classic Florentines.

209. Wisconsin Territorial Centennial half dollar

Wisconsin Territorial Centennial

Like the Old Spanish Trail half dollar, the coin of 1936 that marks the 100th anniversary of Wisconsin's formation as a territory smacks of amateurism (fig. 209). The models were the work of an art student at the University of Wisconsin, and the finished design was made by Benjamin Hawkins, an artist in New York. This half dollar of the United States is, as a work of art, little more than a high school medal of the dullest variety. As a visual experience, it ranks with some of the worst local-society or small-occasion medals, which have timelessness only in the mediocre level of their art.

The obverse is a historical reference expressed in terms of obscure animal symbolism. The reverse, the Great Seal of the territory of Wisconsin, looks like the illustration on a box of Arm and Hammer baking soda. Nothing inspiring, or even really comprehensible, comes through in the design, which is just a hodgepodge of inscriptions and symbols. The heavy lettering and lumpy relief exude an aura of crudity and unappealing, gauche primitivism. Neither simplicity nor imagination appears in this coin. Why, for instance, need the inscription from the Great Seal be painfully written out on the reverse, even to the spelling out of ANNO DOMINI? Use of *all* the statutory inscriptions on the obverse is more than this trifling little mélange of symbols can bear.

Cincinnati Music Center

At the age of 34 Constance Ortmayer produced the designs for the 1936 coin that honored the Cincinnati Musical Center. She had studied under Josef Müllner in Vienna for five years, and her work of the 1930s seemed to capture the angular elongation of the German expressionist sculptor Wilhelm Lehmbruck. Such qualities are visible in the female with the lyre on the half dollar said to commemorate (without great conviction as to precise date) the 50th anniversary of Cincinnati, Ohio, as a center of music in the United States (fig. 210). Part of Ortmayer's claim to connection with such a coin lay in her Germanic background, similar to that of the musicians who made Cincinnati famous, and in the fact that she was for a time technical adviser in sculpture for the Section of Painting and Sculpture of the Treasury Department.

The details and style of this coin perpetuate the slender lettering and weak figures of the John Sinnock school, as exemplified in the Philadelphia Sesquicentennial half dollar of 1926. Surfaces are glazed or rubbed over, and the coin has a worn look even before it has suffered from any use or circulation. Stephen Foster's bust on the obverse is a distorted or compressed lump, and the "goddess of music" on the reverse has much the appeal of a dancer with cramps or a dying daughter of Niobe in the Hellenistic marble group known from several Roman copies.

Long Island Tercentenary

A well-tried combination of designs—jugate heads and a ship—appears again on the Long Island Tercentenary half dollar of 1936. Medalist Howard Kenneth Weinman, son of Adolph Alexander Weinman, carried out the designs (fig. 211). The Dutch pioneer looks like a character out of Shakespeare (a peasant part), and the Indian could easily play professional football any Sunday afternoon across the United States. Otherwise, beyond these clichés brought about in an effort to modernize traditionally idealized subjects, the ship has a correct amount of simplicity, and the lettering seems to fade into the background in a satisfying fashion.

210. Cincinnati Music Center half dollar

211. Long Island Tercentenary half dollar

212. York County Tercentenary half dollar

York County, Maine, Tercentenary

A number of commemorative coins have been criticized in these pages for the low level of their art, and few have deserved ashes and odium more than this half dollar, commemorating the York County, Maine, tercentenary in 1936. The York County seal on the obverse and the stockade on the reverse—Brown's Garrison at Saco—are uninteresting to anyone outside the most parochial native antiquarian circles. The old device of the sun's rays fills the background above the buildings, and the placing of the conventional mottoes in the inner borders easily wins the grand prize for lack of imagination. The awkward lettering around the outer part of the field on both sides dwarfs what passes for the design (fig. 212).

The total performance is pedestrian to an extreme. Rather than a design for a coin, it is more like a medallion on a bottle of vintage brandy. The artist was Walter H. Rich.

213. Bridgeport Centennial half dollar

Bridgeport, Connecticut, Centennial

Henry G. Kreis's half dollar of 1936 honoring Bridgeport, with P.T. Barnum in large, thoughtful profile and a thrusting eagle of conceptual, metallic style, has been cited as one of the more successful commemorative coins within the broad tradition instituted by Augustus Saint-Gaudens (fig. 213). All the mottoes are crowded, not unartistically, into the lower right field on the reverse, and the resulting freedom has been utilized with wisdom to advertise all that is necessary and no more, in lettering that is suave, sturdy, and arresting in its variations.

The reverse ought to have been a lesson to other designers of commemorative coins with local themes, a fact already demonstrated by Kreis in his Connecticut Tercentenary half dollar. When no good local idea or design seems suitable for a coin, success can result only from resorting to a new interpretation of elements, such as the eagle, used in the coins of the regular series. A coin honoring P.T. Barnum could have featured a lion, an elephant, or a performing bear on the reverse, but this product of the civic enterprise of Bridgeport gains great merit for showing an exciting new form of the national bird.

Lynchburg, Virginia, Sesquicentennial

Charles Keck is the last pupil of Augustus Saint-Gaudens to turn his hand to the U.S. coinage. Born in 1875, he was said to have inherited some of his teacher's realistic and pictorial tendencies. One of his famous works was the solid statue of Father Duffy in Times Square. His Lynchburg, Virginia, Sesquicentennial half dollar of 1936 is a successful but not startling combination of conservative elements (fig. 214). A deep bust of Carter Glass in profile to the left is joined with a very Greco-Roman, actually Greek imperial, frontal Liberty placed before local landmarks on the reverse.

The thin, tall lettering and the large, classically draped Liberty demonstrate that Keck was influenced by the Mint medals and commemorative coins of Charles E. Barber and George T. Morgan from 1892 to 1916—the Columbian, Assay Commission, or Panama-Pacific pieces—rather than by the antithetic designs associated with the innovations of Augustus Saint-Gaudens in 1907. The nearly half-figure bust of Senator Carter Glass also recalls the presidential portraits on Assay Commission, inauguration, and other official medals prepared by the Mint designers early in the century. Not only, then, was the name of Charles Keck a link with the great medallic traditions of Saint-Gaudens early in the 20th century, but his style, as manifest in the Lynchburg Sesquicentennial half dollar, was a recollection of the fashions perpetuated by Barber and Morgan in the same decade.

Morgan's own portrait of Carter Glass, the obverse of a medal designed in 1922 to commemorate the Virginian's term from 1918 to 1920 as secretary of the Treasury, is a more modern presentation, a naturalistic treatment with roughened facial surfaces and a truncated bust in coat, shirt, and necktie (fig. 215). The medallic sources of Keck's style, depth of bust, and thin lettering are best demonstrated by comparison with Barber's Treasury series medal of 1913 in honor of Franklin MacVeagh (fig. 216). Precisely the same type of deep bust with hunched shoulders, round skull, and fragile features was also created by Barber for Woodrow Wilson in the Assay medal of 1914 (fig. 152). Certainly the style is one used by tired old men for portraits of their contemporaries, but perhaps it should be counted a greater gift to the official arts than the unnatural, Prussian portrait of Theodore Roosevelt on the inaugural medal of 1905 designated by Saint-Gaudens as the answer to Barber's efforts and executed by A.A. Weinman after the great sculptor's sketches (fig. 119).

In anticipation of subjects that will conclude the series of commemorative half dollars in the 1950s, it might be mentioned that Charles Keck also did a statue of Booker T. Washington "lifting a drapery from a crouching Negro."[14] This work is at Tuskegee, Alabama.

214. Lynchburg Sesquicentennial half dollar

215. Morgan, medal for Glass

Elgin, Illinois, Centennial

It is difficult to find a more aesthetically satisfying, technically superior commemorative half dollar than the Elgin, Illinois, Centennial of 1936. The subject of both obverse and reverse, the Pioneer Memorial in Elgin, is like the obverse of the Stone Mountain half dollar in 1925: an example of a statue group being used as a coin design by the artist who was also sculptor of the group. Triple use or creation can be said to have been achieved here, because the head of the old pioneer on the obverse is also the head of the man with the rifle at the front of the group on the reverse. The three-dimensionality, as well as the precise detail, of the four figures has been cleverly translated onto the reverse of the coin. The lettering is inconspicuous and, especially on the obverse, nobly spaced out (fig. 217). Its format—the relation of major and minor lettering to the head in profile—is that followed by Gilroy Roberts in the obverse of the Kennedy half dollar of 1964 (fig. 240).

The designer of this half dollar, and also sculptor of the statue, Trygve Rovelstad, has produced one of the major documents of sculptural plasticity and vibrant relief in the series of commemorative coins. His obverse is worthy of a Roman medallion, and his reverse rivals the great neoclassic dies of England or Bavaria in the 19th century. A resident of Elgin, Rovelstad worked steadily over the decades at the production of handsome medals similar in style to his 1936 half dollar. In 1970 he created a medallion of silver dollar size for the Lincoln Heritage Trail Foundation of Champaign, Illinois. The young Lincoln's head appears on the obverse, and the future president on horseback in a rural landscape serves as the theme of the reverse. This medallion was designed to resemble a commemorative coin, and the subject, sacred to Kentucky, Indiana, and Illinois, would have been deemed of sufficient interest in the 1930s to have produced a half dollar. Numerous similar medals, made to be as like coins as the law permitted, were sold by many organizations throughout the United States in the 1960s.

216. Barber, medal for MacVeagh

217. Elgin Centennial half dollar

Albany Charter

Gertrude K. Lathrop, born in 1896 and a student of Solon Borglum, was responsible for this half dollar and for the coin of New Rochelle, New York, issued in 1938. The commemorative piece issued for Albany is a mass of symbolism, relieved by the amusing pose of the beaver and the straightforwardness of the three-figure group on the reverse. The lettering is of the thin type and is, properly, set in a low, unobtrusive key (fig. 218).

Lathrop's specialty was animals; thus a beaver gnaws on a maple branch amid statutory inscriptions on the obverse of this important contribution to American numismatics. They appear, presumably, because the beaver is on the seal of the city and the maple is the New York state tree. The design would then seem to become an allegory of municipal government feeding on the rule of the state!

In order to appreciate the scene on the opposite side, Arlie Slabaugh's description of it must be quoted in full:

> Reverse, Peter Schuyler and Robert Livingston, secretary, taking leave of Governor Thomas Dongan in New York. Schuyler is holding the charter. All are dressed in the style of 1686 when the charter for the city was signed by the Governor. Above the group, an eagle with outstretched wings, with the word LIBERTY in minute letters immediately above the eagle. A small pine tree appears behind Governor Dongan at left, which, with the pine cones at lower sides between lettering, and the maple keys (which contain the seeds) in a similar position on the obverse, represent the growth and fertility of the city.[15]

Enough said! That the coin as a whole has considerable appeal can be counted as a credit to the good training and innate taste of the artist, who was able to work in all these allusions to local aspirations and a bygone event with modest, positive precision. The tiny LIBERTY and the miniscule eagle spreading its wings over the three colonial officials are doubtless concessions to federal iconographic tradition. The bird's posture recalls similar compositions, such as the eagle of Zeus or Nike on coins struck under the auspices of imperial Rome.

218. Albany half dollar

219. San Francisco–Oakland Bay Bridge half dollar

San Francisco–Oakland Bay Bridge Opening

Some commemorative half dollars wrestle with the problem of portraying animals, and others essay panoramic landscapes or views of historic sites. None tries animals or vistas on a grander scale on one coin than Jacques Schnier's 1936 coin for California's giant new bridge (fig. 219). Everything is carried out in low relief, with strong outlines and an exceptionally dramatic poising of the bridge in the picture plane. The lettering is solid, but so is California's grizzly bear. The temptation to show comprehensive views of harbors on coins has existed ever since Nero adorned a sestertius with Rome's basin at Ostia or Trajan portrayed the inner port of the same complex. Schnier's grand view from San Francisco to Berkeley is comparable to geography on coins and medals of the 16th or 17th centuries, Medici memorials to the harbor installations at Leghorn or

220. Columbia Sesquicentennial half dollar

221. Delaware Tercentenary half dollar

papal documentation of the enlarged walls of Rome. Contrast the sweep of the Bay Bridge with the cramped distortions of the Aswan Dam area on a crown of Egypt struck in 1964.

In style and in scope this coin departs radically from the dull average of commemorative half dollars honoring municipal impulses. In being so bold it deserves praise for the aesthetic excitement it generates and its artistic success. The bear is a poignant combination of furry power and animal, specifically ursine, sympathies.

Columbia, South Carolina, Sesquicentennial

A. Wolfe Davidson has provided a half dollar of the emblematic type in 1936 to commemorate the sesquicentennial of the founding of Columbia, South Carolina. The coin presents a weak combination of allegorical obverse and symbolic reverse, with disparate lettering, cramped on one side and spread out irregularly on the other (fig. 220). The obverse, Justice flanked by the two State House buildings, is minutely diffused and badly proportioned for the area of the tondo. On this side the inscription says too much. The reverse of palmetto tree, 13 stars, oak branch, and mottoes stuffed in between is boring; it recalls the 19th-century primitivism of a Spanish colonial or newly independent South American country's large denominations in silver, but lacks the spontaneity of those rugged pieces of eight. The Columbia half dollar, of course, lacks the rough feeling of work in a screw press evoked by these coins.

Delaware Tercentenary

Carl L. Schmitz produced the design for the Delaware Tercentenary half dollar in 1936 as the result of a competition. The rivalry must have run the gamut of amateurism. The obverse again is taken up with a ship motif, this time a straightforward, and by now orthodox, view of one of the ships that brought Swedes to the New World in 1638. The reverse demonstrates the convention of a Scandinavian building, a profile view of Old Swedes Church (fig. 221). Above, the sun's rays pour down from puffs of cigar-smoke clouds, like the hand of God in a Byzantine ikon. The same ship, in the same fashion, graces the reverse of the Swedish two-kronor piece struck for the occasion.

Considering that two standard, even popular, and potentially difficult motifs are used, the design comes off with boldness and simplicity. Ships and architecture can offer more pitfalls than they do joys, but Schmitz, wisely, has presented plain solids and solid, yet unusual, lettering. Even the triad of standard mottoes is apportioned to both sides, to their exergues, in such a manner as to avoid irritation. Although offering nothing new, this coin speaks forcefully amid its contemporaries.

Battle of Gettysburg

The 1930s were, supposedly, years of peace and dedication to peaceful pursuits. Authorizations for new commemorative coins were terminated before the shadow of military events in Europe began to fall on America. Because of American desire to avoid art of a military nature and to exclude all recent events from the commemorative coinage, save expositions and an occasional amazing construction such as the Bay Bridge, few U.S. commemorative half dollars of this period are military in theme, and the exceptions all honor ideas or events in the Civil War. The Revolutionary War is hinted at in the Lexington-Concord and Vermont coins, but the Spanish-American War and the First World War were too recent to win places in the repertory of the 1920s or 1930s.

In the half dollar of 1936 honoring the 75th anniversary of the Battle of Gettysburg, Frank Vittor can be praised for good, controlled use of space on obverse and reverse. Jugate busts of a Union and a Confederate soldier present convincing types, timeless in advancing age, that avoid the modern triteness of Howard K. Weinman's early Dutch settler and Indian on the commemorative coin for Long Island. A double-axed fasces, no doubt the influence of the monumental panel on some war memorial, divides the Union and Confederate shields on the reverse. Oak and laurel sprays of peace and war give a vibrant bedding for these shields (fig. 222). Fasces, shields, and wreaths such as these were a stock-in-trade of monuments commissioned by the U.S. government in the 1930s.

The relief of the reverse and the sculptural variations in busts, rim, and lettering on the obverse are sufficiently resonant and more than adequately pitched in directness and subtlety of conception. In many respects this coin is one of the most "American" of our commemorative creations, manifesting the finest of the new government, or "post office," art of the Roosevelt era.

222. Gettysburg half dollar

223. Norfolk Bicentennial half dollar

Norfolk, Virginia, Bicentennial

A low point in coin design can be illustrated in the Norfolk, Virginia, Bicentennial half dollar issued in 1937 and dated 1936 (fig. 223). Skill in spacing the letters, in casting the surfaces, and in modeling the high relief

224. Roanoke Island half dollar

225. Antietam half dollar

saves much of the composition. Still, the commemoration of Norfolk's various anniversaries is a document of epigraphy rather than figural art. A small ship, a plow, and three sheaves of wheat, making up the city seal and providing a full repertory in themselves, are surrounded by too much inscription. To all this has been added the primary designation of commemoration. On the reverse is another special inscription giving more commemorative statistics, plus all three required words and mottoes. The Royal Mace of Norfolk forms the vertical accent, and the statutory inscriptions are packed in to the lower left and right of its handle.

It took a family team, like the Frasers, to produce this coin, with both William Marks Simpson and his wife, Marjorie Emory Simpson, signing the reverse. The coin gives ample evidence that two heads need not be better than one.

Roanoke Island 350th Anniversary

William Marks Simpson, codesigner of the coin for Norfolk's bicentennial, continued his penchant for too much lettering surrounding early American themes. The disparate scale of the lettering on the Roanoke Island, North Carolina, half dollar of 1937, all of which is really too large, sits uneasily on obverse and reverse. Sir Walter Raleigh resembles the movie actor Errol Flynn, who was specializing in historical films at the time Simpson was creating this coin. The frozen, mannered statue of Virginia Dare in the arms of Ellinor Dare, all set on a pedestal on the reverse, is a purely 20th-century neoclassic concept of motherhood, flapping and nobly sentimental even in miniature (fig. 224). It looks like low-relief concepts of Leto, carrying the infants Apollo and Artemis, on Greek imperial coins of Caria in the third century A.D., and ultimately like the Greco-Roman statue of the fleeing daughter of Niobe in the Vatican Museum.

The two little ships on the reverse are as disturbing as, and much less necessary than, the tiny eagle added by Gilroy Roberts to the reverse of John R. Sinnock's Franklin half dollar in 1948. In praise of this coin, it is necessary to note its unusual flavor, which differs somewhat from the usual iconography of founder and early settler commemorative half dollars.

Battle of Antietam

The jugate busts of Generals George B. McClellan and Robert E. Lee are well defined, and Burnside Bridge over Antietam Creek is one of the most relaxed, natural landscapes to grace any commemorative coin (fig. 225). The multitude of inscriptions on the Battle of Antietam issue of

1937 avoid most of the faults exhibited in the two other half dollars, just described, by the same artist. Still, there are too many words, perhaps forced by a desire to spell out all names, titles, and facts, plus inclusion of all the statutory legends. This results in an unnecessary sense of spidery activity across the surfaces of both sides.

There is nothing original in these designs, but a quality of painterly impressionism in handling portraits and landscape makes the coin a satisfying experience, pleasant to contemplate.

226. New Rochelle half dollar

New Rochelle, New York, 250th Anniversary

Gertrude K. Lathrop was described earlier as an artist more at home with animals than humans. She was said to excel in the creation of baby animals. "Fondly amused by the oddities of pets, she has portrayed a Pekingese and an Abyssinian guinea pig. From curly fur and smooth features she extracts lilting line and sweeping contours, dashingly modeled."[16] Excellent credentials for an artist who produced the last half dollar in the boom of commemorative coins before the Second World War!

The issue in question, honoring New Rochelle, New York, in 1938, is a simple, bold, and absolutely tasteless coin. It tries an original obverse and the usual city badge on the reverse (fig. 226). It is profitable, no doubt, to know that John Pell received a fatted calf annually for the lands now embraced by the city, and aestheticians demanding bovine fidelity can take comfort in the fact, noted by Arlie Slabaugh, that "the calf used as a model came from the farm of Parker Corning, New York Representative in Congress at the time."[17]

It is small wonder that, on seeing a coin such as this, President Franklin Roosevelt urged a moratorium on their issue. More distressing is the fact that the accumulated prejudice against commemorative half dollars mounted to such levels that, 25 years later, the centennial of the Civil War could sweep past without the appearance of a single commemorative coin. Fatted calves and gnawing beavers make clever fare in the artistry of American coinage, but events from the raid at Harper's Ferry to the shot that shook the nation in Ford's Theater demand the dignity of commemoration that only a coin can give. Postage stamps are no substitute; they are like writing in the sand. A nation without an artistic, imaginative, and varied coinage of significance is impoverished beyond precise description.

A Quarter Century of Coins and Medals

Numismatics in the United States between 1938 and 1970 was singularly devoid of intellectual excitement in the light of what has been said about the numismatic revolution of 1907 to 1921, when artists from outside the Mint executed designs for the coinage. All the coins being struck at the beginning of 1938 have since been changed in some way or another. The Flanagan quarter dollar merely lost its silver in 1965, but the Weinman half dollar was replaced by Sinnock's Franklin design in 1948, by the silver Kennedy in 1964, and by the partly silver half dollar of 1965 and later. The dime was redesigned by Sinnock to create the Roosevelt memorial in 1946, and the cent received Frank Gasparro's architectural reverse in 1959, a revitalized obverse 10 years later. The first coin to be considered, the nickel five-cent piece, has suffered metallic and aesthetic modifications since its creation in 1938. Medals of these 30-odd years were even less exciting, contributing very little that had not already been conceived in this aspect of numismatic art.

The Jefferson Nickel

Despite the success of James Fraser's Buffalo nickel, the urge to change the type after 25 years was natural and laudable. Since Brenner's cent and Flanagan's quarter dollar had pointed the way to portraits in the regular coinage, a presidential face on the nickel was ordained. Midway through Franklin Roosevelt's second term no candidate was more logical than the man claimed as founding patriot of the Democratic Party. Flanagan's quarter had demonstrated the quick, facile success of Houdon profiles translated into die designs. Like George Washington, Thomas Jefferson had sat for Houdon in Paris about 1789, and replicas of the portrait have been in America since the days of David Rittenhouse, first director of the U.S. Mint. The best likeness by Houdon is the marble bust that has been in the Museum of Fine Arts in Boston since 1934, which H.H. Arnason characterized in such thrilling terms (fig. 227). In his vivid *Sculpture by Houdon*, Arnason wrote:

227. Houdon, Thomas Jefferson

228. Jefferson nickel

> The marble *Jefferson* in Boston is a superb interpretation of the third President of the United States. Jefferson is shown in modern dress, his face tilted upward and angled slightly to the right. The hair is dressed in a manner similar to that of Washington, worn rather long at the sides. The eyes are large and cut unusually deep, shadowed under heavy brows in a manner which gives them an exceptional sense of vitality. The lean symmetrical face, with its sharply aquiline nose, compressed lips and jutting chin is the perfect reflection of the intellectual man of affairs that we know Jefferson to have been. It is at the same time a face of great sensitivity and the face of an aristocrat.[1]

Small wonder, therefore, that when Felix Schlag designed the obverse of the Jefferson nickel his interpretation of the third president should emerge as a verbatim transcription of the Boston bust seen from full left profile, even to the wrinkles in the frock coat (fig. 228). Schlag won an award of $1,000 for his obverse and reverse in a competition involving some 390 artists. There is otherwise nothing particularly thrilling about the obverse, but, given the demands of statutory inscriptions, the sculptor has succeeded in creating an experience of balanced letter sizes and date that differs from the obverse laid out by Fraser in 1912 (fig. 148).

The reverse is a disappointment, but evidently this is not Schlag's fault. The original model showed Jefferson's home somewhat enlarged and cleverly foreshortened at a three-quarters angle with a tree masking the left (facing) or (properly) right front wing. The house is even tilted upward and back slightly, as if the viewer were approaching it while ascending an incline. Official taste eliminated this interesting, even exciting, view and substituted the mausoleum of Roman profile and blurred forms that masquerades as the building on the finished coin. On the trial reverse the name "Monticello" seemed scarcely necessary and was therefore, logically, omitted. On the coin as issued it seems essential lest one think the building portrayed is the vault at Fort Knox, a state archive building, or a public library somewhere. Again, lettering is well balanced and well defined, with slender clarity. The high rim has preserved the broad bust and the blurry, inarticulate columns and windows of the house from much abuse.

Felix Schlag's Jefferson nickel has the distinction of being the last U.S. coin in the regular series until the Bicentennial to be designed by an artist outside the Mint.[2]

Wartime Tokens

During the latter part of 1942 the Mint experimented with various metals, plastic, and glass, to find a substitute for strategic metals in the cent. A number of tokens were produced in several materials. The obverse bears the date 1942, but the Liberty head was that of the 1918 Colombia two-centavo piece struck at the Mint; the reverse wreath was adapted from 19th-century U.S. Mint medalets of George Washington.[3] The 1942 dies show that old designs in modern dress can be very appealing, and that in the future the Mint could do much worse than to use former models and patterns as the basis for new designs in the coinage. The French did just this in the middle 1960s with their new 10-franc and smaller coins, reusing the compositions of Dupré, created at the end of the 18th century, and of Roty, first turned into dies a century later.

The Roosevelt Dime

John R. Sinnock's hand had been absent from the regular coinage for a generation when he was called upon to redesign the dime, the logical memorial for Franklin Delano Roosevelt in the regular coinage. Basing the head on his earlier Roosevelt presidential medal, Sinnock demonstrated his long practice and superior craftsmanship as a die designer in producing a clean, satisfying, and modestly stylish, no-nonsense coin that in total view comes forth with notes of grandeur (figs. 229 and 230). Houdon never modeled Roosevelt in clay and plaster or carved him in marble, but had he done so the results would have surely resembled the profile on the dime. The die designer has achieved a precise, detailed portrait that shows full force of character amid a faithful portrayal. Mottoes sit on the obverse in such a way as to enhance the massive head. A strong rim has protected the obverse from hasty deterioration.

The reverse, a torch of liberty between sprays of laurel and oak, is less satisfying, if only because it is a modern, impressionistic, and therefore blurry version of what A.A. Weinman had conceived for the dime in 1916. Imaginative spacing of the Latin motto between the triad of uprights and a generous, monumental quality to the major lettering, especially the denominator, redeem this side of the small coin from copyism and give it a radiance worthy of the majestic obverse. At the time the new dime appeared many felt Franklin D. Roosevelt should not have been honored with the founding fathers and Lincoln. The hasty, emotional advent of John F. Kennedy to the half dollar in 1964 is evidence

229. Sinnock, models for Roosevelt dime

230. Sinnock, studies for Roosevelt dime

that this reservation never developed tenure. The way for contemporary portraits on coins of the United States had been implemented by Sinnock himself when he sketched out Calvin Coolidge for the Philadelphia Sesquicentennial half dollar of 1926.

In addition to the accepted design, Sinnock sketched a reverse with a hand holding the torch of freedom, along with four other reverses for the 1946 dime, elaborating the themes of freedom, light, and the United Nations.[4] One composition merely added scrolls for the Four Freedoms on either side of the torch, a rather insipid concept since the open documents looked as stiff as a row of tombstones and as architectural as the tablets of Moses. A second design featured a half figure of Liberty holding the flaming lamp of freedom and the branch of peace. With her strongly Phrygian bonnet and her flowing tresses she is a Franco-American type, of World War I vintage. From this idea Sinnock moved on to a capless Liberty in less Grecian costume, gaze directed up at the flaming torch, amid the leaves of an olive tree springing from behind her waist. The draftsmanship is superb, and the concept was certainly refreshing, recalling academic art in the 1930s. The last reverse was one of those unfortunate attempts to adapt a building of mausoleum type, in this instance the War Memorial Opera House in San Francisco, to the tondo form of a small coin amid all the necessary inscriptions. The label UNITED NATIONS CONFERENCE explains why, and the scrolls of Four Freedoms have been placed, like ventilators of a radiator, on a flag below. In all, however, the range of imagination in these suggestions for the dime honoring Franklin Roosevelt and his ideals was stimulating. The coin and its preliminary designs emerged as a perfect demonstration that in Sinnock's case there was no need to go outside the Mint to find numismatic artists of the first rank.

The Franklin Half Dollar

The marble bust of Benjamin Franklin in pseudo-Roman garb, signed and dated "J.A. Houdon, 1780," is one of the treasures of the Nelson-Atkins Museum in Kansas City (fig. 231). Ross E. Taggart wrote of this noble portrait:

> In 1778, the year Franklin concluded the treaty of alliance with France, the old philosopher sat for Houdon, the greatest portrait sculptor of the eighteenth century. Houdon's first portrait of Franklin depicted the statesman wearing the simple Quaker dress which intrigued the French and added materially to Franklin's popularity. Several variants of this bust exist in terra cotta, plaster, and marble. Two years later, Houdon completed this depiction of Franklin clad *à la antique,* or as a Roman statesman, which appears to be unique. . . . The character of the canny, the witty, and the wise old Franklin endures in it.[5]

231. Houdon, Benjamin Franklin

H.H. Arnason had the following to say in his catalog of an exhibition of Houdon's sculpture held at the Worcester Art Museum in 1964:

> Houdon's portrait of Franklin has become so much a part of the iconography of America that it is almost impossible to analyze it objectively. The Metropolitan Museum marble shows him in contemporary dress, simply, even puritanically garbed. He is presented with a somewhat rigid frontality that suggests qualities of forthrightness. He wears his own hair, bald on top and long and flowing down over his ears and

> shoulders. The wrinkles at the corners of the eyes are emphasized, and the eyes themselves look somewhat toward the right. The lips are slightly parted, in what might be the beginning of a smile. The entire expression is one of benevolence, wisdom and humor, as appropriately it should be.[6]

232. Franklin half dollar of 1948 type

Houdon's Franklin in modern dress forms the basis for John Sinnock's half dollar of 1948, a coin issued after the death of the Mint's eighth chief engraver. Sinnock had prepared the designs during the Second World War, but the issue had to wait until postwar pressures on coin production had been satisfied. The reverse was planned without the traditional eagle, and only official worries about the wording of the Coinage Law of 1873, "the figure of an eagle or representation thereof,"[7] led Sinnock's successor to insert the tiny, heraldic bird to the right of the Liberty Bell on the reverse (fig. 232). Numerous critics have observed that this side of the Franklin half dollar is a bolder, rougher version of Sinnock's half dollar for the Philadelphia sesquicentennial of 1926. The fragile uncertainty of the earlier coin has given way to a feeling for texture in the bell and a broad, irregular heaviness of lettering that accords well with this accented style and balances the positive simplicity of the obverse. The fact that on Proof and Uncirculated specimens the lettering on the bell can be deciphered only adds to the interest and immediate visual naturalism of this strong, simple coin, one that speaks with the character of Benjamin Franklin.

Last of the triad of regular coins based on Houdon busts—Washington, Jefferson, and Franklin—the 1948 half dollar set a final standard of excellence, if not great artistry or special excitement, on the round of redesigning that replaced the beautiful issues of Fraser, MacNeil, and Weinman between 1912 and 1916. It is sad that more coins with early patriots on them were not designed and struck. The series could have used a silver dollar, and John Adams, Andrew Jackson, or Alexander Hamilton would have been leading candidates for the honor of being portrayed on the obverse. Among more recent figures of fame, Theodore Roosevelt and Woodrow Wilson had strong claims to this traditional form of recognition. George Washington, whose natural place is on the largest of U.S. coins, could easily have been replaced on the quarter by some lesser figure, since John Flanagan's obverse and reverse soon outlived their original commemorative purpose and their aesthetic appeal as designs in the regular coinage. Indeed, the following decades saw continued neglect of many strong potential subjects for the dollar coin, with the happy exception of Dwight D. Eisenhower, whose conspicuous absence on the coinage of the 1960s would be remedied by the dollar of 1971. Fortunately, the advent of the Presidential dollars series in 2007 would rectify some of the more egregious omissions of the preceding half century (see chap. XI).

Medals by John Sinnock

During his 30 years as an engraver at the Mint in Philadelphia, John R. Sinnock perforce designed a number of medals, including examples in the Presidential Inaugural series (figs. 166 and 167) and the group portraying secretaries of the Treasury. His congressional medal of 1928 in honor of Thomas A. Edison is characteristic of the traditional and eclectic forces that shaped his art as a die designer. It is half Renaissance, in the arrangement of the bust on the obverse, and half modern, of the school of Paul Manship, in the kneeling Spirit of Electricity on the reverse. The previous generation, from the last years of Saint-Gaudens to the decade after the First World War, had been a great age of modern medals in the Renaissance tradition by leading sculptors. Sinnock's Edison medal is an afterglow of this creativity. In trying a pseudoclassical modern reverse, he was casting about for a new style, unfortunately choosing one soon to be typed as a dated product of the generation between the two world wars. In the end he settled for the forthright, conservative simplicity of his Roosevelt dime and Franklin half dollar.

The presidential medal of 1945 inadvertently afforded Sinnock an opportunity to practice portraiture for the Roosevelt dime of 1946 (fig. 233). The full, three-quarters-angle bust traditional to these medals is the vehicle for the famous Roosevelt profile tilted slightly upward and jaw thrust out. Full photographic accuracy has been achieved. The reverse plays on the emotions of World War II and the president's sudden death, showing a leaderless ship of state heading to the left rear into unknown seas. One is mindful that after Roosevelt's death the radio quoted Tennyson's words "may there be no moaning of the bar, when I put out to sea," over and over again. Such must be the implications of the ship in full sail toward the horizon and "the crosses row on row" that are divided by the seated, veiled female with wreath, palm, and gnarled tree or branch at her feet, all symbols of death familiar from the presidential medals to William McKinley and Warren G. Harding.

In this mourning allegory, presumably again Columbia or perhaps Liberty, Sinnock has returned from his phase of Greek archaic– or transitional-style females to those generally classicistic creatures of the earlier part of the century. Curiously enough, there is even something of Augustus Saint-Gaudens in this reverse, for the mourning woman recalls the famous enigmatic figure of the Adams Memorial in the cemetery at Rock Creek Park in Washington, DC. The reverse as a whole has the spirit of a marble memorial in a national cemetery. It is no mean feat to compress such imagery into the tondo of an official presidential medal.

The Princeton University Bicentennial medal of 1946 (fig. 234) marks the culmination of the eighth chief engraver's record of work outside the official demands from the Mint. A straightforward design, with

233. *Sinnock, medal for Franklin D. Roosevelt*

234. *Sinnock, Princeton University Bicentennial medal*

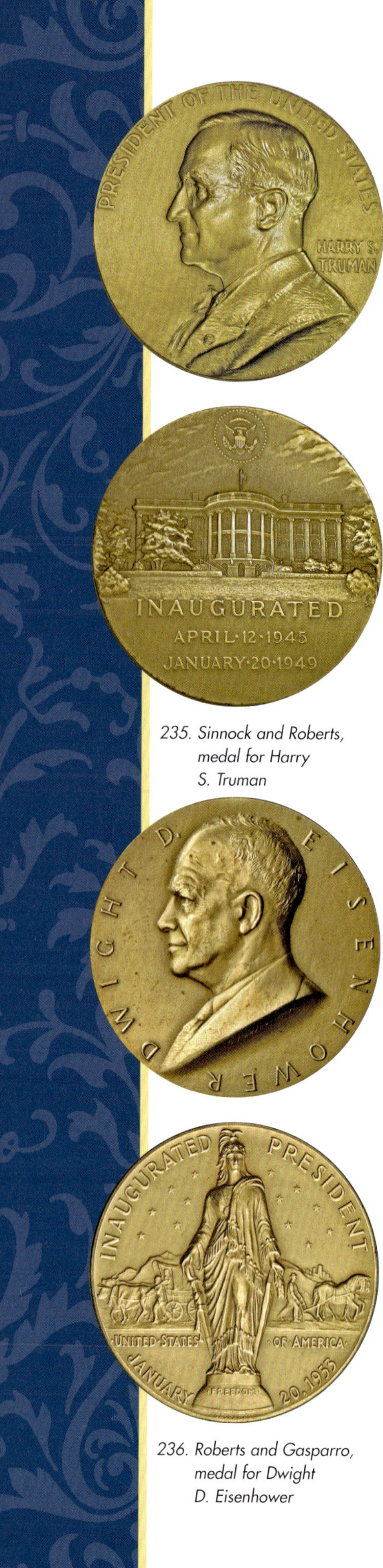

235. Sinnock and Roberts, medal for Harry S. Truman

236. Roberts and Gasparro, medal for Dwight D. Eisenhower

building on one side and university seal on the other, the piece serves as a reminder that what is amply admissible on a medal ought not to appear on a commemorative coin. As a coin type, requiring all the statutory phrases and words of designation, the obverse and reverse would have become crowded, dull, and confused or diffused as to meaning. Nassau Hall, so labeled, is an essay in conventional representation of a building, full and frontal view with the lettering beneath, similar to the "corrected" version of Jefferson's Monticello on the nickel of 1938 or the Lincoln Memorial on the cent of 1959. The academic badge on the reverse is set off by the broad wreath of ivy at the outside border of the tondo. This relieves monotony and gives the entire second side of the medal some status as a work of art.

The vogue for national buildings instead of allegorical females or even eagles on the reverses of our coins and medals grew in the mid-20th century. Paper money had long followed this practice of honoring architecture. The Jefferson nickel of 1938 has its Monticello, and the Lincoln cent received its new reverse with the Lincoln Memorial in 1959. In 1945 Sinnock modeled a characteristic conservative but accurate portrait of Harry S. Truman, and in 1949 this obverse was issued as a presidential medal with a reverse by Gilroy Roberts showing the White House with a tiny presidential seal above (fig. 235). The design reflects Roberts's years of employment in the Bureau of Engraving and Printing, for the building so associated with Truman's actions and personality is presented—amid its leafy planting and finger-brushed clouds above—with an impressionistic force combined with vital accuracy seldom seen heretofore in architectural renderings on medals. The effect is that of a careful engraving or a painting. The building is noble yet human, precise yet sympathetic. The small seal above heralds the popularity of a design that would grace the John F. Kennedy medal by Roberts and Frank Gasparro (fig. 238), the Kennedy inaugural medal by Paul Manship (fig. 239), the Kennedy half dollar (fig. 240), and the two presidential medals for Lyndon B. Johnson, the first by Roberts and Gasparro together (fig. 241) and the second by Gasparro alone.

Medals by Roberts and Gasparro

The medal of 1953 for the first inauguration of Dwight D. Eisenhower might be termed the first example of slick, modern medallic art in the series (fig. 236). The obverse has characteristics of Gilroy Roberts now familiar to all from repetition on several occasions—wide lettering, clean-cut and truncated bust, and a sharp, metallic finish. The portrait is accurate, for—as were his predecessors Charles Barber, George Morgan, and John Sinnock—Gilroy Roberts was a consummate craftsman of the state likeness. To his credit, Frank Gasparro essayed a tour de force for the reverse, a scene of Freedom against a background of progress on the farm, in the city, and along the paths of the pioneers through valley and mountain. All this is set amid a firmament of the canonical 13 stars. This particular image of Freedom had a fascination for Gasparro. He used the same figure—based, for some reason, on the bronze statue that stood atop the dome of the Capitol in Washington—for the sole reverse figure of a First Lady series of medals (fig. 237). The inscription around the detailed projection of the statue reads THE FIRST LADY OF THE UNITED STATES OF AMERICA. Presumably, this refers to Martha Washington rather than to Thomas Crawford's colossal sculpture, a dreadful example of delayed neoclassicism in America on the eve of the Civil War.[8]

237. Gasparro, First Lady medal

238. Roberts and Gasparro, medal for John F. Kennedy

Of the great bronze statue with its fringed himation resembling the dress of a Greco-Roman priestess of Isis, Oliver Larkin wrote:

> Before Crawford died he had completed the plaster model, nineteen feet high, of a bronze *Freedom* for the Capitol dome, a formless, bulky female whose liberty cap, at the suggestion of Jefferson Davis, had become a plumed helmet, and whose every fold and fringe was cut with a minuteness forever invisible to all but the Washington sparrows. After a year's voyage the statue reached Washington in sections and was cast by Clark Mills. At noon of December 1, 1863, guns roared from the field batteries which ringed the wartime capital, a flag went up, and Thomas Walter gave the signal for *Freedom's* bronze head to rise and complete her body. She was not the last of her kind, but perhaps the worst, the questionable plumes and odd silhouette rather suggestive of a pregnant squaw three hundred feet in the air.[9]

Such is the statue that Gasparro chose to symbolize the first administration of Dwight Eisenhower and the public careers of women like Martha Washington and Jacqueline Kennedy.

Little need be added about the presidential medal for John F. Kennedy, the layout of the Kennedy half dollar, and the 1963 medal for Lyndon B. Johnson (figs. 238, 240, and 241). The portraits and obverse lettering follow Roberts's rule, and the reverses are mere inscribed plaques centered on the presidential seal. Paul Manship's medal for Kennedy's inauguration in 1961 is no better (fig. 239). A certain rough boldness is pleasing, but the portrait does not resemble President Kennedy. The head is too round, the nose is too pointed, and the face is too rubbery. It is clear that most medalists of the 1960s had a great deal

239. Manship, medal for Kennedy

240. Kennedy half dollar of 1964

to learn from Gilroy Roberts before they could rival the dignity and accuracy of his portraits. As to reverses, connoisseurs of medal art hoped that Frank Gasparro would return to pictorialism in some form, be it allegory, architecture, or landscape with figures, before death ended his long career with the Mint. Seals, presidential and otherwise, can only be carried so far as works of medallic art.

Commemorative Half Dollars, 1946 to 1954

Three new commemorative half dollars appeared after the Second World War: the Iowa Statehood Centennial, the Booker T. Washington, and the Booker T. Washington–George Washington Carver. The first coin is a passable work of art (fig. 242). The second has features of interest, notably the three-quarters-facing bust on the obverse (fig. 243). The third is a numismatic curiosity but not a work of art (fig. 244).

One side of the Iowa Statehood Centennial comprises a frontal eagle bending over a large ribbon, an adaptation of the upper portion of the state's arms. Twenty-nine stars clustered above signify Iowa's order of entry in the Union. The view on the reverse of the first stone capitol building at Iowa City, with inscription beneath in tiny letters, parallels Sinnock's depiction of Nassau Hall on the medal for Princeton University's bicentennial celebration. The whole coin, the work of longtime Mint engraver Adam Pietz of Philadelphia, is boldly and spaciously laid out. The cloudy background of the capitol adds a touch of interest. The way the eagle hangs down or hovers above its fillet and mottoes recalls carved or painted signs, including ship transoms, made in the 19th century. Characterized by details of planting, with ivy below and around the federalist windows, "The Old Stone Capitol Iowa City" has a liveliness not usually found in these vistas of official architecture and entirely lacking in Sinnock's portrayal of Nassau Hall. The only general criticism of the design, a minor one, is that the major lettering seems a trifle large, out of scale. In sum, conventional motifs have been handled with skill in what is, unfortunately, the last commemorative half dollar in the classic series honoring the states (fig. 242).

Isaac Scott Hathaway designed the two half dollars honoring great African American educators. Both coins suffer from too much lettering, brought about partly by the introduction of biography on the first coin and meaningless aphorisms on the second. The presence of Booker T. Washington may have been necessitated by law on the second coin, but his profile and titles preclude any specific references to George Washington Carver and add nothing that has not been stated on the first coin. A map labeled U.S.A. marks a low point in pictorial imagination, and it is rather sad that the splendid first series of commemorative coins, so much an ornament to the arts of the United States, should reach its conclusion in 1954 with a reverse so impoverished of ideas and devoid of artistry.

The Kennedy Half Dollar

Born of the great emotions following John F. Kennedy's assassination, the half dollar of 1964 is a tolerable, staidly handsome coin, within all the conventional limits. The only unusual feature of the piece might be said to be the monogram of Gilroy Roberts on the truncation of the head, which was taken directly from the bust on the Kennedy presidential medal. Frank Gasparro, successor to Roberts as chief engraver at the Mint, designed the reverse, based on the presidential coat of arms (fig. 240). The motif was not new to numismatic art, having been used three years earlier on the same full scale by Paul Manship for the Kennedy inaugural medal (fig. 239). The obverse portrait on the coin is not completely successful, suffering from confused detail, or lack thereof, and from a compression of the president's face that gives him a simper or, at best, a grimace that could be interpreted charitably as determination. This fault is not present in Manship's Presidential Inaugural medal. Spacing and directness of lettering, however, go far to redeem the portrait on the half dollar. The device of partly concealing the BER of LIBERTY behind the president's hair is a modern elaboration of a technique developed on a wide scale by Charles E. Barber in the reverses of the half dollar and quarter dollar of 1892 (figs. 99 and 100).

The reverse fits the complex presidential emblem within large and extremely handsome lettering. Again, spacing saves the design from pettiness. Without the strong, yet summary, relief of the eagle, the total visual effect would have been too active and too spotty. It was a fashion among die designers of the 1960s to give surfaces a smoothed, almost worn look before they even touched circulation. The British portraits of Queen Elizabeth II displayed this quality. Here, it is seen in the head, wings, and tail of the eagle and on the shield on his stomach.

This is the second presidential or patriot's portrait in the regular coinage that bears no relation to the reverse type, save that in this instance the latter is based on the presidential seal. The other such coin was John Flanagan's quarter dollar of 1932. Jefferson has his Monticello; Franklin appears with the Liberty Bell of his adopted city; and Lincoln traded his ears of wheat for his neo-Roman marble memorial in 1959. No doubt the lack of any specific building or object identified with Kennedy, and the haste with which the half dollar was perforce produced, prevented any more imaginative reverse being contemplated. What appears is serviceable enough, and the coin is a credit to the ideas that brought it to pass.[10]

241. Roberts and Gasparro, medal for Lyndon B. Johnson

242. Iowa Statehood Centennial half dollar

American Numismatic Art After the Years of Kennedy

243. Booker T. Washington half dollar

244. Washington-Carver half dollar design of 1951

Although the death of President Kennedy engendered the half dollar of 1964, his passing seemed to remove any impulse to seek medallic or numismatic artistry outside of official sources. Laws in connection with the coinage tended to suppress rather than to encourage the arts, a major excuse being shortages created by inflation in the middle 1960s. No instinct for artistic patronage came from high government officials, and public pressure toward a revival of the numismatic arts akin to that of the Theodore Roosevelt era or the First World War and the decade following were singularly lacking. The numismatic press contained reports of scattered attempts to stimulate creativity, but in general pessimism reigned in these knowledgeable circles.[11]

So far as a potential future for the U.S. coinage went, one of the most interesting and elucidating "pattern" designs was the series of experimental strikings prepared for the half dollar, quarter dollar, and dime in the new low-silver and base bimetallic combinations. They showed that official numismatic art was ready to make few advances beyond John R. Sinnock's Franklin half dollar of 1948. To avoid any possibility of creating a coin that could be termed a true pattern, as if there were not glorious traditions of patterns in the 19th century, a portrait of Martha Washington in the Houdon tradition was linked with the state of Virginia and dated 1759, the year of her birth (fig. 245). Although her high coiffure and cap intrude into the VIRGINIA, as Kennedy's head does into the LIBERTY, the form and spacing of the lettering on the obverse, as well as the full flavor of the high relief, are very much in the tradition of Sinnock's half dollar.

The reverse is a view of Mount Vernon, so labeled, that presents the Washington home at an angle, such as ought to have been employed for Monticello on the Jefferson nickel. The thinking behind such a sample "coin" is obviously that, if a famous person is portrayed on the regular coinage, the accompanying reverse ought to have a vista of some building connected with that person's career or the honors paid to him or her after death. Thus, Hyde Park might be shown with Franklin Roosevelt, the Hermitage with Andrew Jackson, or the mausoleum on Riverside Drive with Ulysses S. Grant. Such a program of linking men and buildings has, of course, been standard fare for a number of years on U.S. paper currency.

In 1968 the U.S. government restored mintmarks to the coinage and reinstituted the issuance of Proof sets after a lapse of three years. A tiny letter on the obverse or reverse of a coin does not make a new design, and the quality of Proof coins produced in the millions is far from that of the

19th-century issues struck in sets rarely exceeding a thousand. The United States has suffered from long spells of dull coinages punctuated by exciting artistic upheavals, as in 1836 and 1907, and the future could only provide steps forward from the uninspired artistic level of the late 1960s. The dignity of silver as a deep surface texture and a shimmering aesthetic pleasure disappeared from the half dollar, quarter dollar, and dime in 1965. The perpetuation of designs then current in greasy base metals only served to emphasize the need for an imaginative visual break with the past.

Generally speaking, in the 1960s medallic art in America was mired in a phase of facile facing portraits; machine-hewn, regularly squared lettering; and dull reverses that made little pretense at art and did not try to approach the level of the obverse. The font and inspiration of this machined style was the Mint in Philadelphia. Medals were being turned out by the dozens all over the United States every month, and they varied only in the degree that they could be measured downward from the products of the Mint or of the few talented designers whose works were once run off by the Medallic Art Company in New York (later Danbury, Connecticut; fig. 246).

Late in 1965 the Mint issued a medal by Frank Gasparro, known as Presidential List no. 137, to commemorate the new term of office of Lyndon B. Johnson. All the characteristics of official medals and their imitations in the mid-1960s are present in this creation. Johnson, in a dry and capable portrait, faces us, the top of his head barely obscuring some of the letters of his name, as John F. Kennedy and Martha Washington had overlapped their respective inscriptions. The only feature of the reverse that could be classed as art is the small presidential seal at the bottom. Everything else is epigraphy: date and title; a few deathless words from the inaugural address; and, finally, as if to give the whole effort the mark of authenticity, the signature of Lyndon B. Johnson between text and seal (fig. 247). The previous Mint medal of President Johnson had followed Manship's inaugural medal for Kennedy in reproducing the presidential seal on the full surface of the reverse. The second attempt for the favorite son of Texas may be different, but it can scarcely be mentioned in company with medals by Augustus Saint-Gaudens, Charles E. Barber, George T. Morgan, James E. Fraser, Hermon A. MacNeil, or John Flanagan.

The Assay Commission medal for 1966 shows no improvement over or difference from the facing portrait of President Johnson. Also by Chief Engraver Gasparro, the Assay medal presents a bust of Henry H. Fowler, the same master design used for Fowler's appearance in the series for the chief officer of the Treasury. The Assay medal's reverse, modeled by Philip E. Fowler, is, surprisingly enough, no mean work of art. The simple statement ASSAY COMMISSION 1966 is spaced out between the working parts of an analytical balance scale of the type used when the Commission met (fig. 248). The instant impression of this reverse is like that conveyed by a medal of the early Italian Renaissance. This augured well for the future of official medals in the United States.

245. Pattern for Martha Washington coin

246. Roberts, medal for Louis C. West

247. Gasparro, medal for Lyndon B. Johnson

248. Gasparro and Fowler, Assay medal for 1966

In 1968 Frank Gasparro teamed with Edgar Zell Steever to create an Assay medal honoring Albert Gallatin, secretary of the Treasury from 1801 to 1814. The bust and its attendant lettering are vivid yet careful combinations of high, photographic relief and even spacing in the accepted modern formula. The theme of the reverse is Gallatin's introduction of the first official troy pound weight used by the Mint, together with its lesser division, the ounce, and also a gram and a grain. Steever has shown all four, dominated by the large troy pound with its British crown in an imaginative juxtaposition. Shapes dominate this design, a large sphere with a disc on top for the pound and other solids for the smaller weights.[12] Again, it seems that if such was the direction of medallic art in the U.S. Mint at the time, American numismatic aesthetics were well served.

The 1969 Assay Commission medal is as traditional, in the sense of Mint medals by Barber, Morgan, or Sinnock, as any composition could be. Nixon's bust, head in profile, and a modern version of Renaissance lettering, appear on the obverse, while the new (1968) Philadelphia Mint graces the reverse, in the usual tilted, three-quarters vanishing perspective. Frank Gasparro was again responsible for the obverse, and Philip Fowler produced the modern architectural vista that constitutes the design of the reverse.[13]

The presidential medal of Richard Milhous Nixon, Presidential List no. 138 from the Mint at Philadelphia, brought the saga of U.S. medallic art to the threshold of the 1970s. Both obverse and reverse were the work of Frank Gasparro, who deserved credit for having produced handsome designs within the then-accepted official framework. The iconography is so familiar that there is no need to illustrate the piece. Nixon's bust is delineated in sharp profile on the obverse, with PRESIDENT OF THE UNITED STATES in simple capitals above and his full name behind his right shoulder. The presidential seal and encircling stars, similar to the composition on the half dollar for John F. Kennedy, fill much of the reverse, leaving room within the circle for INAUGURATED JANUARY 20, 1969 and the usual presidential quotation.[14] Like the obverse, this reverse attains its success through strength of outlines and simplicity of spacing. It is fortunate that such a successful visual effect has been achieved, for otherwise repetition of a much-used medallic formula would have had little to commend itself in a world increasingly conscious of artistic potentials in medals and coins.

The decade of the 1960s in U.S. numismatic art can be said to have terminated not only with proposals for the Eisenhower dollar but with the rash of medals inspired by the landing on the moon in July 1969. Since most medals are in the shape of full moons to begin with, the possibilities of design to commemorate the latter event were limitless, but most artists who faced the problem preferred to tell some aspect of the heroic flight pictorially within the confines of the medallic circle. Some medals showed the lunar module poised on the surface, while one astronaut plants the U.S. flag. Others showed both spacemen walking across the pitted landscape, with the vehicle at one side or in the background. The earth is often seen in the distance, usually with the western hemisphere clearly outlined. One horrible medal, made in Canada and sold in the United States, shows the astronauts saluting a frozen flag while the main part of the rocket orbits through the background above the module. Another atrocity features a series of modules, like a set of movie frames, traveling from distant earth to the moon's face, where an astronaut is already gathering rocks. Busts of Neil Armstrong, Edwin Aldrin, and Michael Collins have made natural subjects for the other side, set in various juxtapositions amid appropriate inscriptions. The favorite text naturally has been "One Small Step for a Man; One Giant Leap for Mankind." At least, as far as general principles of design go, the vistas of moon medals freed many a second-rate artist from the usual fetters of mere heraldic object coupled with verbose inscription. One of the few symbolic compositions in the old tradition is relatively successful: the American eagle, wings and talons spread, landing on the crater-filled moon with the earth visible in the upper left background, a design later adapted for the Eisenhower dollar in 1971 (fig. 249). The popularity of all these medals, beyond that usually accorded such creations, could be gauged by the fact that one issue of 10,000 serially numbered antique-finish silver pieces was completely sold out nearly a month before the scheduled date of delivery, September 1969.

249. Eisenhower dollar of 1971 type

The Republic of Guinea was the first nation to honor the event with a large silver coin, a showpiece struck under a legal arrangement with a European firm that produced similar souvenir issues for other small nations. Several sources in the United States proposed a commemorative issue, a half dollar, in addition to the official and private medals of various sizes and in a number of metals. The idea of a moon coin may seem almost amusing in the light of other events that had not been commemorated in America at that time, but the theory of such projects prefigured the revival of official commemorative coins by the U.S. government in 1982.

On New Year's Day 1971 the official models for the Eisenhower dollar appeared in the newspapers. Predictably, the obverse bore a portrait, as did the Kennedy half dollar and the Washington quarter dollar. The reverse was based on the emblem of the *Apollo 11* flight to the moon—an attractive variation on the traditional design (fig. 249). It depicted an American bald eagle with an olive branch in its talons, landing on the moon's surface, with the earth seen in the background.

President Eisenhower's head on the new coin seems too brutally sculptural and elongated, like an image hewn from stone rather than anything based on a portrait by Houdon. Admittedly, the president's features had been the despair of political cartoonists as well as artists. His face lacked the craggy and distinctive eyebrow, forehead, nose, chin, and other trademark features that cartoonist or sculptor could draw or chisel.

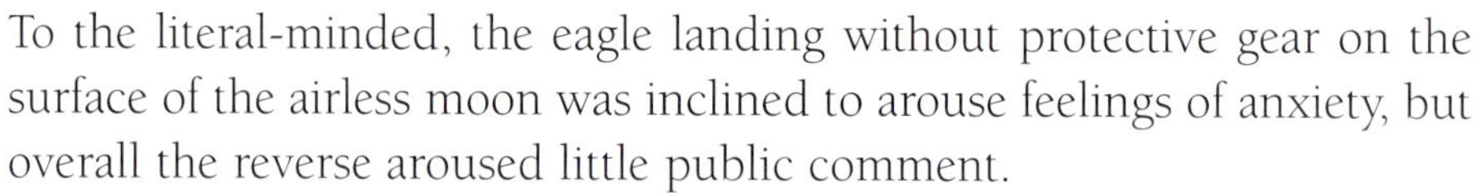
To the literal-minded, the eagle landing without protective gear on the surface of the airless moon was inclined to arouse feelings of anxiety, but overall the reverse aroused little public comment.

Set against the standards of 1907, 1916, and the 1920s, numismatic design from 1938 to 1970 seemed somewhat disappointing. While the newer coins and medals were competent enough, they gave a feeling of having been constricted by official restrictions (the Franklin half dollar), produced in haste (the coin for Kennedy), or partly revised without being thoroughly restudied (both sides of the Lincoln cent). Medals featured excellent obverse portraits, but they relied all too often on dull, trite devices for their reverses (the presidential seal or quotations from speeches). Perhaps the chief quality of these years lay not in what existed but in what had been eliminated. The silver dollar has not been coined since 1935, and commemorative coins, which had not appeared since 1954, would not be issued again until 1982.[15]

XI

Numismatic Art Into the 21st Century

David Thomason Alexander

The Numismatic Horizon Widens: 1972 to 1976

The Kennedy half dollar and the opening of the new Philadelphia Mint were highlights of the tenure of Eva Adams of Nevada as director of the U.S. Mint (October 1961–September 1969). Adams began as an outspoken opponent of coin collecting, on one famous occasion threatening collectors with imprisonment to remedy a largely imaginary coin shortage. She was taking her cue from a former employer, Nevada senator Alan Bible, author of the "Bible bill," who had threatened such sanctions.

Her term coincided with the centennial of the Civil War, which was widely observed but was not marked by any national commemorative coins. After much boosting in the weekly numismatic newspaper *Coin World,* a pillar of the numismatic community since 1960, Adams shifted her position to one much more favorable to the hobby, although she remained firmly opposed to any resumption of commemoratives. She was portrayed on two Mint director medals, the first a distinctly glamorous, Hollywood-esque likeness by Gilroy Roberts, the second a somewhat pinch-featured study by Frank Gasparro (fig. 250). The Gasparro image in reduced size graced the 1967 Assay Commission medal as well.

250. Medals for Eva Adams

An unexpected opening in the private sector was made on October 8, 1964, when the long-serving chief engraver Gilroy Roberts resigned from the U.S. Mint, where he had served since 1938: first as assistant to

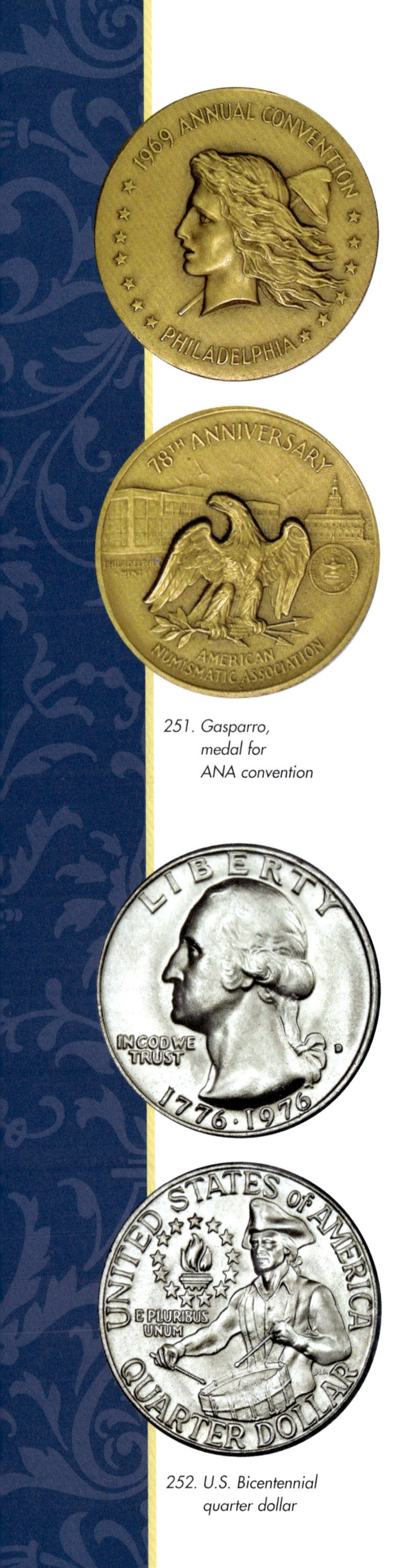

251. Gasparro, medal for ANA convention

252. U.S. Bicentennial quarter dollar

John R. Sinnock, then as chief engraver from 1948. He was succeeded in that post by Frank Gasparro. Roberts rather daringly threw in his fortunes with the newly organized General Numismatics Corporation (GNC) of Yeadon, Pennsylvania, brainchild of merchandising wunderkind Joseph H. Segel. A department of the new firm was called the Franklin Mint, which was immediately engaged in the wholesale manufacture of gaming tokens for the silver dollar–starved Nevada casinos and of Proof-surface coin-relief medals for private medal series such as those of the National Commemorative Society.

GNC went public with a successful stock issue on the national stock exchange underwritten by a New York brokerage house specializing in such new issues, after its Miami Beach–based broker John L. Alexander discovered GNC and researched it for a possible stock issue. In a trice the stock sold out, and the new firm bought quantities of silver bullion before the price rose to dizzying heights. Roberts's gamble paid off handsomely, making him a wealthy man when GNC achieved fame as the Franklin Mint. In its early years, the firm offered many opportunities to aspiring medallic sculptors and widely advertised their achievements, although after several years the sculptors' role was played down and ultimately nearly forgotten. Although the Franklin Mint was a historic merchandising phenomenon, its long-range effect on the numismatic world would remain intensely controversial.

Gasparro continued his unmistakable style in the medal world even after his retirement from the Mint, where his efforts included medals of presidents Johnson, Nixon, and Carter, several secretaries of the Treasury, and congressional honorees including Marian Anderson and John Wayne. His National Bicentennial medals struck in gold, silver, and bronze were among the few medallic standouts of that event, as was his private commission from the City of Philadelphia for its bicentennial medal. Late in his career he was bitterly disappointed by the rejection of his design for the new small-size dollar coin in 1979, a Liberty head with cap on pole, inspired by the 1793 large cents and half cents and prefigured by his obverse for the 1969 American Numismatic Association (ANA) convention medal (fig. 251).

Eva Adams's successor, Mary Brooks, served as director from 1969 to 1977 and began as an opponent of commemoratives, repeating the hoary official line against such coinage. However, the nation was looking forward to the approaching American Revolution Bicentennial, an event of even greater importance than the Civil War centennial. As early as 1966, at the Chicago ANA convention, Medallic Art Company president William T. Louth advocated one or more commemorative coins for the nation's birthday. This voice was hard to ignore, as Medallic Art had been the recognized leader in the design and production of fine art medals since the 1920s, and had struck most official Presidential Inaugural medals issued since the 1953 inauguration of Dwight D. Eisenhower along with innumerable significant award medals and official issues of all kinds for states and cities. In the event, Louth's firm would soon be striking most of the high-quality official state and local medals for the Bicentennial in 1974 through 1976.

In January 1973, Representative Richard C. White, Democrat from Texas, proposed Bicentennial dollar and half dollar coins, and his concept received wholly unexpected U.S. Mint endorsement on March 2. Hearings and additional proposals soon followed, some advocating that all six circulating coins bear Bicentennial designs; an innovative suggestion by Oregon's Mark Hatfield called for a Bicentennial gold $25 piece. The idea of a gold coin violated another Treasury position, which dated from the 1933 presidential executive order halting gold coinage and its circulation.

Eventually, in October 1973, legislation passed both houses of Congress to change the reverse of the quarter dollar, half dollar, and dollar to bear the dual dates 1776–1976 on coins struck from July 4, 1975, through January 1, 1977. Circulating coins would be struck in the standard copper-nickel clad copper composition at Philadelphia and Denver, with auxiliary coinage to be struck at the West Point Bullion Depository. Provision was made for as many as 60 million Bicentennial coins in 40 percent silver alloy to be struck at San Francisco at the discretion of the secretary of the Treasury.

A nationwide design competition attracted almost a thousand entries, which were sifted by a five-member judging panel chosen by the National Sculpture Society: sculptor Robert A. Weinman, former chief engraver and Franklin Mint executive Gilroy Roberts, sculptor Adlai S. Hardin, Smithsonian numismatic curator Elvira Clain-Stefanelli, and Medallic Art Company executive Julius Lauth. The winning quarter design was the Colonial drummer boy created by businessman and designer Jack L. Ahr (fig. 252). Minneapolis commercial artist Seth Huntington's view of Independence Hall was chosen for the half dollar, and 22-year-old student Dennis R. Williams of the Columbus, Ohio, College of Art and Design juxtaposed the Liberty Bell and the moon on the winning dollar (figs. 253 and 254). Only minor changes were made before coinage began, and the new coins received a generally favorable reception.

Most widely acclaimed was the drummer on the quarter, the coin most widely circulated in a country that had effectively forgotten the "Ike" dollar and Kennedy half dollar. The spirited youth beating the drum fills the field, making the torch in a circle of stars at the upper left somewhat superfluous, especially since E PLURIBUS UNUM is crowded in below. The half dollar was criticized for its lifeless reiteration of Independence Hall, already familiar to collectors from Sinnock's gold quarter eagle hailing the 1926 sesquicentennial. The dollar was more appealing in its first variety with thick sans serif lettering, a contrast to the visibly thinner letters on the more common second variety. The Liberty Bell, of course, would have been remembered from another Sinnock effort, the 1948 Franklin half dollar.

253. U.S. Bicentennial half dollar

254. U.S. Bicentennial dollar

Proof sets without the now-standard S mintmark were struck to exhibit the new coinage, while three-coin sets bearing the regular S mintmark were soon for sale in both clad and 40 percent silver. Sales would prove disappointing; the large remainder left after the announced sale period was over eventually sparked debate over proper disposition. Sets in storage were found to be developing spots on their mirror surfaces, while the cost of simply melting unsold sets was increased by the necessity of shelling the coins out of their rigid plastic packaging. In 1977 the more familiar reverses resumed, to some expressions of regret among collectors and members of the public who had particularly liked the drummer boy.

An entire volume could be written on other aspects of Bicentennial numismatics, especially in the field of the medal. Frank Gasparro placed a half-length figure of the Statue of Liberty and the Great Seal of the United States on the seven sizes of the National Bicentennial medals (fig. 255). Struck in three-inch .900 fine gold was a massive medal containing 13.18 troy ounces, of which 423 were sold for $4,000. Less costly gold medals were the 1-5/16-inch (1.167 troy ounces) and .906-inch (.37 troy ounces) issues, at $400 and $100, respectively. Struck in .925 (sterling) silver were three-inch and 1-1/2-inch medals; bronze and gold-plated bronze 1-1/2-inch medals brought up the rear.

The American Revolution Bicentennial Administration (ARBA), successor to the earlier American Revolution Bicentennial Commission, commissioned four annual medals from 1972 to 1975. The first was designed by the prolific Ralph J. Menconi of Pleasantville, New York, who donated time from a busy schedule to create a 1-1/2-inch bronze medal bearing the Houdon bust of Washington with a reverse recalling colonial resistance to the Stamp Act (fig. 256). Richard Layton designed the 1973 issue, with busts of firebrands Patrick Henry and Samuel Adams and the Committees of Correspondence (fig. 257). Robert Weinman's 1974 John Adams–Continental Congress design was acclaimed a success, and Margaret Grigor's 1975 Paul Revere–Minute man design was another triumph, combining outstanding medallic sculpture with carefully crafted historical imagery (figs. 258 and 259).

Generally speaking, Bicentennial medals struck for states and cities by Medallic Art Company were the most successful in design and execution. Those cobbled together by less experienced makers—notably the Ohio and Florida medals struck by knockoff firms founded by ex–Franklin Mint employees—faded from sight most quickly. As 1976 came to its end, the flood of Bicentennial medals was abruptly halted. No professional catalog of the issued medals was ever prepared, despite the availability of a $30,000 federal grant for this purpose, and what might have been an invaluable artistic resource was never created. While medal collecting is now in a more vigorous state in the United States than at any other time since the years before the Civil War, appreciation or even recollection of the Bicentennial and its medals is nonexistent. Coincidentally, another

255. *Gasparro, medal for national Bicentennial*

256. *Menconi, medal for American Revolution Bicentennial Administration*

257. *Layton, medal for ARBA*

258. *Weinman, medal for ARBA*

259. *Grigor, medal for ARBA*

landmark in the history of the American medal vanished early in 1977 when President Jimmy Carter abolished the annual Assay Commission, the longest-serving citizens' regulatory body in the United States, whose medals had been issued since 1860.

American Arts Gold Medallions

The word *art* has appeared in many odd contexts in modern times, but few are odder than the American Arts gold medallions struck very unwillingly by the U.S. Mint in 1980 through 1984 under the direct mandate of Congress (fig. 260). Properly speaking, a medallion is a very large medal, greater than 100 millimeters in diameter. These American bullion pieces were not coins but were approximately the size of the South African krugerrand and Canadian maple leaf, legal-tender coins with which the new U.S. Mint pieces were supposed to compete. The first two years' strikings of these medallions were made to look as little like coins as possible: they bear no mark of fineness and lack the reeded edge typical of modern precious-metal coins. The Mint made the ordering procedures as cumbersome as possible, packaged them in thoroughly ugly Styrofoam holders, and spared no effort to impede the sale of the gold pieces.

One-ounce and half-ounce issues were struck each year from 1980 through 1984, ostensibly to honor the arts, as their legend AMERICAN ARTS COMMEMORATIVE SERIES proclaims, while intending to cut into the active bullion-coin market. Frank Gasparro designed the 1980 medallions: the larger honored painter Grant Wood and his famed painting popularly called *American Gothic,* and the smaller companion piece portrayed singer Marian Anderson. Next year featured writer and social critic Mark Twain as portrayed by Matthew Peloso, with writer Willa Cather portrayed by Sherl Winter.

Since the program was plainly foundering by 1982, coinlike denticles and edge reeding were introduced for the pieces portraying musician Louis Armstrong (by John Mercanti) and architect Frank Lloyd Wright (by Edgar Z. Steever). In 1983, the great American poet Robert Frost, by P. Fowler, joined sculptor Alexander Calder, by Michael Iacocca. Ending the ill-fated series were the 1984 issues bearing portraits of actress Helen Hayes and writer John Steinbeck by John Mercanti. Near the end of the series an effort was made to market the pieces through a leading bullion firm under the slogan "America Strikes Gold!" Despite outstanding designs, the American Arts gold medallions became the vermiform appendix of U.S. numismatics, unknown to the collecting community and scorned by their intended beneficiaries, the bullion buyers.

260. American Arts medallions

260. American Arts medallions

260. American Arts medallions

The Susan B. Anthony Dollar: From Hope to Fiasco

261. Gasparro, model for Liberty dollar

262. Susan B. Anthony dollar

A major innovation for U.S. circulating coinage began its long gestation in May 1975 with a contract between the U.S. Mint and the Research Triangle Institute (RTI) to study the practicality of a small-diameter, base-metal circulating one-dollar coin. After four months, RTI made its recommendations for the new dollar, and Chief Engraver Frank Gasparro wasted no time in beginning the work of designing the proposed piece, basing his obverse on the medal he had designed for the 1969 Philadelphia American Numismatic Association convention. Treasury secretary William Simon recommended a diameter of 25.5 mm, although 26.5 mm was the diameter actually adopted. This was the first step that led to the coin's failure, as the quarter dollar had a diameter of 24.3 mm.

A model of Gasparro's proposed design was soon publicized (fig. 261), showing a Liberty head with flowing hair facing left, with a Liberty cap on a pole, inspired by Augustin Dupré's obverse for the Libertas Americana medal and the first U.S. copper cents and half cents of 1793. Circling the Liberty head were 13 five-pointed stars, LIBERTY at the top, the large date 1977 below; IN GOD WE TRUST was placed at left, and the artist's initials, FG, at right. The reverse bore an eagle flying to the right against a starry sky with brilliant sunbeams streaming from mountains in the background. UNITED STATES OF AMERICA appeared above, E PLURIBUS UNUM and ONE DOLLAR below. Interest in the new dollar was running high, and much comment was generated by Gasparro's models.

While the merits of the new dollar's design were being debated, legislation was quietly prepared that mandated a portrait of 19th-century women's rights leader Susan B. Anthony (1820–1906) for the coin's obverse. The Susan B. Anthony dollar may well have been one of the few coins whose public rejection can be attributed in some measure to the sheer ugliness of its obverse design (fig. 262). Gasparro's flying-eagle reverse was also jettisoned in favor of a reprise of the eagle landing on the moon, which was viable on the large Eisenhower dollar but is lost on the smaller coin. However, the greatest roles in the coin's ultimate failure were played by size, alloy, and color. Initial Mint discussions favored the adoption of a highly innovative 11-sided planchet, to be struck in a bright yellow alloy resembling the aluminum-bronze or nickel-brass used by several industrial nations, such as the United Kingdom. In shape and color the new dollar would be a visual and tactile standout.

It is now known that such multisided planchets were actually prepared and that the Mint's technology chief, Alan Goldman, carried a couple of them in his pocket as a field test of the proposed shape and color. The dollars were struck for circulation, however, on round planchets dangerously close to the quarter dollar in size, presenting the same reeded edge, clad copper composition, and silvery color. The Mint made much of the 11-sided inner border placed on the new coins, but the public found these useless in distinguishing the dollar from the quarter dollar. The uninspiring obverse certainly played a part in the public's rejection of the coin, but confusion with the quarter, continuing public attachment to the paper dollar bill, and the absence of any convenient place for the coins in the nation's cash registers and money-handling machines also worked powerfully to doom the new coin.

A major beneficiary of the new dollar was to have been the nation's vending-machine industry, to whose needs the U.S. Mint had long been exceptionally attentive. This industry had been ceaselessly invoked in the planning stages for the new dollar, and the nearly complete rejection of the coin by this powerful industry must have been especially shocking to the Mint. The harbinger of a death knell was audible at the 1979 ANA convention in St. Louis, where workmen industriously applied self-adhesive notices proclaiming "This machine does not accept the new silver dollar" to row upon row of hotel vending machines. The coin, of course, had no silver content, but this inappropriate name persisted.

Ex Tenebris: The Return of Commemorative Coinage

In retrospect, the Bicentennial coins, the small-size dollar, and the gold medallion fumble can be viewed as the first feeble wavelets of what became a numismatic tsunami: the wholly unexpected rebirth of commemorative coins. The celebration of the 250th anniversary of George Washington's birth in 1982 proved strong enough to sweep away 28 years of increasingly meaningless and ritualized Treasury cant against commemoratives: they had been plagued by profiteering and abuses in distribution ("Goodness, the three-coin Cincinnati set cost a whole seven-fifty!"), they confused the public, they encouraged counterfeiting, they defeated the primary purpose of the Mint—to make money—and on and on. Bulldozing these hoary objections was legislation approving a Washington commemorative coin introduced in the House early in March 1981 and in the Senate in May 18. Passage was almost giddily rapid, and congressional approval was voted on December 13. The bill was signed into law by President Ronald Reagan in December 1981.

The first commemorative in nearly 30 years was designed by the newly installed chief engraver, Elizabeth Jones, the first internationally acclaimed sculptor in history to hold this post. Struck in 90 percent silver, the new half dollars were identical in size and weight to the coins struck before 1964. This coin and its several successors were subjected

263. Washington 250th Anniversary half dollar of 1982

to close scrutiny and abundant comment by collectors and the public, after which new commemoratives arrived so quickly that fatigue set in and collectors lost the immediacy of interest that had led to careful analysis of the new designs. Another development that separated the new commemoratives from their pre-1954 counterparts was the offering of both Proof and Uncirculated versions and the increasing use of the silver dollar denomination. Breaking with long-standing tradition, the Proofs would be struck in larger numbers, making a number of the new issues scarcer in the business strike or Uncirculated form.

The obverse of the new half dollar presented Washington on horseback facing the viewer, his uniformed figure shown from the knee upward, mounted on a steed turning to face the viewer with fine muscular power (fig. 263). The legend GEORGE WASHINGTON / 250th ANNIVERSARY OF BIRTH 1982 is well spaced, the smaller LIBERTY at left unobtrusive. The reverse placed the concentric upper legend UNITED STATES OF AMERICA / IN GOD WE TRUST above a view of Washington's beloved estate, Mount Vernon. The building is not shown head on, as in the trolley car–like Monticello or Lincoln Memorial on the nickel and cent, but in an angled perspective that creates outstanding visual effect. A tiny eagle and shield and the legend HALF DOLLAR appear below but do not crowd the main device. Jones's assistant Matthew Peloso had contributed to the reverse design and had received permission to place his initials on the coin. He chose to conceal them in the shrubbery left of the building, an act that ruffled the feathers of Mint director Donna Pope and impacted negatively on his career.

In a short time, some 4.9 million Proof Washington half dollars had been struck at San Francisco and 2.2 million business strikes at the Denver Mint, priced at $10.50 and $8.00, respectively. Pricing offered an important insight into the dramatic change in the official position on supposed abuses. Treasurer of the United States Angela M. "Bay" Buchanan told Senator Frank Annunzio's coinage panel in May 1981, "While the Department of the Treasury has a history of objecting to the issuance of commemorative coins for the benefit of private sponsors and organizations, it has not objected to special coinage authorized by Congress for the government's own account." Collectors were soon shaking their heads over the voraciousness of "the government's account," as the new Washington coins' prices on the secondary market swiftly declined well below issue price and remain today at even lower levels. In quick succession, 82 commemorative types appeared between 1982 and the end of 2006; if Proof and Uncirculated versions were counted separately, this total would effectively double. In a short time problems of issue prices, surcharges, and themes chosen for commemoration came to trouble collectors and ultimately drove most of them away from the rapidly expanding series.

The full story of the ins and outs of the second series of U.S. commemoratives could fill volumes. While our primary focus must be on the aesthetics of the new coins, four examples of the problem of costs will explain the response of the collecting community. A collector setting out to acquire all sets and packaging options of several of the most important commemorative coins would have needed an industrial-strength purchasing budget: $1,300 for all options of the 1983 and 1984 Los Angeles Olympics coins; $1,006 for all options of the Statue of Liberty Centennial issues; $2,375 for all of the combinations of the Civil War Battlefields issues; and a whopping $10,628 for all options of the extensive series honoring the 1996 Atlanta Olympics.

An in-depth review of all issues would overwhelm the purposes of this book, but it can be said that between 1982 and 1996 the broad outlines of new commemorative programs emerged, revealing stark extremes in the quality and relevance of designs. Following the success of the Washington half dollar, the silver dollar emerged as the denomination most widely used for commemoration. Its large diameter offered a more far more adequate area for bas relief art than the traditional half dollar, but this additional space could not in itself ensure any greater degree of artistic excellence.

Coins marking the Los Angeles Games of the 23rd Olympiad took center stage in 1983 and 1984. The first games in the City of Angels since 1932 immediately elicited an audacious proposal for a total of 53 coins to be struck in gold, silver, and copper-nickel and marketed by a consortium of Occidental Petroleum, the Franklin Mint, and the investment house of Lazard Frères. This effort would include gold $100 and $50 pieces, silver $10 pieces, and copper-nickel $1 coins, with a percentage of the proceeds going to the U.S. Olympic Committee but more to the consortium. Alternate proposals were quickly made calling for 25 or 17 coins hailing the Los Angeles event. Thanks to Representative Frank Annunzio, the numismatic watchdog of the U.S. Congress, the final nod went to the Mint's own proposal for a three-denomination set to include a .900 $10 gold piece and two .900 silver dollars.

The three coins finally struck for the Los Angeles games offered varying design quality. The silver dollars were the first commemoratives in this denomination since 1900 and employed the word *Olympiad* carelessly. This term does not refer to the games themselves but to the four-year interval between the games, thus: "Games of the 23rd Olympiad." Elizabeth Jones's dollars dated 1983 bear a masterful stylization of the ancient sculptor Myron's *discolobus* or discus thrower, shown as a reiteration of three figures in a successful update of an ancient artwork identified with the Olympics (fig. 264). At the insistence of Treasury secretary Donald Regan, the Olympic star logo was placed in the right field above the Olympic rings, detracting from the simplicity of the basic design. The frosted devices on the Proof version highlight this design, wonderfully emphasizing its intrinsic feeling of motion. John Mercanti's reverse, however, shows a head-and-shoulders view of the American eagle, not identifiable as an Olympic element.

264. Los Angeles Olympics dollar of 1983

Attracting much dismissive criticism were the 1984 dollars depicting the gate of the Los Angeles Olympic stadium, which are dominated by

265. Los Angeles Olympics dollar of 1984

266. Los Angeles Olympics eagle

Robert Graham's sculptures of two human forms that were promptly derided as automobile hood ornaments or as the "headless torsos." The obverse legend is exceptionally tiny in proportion to the coin's size, and while the full-form eagle occupying the reverse is an excellent rendering of the national bird, it offers no specific Olympic imagery (fig. 265).

The first gold commemorative to appear since 1926 bears the eagle or $10 denomination and presented male and female runners upholding the Olympic torch, the five Olympic rings at the left (fig. 266). The reverse bears an eagle display that was described as the Great Seal of the United States but in fact is not, as it lacks the shield on the eagle's breast. In photographs, this gold coin seems to lack all muscular tension, and it was ridiculed as "Dick and Jane jogging" (a quotation attributed to Congressman Annunzio). The obverse design concept was officially attributed to Mint artist Jim Peed, the relief modeling to John Mercanti, and both artists' initials appeared on the obverse. Examination of the actual coin shows that the obverse possesses much more vitality and visual appeal than the illustrations suggest. The coin was further troubled by controversy swirling around the four mintmark varieties created by striking at the Philadelphia, Denver, San Francisco, and West Point mints, which gave collectors an unexpected and costly challenge when they tried to assemble a complete set of these coins.

The 1986 centenary of the erection of Auguste Bartholdi's Statue of Liberty, properly *Liberty Enlightening the World*, on Bedloe's Island in New York harbor called forth three coins: the nation's first commemorative half eagle or $5.00 gold piece, a silver dollar, and the first clad commemorative half dollar. The obverse of the gold coin by Elizabeth Jones looks upward at the face of Liberty gazing into the future, the rays of her coronet extending boldly to the outer rim, and LIBERTY spelled out with four relief and two incuse letters (fig. 267). The arresting reverse eagle appears to be striking downward, with talons spread.

The dollar's obverse bears the entire statue minus its distinctive pedestal, with the great hall of immigrants in the left background (fig. 268). Bursts of lettering identify ELLIS ISLAND, GATEWAY TO AMERICA, joining statutory inscriptions LIBERTY and IN GOD WE TRUST, the mintmark, and incuse date at the base. If the obverse is busy, the reverse is positively cluttered, with flaming torch and huge rays, UNITED STATES OF AMERICA, and three lines (12 words in all) of Emma Lazarus's poem "The New Colossus," with E PLURIBUS UNUM and the denomination below, followed by MP-JM for Peloso and Mercanti. This coin's Proof version creates the boldest contrast of field and reliefs, which highlights the reliefs and rescues them from some of the visual confusion.

The half dollar by Edgar Z. Steever IV and Sherl J. Winter (fig. 269) shows a side view of Bartholdi's great statue facing a tiny Manhattan skyline of 1913 in the distance, dwarfed by a massive rising sun nearly the size of the planet Jupiter. The reverse presents a charming concept, an immigrant family fortunate enough to have navigated its way through the Ellis

Island gauntlet and now facing the same skyline across the choppy waters of the harbor. Here is a coin that redefines "busy," with nearly all surfaces occupied by something in relief, including two separate skyline views. The hands-down artistic winner in this trio must be the gold half eagle.

The bicentennial of the Constitution was celebrated in this early learning stage of renewed commemorative design. It was hailed by two denominations notable for their multiplicity of quill pens. The second commemorative gold half eagle was designed by veteran medalist Marcel Jovine (fig. 270). His obverse bears a massive eagle with coarse and rugged feathers walking left and holding a quill pen the length of its own body; LIBERTY, a minute IN GOD WE TRUST, and the date are squeezed into the narrow outer field, the only area not occupied by feathers. The reverse is dominated by a second upright quill, "We the People" in Old English lettering, 13 tiny stars, FIVE DOLLARS, and an outer legend consisting of the national name and BICENTENNIAL OF THE CONSTITUTION. That so much can be shoehorned into so limited a space is a credit to Jovine's inventiveness if not to artistic restraint.

The silver dollar by Patricia Lewis Verani repeats the Old English "We the People" and quill pen, now placed over rippling sheets of parchment (fig. 271). On this coin the event celebrated is called the U.S. CONSTITUTION 200th ANNIVERSARY. Squeezed in below are 13 stars and the inscription 1787 • LIBERTY • 1987. Verani's reverse triggered immediate amusement with its group of 13 figures in historical costumes coming to a point in the center over the denomination (oddly expressed as DOLLAR 1). The tightly bunched figures' resemblance to bowling pins was inescapable and effectively negated the dignity this design might otherwise have possessed.

The growing importance of sport in U.S. commemoratives was underscored by the coins struck to assist the training of American athletes participating in the games of the 24th Olympiad. Held outside the United States, the winter games took place in Calgary, Alberta, Canada, and the summer events in Seoul, South Korea. This two-coin set included what collectors generally agree is the finest commemorative obverse of the new series, Elizabeth Jones's Nike on the gold $5 coin (fig. 272). The Proof edition is especially striking, with its laurel-crowned head of Nike or Victory nearly facing the viewer, a jewel-like microscopic IN GOD WE TRUST on her narrow hair ribbon; the small date and LIBERTY legend offer minimal visual fatigue. Marcel Jovine's reverse is an interesting contrast, with a small USA inside the top three Olympic rings, directly above a compressed flaming torch over three concentric legends in graduated sizes.

The obverse of the silver dollar by Patricia Lewis Verani is somewhat labored, with the large and incorrectly used legend OLYMPIAD (without "Games of," ordinal number, or locale; fig. 273). Laurel sprays frame hands that light the Olympic torch with the blazing torch of the Statue of Liberty, an icon that could not have been recognized by many collectors. At first glance, the reverse suggests the 1849 Type I gold dollar,

267. Statue of Liberty half eagle

268. Statue of Liberty dollar

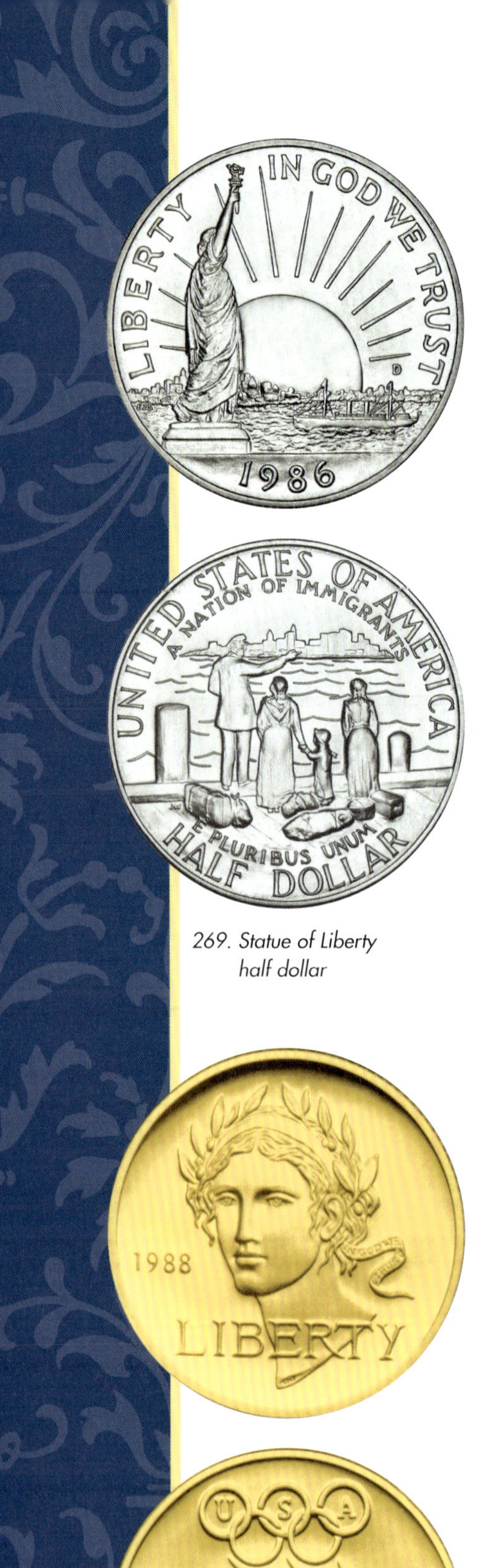

269. Statue of Liberty half dollar

270. Constitution Bicentennial half eagle

271. Constitution Bicentennial dollar

272. Seoul Olympics half eagle

273. Seoul Olympics dollar

274. Congress Bicentennial half dollar

with its value in a wreath, but here 1 DOLLAR is almost rudely elbowed aside by seven lines of lettering and symbol. The resulting composition is a disconnected mixture of semirelated elements that can be charitably described as unexceptional.

Another three-coin set notable for repeated design elements hailed the 1989 bicentennial of Congress. Chosen for the clad half dollar and silver dollar were different views of Thomas Crawford's statue *Freedom,* which stands more than 300 feet above the ground on the pinnacle of the U.S. Capitol. The clad half dollar bears the head and shoulders, the silver dollar the full standing figure, of this little-known Civil War–era sculpture. William Woodward created a somewhat compressed view of the whole Capitol for the reverse of the half dollar (fig. 274). The mace of the House of Representatives on the dollar was also by Woodward, from models by Chester Y. Martin (fig. 275). A gold $5 piece combines a disembodied Capitol dome, the nubbinlike statue at its peak, with an eagle from the Old Senate Chamber, both by John Mercanti (fig. 276). Congress is the subject of commemoration, but a casual observer might be excused for believing that all three coins commemorate the Capitol itself.

A blow to hopes for higher-quality commemoratives came with the ousting of Chief Engraver Elizabeth Jones in December 1990. Her efforts had brought unprecedented international acclaim and honors for her work as a private medalist and as a coin designer, especially in Italy, where she had lived and worked before becoming chief engraver. She was honored by the American Medallic Sculpture Association (AMSA), National Sculpture Society, American Numismatic Society, FIDEM (the International Medal Federation), Italy's Scuola dell'Arte della Medaglia, and the ANA. The shock was profound when her pro forma resignation, submitted at the beginning of the Ronald Reagan presidency, was unexpectedly accepted on December 13, 1990. She was the first chief engraver to leave the post by any path other than retirement or death and, as it turned out, was the last to hold the historic office. The resignation was widely credited to the efforts of Mint director Donna Pope and an ambitious underling who hoped to succeed Jones but failed to realize his goal: the position of chief engraver was abolished under President Bill Clinton in 1996.

By 1992, collector unhappiness with the escalating numbers of new commemoratives, their pricing, and surcharges led to the establishment of the Citizens Commemorative Coin Advisory Committee (CCCAC), which included seven members appointed by the secretary of the Treasury from the public and the collecting community. Like the historic Commission of Fine Arts, the CCCAC was to exercise a purely advisory role, which was not binding on the Treasury and was in fact frequently ignored.

The first commemorative to appear only as a silver dollar marked the 100th anniversary of the birth of Dwight D. Eisenhower in 1990, with an innovative obverse presenting civil and military busts facing in opposite

275. Congress Bicentennial dollar

276. Congress Bicentennial half eagle

directions (fig. 277). The retirement home granted to Ike and Mamie Eisenhower on the Gettysburg National Military Park provided the reverse, although this was not Eisenhower's birthplace. Considerable comment arose from the fact that Eisenhower had already been portrayed on the circulating dollar coins of 1971 to 1978, some of which were sold as Proofs for the benefit of an underfinanced and badly managed institution called Eisenhower College.

The golden jubilee of the Mount Rushmore National Memorial in 1991 saw a clad half dollar designed by Jovine and T. James Ferrell, a silver dollar by Hungarian-born sculptor Marika Somogyi and Frank Gasparro, and a gold $5 piece by Mercanti and Robert Lamb. Once more, two obverses repeat the same device, in this case the monumental sculpture of George Washington, Thomas Jefferson, Theodore Roosevelt, and Abraham Lincoln created by Gutzon Borglum. His was the troubled project for the Confederate memorial on the side of Georgia's Stone Mountain that had been depicted on the 1925 half dollar (fig. 181).

The half dollar and dollar provide a fascinating contrast in the treatment of the same artifact, both crowned by the word LIBERTY but each offering a highly distinctive view of the monument. The buffalo or American bison returned to U.S. coinage on the half dollar reverse within a bold beaded rim (fig. 278). The dollar presents an odd treatment of the Great Seal, placed in what looks like an exploding cloud that merges imperceptibly into a map of the continental United States, inscribed SHRINE OF DEMOCRACY (fig. 279). The obverse of the gold $5 piece is almost wholly occupied by a gigantic eagle, plunging aggressively toward the dwarfed monument, which peers anxiously upward from the extreme lower border, looking for all the world like a bewildered last-minute afterthought to the design (fig. 280). The reverse consists almost entirely of an ornate four-line inscription.

The next two single-coin commemorations plumbed the depths of design trivialization and brought the question of theme into sharp focus. The year 1991, Americans were informed, was the 38th anniversary of the end of the bloody and indecisive war that President Harry S. Truman had stubbornly called the "Korean conflict" or "police action." The Americans fighting in the peninsula called it the Korean War. It was undertaken by United Nations vote to repel the invasion of South Korea by the Communist armies in the North. No other 38th anniversary in history had been marked by a commemorative coin, and the issue was little more than a fund-raiser for the long-delayed monument to this struggle in Washington, DC.

John Mercanti and James Ferrell created the Korean War silver dollar, which immediately became the poster child for regrettable design (fig. 281). The obverse, with its jumbled and totally disproportionately sized elements, strongly suggests a plastic novelty found in a Cracker Jack box in the 1950s. A colossal GI in full battle gear steps off minute ships to climb a dunelike hill while two Sabre jets fly overhead. The

277. Eisenhower Centennial dollar

278. Mount Rushmore Golden Anniversary half dollar

reverse presents a map of the Korean peninsula divided by the 38th parallel, with the Communist north darkly shaded and the south bearing the yin-yang symbol of the Republic of Korea; an eagle's head glowers down from the right. U.S. Mint literature consistently referred to the event as the Korean "War," which must have given belated satisfaction to veterans of the so-called conflict, and coin sales provided some $5.8 million for the war memorial project. Hopefully the storm of criticism over the coin's "carnival throw" design did some long-term good in the preparation of future commemoratives.

From this point, single-coin commemoration became more common, and the release marking the 50th anniversary of the United Service Organization (USO) followed in 1991 (fig. 282). The coin recalled the stirring times of World War II to many veterans but offers an uninspired design that joins the Korean War coin near the bottom of the artistic roster. The obverse by Robert Lamb, modeled by William C. Cousins, presents the script legend "50th Anniversary" over a large USO pennant with statutory mottos. Mercanti's reverse bears an eagle with USO streamer in its beak standing on a beach ball–sized globe. Up to this point the secondary-market performance of modern commemoratives had been uniformly dismal, but the USO coin enjoyed a startling surge into the $60 range before slumping to the now-usual half-issue-price value.

279. Mount Rushmore Golden Anniversary dollar

280. Mount Rushmore Golden Anniversary half eagle

281. Korean War dollar

282. United Service Organizations dollar

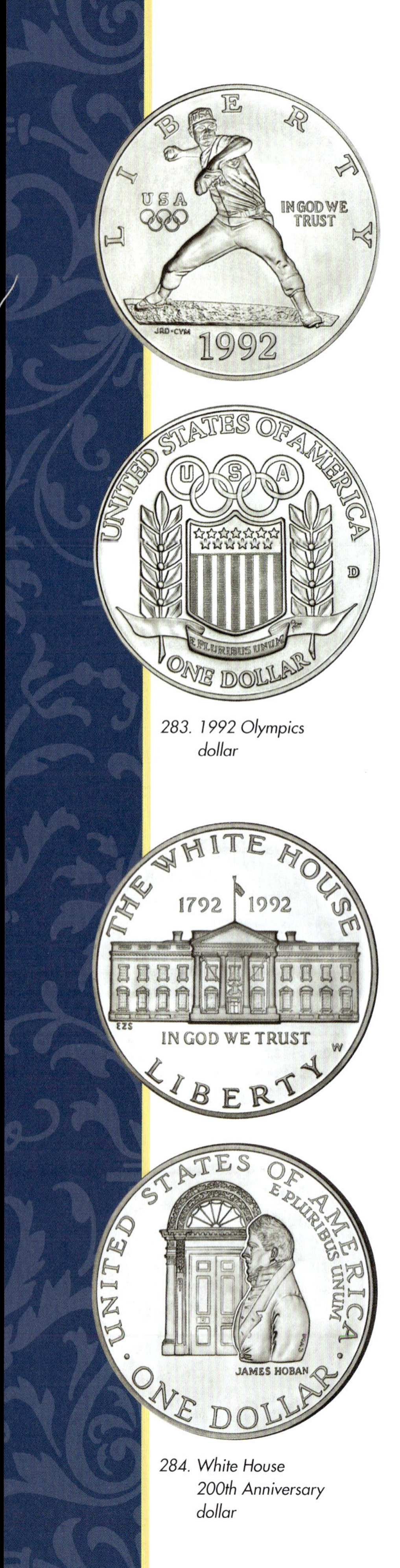

283. 1992 Olympics dollar

284. White House 200th Anniversary dollar

A 1992 commemorative set of clad half dollar, silver dollar, and gold $5 coin hailed the Games of the 25th Olympiad, held in Albertville, France, and Barcelona, Spain. This set offered one newsworthy design element, John R. Deecken's silver dollar obverse, with its baseball pitcher throwing to home plate (fig. 283). Sports-card collectors quickly pointed out that this especially spirited figure is virtually identical to a popular baseball card's portrayal of Texas Rangers star Nolan Ryan. Possibly a more significant feature is the coin's incuse-lettered edge, which repeats XXV OLYMPIAD four times around the circumference.

This year also marked the bicentennial of the White House with a silver dollar designed by Edgar Z. Steever and Chester Martin, which was an outstanding sales success (fig. 284). While its obverse view of the building's north portico is necessarily static, the reverse bears a half-length portrait of Irish-born architect James Hoban and the fan-lighted main entrance, which President John Adams had intended should bear the inscription "May none but wise men rule under this roof." The fashionable pursuit of political correctness no doubt ensured that this sentiment was deleted from the coin design.

The quincentennial of Christopher Columbus's discoveries brought another three-coin set, whose clad half dollar by T. James Ferrell captures the navigator's landing and his three ships with considerable vitality and skill (fig. 285). The silver dollar obverse by Mercanti was thought by many to show Columbus with a telescope, a navigational aid not yet invented in 1492 (fig. 286). The object is, however, a rolled-up chart, but additional debate centered on Thomas D. Rogers's reverse with its jarring juxtaposition of the *Santa Maria* and space shuttle *Discovery.* The gold $5 coin bears a well-balanced Columbus bust facing left against a Western Hemisphere map, with the reverse displaying a chart with compass rose and the coat of arms granted to Columbus as Admiral of the Ocean Sea, as preserved in the *Cronica de Oviedo* (fig. 287). The three coin sets of 1993, 1991 through 1995, and 1994—honoring James Madison and the Bill of Rights, the 50th anniversary of World War II, and the 15th FIFA World Cup soccer playoff—present a panorama of busy designs studded with repetitious portraiture and generous application of inscriptions. The World War II gold $5 coin strongly evokes the spirit of stamps and documents of the war with its triumphant GI and huge reverse V (fig. 288). The World Cup coins all employ the same "World Cup / USA 94" logo on their reverses, unifying the set while sacrificing originality.

The 1993 silver dollar honoring the 250th anniversary of Thomas Jefferson's birth bears a long-necked bust based on a portrait by the great painter Gilbert Stuart (fig. 289). By coincidence, a plaster model for the 1938 Jefferson nickel by Dutch artist Frans Karel Hejda was discovered by Stack's in New York City at this time (fig. 290). The model used a virtually identical Stuart portrait but had lost out to Felix Schlag's design, which featured a bust after Houdon. The dollar's reverse places Monticello off center toward the left, presenting marvelous vitality compared to the same building's lifeless facade on the nickel.

285. *Columbus Quincentenary half dollar*

286. *Columbus Quincentenary dollar*

287. *Columbus Quincentenary half eagle*

288. *World War II 50th Anniversary half eagle*

289. *Thomas Jefferson 250th Anniversary dollar*

290. *Plaster model for 1938 Jefferson nickel, after Stuart portrait*

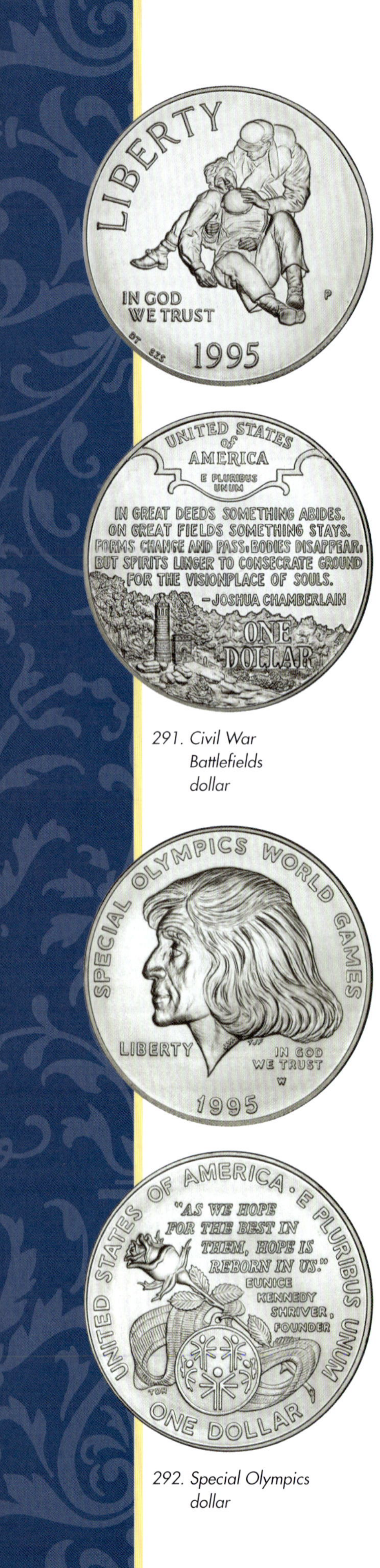

291. Civil War Battlefields dollar

292. Special Olympics dollar

During 1994, four silver dollars appeared in rapid succession, devoted to the Vietnam Veterans Memorial, prisoners of war, women in military service, and the bicentennial of the Capitol. By this point most established collectors of U.S. coins had become jaded and showed less and less interest in this continuing flood of costly commemoratives. That most deadly of modern attributes, irrelevance, had overtaken the series. The new commemoratives might have attracted enough new collectors from the general public to compensate, but cost and the often disconcerting results of attempts to resell these coins for anything near issue price effectively kept many such buyers from progressing into the mainstream of the hobby.

A kind of numismatic time travel distinguished 1995, with the appearance of three coins dedicated to Civil War battlefields—coins that would have been ideal 31 years earlier for the centennial of the War Between the States. All obverses were the work of the greatest modern Civil War artist, Connecticut's Don Troiani, who gave the trio a dignity and simplicity unequaled in the new commemorative series. The reverses of the half dollar and silver dollar, however, tend to the wordiness that afflicts the series as a whole. Even the haunting quotation from Gettysburg hero Joshua Chamberlain, describing battlefields where "spirits linger to consecrate ground for the visionplace of souls," is muted by the general clutter (fig. 291).

During 1995 and 1996, the Atlanta Centennial Olympic Games brought forth a record issue of four clad half dollars, eight silver dollars, and four gold $5 pieces, offered in both Uncirculated and Proof. The obverses illustrated a bewildering variety of sports, while the reverses were standardized for each denomination and date. This effusion can only be described as exhausting, and it is unlikely that many living collectors could list all the Olympic subjects from memory even if a substantial reward were offered for such a feat. Although some remarkably small mintages are included in this mass of coins, collector indifference to them has remained fixed.

Tagging along with the Atlanta coins was the 1995 silver dollar devoted to the Special Olympics, the sports competition that encourages the active participation of those with disabilities (fig. 292). The Special Olympics were originally conceived by Anne Burke of the Chicago Park District in 1965. Eunice Kennedy Shriver became associated with the event through a grant from the Joseph P. Kennedy Foundation in 1968. The Uncirculated 1995 commemorative dollars portraying Shriver were struck at West Point, and the Proofs at Philadelphia. The reverses named her "Founder of the Special Olympics," despite the opposition of the CCCAC and the Commission of Fine Arts to this designation. Both organizations also objected to the portrayal of a living person. Whatever the merits of this debate, it is impossible not to feel regret for the portrait employed, which is profoundly unflattering to its subject. Its pitiless clarity recalls a remark of inaugural-medal sculptor Frank Eliscu, who softened the realism of his 1974 inaugural medal portrait of the 66-year-old vice president, Nelson A. Rockefeller, because "if you portray every wrinkle, you get a piece of taxidermy."

One result of this outburst of Olympic commemoration was 1996 legislation that attempted to set a limit of two issues per year for future commemoratives and limited coinage of each issue to no more than 750,000 clad half dollars, 500,000 silver dollars, and 100,000 gold $5 or $10 coins of each approved issue. Ways were still found to escape some of these restrictions, but the legislation did make a start at reining in the more exuberant proposals.

By the end of 1996 the general trends set by these early commemoratives had become fixed. A new development was the recycling of earlier medallic art, exemplified by the obverse of a decidedly confusing silver dollar dedicated to a very general subject, "national community service" (fig. 293). This coin commemorated no specific organization or cause, or even a definite anniversary, and its obverse was borrowed from a 1906 medal by Augustus Saint-Gaudens for the Women's Auxiliary of the Massachusetts Civil Service Reform Association. The reverse wreath, layout, and lettering are of the style seen in U.S. Mint medals of 1880 through 1900.

Commemoratives from 1997 to 2006 varied profoundly in their focus, from the 150th anniversary of the Smithsonian Institution (marked by a fascinating James Smithson gold $5 piece; fig. 294) to the vastly more trivial dollar for the National Botanic Garden and the poignant 1997 National Law Enforcement Officers Memorial. Coins honored Jackie Robinson's role in breaking the color barrier in professional baseball and the opening of the Franklin D. Roosevelt Memorial in the nation's capital. The latter coin was another gold $5 piece, whose depiction of a wind-blown FDR suggested to numismatist Tom DeLorey a dog out for a Sunday ride in the family Studebaker (fig. 295).

Actual portraiture included Robert F. Kennedy on the 1998 silver dollar (fig. 296), struck on the 30th anniversary of his assassination by Palestinian terrorist Sirhan Bishara Sirhan. Fictitious portraiture appeared on the 1998 Black Revolutionary War Patriots silver dollar (fig. 297), with its bold African American bust identified as Crispus Attucks (1723–1770). No authentic likeness is known of Attucks, who is considered the first martyr to the cause of American independence; he was killed when British soldiers opened fire during a street disturbance that went down in history as the Boston Massacre.

Righting what many numismatists viewed as a historic wrong was the 1999 gold $5 coin marking the bicentennial of George Washington's death (fig. 298). This remarkable coin brought back from obscurity the Laura Gardin Fraser design that had been twice chosen in the 1932 Washington quarter dollar contest and was so unjustly rejected

293. National Community Service dollar

294. Smithsonian 150th Anniversary half eagle

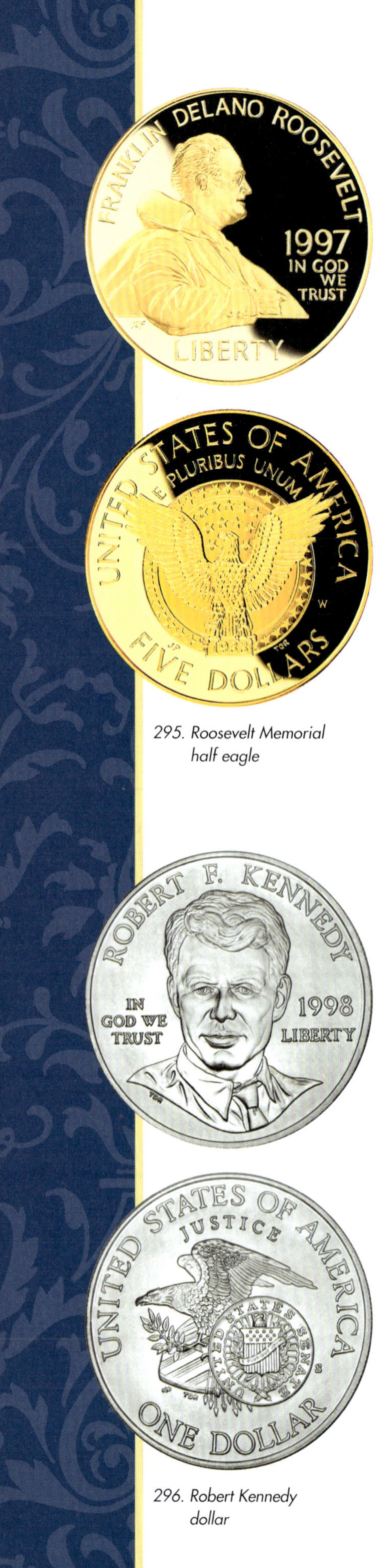

295. Roosevelt Memorial half eagle

296. Robert Kennedy dollar

by secretary of the Treasury Andrew Mellon (see chap. IX and fig. 194). Like the 1995 Civil War coins, this issue achieved a significant if belated purpose 57 years after it was completed. Another retro issue was the 1999 Dolley Madison dollar (fig. 299), whose bold décolleté portrait is a latter-day companion to her husband's portraits on the 1993 Bill of Rights coins, and which includes yet another view of the Madison home, Montpelier.

A startling innovation for the entire U.S. coinage was the bimetallic gold-and-platinum $10 coin honoring the bicentennial of the Library of Congress in 2000 (fig. 300). This issue was America's introduction to the bimetallic coinage in widespread use in Europe, Asia, and Africa. This complex two-color coin's obverse presents a flaming torch that spills over from the platinum center onto the outer gold ring, with the library dome occupying the background. The reverse bears a slightly compressed eagle from the Great Seal, confined entirely to the inner circle. Many collectors today would be surprised to learn of this coin's existence, yet less than a decade after its issue the Uncirculated version bore a catalog value of well over $1,000; its Proof companion listed at over $500. In either version this was not a coin for the fainthearted.

There had always been some on-and-off debate over abstruse historical points of some of the commemoratives of 1892 to 1954: was the 1892 Columbus portrait historically accurate? Was Lord Baltimore's Puritan collar correct? Did Old Swedes Church have the belfry shown on the Delaware half dollar? and so on. The Special Olympics and 2000 Leif Ericson Millennium dollars spurred further debate by introducing a far more disquieting unconcern for factual accuracy in commemorative inscriptions (fig. 301). The questions arising from the term *founder* on the 1995 dollar have been noted. The ruggedly handsome Ericson coin by Mercanti and Ferrell bears an even more debatable assertion: that the Norse explorer was the "founder of the New World." Here is revisionism at its most dramatic, since the founder by any reasonable standard of discovery, exploration, and continuous subsequent development could only be Christopher Columbus, who had been commemorated on the 1992 set.

Ericson, properly Leifur Eriksson, briefly explored a ribbon of coast in the Newfoundland–Nova Scotia region, leaving only a few stone hearths at Anse aux Meadows and the vaguest of historical recollections. Although he was also hailed as "Fundur Norður-Ameríku" on the companion 1,000-krónur coin released by the Republic of Iceland and marketed with the U.S. commemorative, the claim is historically fallacious and unworthy of either issuing nation. A coin commemorating the spurious Kensington Rune Stone of Minnesota would have been almost as fitting a memorial to historical fantasy fulfillment.

Undoubtedly the most startling example of the vast popularity of America's historic-coin designs was the American Buffalo commemorative coin, struck in 2001 to benefit the Smithsonian Museum of the American

297. Black Revolutionary War Patriots dollar

298. Washington Death Bicentennial half eagle

299. Dolley Madison dollar

300. Library of Congress Bicentennial eagle

301. Leif Ericson Millennium dollar

302. American Buffalo dollar

303. $50 gold bullion coin

Indian, created by Public Law 101-185. This new and highly innovative institution grew out of the former Museum of the American Indian, built by the George Heye Foundation as a next-door neighbor to the American Numismatic Society in the Audubon Terrace museum complex at 155th Street and Broadway in New York City. All institutions on the terrace had been endowed by the great benefactor Archer M. Huntington, but starting in the 1980s, three left that site, including the Indian museum.

These American Buffalo coins were silver dollars struck in Proof and Uncirculated at Philadelphia and Denver, respectively (fig. 302). They were enlargements of James Earle Fraser's 1912 designs for the nickel that was struck from 1913 through 1938 (fig. 147); the new dollars displayed incuse dates and denominations but lacked the distinctive textured fields that had distinguished the smaller denomination. The obverse presented the composite Indian head that showed Fraser's mastery of Western art and history at its finest, and the combination of Indian and buffalo made this the most American of all American coin designs. The smooth fields on the silver dollars were a disappointment, however, and did not provide the dimensionality that had made the original nickel such an enduring visual success. Nonetheless, the new Buffalo silver dollars were a dramatic sellout, and the Mint managed to resist the temptation to exceed the mintage limits or create another date of this wildly popular type. Some 227,131 business strikes and 272,869 Proofs were struck, and they soon cataloged at well over $100 for each type.

Retro design was now a powerful factor in American coinage, not only in the commemorative field but in the area of gold and silver bullion coinage as well. To understand this latter phenomenon, it is necessary to go back in time to the aftermath of the unfortunate American Arts gold medallions. The Treasury's determination to block the creation of U.S. bullion coins failed, and only two years after the medallion fiasco both silver and gold pieces were struck that were declared legal tender and given official denominations, although it is unlikely that a single piece ever circulated at its stated value.

First came the $50 denomination (fig. 303), struck in .9167 fine gold but containing a full troy ounce of precious metal. Joining it were the half-ounce ($25), quarter-ounce ($10), and 1/10-ounce ($5) pieces. All bore an obverse that was said to be an updated version of the Augustus Saint-Gaudens high-relief double eagle of MCMVII (1907), and they actually employed Roman-numeral dates from MCMLXXXVI (1986) to MCMXCI (1991), when the complexity made it desirable to switch over to the simpler Arabic numerals. These obverses were retro designs with a switch: the striding Liberty was slimmed down, a size or two having been trimmed from her waist and hips. Much controversy greeted this tampering with the work of the great Saint-Gaudens, but the coins were an immediate commercial success and continue to sell well to the present day.

A new reverse joined the striding Liberty: Texas artist Miley Busiek's "family of eagles," showing a mother, two nestlings, and a wide-winged incoming father about to alight in the family's untidy nest. The new design annoyed many observers already bristling over the weight-loss program for the Saint-Gaudens Liberty, but the design was still being struck 20 years later. For silver-bullion buyers the Mint created a $1 piece (one troy ounce; fig. 304) that brought back Adolph Alexander Weinman's Walking Liberty of 1916, subtly reconfigured to allow the striking of full detail on the hand, which had generally eluded the Mint's efforts from 1916 to 1947. John Mercanti designed the silver bullion coin's reverse, which displays a spread eagle based on the Great Seal but boasts little visual distinction.

The success of the 2001 Buffalo dollar played a role in the next triumph of traditional design, the instantly popular .999 fine gold Buffalo $50 piece of 2006 (fig. 305), which brought back not only Fraser's beloved Indian and buffalo but the irregular surfaces that had been omitted from the 2001 silver dollars as well. This new bullion coin was greeted with a surge of public enthusiasm, and coinage was continued into 2007; sales were largely confined to the United States, without the addition of the fractional pieces.

The dramatic popularity of these retro designs raises an uncomfortable but unavoidable question: are there artists now living who are capable of creating such great bas-relief art? If they exist, where are they, and why is their input not seen on modern commemorative or bullion coins? The designers of the pre-1954 commemoratives were generally sculptors in the round who were put to work creating bas-relief art. The designers of the post-1982 coins have nearly all been graphic artists trying to make bas-reliefs out of two-dimensional images. Without artists of the caliber of the Frasers, the Weinmans, Brenner, Manship, Donald DeLue, Menconi, Margaret Grigor, Walker Hancock, Gertrude Lathrop, Chester Beach, and all the rest, coin design faces a very grim future. There is no way to escape a fundamental reality: modern sculpture of the welded-steel-and-mud-pie school simply cannot serve as viable numismatic art. Recourse will be made again and again to classic designs of the past to answer this very real need.

The first decade of the 21st century is hopefully seeing continuing improvement in commemorative coin design, with the West Point Bicentennial dollar, First Flight Centennial coins, and Benjamin Franklin dollars validating this belief (figs. 306–310). It was a long struggle from 1982 to 1996, but perhaps collectors of the future will study commemoratives of that era with the same determination that earlier generations devoted to the coins of 1892 to 1954. In any case, the modern commemoratives will always retain something of an elitist air, due to their cost and methods of distribution.

304. Sillver bullion dollar

305. Buffalo $50 gold bullion coin

306. *West Point Bicentennial dollar*

307. *First Flight Centennial dollar*

308. *First Flight Centennial eagle*

309. *First Flight Centennial half dollar*

310. *Benjamin Franklin dollars*

The Statehood-Quarter Revolution

The total popularization of numismatic art will result not from traditional commemoratives but from a revolutionary new approach adopted in 1999: the circulating statehood quarter dollars. These feature all 50 states and may include territories such as Washington, DC, Puerto Rico, the U.S. Virgin Islands, and Guam, conditional on the securing of enabling legislation.

The statehood program was a logical outgrowth of concerns over the direction taken by the Mint in selecting subjects, developing designs, and above all, marketing commemorative coins in the mid-1990s. On July 12, 1995, professional numismatist Harvey G. Stack of New York City suggested the statehood concept in testimony before the congressional Subcommittee on Domestic and International Policy. He drew attention to public dissatisfaction with high issue prices and the mere fractions of these prices that buyers of modern issues received when they attempted to sell their coins on the secondary market. Many went away angry and disillusioned at what they thought the coin market had done to them, although in fact they had not dealt with the coin market but solely with the U.S. Mint.

Harvey Stack notes that in explaining his concept to the subcommittee, "I also advocated a circulating commemorative. I spoke to the Commemorative Coins Committee about this. I suggested that we start off as the Canadians did with their coins for the 12 provinces and territories. We could start with the first 13 states and issue new commemorative coins every year or two that would commemorate the other states as they came into the Union, covering all 50 states. These coins would be historical. They would perpetuate history and give an idea when each state entered the Union." The key to the Stack proposal was the issue of the new state quarters at face value, which would enable masses of people to collect them out of circulation, from pocket change, as had been so widely done before the disappearance of silver from U.S. coinage in 1965.

The proposal was spelled out in the summer of 1996 by Michael N. Castle (Republican from Delaware) in legislation termed HR 3793, the 50 States Commemorative Coin Program Act. The act provided for five state issues each year for 10 years, with the states appearing in the order in which each joined the Union. Final approval came when President Clinton signed PL 105-124 in December 1997. The U.S. Mint registered the program name under the title of the 50 State Quarters® Program to head off the private imitations of other government issues that had been widely sold in earlier years, to the public's confusion. Lamentably, even copyright registration did not prevent infringements such as private

311. Statehood quarter dollar obverse

gold-plating of coins, which were sold via Sunday supplements and television amid a welter of inaccurate claims of value and investment potential; in fact, such potential was effectively nonexistent.

All obverses were standardized at the beginning of the program (fig. 311). John Flanagan's 1932 Washington bust would appear on all, with significant modifications by sculptor-engraver William Cousins, including an attempt to strengthen the hair, a feature of the 1932 design that was notoriously weak even on Proofs. Unfortunately, the result suggested that the hair had been worked over by a child wielding a rusty nail. Surrounding the bust would be UNITED STATES OF AMERICA, LIBERTY, IN GOD WE TRUST, and QUARTER DOLLAR.

The reverse would be the "action side," the 24.26 mm stage upon which all state symbols and devices had to be fitted along with the state name, date of admission to the Union, date of issue, and E PLURIBUS UNUM—a tall order for so small a space. Fortunately, a number of perceived problems were eliminated at the start of the design process. Outlawed were state seals and flags, portraits of living persons, and emblems of local organizations, all to assure "a dignity befitting the nation's coinage" and designs that would "have broad appeal to the citizens of the state and avoid controversial subjects or symbols that are likely to offend." Regrettably, outline and relief maps, state birds, and obscure public buildings did not fall under the ban and would repeatedly surface, to general confusion, over the following years.

From the start, state governors and committees were central to a selection process that differed in detail from state to state. Generally, five semifinalists would be winnowed from a larger flotilla of entrants called for by each state. These five would be sent to Washington for review by the Commission of Fine Arts and CCCAC, then by the Mint, then returned to the governor for the final pick unless the secretary of the Treasury invoked his right of absolute veto of any specific design. The results of this process were decidedly mixed, due to the volatile elements of local and national history, community pride and boosterism, and varying concepts of what constituted art or would-be art, topped off with a hearty dose of politics on the local, state, and federal levels.

Considerable ill will was generated from the start by a firm Mint decision not to credit local artists who created the winning designs and to place only its own staff members' initials on the reverses adopted. This practice was extended to states in which the actual designer had been publicized and lionized and might even have received a significant prize for his or her work. Begun under Mint director Philip N. Diehl, this ungenerous policy continued under his successors Jay Johnson and Henrietta Holsman Fore. During 2004 the Mint announced the Artistic Infusion Program, which specifically addressed the need to foster artistic talent in the private sector and secure it for the Treasury and Mint. From many applicants the Mint selected 18 "master designers" and six "associate designers" to whom the development of future coin and medal designs could be entrusted. Fore stated, "The Artistic Infusion Program artists will also receive other new coin and medal assignments as they become available. The initials of both the artists and engravers will be on all coins and medals, *except the state quarters, which will carry only the sculptor-engravers' initials*" (author's emphasis).

This exclusion can only be described as puzzling and grossly inconsistent. When all coin and medal design cried out for new talent, discouraging artists from participating in the area most desperately in need of such help, the statehood quarters, was simply inexplicable. The extensive new rules for design selection released during 2005 merely placed the selection process even more firmly under the Mint's control. Here an overview will be formed on the basis of the artistic achievements of the first 40 issues. It should be noted that in addition to the circulating copper-nickel clad coins, Proofs were struck in clad metal and .900 silver for those wishing to see the coins at their finest. Like the commemorative coins, the statehood Proofs had to be ordered from the Mint. The general public knew little of this and contented themselves with circulating examples taken from pocket change, as Harvey Stack had originally suggested.

Nearly all observers praised the first coin, the Delaware quarter (fig. 312), which depicted patriot Caesar Rodney riding to Philadelphia to ensure that his state voted for independence, the same subject chosen for Delaware's bicentennial medal in 1975. The design offered historical relevance and simplicity, adding only THE FIRST STATE (i.e., the first to ratify the Constitution) and CAESAR RODNEY to the standardized elements.

Pennsylvania came next, and this coin introduced two problems that would recur again and again: the outline map and obscure symbol (fig. 313). The mysterious female figure holding an eagle-topped staff by Donald Carlucci was identified (though not on the coin) as the statue *Commonwealth,* which stands atop the capitol dome in Harrisburg, the work of sculptor Roland H. Perry. Few observers had ever seen this statue, which to history-minded collectors suggested a druid holding a storm trooper standard of the 1930s. On the next quarter New Jersey offered the heroic image of the painting *Washington Crossing the Delaware*, by Emmanuel Leutze, an intricately detailed scene reduced to 21 × 11 mm and placed over the legend CROSSROADS OF THE REVOLUTION (fig. 314). Georgia offered a peach inside an outline map, framed by branches and a ribbon inscribed WISDOM JUSTICE MODERATION—a simple if undeniably bland composition (fig. 315). Andy Jones was positively identified as designer of the Connecticut quarter, which completed the issues of 1999 (fig. 316). It presented what was said to be the Charter Oak, but it resembles a leafless sea fan more than the boldly leafed tree that graced Henry Kreis's design for the Connecticut Tercentenary half dollar of 1935 (fig. 201).

Massachusetts led off the 2000 coins, offering a relief map of the Bay State with a star at Boston and a view of the famous Daniel Chester

312. Delaware quarter dollar reverse

313. Pennsylvania quarter dollar reverse

314. New Jersey quarter dollar reverse

315. Georgia quarter dollar reverse

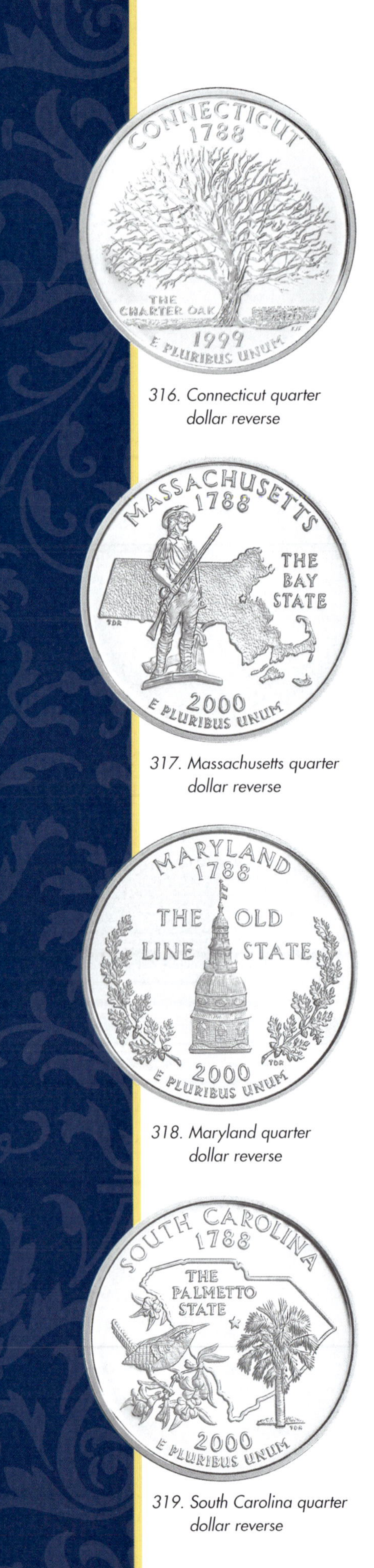

316. Connecticut quarter dollar reverse

317. Massachusetts quarter dollar reverse

318. Maryland quarter dollar reverse

319. South Carolina quarter dollar reverse

French statue *The Minute Man* (fig. 317). This design was created by two unidentified schoolchildren and evoked for older collectors memories of World War II stamps and savings bonds. Maryland's contribution provided the second obscure public building of the series, the wooden dome of the Capitol at Annapolis, flanked by a chopped-up Washington quotation, THE—OLD / LINE—STATE (fig. 318). This somewhat enigmatic state nickname, along with white oak sprays, was added by Mint sculptor Thomas D. Rogers Sr. to the basic design of Bill Kraczewicz, later one of the "master designers" named under the 2004 Artistic Infusion Act. Most collectors wrote it off as an oddly decorated dinner bell and dismissed it from their minds. South Carolina's quarter has a distinct resemblance to sentimental postcard art with its perky wren, outline map with a star for Columbia, palmetto tree, and somewhat redundant legend THE PALMETTO STATE (fig. 319). This is a charming composition, but it possesses none of the gravitas expected from a state tribute.

Natural landmarks take center stage on New Hampshire's quarter (fig. 320), with its rendering of the Great Stone Face or Old Man of the Mountain, the granite cliff that had already symbolized the state on its World War I service medal, on a commemorative stamp, and most recently on brass New Hampshire Department of Transportation highway toll tokens. LIVE FREE OR DIE joined the design, which was made unusually historic only three years later when the rocky outcropping collapsed into a pile of talus after untold millennia of water seepage freezing and thawing. Plans for its restoration have thus far come to naught. Virginia focused on an actual historical event for its quarter, the 400th anniversary of the settling of Jamestown (fig. 321). Three graceful ships approach from the left, with the legends JAMESTOWN 1607–2007 and QUADRICENTENNIAL in the field. Citing a specific event gives this coin a more than ordinarily apparent commemorative quality.

The year 2001 opened with the New York quarter, which placed the Statue of Liberty over a topographical map featuring the Erie Canal and lower Hudson River (fig. 322). The design also features 11 stars and the slogan GATEWAY TO FREEDOM, a reference to the great wave of 19th-century immigration that entered the United States through the city and later via Ellis Island. North Carolina highlighted the first flight of a heavier-than-air craft by Wilbur and Orville Wright at Kitty Hawk on December 17, 1903 (fig. 323). The art was derived from a contemporary photo of the 120-foot flight, and the theme ruffled feathers in Ohio, the Wrights' home state. The prolific artist Daniel Carr created the graceful seascape on the Rhode Island quarter, which honors the 13th and most unwilling state to ratify the Constitution (fig. 324). Pell Bridge forms the background for the sailboat at the center, which is flanked by the legend THE OCEAN STATE. Carr also designed two later state quarters, neither of which was officially linked to him, in accordance with the mean-spirited policy that continued throughout the series.

Vermont chose a maple-tapping scene backed by a profile of the Camel's Hump of the Green Mountains and the slogan FREEDOM AND UNITY (fig. 325). No attempt was made to recall the state's Revolutionary history, which had already been highlighted by the 1927 Vermont Sesquicentennial half dollar. A thoroughbred racehorse and the hilltop mansion near Bardstown where Stephen Collins Foster wrote "My Old Kentucky Home" give the Kentucky quarter a cheerful tone (fig. 326). More than 50,000 entries were received in the state contest, but there were only two finalists: the horse and a design hailing the birthplace of Abraham Lincoln. The unusually hostile interaction of the Mint and the Kentucky contest representatives appointed by Governor Paul E. Patton represented a low point in the overall program.

Tennessee's rich musical heritage inspired its 2002 quarter, whose designer, elementary-school teacher Shawn Stookey of New Johnsonville, was actually credited by the Mint with the winning design, which features fiddle, trumpet, and guitar (fig. 327). Both fiddle and trumpet display inaccuracies, to the delight of sharp-eyed collectors. Ohio zeroed in on its contributions to aviation and space exploration, displaying an outline map with the Wright Brothers' 1905 *Flyer III* emerging at left, and an astronaut modeled on a photograph of Col. Edwin "Buzz" Aldrin in full space gear at right (fig. 328). A nagging disagreement with North Carolina led to the peculiarly worded legend BIRTHPLACE OF AVIATION PIONEERS. Humorists noted the noose-like state border directly over the suited figure and promptly dubbed this the "hanging astronaut" quarter.

The ultimate development of the ubiquitous map had to be that on the Louisiana quarter (fig. 329). The design features an outline map of the continental United States, with a smaller relief map of the Louisiana Purchase near its center, on which the modern state is demarcated. A brown pelican and a trumpet (criticized for valve construction details) emitting three musical notes complete the complex composition. Indiana, "Crossroads of America," provided yet another map and star, plus a circle of 19 stars and a modern racing car of the Indianapolis 500 (fig. 330). This race is a commercial event, held on the raceway built by automotive pioneer Carl G. Fisher, which opened with an asphalt track in the hot summer of 1908. Fisher called the race off after the heat-softened pavement caused accident after accident. Rebuilt with brick, the track reopened in 1911. There was some comment on the commercial nature of the great event, but Governor Frank O'Bannon and the Mint were unconcerned. Ending this year was the Mississippi effort, a spray of blossoms from the state tree and flower, justifying the script name "The Magnolia State" (fig. 331). Here was a design at once elegant and simple, without a map!

The quarter for Illinois, "Land of Lincoln," features a busy and distinctly crowded design that still manages to exert its own unique charm (fig. 332). The reverse depicts the Chicago skyline, dominated by the Sears Tower, and an outline map that encloses the standing figure of

320. New Hampshire quarter dollar reverse

321. Virginia quarter dollar reverse

322. New York quarter dollar reverse

323. North Carolina quarter dollar reverse

324. *Rhode Island quarter dollar reverse*

325. *Vermont quarter dollar reverse*

326. *Kentucky quarter dollar reverse*

327. *Tennessee quarter dollar reverse*

328. *Ohio quarter dollar reverse*

329. *Louisiana quarter dollar reverse*

330. *Indiana quarter dollar reverse*

331. *Mississippi quarter dollar reverse*

332. *Illinois quarter dollar reverse*

333. *Alabama quarter dollar reverse*

334. *Maine quarter dollar reverse*

335. *Missouri quarter dollar reverse*

a youthful, beardless Abraham Lincoln. Another human form appears on the Alabama quarter: Helen Keller, seated in a chair labeled SPIRIT OF COURAGE (fig. 333). Blind, unable to speak, and deaf from her 19th month, Keller (1880–1968) became a world-renowned symbol of triumph over physical challenges, although her connection with Alabama was unsuspected by most collectors and the general public. Another appealing seascape made the Maine quarter memorable, along with an exceptionally harsh struggle between the Mint and designer Daniel J. Carr that resulted when a generic scene (fig. 334) emerged from what had been a specific representation of the Pemaquid Point lighthouse.

The most vigorous and public contention of the whole series centered on the Missouri quarter. Designer Paul Jackson squared off against the Mint leadership over the drastic redrafting of his original concept, which showed Lewis and Clark paddling a canoe down a river with heavily wooded banks, with a view of the Jefferson National Expansion Monument, the famous St. Louis Arch, in the distance. The Mint moved an enlarged arch to the center and placed a heavy river pirogue with six paddling men in the river. The legend CORPS OF DISCOVERY 1804 2004 identified the scene. The Commission of Fine Arts panned the second version, and an enraged Jackson went public with his denunciations. As the coin was finally struck, three men are shown paddling an awkward vessel closely resembling a bathtub between leaning trees that are altogether too similar to broccoli on a salad plate (fig. 335).

The Arkansas coin presented another cluttered design of the postcard genre with its mallard duck flying over a river bordered in trees, rice stalks at left, and a faceted diamond suspended over all, recalling the state's possession of America's only active diamond mine (fig. 336). Numismatists recalled the bold diamond shape on the Arkansas Centennial half dollars of 1935 to 1939, which drew attention to the same historic mine (fig. 202).

Michigan led the 2004 parade with its field-filling map of all the Great Lakes, featuring a relief state map separating Lakes Michigan and Huron, and the Upper Peninsula separating Lakes Michigan and Superior (fig. 337). This crisp, clear, field-filling design is the first appearance of the lakes since the 1936 Great Lakes Exposition (Cleveland) half dollar. The Florida quarter is reminiscent of the Columbus Quincentennial dollar, but the quarter depicts the space shuttle *Discovery* soaring into space, the Spanish galleon sailing below, with the punning inscription GATEWAY TO DISCOVERY (fig. 338). The overall effect, unfortunately, is that of the "Sand Dollar" tokens issued earlier by service clubs near Cape Canaveral. The Texas coin offered stark simplicity, the "lone star" superimposed on a relief map inside a rope border (fig. 339). The stark contrast between the 2004 Texas quarter and the Texas Centennial half

336. *Arkansas quarter dollar reverse*

337. *Michigan quarter dollar reverse*

338. *Florida quarter dollar reverse*

339. *Texas quarter dollar reverse*

340. Iowa quarter dollar reverse

341. Wisconsin quarter dollar reverse

342. California quarter dollar reverse

343. Minnesota quarter dollar reverse

dollar of 1934 to 1938 would be hard to exaggerate. This may be the only map design to attain this high degree of artistic integrity.

Iowa's quarter offered a fairly thorough revision of a Grant Wood painting (recall the first American Arts medallion), in this instance his canvas entitled *Arbor Day,* a scene of tree planting set at a one-room schoolhouse on the rolling prairie that makes up so large a part of the state's topography. As struck, the sapling being planted has become a tall tree, and most of those taking part in the planting have been omitted, but GRANT WOOD is placed just below the teacher and children, who are struggling with the massive roots of the tree they are planting (fig. 340). The scene is pleasing enough and certainly evocative of the Great Plains. The Wisconsin quarter groups together a cow's head, a cut wheel of cheese, and an ear of corn, creating a wholly agricultural theme (fig. 341). Several relatively bold varieties with extra leaves at the lower left of the corn were soon discovered and dubbed "Extra Leaf" varieties. Of uncertain cause, these varieties brought added specialist interest to the Wisconsin issue.

California, like New York, is a state deeply divided into north and south. Suggested for its quarter were themes of Hollywood, the sea, Golden Gate Bridge, the gold rush of 1849, and wilderness conservation as personified by John Muir, father of Yosemite National Park. Amid much vocal advocacy by the politically powerful Sierra Club, Governor Arnold Schwarzenegger chose a standing bearded figure of Muir, a soaring condor, and Yosemite's Half Dome peak (fig. 342). The result is of more or less universal rather than parochial California interest, which is not wholly a bad thing.

Minnesota, by comparison, was a shoo-in: its small map and legend LAND OF 10,000 LAKES appear to the left of a lake scene with a fishing boat and a common loon, pine trees towering on shore (fig. 343). Oregon followed with its own scenic Crater Lake, also edged in pines, and offering one of the most serene landscape images in the statehood coin program (fig. 344). Kansas achieved simplicity and popularity at one stroke—if not particular originality—with its reverse design of a buffalo seen nearly full face on a grassy mound flanked by sunflowers growing at left (fig. 345). The final 2005 coin honored the mountain state of West Virginia with a view of the graceful bridge spanning New River Gorge, a 3,030-foot steel span (fig. 346).

Nevada's 2005 quarter is an unusually beautiful object, if not the "Morning in Nevada" theme approved by the state's citizens. Instead, three sleek, glistening horses race toward the left between sagebrush sprays (fig. 347). In the background the sun rises over mountains just slightly taller than the horse in profile. The beauty is somewhat precious, and the horses resemble a trio of well-fed Lipizzaner stallions or a Louis XIV carousel more than the wild mustangs they are supposed to represent. Nebraska chose the solitary, needlelike Chimney Rock under a blazing sun for its design (fig. 348). An ox-drawn Conestoga wagon at left represents the innumerable wagon trains heading West that used this natural feature as a vital landmark.

Colorado also chose to focus on the state's natural beauty, depicting the jutting Rocky Mountains and a pine forest over a banner with the incuse inscription COLORFUL COLORADO (fig. 349). Debate over the Colorado design coincided with the replacement of the CCCAC by the Citizens Coinage Advisory Committee, which included the dynamic Ohio coin dealer Tom Noe, who began making a vastly different kind of headline soon after. North Dakota received only 400 entries in its state quarter contest and settled rapidly on a pair of grazing buffalo before the Badlands' buttes (fig. 350). Here was another simple, almost bucolic design of some artistic distinction and free of objectionable clutter—and, above all, maps.

The year 2006 closed with the South Dakota quarter, modeled by John Mercanti (fig. 351). This was a remarkable reprise of the obverse for the 1991 Mount Rushmore Golden Anniversary silver dollar by Marika Somogyi. There are differences, to be sure: wheat ears replaced the laurel flanking the view of the monument, and Lincoln on the quarter has been given distinctly anthropoid features, while Jefferson more closely suggests a Jivaro Indian treatment of the human head than the well-detailed bust on the earlier dollar.

344. Oregon quarter dollar reverse

345. Kansas quarter dollar reverse

346. West Virginia quarter dollar reverse

347. Nevada quarter dollar reverse

348. Nebraska quarter dollar reverse

349. Colorado quarter dollar reverse

350. North Dakota quarter dollar reverse

351. South Dakota quarter dollar reverse

While the statehood program presented many fascinating quirks, it created a splendid new collectible. It offered at least the opportunity for development of real numismatic art and evoked an outstanding range of questions deserving of in-depth research in the future. Its very real overall success also led to further democratization of U.S. commemorative coinage. In 2004 through 2006, the bicentennial of Lewis and Clark's exploration of the Louisiana Purchase was celebrated by another name-protected program, the Westward Journey Nickel Series™.

The 2004 release paired the 1938 Felix Schlag bust of Jefferson with two different reverses (fig. 352). First was a re-creation of the reverse of the Thomas Jefferson Indian Peace medal by Norman E. Nemeth, showing crossed hatchet and peace pipe over the clasped hands of an American military officer with stripes on his sleeve and an Indian wearing a bracelet with the American eagle of the 1804 pattern. The appearance of this coin brought many calls to coin dealers: "I got an 1803 nickel! Says so right under LOUISIANA PURCHASE!" Later in the year there appeared the Keelboat reverse by Alfred Maletsky, with its ungainly river craft with seven men on deck, two in uniform chapeaus, five poling. A sail and tent at the stern re-create the watercraft used by the Corps of Discovery and present a remarkably detailed treatment for an area of just 21.2 mm.

For the 2005 release (fig. 353), John Fitzgerald and Don Everhart presented a new obverse with an innovative Jefferson profile facing right and the back of the head extending off the planchet; the script legend "Liberty" is at right. The first 2005 reverse, by Jamie Franki and Norman E. Nemeth, presented a buffalo facing right on a mound so thin as to suggest a tree branch. The next reverse offered a seascape from a tall bluff near the Columbia River with an excerpt from Captain William Clark's ecstatic journal entry on reaching the broad Pacific: "Ocean in view! O! The joy!"

The final Westward Journey nickel (fig. 354) bore a tall, nearly full-face Jefferson bust by Jamie Franki and Donna Weaver. The reverse was confusingly publicized as the return of the "original" Monticello, the lifeless trolley car that the Mint had substituted in 1938 for Schlag's real original design showing the building in three-quarters perspective with its trees and delightful 1930s lettering. Excepting this part of the design, all of the new nickels were praiseworthy and represented a solid contribution to numismatic art.

At this time Lewis and Clark seemed to permeate several areas of U.S. coinage, including the 2004 commemorative silver dollar (fig. 355), which features standing figures of both explorers and a small-diameter Indian Peace medal on the reverse, which was soon adapted to the first Lewis and Clark nickel, just described. More significant to the public was the Mint's second attempt at a small-size circulating dollar, the 26.49 mm infelicitously named "golden dollar" struck in 2000 in a complex alloy of 6 percent zinc, 3.5 percent manganese, 2 percent nickel, and 88.5 percent copper, bearing a plain edge. The obverse, by Glenna Goodacre, portrays the Shoshone Indian woman Sacagawea, who, with her husband,

352. *Westward Journey nickels of 2004*

353. *Westward Journey nickels of 2005*

354. *Westward Journey nickel of 2006*

355. *Lewis and Clark Bicentennial dollar*

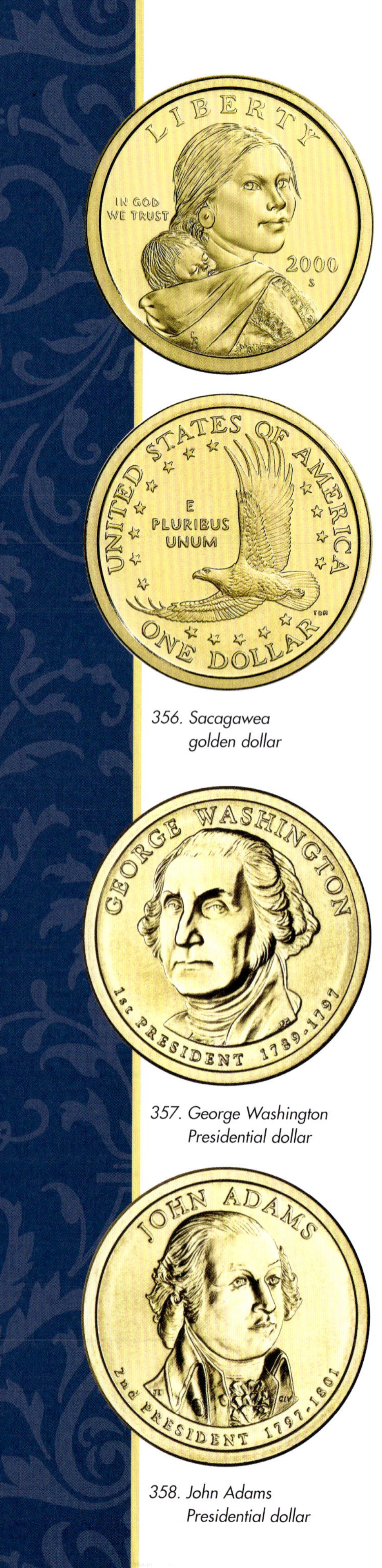

356. Sacagawea golden dollar

357. George Washington Presidential dollar

358. John Adams Presidential dollar

French wood-runner Pierre Charbonneau, accompanied the Corps of Discovery (fig. 356). Many history books refer to her as the expedition's guide, but her knowledge of geography was little more advanced than that of Lewis and Clark. Goodacre portrays her carrying her infant son, nicknamed Pompey by Clark, thus underlining the real value of her presence: as a woman and mother, she testified to the expedition's peaceful intent. Thomas D. Rogers's reverse shows an eagle soaring on wide wings within a circle of stars.

When new, these coins radiated a glorious mint luster, but manganese is notoriously hard to mix, as the Mint discovered with its "silver" nickels of 1942 through 1945, and some degree of discoloration was soon apparent. Moreover, although color and edge distinguished the Sacagawea dollar from the quarter dollar and the doomed Susan B. Anthony dollar, there was still no place in the till for the new coins. The Treasury decision to launch the coins through Wal-Mart rather than through the nation's banks antagonized the latter institutions, which then folded their arms and waited for the coin's failure. Sculptor Goodacre showed rare commercial acumen in requesting payment in 5,000 of the new dollars, which she then had encapsulated by International Coin Grading with a special filament announcing, "Presented to obverse sculptor Glenna Goodacre by the U.S. Mint."

By 2007, circulation of the Sacagawea dollar was only sporadic, and the announcement that the U.S. Postal Service was phasing out the stamp-vending machines that gushed the dollars as change was an unexpected blow to continued circulation. Nonetheless, in early 2007 the Mint began coinage of a new circulating commemorative series of dollars in the golden alloy, which portrays all deceased presidents of the United States. Each coin bears an incuse-lettered edge with mintmark, E PLURIBUS UNUM, and IN GOD WE TRUST, thus eliminating some of the clutter that cursed the statehood quarter dollars and commemorative coins. An early ploy called for recycling the stilted busts on the U.S. Mint presidential medals, an idea instantly shot down by the advisory and fine arts bodies. Instead, all-new busts of Presidents Washington, John Adams, Jefferson, and Madison appeared in the first year (figs. 357–360) with a new reverse inscribed UNITED STATES OF AMERICA around the Statue of Liberty and a large denomination expressed as "$1" (fig. 361). Upon the release of the first presidential dollar, observers noted that the somewhat lumpy features of Washington suggested that he had been in a bare-knuckle boxing match with a prominent pugilist. Hopefully future releases will be less startling to the public eye.

A new and dynamic mint director, Edmund C. Moy, came into office as the new dollar program took off and offered a delightfully upbeat view of the new series that may well impact on its eventual success. The legislation specifies that Sacagawea production must continue for at least one third of each year's dollar coin production, and Moy expressed hope that the Treasury could spread dollar coin use in such wholesale coin-consuming areas as parking meters in major cities, including New York. It can be safely said that the new dollars are a direct legacy of the statehood quarter dollars and may provide additional "out-of-pocket" collectibles for the nation at large.

The more than 200-year saga of American coinage contains many outstanding successes and a few dismal failures. One thing it cannot be called is dull. The continuing struggle for acceptable numismatic iconography for a republic that grew from a few million settlers on the Atlantic seaboard to a world power in little more than two centuries is recorded in the nation's coins and medals. Hopefully this book has provided insight into the landmarks of this struggle.

359. Thomas Jefferson Presidential dollar

360. James Madison Presidential dollar

361. Reverse for all Presidential dollars

Notes • Bibliography • Index

Notes

Abbreviations

AJN	*American Journal of Numismatics,* 1866–1919.
Judd	J.H. Judd, W.H. Breen, and A. Kosoff, *United States Pattern, Experimental and Trial Pieces.* Racine, WI: Whitman Publishing, 1965.
Morey	C.R. Morey, "Sculpture Since the Centennial," in *The Pageant of America,* vol. XII, *The American Spirit in Art.* New Haven, CT: Yale University Press, 1927.
Saint-Gaudens	H. Saint-Gaudens, *The Reminiscences of Augustus Saint-Gaudens.* New York: Century, 1913.
Selections From The Numismatist	American Numismatic Association, *Selections From* The Numismatist: *United States Coins.*
Slabaugh	A.R. Slabaugh, *United States Commemorative Coinage: The Drama of America as Told by Our Coins.* Racine, WI: Whitman Publishing, 1963.
Taxay, *Commemorative Coinage*	D. Taxay, *An Illustrated History of U.S. Commemorative Coinage.* New York: Arco Publishing, 1967.
Taxay, *U.S. Mint*	D. Taxay, *The U.S. Mint and Coinage: An Illustrated History From 1776 to the Present.* New York: Arco Publishing, 1966.
Yeoman	R.S. Yeoman, *A Guide Book of United States Coins.* 23rd ed. Racine, WI: Whitman Publishing, 1969.

CHAPTER I. Background of the Federal Coinage

1. The Greco-Roman sources and Renaissance parallels, including coins, are discussed in detail and illustrated in an article by O. Brendel, "Die Friedensgottin: Numen und Allegorie," in *Corolla Ludwig Curtius* (Stuttgart: W. Kohlhammer, 1937), 212–216, plates 68–71.

2. Rhys Carpenter, *The Esthetic Basis of Greek Art* (Bloomington: Indiana University Press, 1962), 21.

3. The reverse legend is taken from one of Horace's *Odes*, one filled with harmless mental ramblings, and Benjamin Franklin had a hand in this part of the design, receiving the suggestion for the mottoes from one Sir William Jones. The two snakes being throttled by the infant Hercules are said to symbolize the surrender of Burgoyne at Saratoga, October 17, 1777, and Cornwallis at Yorktown, October 19, 1781, the dates appearing below. "Two were struck in gold and presented to the King and Queen of France [Louis XVI and Marie Antoinette]. Silver ones were given to the French Ministers of the Chamber of Deputies as well as to some of the higher dignitaries in the U.S. The bronze pieces were presented to the members of Congress." *Stack's Auction Catalog,* September 30 and October 1, 1966, 40, number 652. It is clear the piece had much more French than American orientation. See C.W. Betts, *American Colonial History Illustrated by Contemporary Medals* (New York, 1894), 300, under number 615; and J.F. Loubat, *The Medallic History of the United States of America, 1776–1876* (New York, 1878), 86–92, under number 14. Franklin's original idea for the reverse had the infant Hercules in his cradle and France/Minerva "sitting by as his nurse," "her robe specked with a few 'fleurs-de-lis.'"

A contemporary account quoted from J.U. Niemcewicz's "A Visit to Mount Vernon," *American Heritage* 16 (February 1965): 70, confirms that the allegorical or mythological aspects of this medal by Dupré were taken literally: "Mrs. Washington

showed me a small collection of medals struck during the Revolution . . . one with the head of Liberty on one side and on the reverse France defending America with her shield against Gr[eat] Britain."

A curious modern echo of the Liberty with flowing hair and cap on pole over her right shoulder appears on the 1969 Annual Convention medal of the American Numismatic Association, the work of Frank Gasparro. The chief engraver has chosen traditional themes, including an eagle based on those used on silver coinage from 1807 through 1891, because the convention was held at Philadelphia in connection with the dedication of a new, "$37 million" U.S. Mint building. The style of Gasparro's Liberty is not that of the 1790s but that of Augustus Saint-Gaudens about 1907, specifically his studies for the head of General Sherman's Nike and the Liberty on the gold coinage. See the *New York Times,* July 27, 1969, D27. See also *The Numismatist* (May 1969): 625–626, with drawings.

4. C.T. Tatman, "The Beginnings of United States Coinage," *AJN* 29 (1895): 72.

5. "The Eagle on Our Coins," *AJN* 29 (1894): 32.

6. "The Coin Cabinet at the Philadelphia Mint," *AJN* 29 (1894): 20.

7. See address by Nellie Tayloe Ross, director of the U.S. Mint, quoted in Arthur Sipe, "Franklin Institute Celebrates Debut of the Benjamin Franklin Half-Dollar," *Selections From* The Numismatist, 172.

8. Yeoman, 194.

9. The description is taken from an editorial comment by William Sumner Appleton in 1874, "Medal Commemorative of American Independence," *AJN* 9 (1875): 65–66.

10. Ibid., 66, with letter quoted from T.J. Randolph, *The Writings of Thomas Jefferson,* vol. III (Boston, 1830), 56–57. Jefferson was concerned about the value of these potential "Diplomatic" or presentation medals—that is, the amount of gold in the links of chain per important recipient. He then goes on to talk about the hiring of "Drost," a Swiss, to undertake assaying in the confidential operation of coining. This was the medalist and die engraver Jean-Pierre Droz, to whom at one time the dies for the first or Chain cent of 1793 were attributed (fig. 15).

11. Two gold medals and six examples in bronze were finished by January 1792. One of the dies was broken in the coining press, causing considerable delay. In April 1790, when the medal was being planned, Jefferson felt the female should be "a Columbia." See Loubat, *Medallic History of the United States of America,* 115ff., under number 19, where the side with the allegorical figures is considered the obverse. The copies by C.E. Barber were made at the behest of H.R. Linderman, director of the Mint, in order that the piece might be added to the "list of public medals." See *Numismatic Scrapbook Magazine,* January 25, 1967, 199–200, for the letter of authorization from Linderman to James Pollock, superintendent of the Philadelphia Mint. Barber's version of the so-called Diplomatic medal (no. 635) was sold at the Mint until the 1980s. Barber also made a "Great Seal Centennial Medal, 1782–1882" (no. 636).

12. "The New Dime," *Selections From* The Numismatist, 155.

13. R. Morris, "The Liberty Cap on American Coins," *AJN* 13 (1879): 52–53.

14. T. Spicer-Simson, "Portrait Reliefs, Medals and Coins in Their Relation to Life and Art," *AJN* 51 (1917): 183.

15. See B.L. Belden, *Indian Peace Medals Issued in the United States* (New Milford, CT: N. Flayderman, 1966).

16. From the earliest decades of the United States to the present, private medals have been important in shaping the course of numismatic art. Artists trained in the Mint have worked for private concerns, and designers normally retained by outside firms have created dies struck at the Mint. Fame as an engraver in private practice in America or abroad has at times led to employment by the Mint. The arts of public and private enterprise have long been closely allied. In several periods of American history—notably the decades after the Civil War, the years after 1915, and the generation from 1950 to 1970—the demand for private medals has been great, and many distinguished artists have fashioned works of exceptional beauty in the medium of medals of all sizes in a number of metals.

17. Illustrated in A.T. Gardner, *American Sculpture: A Catalogue of the Collection of the Metropolitan Museum of Art* (New York, 1965), 131. Albert Laessle (1877–1954) was born in Philadelphia and worked continuously there, hence his penchant for eagles; this one was exhibited at the Sesquicentennial Exposition, Philadelphia, in 1926.

18. The distributor's announcement of the President Nixon official inaugural medal shows that the relation between needlework and numismatic art was as valid in 1969 as it was in 1806 or 1825. "A sculptured miniature of the crewelwork pattern depicting the Great Seal of the United States, embroidered by Julie Nixon for her father, appears on the reverse side of the medal, along with the wording 'To RN—JN.' The introduction of a personal family touch in the design is a first in the medal's 68-year history. Following tradition, a sculptured portrait of the President appears on the obverse side." Advertisement of Presidential Art Medals, Inc., *The Numismatist* (March 1969): 375.

19. The postage stamp of course came to offer outlets for portraiture as yet inadmissible on the regular coinage, and in time of necessity the encased stamp more than the banknote brought the art of the engraver for paper in direct relation with the message of the die cutter.

CHAPTER II. Early Coins and Medals of the United States

1. The schema for the reverse, ONE CENT in a wreath, fraction below, and (in this case) UNITY STATES OF AMERICA around, appears on a Washington coin dated 1783. The design was also used on the very rare Birch Cent of 1791, made from dies evidently engraved by Robert Birch when Congress first authorized issues by the U.S. Mint. See Yeoman, 52 and 58.

2. New Hampshire *Gazette,* December 2, 1794, quoted in "Dollar of 1794," *AJN* 9 (1874): 9.

3. On the general subject, especially in connection with sculpture, see chapter 61, "Neoclassicism in America," in Benjamin Rowland Jr.'s *The Classical Tradition in Western Art* (Cambridge, MA: Harvard University Press, 1963), 311–318.

CHAPTER III. America's Classical Coinage

1. Gobrecht also did a rather different medal in 1826, in honor of Charles Carroll of Carrollton, last surviving signer of the Declaration of Independence. The design was traditional and prosaic, a bust on the obverse and lettering in and around a wreath and scroll on the reverse. See V. Clain-Stefanelli, *History of the National Numismatic Collections* (Washington, 1968), 46, figure 97.

2. Sully's connections with the officials of the Philadelphia Mint are implied but not stated in E. Biddle and M. Fielding's *The Life and Works of Thomas Sully (1783–1872)* (Philadelphia, 1921), 47ff. On the eve of Sully's departure early in October 1837 for London to paint Queen Victoria's portrait, "friends and admirers in Philadelphia, opened a subscription paper 'for the purchase of a memorial of respect and friendship to be presented to Mr. Sully.' A sum approximating $300 was promptly raised." The committee of leading citizens included Dr. Robert M. Patterson and James B. Longacre; they are listed again as contributors, along with C. Gobrecht and Wm. Kneass. Ten dollars was the standard donation. Since Sully's biographers make no mention of a sketch for the coinage, the design must have been produced very quickly and not considered important or worthy of notation by the artist. Such had evidently been the case with Gilbert Stuart's alleged restyling of the bust of Liberty for the dollar of 1795 and other coins of 1796.

3. "Peter, the 'Mint Bird,'" from *Harper's Young People,* as reprinted in *AJN* 27 (1893): 85.

"On the Dollars of 1836, 1838 and 1839, and the nickel Cents coined in 1856, is the portrait of an American eagle which was for many years a familiar sight in the streets of Philadelphia. 'Peter,' one of the finest eagles ever captured alive, was the pet of the Philadelphia Mint, and was generally known as the 'Mint bird.' Not only

did he have free access to every part of the Mint, going without hindrance into the treasure vaults, where even the treasurer of the United States would not go alone, but he used his own pleasure in going about the city, flying over the houses, sometimes perching upon lampposts in the streets. Everybody knew him, and even the street boys treated him with respect.

"The Government provided his daily fare, and he was as much a part of the Mint establishment as the Superintendent or the Chief-coiner. He was kindly treated and had no fear of anybody or anything, and he might be in the Mint yet if he had not sat down to rest upon one of the great flywheels. The wheel started without warning, and Peter was caught in the machinery. One of his wings was broken, and he died a few days later. The Superintendent had his body beautifully mounted, with his wings spread to their fullest extent; and to this day Peter stands in a glass case in the Mint cabinet. A portrait of him as he stands in the case was put upon the coins named."

Since Titian Peale, an ornithological artist, made the design for the flying eagle, it seems more likely that this is another "identification" legend given a greater degree of seeming reality by the fact that Peter was mounted to match the coin-design.

In a now-famous letter of April 9, 1836, Robert M. Patterson, director of the Mint, wrote to Levi Woodbury, secretary of the Treasury: "The die for the reverse is not yet commenced, but I send you the drawings which we propose to follow,—the pen sketch being that which we prefer. The drawing is true to nature, for it is taken from the eagle itself,—a bird, recently killed, having been prepared, and placed in the attitude which we had selected." In a letter of April 14, Patterson refers to the behavior of feathers on the neck of a (seemingly) living eagle, and this has led Walter Breen to suggest that "perhaps 'Peter' had entered the Mint ménage by then." *The Coin Collector's Journal* (September–December 1954): 9; see also Taxay, *U.S. Mint*, 171–174.

Titian Peale and Christian Gobrecht labored excessively to produce sketches of and patterns showing eagles in various poses of flight. All was, alas, in vain, for the regular coinage continued to bear the same old, flat, heraldic eagle with the sandwich-board shield on its stomach. Instances are all too numerous in American coinage where an artistic design has been jettisoned at the 11th hour in favor of a mediocre stereotype, for no apparent reason. These disasters have occurred often at the whim of a high official in the government after his subordinates have expended measureless effort to secure drawings, models, and patterns worthy of our heritage.

A model, the mechanical reduction, a bronze trial, and an ink drawing of the flying and perched eagles prepared by Gobrecht in the late 1830s are illustrated in V. Clain-Stefanelli, *History of the National Numismatic Collections*, figures 80–83. The eagles are, however, attributed to Franklin Peale, for many years chief coiner at the Philadelphia Mint. Franklin and Titian Ramsay were brothers, sons of Charles Wilson. Titian Peale prepared the colored plates in the first and last volumes of Bonaparte's *American Ornithology*, published in 1825 and 1833. At this time Franklin Peale was moving from assistant assayer (1833) to melter and refiner (1836), and in 1839 to the office which he held until 1854. See Taxay, *U.S. Mint*, 178.

4. What Oliver Larkin of Smith College wrote about Thomas Sully in his Pulitzer Prize–winning *Art and Life in America* (New York, 1964), 125, applies to the seated Liberty, which was originally based on a sketch by that artist: "It was in England that Sully learned from Lawrence how to suppress those elements of form which did not yield a lush femininity, how to draw loosely and carelessly, how to destroy the shape of chin and cheeks in order to emphasize the glowing eyes, how to contrast pearly skin with soft shadow accents of a pinkish orange and reduce modish curls to a few silken highlights."

5. The extensive issuance of private or territorial gold coins began in 1849, with the demands for coined gold in California. As works of art their designs are relatively uninspired. They tend to echo the regular U.S. gold dies of Gobrecht and Longacre. One of the handsomest coins in the series is a $50 coin struck by Kellogg and Company in 1855 and bearing the signature of F. Gruner on the obverse. The head of Liberty is a careful version of the contemporary federal dies, but the reverse shows an

eagle crouching over a U.S. shield, ribbon in its beak, a splendid design employed four years earlier on the U.S. Assay Office $50 piece of Moffat and Company in the name of the assayer, Augustus Humbert. The composition looks very much like some of the unused designs by Longacre. See Yeoman, 348–359.

In one instance these private issues used a design that echoed a rare pattern made at the Philadelphia Mint by Gobrecht early in 1836. The gold coins of the Pacific Company, struck at San Francisco in 1849, bear an obverse with a radiate Liberty cap against a field of stars (Yeoman, 354). Gobrecht's simpler version of this motif was designed as a gold dollar (Judd, 24). It appeared again in 1850 as a trime or silver three-cent piece, Longacre's interpretation of the idea (ibid., 37).

6. They came from Dr. Andrew Longacre, the artist's grandson.

7. This is undoubtedly the same J.G. Bruff who teamed with William Barber to design the congressional medal presented to Cyrus W. Field. It was authorized in a resolution of March 2, 1867 and is no. 625 in the *List of Bronze Medals for Sale* by U.S. Mint, Philadelphia.

From time to time other persons outside the Mint submitted designs for the coinage, especially when changes were contemplated. In response to a competition on the occasion of the Coinage Act of 1853, John R. Chapin of Newark, New Jersey, submitted excellent sketches of rather crowded obverses and reverses for the silver dollar, half dollar, and quarter. See C.L. Coffing, "New Coins, New Designs Tax 1853 Mint," *Numismatic Scrapbook Magazine,* February 25, 1969, 294.

8. The remaining drawings are just what would be expected from a man whose concern was not with a major redesigning of the coinage but with minor modifications and updatings. It is, of course, unfair to draw pregnant conclusions from a segment of a man's artistic production. The drawings preserved in several Philadelphia institutions do nothing to invalidate the observations that Longacre was a perfectly capable artist for the Mint but a man much more at home producing his gallery of national portraits than in concocting metallic money for the United States. He seems to have left behind more papers, notes, and drawings, than any other die designer of the 19th century, and for his sense of history we must be extremely grateful.

9. Yeoman, p. 231. A history of the $3 gold piece is given by Walter Breen, in *Coins: The Magazine of Coin Collecting,* August 1968, 27–31.

10. J.C.F., "The 'Emblem of Liberty' on Our Coins," *AJN* 41 (1906): 75–76.

CHAPTER IV. The Civil War and Its Aftermath

1. G.S. Chamberlain, "Horatio Greenough's Proposed Designs for the United States Coinage," *Art Quarterly* 22 (1959): 261, reprinted in *American Medals and Medalists* (Annandale, VA, 1963), 118.

2. "The Trade Dollar," *AJN* 8 (1873): 32.

3. In a pencil drawing, dated 1876, for a proposed $100 gold piece, George T. Morgan gave further artistic depth to the notion of "Liberty seated at the seashore." The goddess is placed in a relaxed pose in three-quarters right profile, symbols of the land behind her at the left, mountains including a volcano across the background, and a side-wheel steamship on the sea at the right. See V. Clain-Stefanelli, *History of the National Numismatic Collections* (Washington, 1968), 41, figure 84. This most effective composition had to wait until the early part of the 20th century for adoption, notably on presidential medals such as the Hampton Roads medal for Theodore Roosevelt in 1907 (fig. 120).

4. "From the Mint Archives," *Numismatic Scrapbook Magazine,* March 25, 1966, 730. A wide range of half dollar patterns by all the engravers from Gobrecht to the Barbers and Morgan, including unpublished specimens, is illustrated in *A "Gentleman's Study Collection" of United States Half Dollars, Offered at Fixed Prices by Coronet Coin and Stamp Shop* (Manhasset, NY, 1968). The "1838 Gobrecht Group" is particularly rich, as is "The Beautiful 1877 Series." It is rightly pointed out in connection with the "Sailor Head" obverse of 1877 (Judd, 167, no. 1502) that the features resemble the young head of Queen Victoria (10, no. 76). This was logical since the Britisher

William Barber, trained in the Royal Mint traditions of the Wyon family, created the design following the Coinage Act of March 3, 1875 (Judd, 156).

5. "From the Mint Archives," 730.

6. "To Marry a Goddess," *Selections From* The Numismatist, 131.

7. "Opinions on the New Dollar," *AJN* 12 (1878): 107.

8. "The New Dollar," *AJN* 12 (1878): 106.

9. "Opinions on the New Dollar." One slightly disturbing report, which came to the attention of numismatists through the *American Journal of Numismatics* for 1882, suggests that the modest and virtuous Williams might have been tempted to turn her famous profile to the show business. At least the news is evidence that at this date a considerable public might have been ready to believe that the neo-Pheidian profile on the Liberty Head dollar was hers. "It is announced that Miss Anna W. Williams, the Philadelphia lady whose portrait may be seen by anyone who possesses or can borrow a 'Morgan' silver dollar, has been engaged by a theatrical manager who proposes to make a 'star' of her. When the dollar was first issued the face was criticized considerably, as was also the figure of the 'scared hen' on the reverse; but there will now be an opportunity for the critics to see how they fancy the original. The lady certainly has a beautiful profile, if the likeness on the coin is good, and if successful will draw many of her portraits into her treasury" (47).

10. "Our Silver Currency," *AJN* 11 (1876): 23, from *Galaxy.* In a letter dated June 13, 1876, to director of the Mint James Pollock, Samuel Longfellow of Cambridge, Massachusetts (brother of Henry Wadsworth Longfellow), suggested that Franklin's head be placed on the twenty-cent piece and the denomination be named the "Franklin." He also suggested Washington's head and name for the double eagle. See *The Numismatic Scrapbook Magazine,* January 25, 1969, 94.

11. "Art in Our Coinage," *AJN* 22 (1887): 17–18, from *The Century.*

12. The general source or proto-parallel for the reverse of Paquet's presidential medal to Andrew Johnson can be seen in the design attributed to Conrad H. Kuchler for a posthumous Peace medal in Washington's name. A Native American and Liberty-Columbia-Minerva flank the altar with a bas-relief of rural prosperity on the front, a Rococo bust of Washington on the top. See V. Clain-Stefanelli, *History of the National Numismatic Collections*, 45, figure 94.

13. The first medal is described in J.F. Loubat's *The Medallic History of the United States of America, 1776–1876* (New York, 1878), vol. I, 411–417, and vol. II, pl. LXXVI; the second is described in the same source, vol. I, 430–433, and vol. II, pl. LXXX. Loubat gives the documents, especially the description of Payne's attack on Secretary Seward, which are the literary counterparts to Paquet's models.

CHAPTER V. The Columbian Exposition and Modern Design

1. "The New Designs for Our Coinage," *AJN* 26 (1891): 1–3.

2. M., "The New Silver Coins," *AJN* 26 (1892): 55.

3. O.W. Larkin, *Art and Life in America* (New York, 1964), 311.

4. Slabaugh, 12.

5. "The Columbian Half Dollar," *AJN* 27 (1893): 65.

6. "New Columbian Medals," *AJN* 28 (1893): 35.

7. "The 'Isabella' Quarter Dollar," *AJN* 28 (1893): 40.

8. "The St. Gaudens Columbian," *AJN* 314 (1896): 28.

9. Saint-Gaudens, 66–67.

10. Editorial, *AJN* 28 (1894): 108. At the same time, between 1890 and 1895, Saint-Gaudens used a pair of these youths, with their torches (of learning) and without their ribbons of modesty, on either side of the coat of arms in the central relief over the main doors of the Boston Public Library. The perennial question of possible indecency was ultimately settled, although the statement "Free to All" carved just below might have evoked ribald remarks and strong actions in these connotations. See Walter M. Whitehill, *Boston Public Library: A Centennial History* (Cambridge, MA: Harvard University Press, 1956), 159ff. Proper Bostonians were basically too busy

banishing Frederic MacMonnies's naked, lusty young bacchante from the courtyard of the McKim, Mead, and White palace to notice nudity on the doorstep. See Larkin, *Art and Life in America,* 299–300; Walter M. Whitehill, "The Vicissitudes of Bacchante in Boston," *The New England Quarterly* 27 (1954): 435–454.

11. Lorado Taft, *The History of American Sculpture* (New York, 1930), 382.

12. Ibid., 382–383.

13. Taxay (*U.S. Mint,* 312) implies that, although Barber made finished patterns, Theodore Roosevelt never saw them while the change in design was being considered and effected. Barber obviously never had a chance against Saint-Gaudens's powers of persuasion over the brandy and cigars.

14. "The Annual Assay Medals of the U.S. Mint," *AJN* 40 (1906): 78.

15. Assay Commission medals did seem to offer more opportunity for creating personal or genre designs than medals commemorating presidential terms of office. In their final years Assay medals were as commonplace design-wise as coins, but in the days of the two Barbers and Morgan they were characterized as an unusual series, with some amusing and interesting expressions of medallic art. The extremely limited editions of these pieces and their relation to a single theme made them imaginative on occasion, where otherwise more stereotyped heraldry or mere inscriptions in wreaths would have existed. Such scenes as "The monetary deities before a coining press" (1881), "Kneeling female exhibiting scales to child" (1884 and 1890), or "Science seated with testing cup, which young child waits to receive" (1894) cannot fail to excite aesthetic curiosity. The "Interior of smelting room at mint; men withdrawing metal from a furnace" (1891 and 1901) adds the practical note of coining processes depicted in medallic art, a theme revived by Laura Gardin Fraser in her American Numismatic Society Centennial medal of 1958. The Titian Peale flying eagle of the Gobrecht dollar of 1836 or the cent of 1856 to 1858 even made his appearance on the 1922 medal, with Andrew Mellon on the obverse. Sinnock's designs of 1931 and 1933 took refuge in the architectural theme, as if in anticipation of later coins, showing the front entrance of the U.S. Mint. The 1928 offering was historical, the "first coining press of the U.S. Mint with two men at work."

A full aesthetic history of official medals since the Civil War would have to include a major chapter on the Assay Commission medals. Their obverses are, naturally, official portraits, usually the dies used in the presidential series and the series for secretary of the Treasury or director of the Mint. Charles Barber's influence shows clearly in the numerous combinations of allegorical personifications and children, a motif found on his 1907 medal commemorating Theodore Roosevelt's dispatch of the fleet around the world and on his 1915 half dollar for the Panama-Pacific Exposition. In general, therefore, the styles, compositions, and details encountered in other Mint medals or even in patterns for the coinage had their echoes in this special series. See the Assay medals described in *Abner Kreisberg, Auction Catalog, Mail Bid Sale* (October 31, 1966), 215–217, lots 3936–3959, embracing the years 1868 to 1933. Hathaway, Bowers, Cat. no. 3 (1969), 31–35.

16. P.C.W., "The Souvenir Gold Dollars," *AJN* 39 (1904): 26.

17. M., "The Assay Medal of 1910," *AJN* 44 (1910): 131–132.

CHAPTER VI. Theodore Roosevelt and Artistic Revolution

1. C.R. Post, *A History of European and American Sculpture From the Early Christian Period to the Present Day,* vol. II (Cambridge, MA, 1921), 238.

2. In 1900 Theodore Roosevelt stated that he considered Kelly's equestrian *Sheridan's Ride,* Saint-Gaudens's *Puritan,* Kerney's *Leopard,* and Remington's *Broncho Buster* "the finest type of American bronzes." He had purchased a reduction of the first statue, not the centerpiece of Sheridan Circle in Washington, "when a student at Harvard, with the last fifty dollars I had at the time." See Robert Bruce, *Art and Sculpture of James Edward Kelly, 1855–1933,* vol. I (New York, 1934), 20, references I owe to a monograph on equestrian statues in America by Anna C. Hunt of Boston University. See chapter VIII, note 12.

3. "The New United States Coins," *AJN* 42 (1907–1908): 25.

4. Liberty owes an obvious debt to a frontal view of the Victory of the Sherman Monument, unveiled in 1903. The small bronze in the Metropolitan Museum points up the similarities. It is amusing to note that here a modern, heraldic eagle is embroidered on the rectangular chest piece of Victory's chiton. See A.T. Gardner, *American Sculpture: A Catalogue of the Collection of the Metropolitan Museum of Art* (New York, 1965), 55.

5. It is now known that Hettie Anderson was the last model Saint-Gaudens used for the coin.

6. Saint-Gaudens, 329–333. Henry Hering (1874–1949), mentioned in the previous paragraph, was described in L. Taft's *History of American Sculpture* (556) as a sculptor, who "enjoyed for several years the privileges of Saint-Gaudens's studio and is equipped for any form of sculpture." He executed an impressive Civil War Memorial for Yale in 1913 and sculpture for the Field Museum in 1917. "He has chosen to specialize in architectural art, and the 'strait and narrow way' is opening to a very opulent reward." This is by way of saying that, while a medalist of conservative clarity, as a monumental sculptor he was a carver of massive, neo-Roman, academic statuary, the memorials and allegories so beloved of officials decorating the grounds and buildings of world's fairs and regional expositions. Typical of these was the great seated goddess of Dea Roma type known as the *Spirit of Water Transportation.* His *Pro Patria,* the Indiana World War Memorial, was one of those pseudonatural athletic soldier-Mercury young men so popular in this class of art in the 1920s.

7. Some sources have it that a popular living subject employed by Saint-Gaudens, one Alice Butler of Windsor, Vermont, posed for the head of Liberty in the Indian bonnet. (The latter was evidently supplied by A.A. Weinman.) Butler was also said to have served as a model for the head of Sherman's Nike. A photograph of her posing for Saint-Gaudens in Junoesque attire shows that she did have a Pergamene Greek profile, open mouth, and heavy jaw. She would thus provide still another instance of the close connections between living models, their costumes, the Greek sculptural ideal, and the work of sculptors at the start of the 20th century.

8. Modern research indicates that Pratt's design was in fact a modification of Saint-Gaudens's original, and that the modification was made at the request of President Roosevelt, who wanted the image of the bird to be more accurate.

9. "New U.S. Gold Series Criticized and Defended," *Selections From* The Numismatist, 208–209.

10. Ibid., 209.

11. Ibid., 210. The Chapman and Bigelow letters cited in notes 7–9 were also quoted by Taxay, *U.S. Mint,* 326–329.

12. Morey, 208. Bela L. Pratt did design (1910–1912) the impressive bronze personifications of Art and Science on the terrace of the Boston Public Library. In this connection his monumental work stood side by side with that of his erstwhile teacher Augustus Saint-Gaudens, on pedestals intended for bronze groups that Saint-Gaudens never completed.

13. Ibid., 212. Brenner's grandfather was a blacksmith and his father a learned carver of gravestones, rings, brooches, and other local artifacts in the Russo-German Baltic (Latvian) town of Shavli, where the future sculptor-medalist was born. Brenner achieved no fame as a monumental sculptor, producing only the Schenley Memorial Fountain in Pittsburgh (1916) and a number of busts. The marble *Charles Eliot Norton* in the Fogg Museum at Harvard is perhaps the best known, a work commissioned by Brenner's great patron, the philhellene banker James Loeb.

14. See "Redesigned Lincoln Cent Returns Design to 1909 Sharpness; New Lettering Used," *Numismatic Scrapbook Magazine,* February 2, 1969, front cover and page 258; see also *The Numismatist* (March 1969): 329.

15. The success of the 1909 obverse for the cent was exploited in a bronze relief of the Gettysburg Address, which has the numismatic tondo at the upper left. The date of Lincoln's birth has replaced the LIBERTY; the invocation has been removed;

and the sculptor's name is written out behind the right shoulder. A casting was advertised and illustrated by Victor D. Spark in *Art Journal* 26 (1966–1967): 197.

16. Morey, 217.

17. L. Taft, *The History of American Sculpture* (New York, 1930), 557.

18. Saint-Gaudens, 330.

19. A.T. Duffield, "The Nickel," *Selections From* The Numismatist, 142.

20. T.L. C[omparette], "Coins and Medals in the United States in 1913," *AJN* 47 (1913): 145.

21. Duffield, "The Nickel," 142.

22. W.H. De Shan, "The New Five-Cent Piece," *Selections From* The Numismatist, 144. See also Judd, 216.

23. Despite the claims of the quoted news article, neither John Big Tree nor any other Indian posed expressly for the nickel design. Fraser had been making Indian portrait busts for several years prior to his first 1911 contact with the Mint.—*Editor*

24. *Numismatic News,* April 2, 1966, 16.

25. Judd, 216.

26. Chief John Big Tree died on July 6, 1967, at the reservation near Syracuse, New York. His age was given as 102 in some accounts, 92 in others that seem most reliable. At the same time the statue for which the chief posed entered the news again. Through the family connections with Theodore Roosevelt, a casting of *The End of the Trail* passed to the Delano family. In 1967 it was sold to the Whitney Gallery of Western Art at Cody, Wyoming; see *Coin World* (July 19, 1967): 3. The "original" bronze, cast from the statue shown at the Panama-Pacific Exposition of 1915 in San Francisco, is in the National Western Heritage Museum and Cowboy Hall of Fame in Oklahoma City, Oklahoma.

27. *Boston Globe,* May 11, 1966, 29.

28. M., "The Pan-American Medal," *AJN* 36 (1901): 40.

29. Ibid., 40–41.

30. Slabaugh, 31.

31. E.H. Adams, "The Panama-Pacific Commemorative Coins," *Selections From* The Numismatist, 250.

32. Barber is credited with both obverse and reverse of the half dollar, the latter coming from a repertory of designs practiced at the Mint at least since 1877; this was also the period in which Morgan first worked out his reverse composition used with modifications on the Panama-Pacific quarter eagle. Compare Judd, 168ff. Barber had created similar eagles on shields in sketches for the reverse of the Columbian Exposition quarter dollar during April 1893. See Taxay, *Commemorative Coinage,* 7 and 11. All this is further evidence of the seemingly harmonious interchange of ideas and designs that marked Barber's and Morgan's long careers as artists in the Mint.

CHAPTER VII. New Silver Coins, 1916 to 1929

1. The story that Liberty's bare breast was subsequently covered due to public outcries of immodesty is often accepted as fact. Years of research, however, have found no documentation to support this story, which likely would have made headlines had it been true. It is more likely that, in covering her bosom with chain mail, Liberty, like her country, was preparing for war.

2. L.W. Culver, "The Sesquicentennial of the Quarter Dollar," *Selections From* The Numismatist, 163.

3. When Hermon MacNeil turned his hand to the ever-popular sculptural theme of George Washington, he could not resist setting the first president against a monumental wall and placing a figure like his armed Liberty of the 1916 quarter dollar in the background. The statue of Washington standing in field dress with triangular hat and ample cloak was executed for the arch at the start of Fifth Avenue in New York. The inspiration for this type of group was the Saint-Gaudens monument to the preacher Phillips Brooks beside Trinity Church in Copley Square, Boston. In that

work, the sculptor's last, the good divine is overshadowed by Christ. MacNeil's Washington has a militant female with Liberty at the left rear and a helmeted, cuirassed man of undetermined aspirations on the other side, beyond the U.S. shield against a large Christmas wreath.

4. *Coins: The Magazine of Coin Collecting*, February 1966, 27.

5. G.F. Kunz, "The Late Louis Oscar Roty," *AJN* 47 (1913): 107–108.

6. "The Girl on the Quarter," *Selections From* The Numismatist, 167. On April 4, 1966, Doscher, then a matron of 72, appeared on the television program *I've Got a Secret*, challenging the panel to guess her connection with the quarter dollar by Hermon MacNeil. Doris (not Dora) Doscher Baum died on March 9, 1970 (*New York Times*, March 13, 1970, 39).

7. Morey, 211.

8. B.G. Proske, *Brookgreen Gardens: Sculpture* (Brookgreen, SC, 1943), 119.

9. Ibid., 121.

10. Since Weinman and his contemporaries knew ancient coins well, it is natural to compare this reverse with its obvious Greek prototype, the large dekadrachm of Carthage struck in the third century B.C. With its broad, flat flan, this is one of the most medallic of all Greek coins. See A.B. Brett, *Catalogue of Greek Coins* (Boston: Museum of Fine Arts, 1955), 68, no. 506.

11. "The New Dime," *Selections From* The Numismatist, 154.

12. Ibid., 156.

13. *Letters of Wallace Stevens*, selected and edited by Holly Stevens (New York, 1966), 155, note 2. The bust is plate 9. I owe the discovery of this Stevens-Weinman numismatic connection to Mr. and Mrs. Barry F. O'Connell.

14. Saint-Gaudens, 253–257.

15. Morey, 222.

16. Kunz, "The Late Louis Oscar Roty," 109.

17. J. Moss, "Peace Dollars," *Selections From* The Numismatist, 132–133.

18. Taxay, *U.S. Mint*, 355–356.

19. The statements and correspondence in connection with the designs for the Peace dollar, Teresa Cafarelli de Francisci's participation, and the final modifications of the height of the relief by Chief Engraver George T. Morgan, are set forth in Taxay, *U.S. Mint*, 354–359. Of the eagle he writes (358): "It is de Francisci's conception of America, and it is a beautiful conception." Oddly enough, this American eagle can be traced back through a number of Italian 16th-century birds to the creature perched over rocks on a branch in the upper left reverse of Pisanello's medal of 1444, made for the marriage of Leonello d'Este with Maria of Aragon. Here the eagle symbolizes the Este family (figs. 121 and 109). See G.F. Hill, *A Corpus of Italian Medals of the Renaissance Before Cellini* (London, 1930), 6, number 32; C. Vermeule, *European Art and the Classical Past* (Cambridge, MA, 1964), 53.

CHAPTER VIII. Commemorative Coins, 1918 to 1928

1. There were two thorough books on commemorative coins in print as the first edition of this book went to press. *United States Commemorative Coinage*, by A.R. Slabaugh, presents all the folklore and much of the public or historical background for each type and issue. *An Illustrated History of U.S. Commemorative Coinage*, by D. Taxay, publishes the contents of the national archives, principally the files of the Commission of Fine Arts. This includes correspondence from 1915 to 1951 and models or sketches for many of the coins, additional illustrations having been secured from the families of the artists involved. Both books are necessary for a complete understanding of the series.

2. Morey, 215.

3. In the years since the first edition of this book was written, it has been confirmed by researcher Roger W. Burdette that local Maine artist Harry H. Cochrane provided the design for the Maine Centennial. "Because Cochrane did not know how to create the necessary models, the Commission of Fine Arts commissioned

de Francisci to do so. De Francisci did the best he could with a design imposed upon him, and it is not to his discredit that he accepted the work," asserts Burdette.

4. Morey, 202.

5. Taxay, *Commemorative Coinage,* 52–58. For Morey's comment see chapter IX, note 9.

6. Here I differ from Taxay (*Commemorative Coinage,* 43–47), who asserts that the eagle seal is the obverse and the jugate bust the reverse.

7. Morey, 220.

8. Ralph Beck took credit for the motif, having been the designer of the Pan-American Exposition seal, but James E. Fraser was responsible for the idea of turning North and South America into draped females on the reverse of the Monroe Doctrine Centennial half dollar. His suggestion to Chester Beach was recorded more than once in the correspondence of the Commission of Fine Arts. See Taxay, *Commemorative Coinage,* 62–68. The Pan-American Exposition medal attributed to Beach is illustrated on page 49 of Slabaugh's *Commemorative Coinage,* and the familiar Beach monogram seems to be visible to the right of the female embodying North America; in poses and details the ladies are more like those of the Ralph Beck seal than the Monroe Doctrine Centennial half dollar. As is so often the case in the fine arts, by 1923, Beck, Fraser, and even Beach himself may have forgotten about the latter's connections with the designs of 1901.

9. Many medals issued since the First World War have been accompanied by brochures as well as the traditional velvet-lined boxes. As in this instance, these brochures are often prime sources of information about the medals in question.

10. The spirit that motivated French's statue and the coin is told best by D.B. Little, *America's First Centennial Celebration: The Nineteenth of April 1875 at Lexington and Concord, Massachusetts* (Boston: The Club of Odd Volumes, 1961).

11. C.R. Post, *A History of European and American Sculpture From the Early Christian Period to the Present Day,* vol. II (Cambridge, MA, 1921), 260.

12. Morey, 209. See chapter VI, note 2, on the other equestrian *Sheridan.*

13. Taxay, *Commemorative Coinage,* 74–78. Translation of the Stone Mountain sculptures to the small, circular area of a medal or coin brings to mind the later parallel of the presidents on the side of Mount Rushmore, South Dakota, where Gutzon Borglum worked after he abandoned Stone Mountain. The faces of Mount Rushmore have appeared as at least one medallic obverse, and in 1968 and 1969 bills were introduced in Congress to make them part of the reverse design of the dollar bill. See *The Numismatist* (February 1969): 169 and *Numismatic News,* February 4, 1969, 1. See chapter XI for discussion of the 1991 Mount Rushmore Golden Jubilee commemoratives and the 2006 South Dakota statehood quarter.

14. The sketches for the sesquicentennial of American Independence half dollar attributed to John Frederick Lewis in Taxay's *Commemorative Coinage,* 111–117, are obviously from the hand of John Sinnock; the credit for the coin, therefore, must remain his.

15. Morey, 215.

16. The various models for the (Bennington) Vermont Sesquicentennial half dollar are illustrated in Taxay, *Commemorative Coinage,* 91–94.

17. Slabaugh, 75.

CHAPTER IX. Washington's Bicentennial and Commemorative Half Dollars, 1932 to 1938

1. H.H. Arnason, *Sculpture by Houdon: A Loan Exhibition* (Worcester, MA, 1964), 90.

2. The foremost painter of Washington, Gilbert Stuart, was attracted to this strong profile, for the Museum of Fine Arts in Boston possesses his study after one of the Houdon busts in civic attire. A note on the bottom of the oval states, "Stuart pencil'd over a profile from Houdon's bust." A thin line gives the shape to which the paper was subsequently cut (fig. 191). The results are very like a study for a giant cameo, the center of a banknote, or even a coin such as the Jefferson nickel of 1938,

where a similar view of a draped bust by Houdon was the source. Like the story of Stuart's participation in the draped bust of Liberty for the coinage of 1796, this sketch is further evidence of the painter's interest in the relation between the human figure and the medallic tondo, a basic element of coin design.

Stuart's unfinished "Athenaeum Heads" of George and Martha Washington, also in the Boston Museum and "probably the best known paintings in American art," were done from life in Philadelphia in 1796, the year he redesigned the coinage. Coincidentally enough, these prototypes for America's classic national portraits are set off by painted ovals as background for the heads and shoulders. Stuart, therefore, seemed to think in images suited to coinage and, of course, the dollar bill. For the pair of Washington portraits, see *American Painting in the Museum of Fine Arts, Boston,* vol. I (Boston: Museum of Fine Arts, 1969), 243–245, numbers 907 and 908, figures 118 and 117.

3. "A New Washington Medal," *AJN* 23 (1889): 92.

4. The whole sad story is set forth in detail, with copies of letters involved, in Taxay, *U.S. Mint*, 360–366.

5. This medal was struck for the American Numismatic Society by the Medallic Art Company, New York. Its obverse is stamped in relief in the cover of the *Centennial Publication of the American Numismatic Society,* edited by Harald Ingholt (New York: American Numismatic Society, 1958). Laura Fraser died at Norwalk, Connecticut, in 1966.

6. Morey, 213.

7. B.G. Proske, *Brookgreen Gardens: Sculpture* (Brookgreen, SC, 1943), 211.

8. Ibid., 213.

9. Morey, 219.

10. Slabaugh, 95–96.

11. See M.R. Scherer, *The Legends of Troy in Art and Literature* (New York: Phaidon Press, 1963), 165, figure 139.

12. Slabaugh, 98.

13. Proske, *Brookgreen Gardens,* 259–261.

14. Ibid., 131.

15. Slabaugh, 113.

16. Proske, *Brookgreen Gardens,* 403.

17. Slabaugh, 133.

CHAPTER X. A Quarter Century of Coins and Medals

1. H.H. Arnason, *Sculpture by Houdon: A Loan Exhibition* (Worcester, MA, 1964), 104.

2. Schlag executed few medals or coins, reportedly three as of his death in 1974. For the Commemorative Society of Celebrated Women he designed in 1966 "a tribute to Betsy Ross and her home where the first Stars and Stripes flag was made." The kneeling seamstress is conceived in a kind of Afro-archaic-Greek smooth style, like Paul Manship's art of the 1930s. The round yet rhythmic figure in sleek "homespun" dress is not unbecoming to a medallic tondo. The little colonial house on the reverse and the accompanying lettering have given the artist an outlet for all those creative urges suppressed when the Monticello reverse of the 1938 nickel was altered. The side of the Ross house, seen at the angle denied Jefferson's home, is dissolved into a flaming carpet. See *The Numismatist* (September 1966), 1181.

3. See R.H. Lloyd, "Our War Time 'Plastic' Cent," *Numismatic Scrapbook Magazine,* August 1967, 1401–1405, and figure on page 1403.

4. They are illustrated in an article by Gilroy Roberts, "Birth of a Dime Design," *Coins: The Magazine of Coin Collecting,* October 1967, 22–25.

5. Ross E. Taggart, *Handbook of the Collections in the William Rockhill Nelson Gallery of Art and Mary Atkins Museum of Fine Arts* (Kansas City, MO: University Trustees Vol. R. Nelson Trust, 1959), 118.

6. Arnason, *Sculpture by Houdon,* 56. For a detailed discussion of all Houdon's Franklins, see, in addition to the Worcester Exhibition Catalog (cited in the

bibliography), J. Montague Massengale, "A Franklin by Houdon Rediscovered," *Marsyas* 12 (1964–1965): 1–15. The Kansas City bust is classified as a version in ancient dress of the 1778 portrait in civilian ("Quaker") costume. The Angers-Athenaeum bust, in heavy classical drapery, has been dated 1786, when Houdon, then back in Paris, and Jefferson were "conferring" on work for the Virginia capitol. This was shortly after Houdon had visited Mount Vernon to make his master *modello* of Washington, the basis for the 1932 quarter. Houdon and Franklin crossed the Atlantic from France on the same ship, the latter returning home to stay. Since Houdon's Franklins have always formed illustrations for any biography of the statesman, an engraver at the Philadelphia Mint would have no trouble in securing good photographs. The Metropolitan Museum's Franklin, a marble version of the 1778 likeness, has been a treasure of that institution since 1872.

7. See chapter I, note 7.

8. See American Numismatic Association, 75th Annual Convention, Chicago, August 16–20, 1966, *Auction Sale Catalog,* lot 219. See also chapter XI.

9. O.W. Larkin, *Art and Life in America* (New York, 1964), 184. The collaboration of Roberts and Gasparro took on reversed form in the August 19, 1958, congressional medal for Admiral Hyman G. Rickover, Gasparro doing the obverse and Roberts the reverse. In the former Frank Gasparro presents a good, uniformed likeness of the nautical scientist in the nearly frontal format made standard by Roberts, while the reverse displays a figure of a nude, muscular man kneeling to harness the whirling atoms. This essay in the creative arts by Gilroy Roberts seems to have been much influenced by the architectural sculpture of Paul Manship in the 1930s.

10. Roberts (d. 1992) wrote about his own part in the coin honoring John F. Kennedy in "Reminiscences on the Creation of the Kennedy Half Dollar," *Coins* (August 1965). The former chief sculptor-engraver of the U.S. Mint also described the processes of preparing and manufacturing modern coins and medals in "Creating Designs in Circles," *Coins* (May 1968): 32–35. At the time of writing Roberts was serving as the first sculptor-engraver at the Franklin Mint in suburban Philadelphia, the nation's largest private producer of commemorative medals, gaming tokens, and special coins.

11. Thanks to the interest taken by the popular coin weeklies and monthly magazines, famous die designers in addition to Gilroy Roberts commented on their work. See "Thomas Humphrey Paget Tells Own Story of Designing Coins for Kings," in *Coin World* (September 28, 1966): 28. Paget, who signed with the initials H.P., designed some of the most familiar and appealing, essentially heraldic, British, British imperial or colonial, and foreign coins. The fashion for presenting engravers, their preliminary sketches, and plaster models in the popular press was even extended to commercial appeals for issues of medals. Albino Manca is shown alongside his three preliminary drawings and a plaster model for a medal honoring the heavyweight boxer Jack Dempsey in an advertisement for the Cavalcade of Sports series, issued by Paramount International Coin Corporation of Ohio, in the issue of *Coin World* just cited (p. 25). The other two plaster models derived from the drawings appear, without Manca, in another advertisement by the same firm, in *Numismatic News,* December 5, 1966, 11.

12. See *Coins* (May 1968): 16. The Assay medal for 1967 can hardly be considered a work of art. It shows the facing head and shoulders of Eva Adams, director of the Mint, on the obverse and the then uncompleted fourth U.S. Mint in Philadelphia on the reverse. See *Numismatic News,* February 27, 1967, 16. See also chapter XI.

13. *Coins* (March 4, 1969): 1.

14. *Coins* (May 20, 1969): 1. The portrait was that used for the Assay Commission medal of 1969; the quotation is from Nixon's acceptance speech at the August 1968 Republican national convention. See *Coins* (July 1969): 14.

15. *Numismatic News,* June 3, 1969, 1, contained a staff artist's conception, widely illustrated in the general news media at the time, of how a proposed nonsilver dollar for Dwight D. Eisenhower should appear. A Houdonesque bust was combined with the lettering of the Franklin half dollar. Such traditional taste was entirely predictable.

Bibliography

This listing will suggest published sources of information on art and design, sculptors, engravers, and the history of American coinage and medallic art. Obviously a vastly greater number of titles exist, but such specifics as a study of die varieties of early half dimes are of less interest to the field of art than a study of U.S. historical medals.

Periodicals

American Journal of Numismatics. Among journals, this was a great early source for history and aesthetics of American coinage and medals before 1918.

The Numismatist, journal of the American Numismatic Association, 1888 to the present. This publication contains a wealth of valuable general and in-depth articles, and in the past anthologies of these have appeared in hardcover.

Numismatic Scrapbook Magazine was published from 1935 to 1976, initially by Lee F. Hewitt in Chicago, and after 1968 by Amos Press of Sidney, Ohio.

Coin World, a tabloid weekly newspaper of the entire numismatic field, has been published since 1960 and has included a greater number of in-depth articles in the art field than is generally realized, including David T. Alexander's column, "The Research Desk," which has appeared monthly since 1991.

COINage magazine, based in Ventura, California, has appeared monthly since 1966 and includes numerous historical and artistic features by qualified writers and researchers.

MCA Advisory and *The Medal Cabinet* are publications of Medal Collectors of America, founded 1998. The *Advisory* is edited by John W. Adams of Boston.

Medallic Sculpture was the journal of the American Medallic Sculpture Association (AMSA), which more recently has offered a number of other informative publications relating to medallic sculpture.

Numismatic News is a weekly publication based in Ohio.

TAMS Journal is the publication of the Token and Medal Society, founded in 1961. The first decades of the journal were rich in significant medal research, but in recent years the token sector has come to dominate TAMS's publishing activities. `

Books and Journal Articles

HISTORY OF U.S. COINAGE AND MEDALS

Adelson, H.L. *The American Numismatic Society, 1858–1958.* New York: American Numismatic Society, 1958.

Alexander, D.T. *The Society of Medalists History, Appreciation and Variety Catalogue.* Boston: Medal Collectors of America, 2005.

Alexander, D.T., and T.K. DeLorey. *Coin World Comprehensive Catalog and Encyclopedia of United States Coins.* 2nd ed. Sidney, OH: Amos Press, 1998.

American Numismatic Association. *American Numismatic Association Centennial Anthology.* Edited by Carl W.A. Carlson and Michael J. Hodder. Colorado Springs, CO: Author, 1991.

———. *American Numismatic Association Centennial History, 1891–1991.* Edited by Q. David Bowers. Colorado Springs, CO: Author, 1991.

———. *Selections From* The Numismatist: *United States Coins.* Racine, WI: Whitman Publishing, 1960.

American Numismatic Society. *Catalogue of the International Exhibition of Contemporary Medals.* New York, 1911.

Baxter, B.A. *The Beaux-Arts Medal in America.* New York: American Numismatic Society, 1988.

Betts, C.W. *American Colonial History Illustrated by Contemporary Medals.* Edited by W.T.R. Marvin and L.H. Low. New York: Scott Stamp and Coin, 1894.

Bowers, Q.D. *American Numismatics Before the Civil War, 1760–1860, Emphasizing the Story of Augustus B. Sage.* Foreword by Joel Orosz. Wolfeboro, NH: Bowers and Merena Galleries, 1998.

———. *Commemorative Coins of the United States: A Complete Encyclopedia.* Wolfeboro, NH: Bowers and Merena Galleries, 1991.

Breen, W. *A Coiner's Caviar: Encyclopedia of U.S. and Colonial Proof Coins, 1722–1989.* Rev. ed. Wolfeboro, NH: Bowers and Merena Galleries, 1989.

———. *Complete Encyclopedia of U.S. and Colonial Coins.* New York: Doubleday, 1988.

———. *Encyclopedia of United States and Colonial Proof Coins, 1722–1989.* Rev. ed. Wolfeboro, NH: Bowers and Merena Galleries, 1989.

———. "The Secret History of the Gobrecht Coinages, 1836–1840." Pts. 1 and 2. *Coin Collector's Journal* 21, nos. 5–6 (1954).

———. "Silver Coinages of the Philadelphia Mint, 1794–1916." *Coin Collector's Journal* no. 159 (1958).

———. "The United States Minor Coinages, 1793–1916." *Coin Collector's Journal* 21, no. 3 (1954).

Chamberlain, G.S. *American Medals and Medalists.* Annandale, VA: Turnpike Press, 1963.

Clain-Stefanelli, E.E. "Numismatics—An Ancient Science: A Survey of Its History." Paper 32, bulletin 229 of *Contributions From the Museum of History and Technology.* Washington, DC: U.S. Government Printing Office, 1965.

Clain-Stefanelli, V. "History of the National Numismatic Collections." Paper 31, bulletin 229 of *Contributions From the Museum of History and Technology.* Washington, DC: U.S. Government Printing Office, 1968.

Crosby, S.S. *The Early Coins of America; and the Laws Governing Their Issue. Comprising Also Descriptions of the Washington Pieces, the Anglo-American Tokens, Many Pieces of Unknown Origin, of the Seventeenth and Eighteenth Centuries, and the First Patterns of the United States Mint.* Boston, 1875.

Dusterberg, R.B. *The Official Inaugural Medals of the Presidents of the United States.* Cincinnati, OH: Medallion Press, 1971.

Hibler, H.E., and C.V. Kappen. *So-Called Dollars.* New York: Coin and Currency Institute, 1963.

Judd, J.H. *United States Pattern Coins: Experimental and Trial Pieces.* 9th ed. Edited by Q. David Bowers. Atlanta: Whitman Publishing, 2005.

Julian, R.W. *Medals of the United States Mint: The First Century, 1792–1892.* El Cajon, CA: Token and Medal Society, 1977.

Levine, H.J. *Collectors Guide to Presidential Inaugural Medals and Memorabilia.* Danbury, CT: Johnson and Jensen, 1981.

Loubat, J.F. *The Medallic History of the United States of America, 1776–1876.* New York, 1878. Reprint, New Milford, CT: Flayderman, 1967.

MacNeil, N. *The President's Medal, 1789–1977.* New York: Clarkson N. Potter in association with the National Portrait Gallery of the Smithsonian Institution, 1977.

Noe, S.P. *The Medallic Work of A.A. Weinman.* New York: American Numismatic Society, 1921.

Pollock, A.W., III. *United States Patterns and Related Issues.* Wolfeboro, NH: Bowers and Merena Galleries, 1994.

Prucha, F.P. *Indian Peace Medals in American History.* Lincoln, NE: University of Nebraska Press, 1971.

Rulau, R. *Discovering America: The Coin Collecting Connection.* Iola, WI: Krause Publications, 1989.

———. *Standard Catalog of United States Tokens, 1700–1900.* 4th ed. Iola, WI: Krause Publications, 2004.

Rulau, R., and G. Fuld. *Medallic Portraits of Washington: An Illustrated, Priced Revision of W. S. Baker's 1885 Catalog of the Coins, Medals and Tokens of the Father of His Country*. 2nd ed. Iola, WI: Krause Publications, 1999.
Slabaugh, A.R. *United States Commemorative Coinage: The Drama of America as Told by Our Coins*. Racine, WI: Whitman Publishing, 1963.
Smith, P. *American Numismatic Biographies*. Rocky River, OH: Gold Leaf Press, 1992.
Stahl, A.M., ed. *The Medal in America: Coinage of the Americas Conference Proceedings*. New York: American Numismatic Society, 1988.
Swiatek, A., and W. Breen. *The Encyclopedia of United States Silver and Gold Commemorative Coins, 1892–1954*. New York: Arco Publishing, 1981.
Taxay, D. *Counterfeit, Mis-Struck, and Unofficial U.S. Coins*. Introduction by John J. Ford Jr. New York: Area, 1963.
———. *An Illustrated History of U.S. Commemorative Coinage*. New York: Arco Publishing, 1967.
———. *The U.S. Mint and Coinage: An Illustrated History From 1776 to the Present*. Foreword by Gilroy Roberts. New York: Arco Publishing, 1966.
Yeoman, R.S. *A Guide Book of United States Coins*. 61st ed. Edited by Kenneth Bressett. Atlanta: Whitman Publishing, 2007.

Sources of American Numismatics

Arnason, H.H. *Sculpture by Houdon: A Loan Exhibition*. Worcester, MA: Worcester Art Museum, 1964.
Aspet, H., J.W. Beatty, G. Brown, et al. *Catalogue of Sculptured Works of Augustus Saint-Gaudens With Biographical Sketch: Memorial Exhibition*. New York: Metropolitan Museum of Art, 1908.
Augustus Saint-Gaudens: The Portrait Reliefs, The National Portrait Gallery. Washington, DC: Smithsonian Institution, 1969.
Chamberlain, G.S. *Studies on American Painters and Sculptors of the Nineteenth Century*. Annandale, VA: Turnpike Press, 1965.
Contemporary American Sculpture Issued for the Exhibition Held by the National Sculpture Society in Cooperation With the Trustees of the California Palace of the Legion of Honor, 1929. Foreword by A.A. Weinman. New York, 1929.
Craven, W. *Sculpture in America: From the Colonial Period to the Present*. New York: Thomas Y. Crowell, 1968.
Exhibition of American Sculpture. Preface by Hermon A. MacNeil. New York: National Sculpture Society, 1923.
Francis, R.G. *Cyrus E. Dallin: Let Justice Be Done*. Springville, UT: Springfield Museum of Art in cooperation with the Utah American Revolution Bicentennial Commission, 1976.
Gardner, A.T. *American Sculpture: A Catalogue of the Collection of the Metropolitan Museum of Art*. New York: Metropolitan Museum of Art, 1965.
———. *Yankee Stonecutters*. New York: Columbia University Press, 1945.
Great Americans: From the Revolution to the Civil War. Museum of Fine Arts Picture Book no. 1. Prepared by R.B.K. McLanathan. Meriden, CT: Meriden Gravure, 1954.
Harbeson, G.B. *American Needlework: The History of Decorative Stitchery and Embroidery From the Late 16th to the 20th Century*. New York: Coward-McCann, 1938.
Hind, C.L. *Augustus Saint-Gaudens*. New York: The International Studio, 1907–1908.
Hornung, C.P. *Handbook of Early American Advertising Art*. New York: Dover, 1947.
Howlett, D.R. *The Sculpture of Donald De Lue: Gods, Prophets and Heroes*. Boston: David R. Godine, 1990.
Jenkins, D.H. *A Fortune in the Junk Pile: A Guide to Valuable Antiques*. New York: Crown, 1963.
Larkin, O.W. *Art and Life in America*. New York: Holt, Rinehart and Winston, 1964.
McClinton, K.M. *Antique Collecting for Everyone*. New York: McGraw-Hill, 1951.

———. *The Complete Book of Small Antiques Collecting*. New York: Coward-McCann, 1965.

McGill, J. *The Joy of Effort: A Biography of R. Tait McKenzie*. Bewdley, Ontario: Clay Publishing, 1980.

Moore, N.H. *Old Pewter, Brass, Copper and Sheffield Plate*. Garden City, NY, 1933.

Morey, C.R. "Great Sculpture Since the Centennial." In *The Pageant of America*, vol. XII, *The American Spirit in Art*. New Haven, CT: Yale University Press, 1927.

Post, C.R. *A History of European and American Sculpture From the Early Christian Period to the Present Day*, vol. II. Cambridge, MA: Harvard University Press, 1921.

Proske, B.G. *Brookgreen Gardens: Sculpture*. Brookgreen, SC, 1943.

Rand, H. *Paul Manship*. Washington, DC: Smithsonian Institution Press, 1989.

Revi, A.C. *American Pressed Glass and Figure Bottles*. New York: Thomas Nelson, 1964.

Sack, A. *Fine Points of Furniture: Early American*. New York: Crown, 1950.

Schmeckebier, Lawrence. *Ivan Meštrovic: Sculptor and Patriot*. Syracuse, NY: Syracuse University Press, 1959.

Taft, L. *The History of American Sculpture*. New ed. with supp. chapter by Adeline Adams. New York: Macmillan, 1930.

Tharp, L.H. *Saint-Gaudens and the Gilded Era*. Boston: Little, Brown, 1969.

Vermeule, C. *European Art and the Classical Past*. Cambridge, MA: Harvard University Press, 1964.

ART AND COINAGE

Adams, J.W., and A. Bentley. *Comitia Americana and Related Medals: Underappreciated Monuments to Our Heritage*. Crestline, CA: George Frederick Kolbe, 2007.

Becatti, G. *The Art of Ancient Greece and Rome: From the Rise of Greece to the Fall of Rome*. Englewood Cliffs, NJ: Prentice-Hall, 1967.

Groenewegen-Frankfort, H.A., and B. Ashmole. *Art of the Ancient World*. New York: New American Library, 1967.

Saint-Gaudens, H. *The Reminiscences of Augustus Saint-Gaudens*. New York: Century, 1913.

Strong, D.E. *The Classical World*. New York: McGraw-Hill, 1965.

Sutherland, C.H.V. *Art in Coinage: The Aesthetics of Money From Greece to the Present Day*. New York: Philosophical Library, 1956.

Taxay, D. "Augustus Saint-Gaudens and the United States Mint." *Coins: The Magazine of Coin Collecting* 16, no. 2 (1969).

Catalogs of Coins and Medals

UNITED STATES

Catalogue of the International Exhibition of Contemporary Medals. New York: American Numismatic Society, 1911.

Judd, J.H. *United States Pattern Coins: Experimental and Trial Pieces*. 9th ed. Edited by Q. David Bowers. Atlanta: Whitman Publishing, 2005.

Noe, S.P. *The Medallic Work of A.A. Weinman*. New York: American Numismatic Society, 1921.

Vlack, R.A. *Early American Coins: A Comprehensive Listing With Valuations of Early American Coins and Tokens Used in the American Colonies and Early America, Prior to the Establishment of the United States Mint Issue of 1793, Including the Washington Issues up to 1796*. 2nd. ed. Johnson City, NY: Windsor Research, 1965.

Yeoman, R.S. *A Guide Book of United States Coins*. 61st ed. Edited by K. Bressett. Atlanta: Whitman Publishing, 2007.

The U.S. Mint in Philadelphia and the private Franklin Mint in Franklin Center, Pennsylvania, have both produced illustrated catalogs of their commercial medals. These lists were supplemented annually with new issues for a number of years.

EUROPEAN

Carson, R.A.G. *Coins of the World.* New York: Harper, 1962.

Hill, G.F. *A Corpus of Italian Medals of the Renaissance Before Cellini.* London: British Museum, 1930.

Krause, C.L., C. Mishler, and staff. *Standard Catalog of World Coins.* 4 vols. Iola, WI: Krause Publications, numerous editions.

Pollard, G. *Renaissance Medals From the Samuel H. Kress Collection at the National Gallery of Art. Based on the Catalogue of Renaissance Medals in the Gustave Dreyfus Collection by G.F. Hill.* Rev. ed. London: Phaidon, 1967.

Yeoman, R.S. *A Catalogue of Modern World Coins.* 8th ed. Racine, WI: Western, 1968.

———. *Current Coins of the World.* 2nd ed. Racine, WI: Western, 1968.

Index

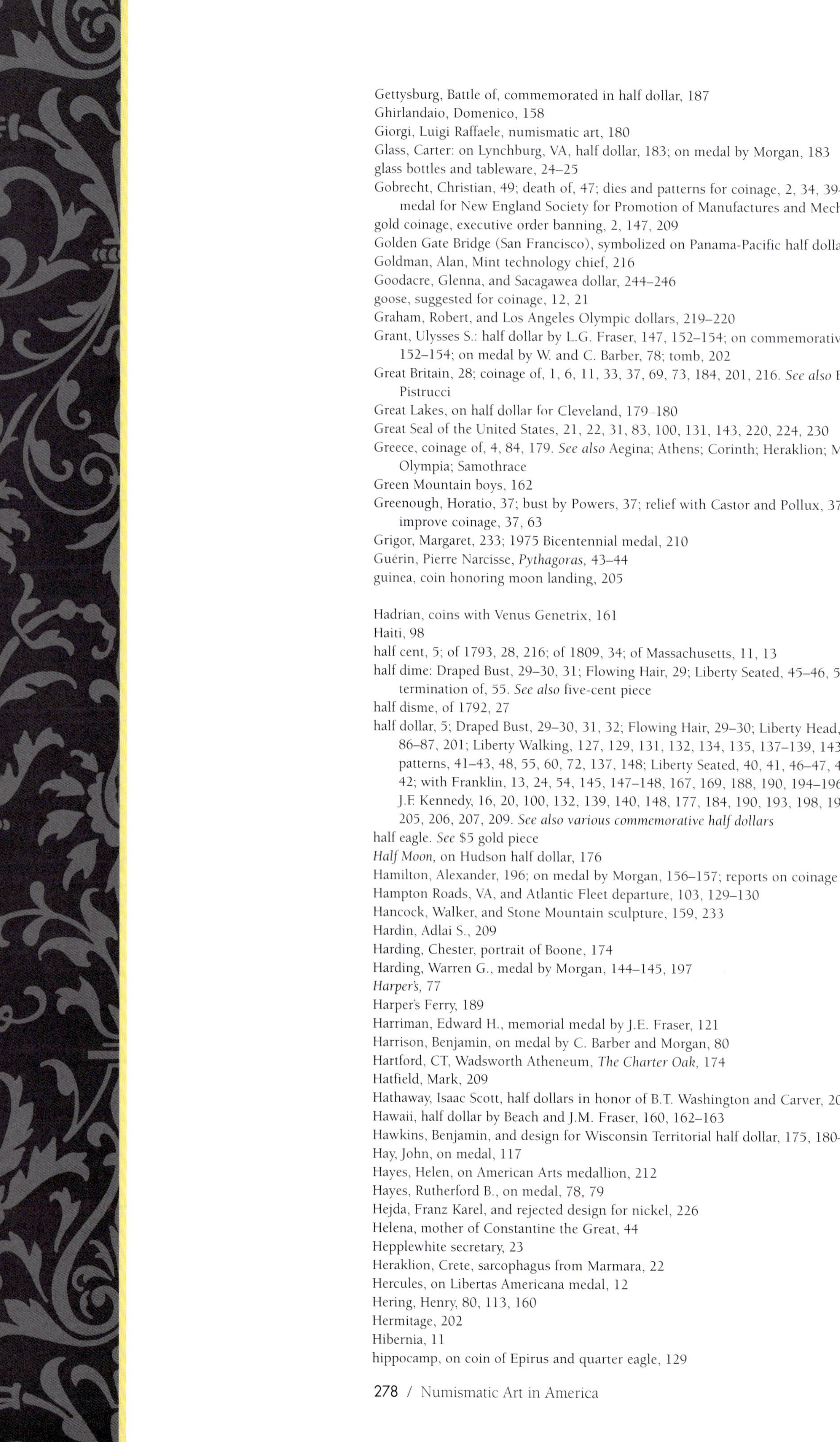

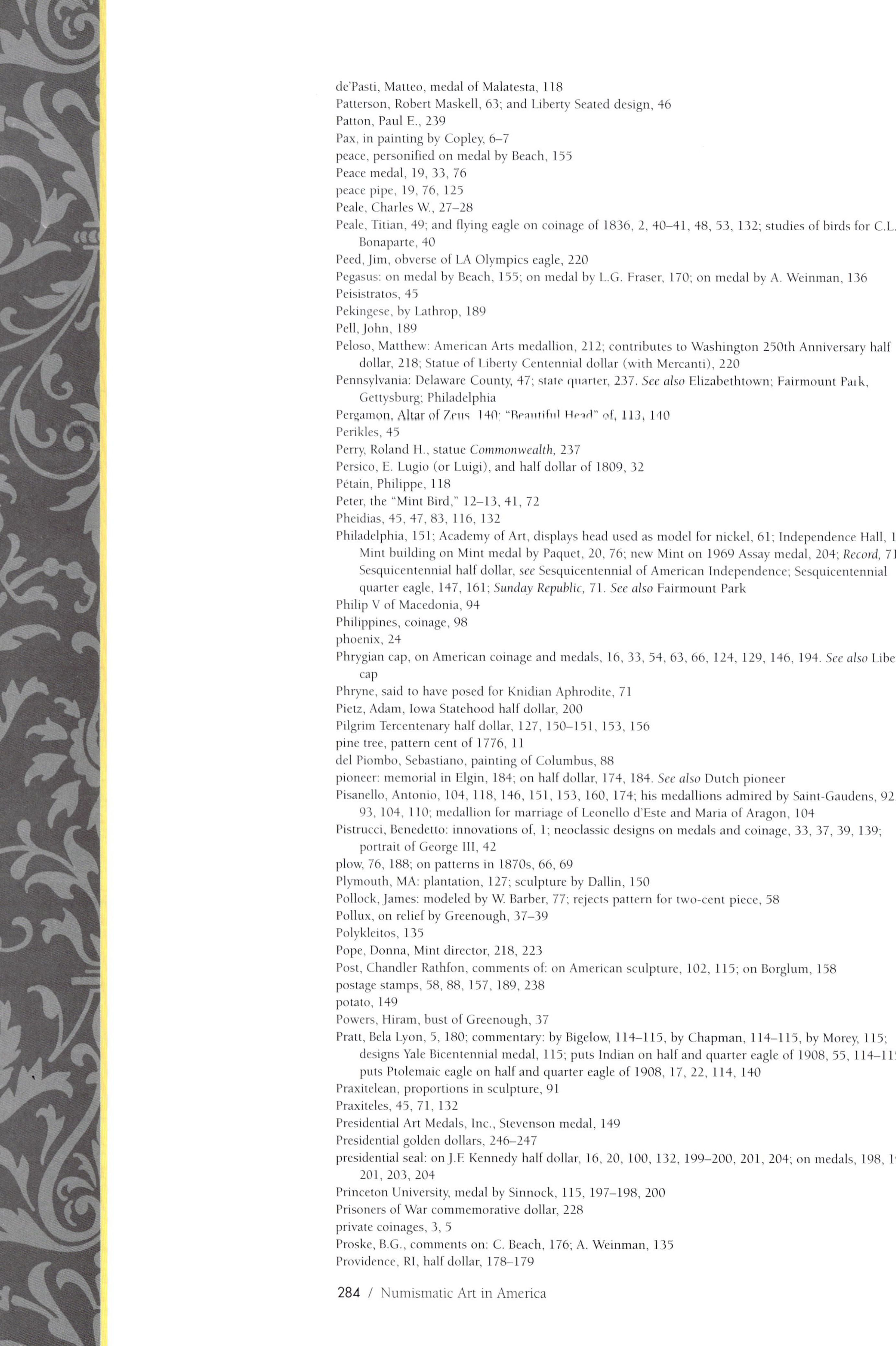

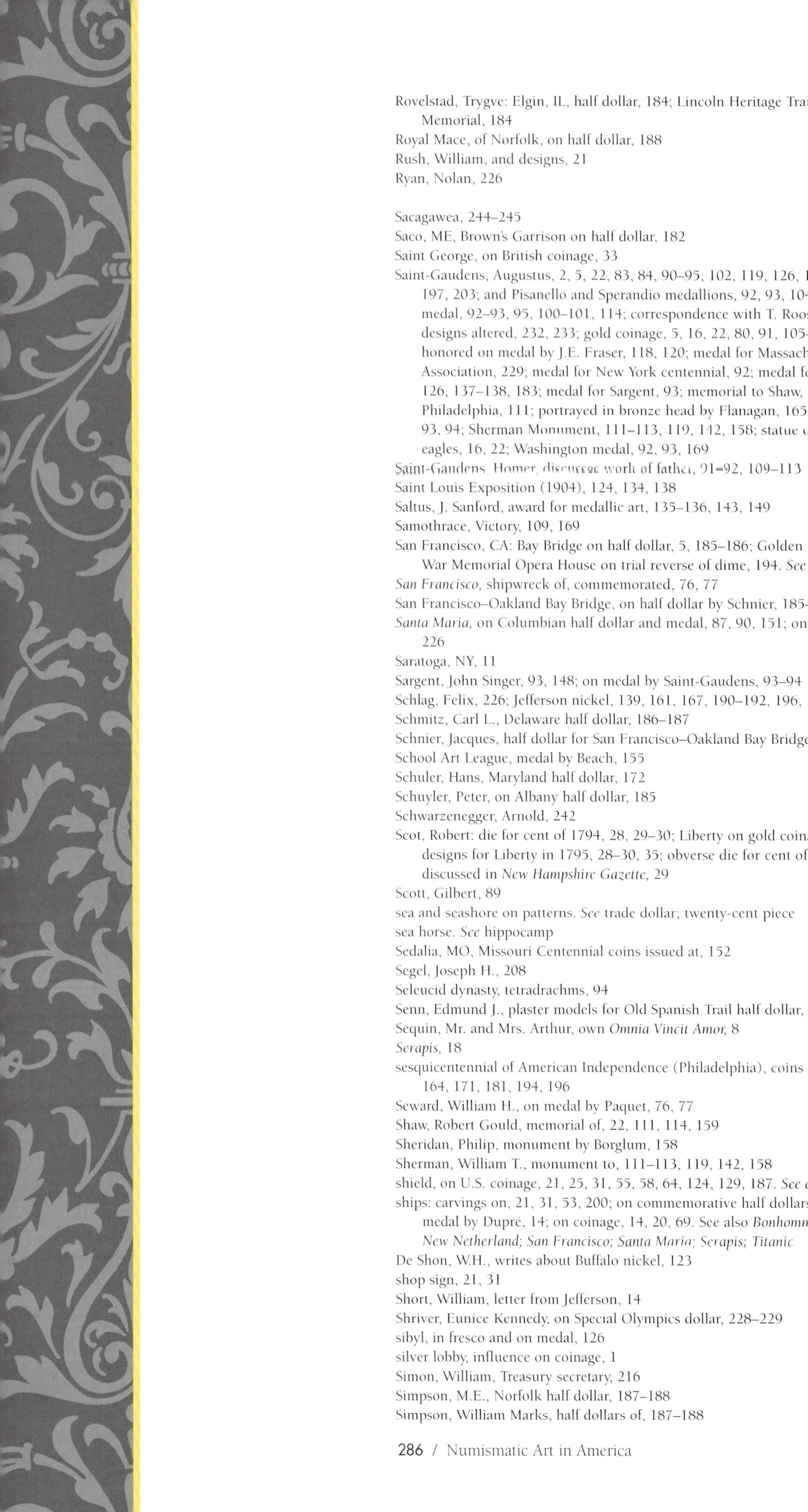

EID·MAR

The Expert's Guide *to* COLLECTING & INVESTING IN RARE COINS

Coin collecting—the "Hobby of Kings"—pays rich dividends in fun and enjoyment. But it can also pay the old-fashioned way: with a huge return on your investment. Now you can learn how to be a smart collector and investor, straight from the expert: award-winning author and numismatist Q. David Bowers.

With hands-on advice, real-life examples, and entertaining storytelling, the "dean of American numismatics" shares 50 years of experience buying and selling rare coins, tokens, medals, and paper money.

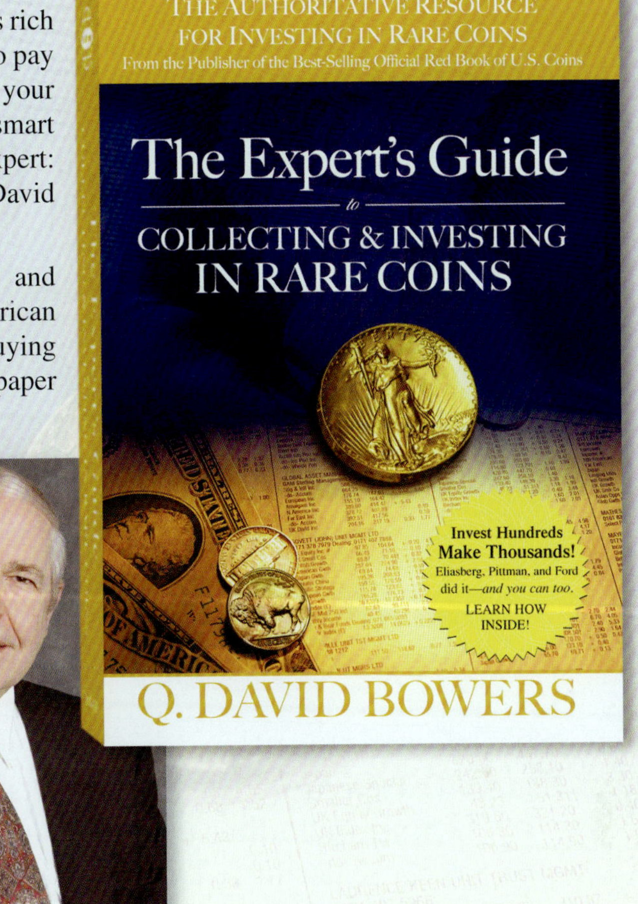

Want to know how to evaluate a coin's potential? Use the four-step process in chapter 2. What's the best way to predict the rare-coin market? It doesn't take a crystal ball; find out in chapter 13. To avoid getting burned in online auctions, read chapter 15. And if you want to be a smart seller, you can learn the ropes in chapter 34. All of these expert secrets, and more, are waiting inside. . . .

"[Bowers brings] proper balance to the interplay of collecting and investing in our hobby community."

—Clifford Mishler, numismatic author and researcher

"Are there really 'secrets' to successful coin buying? You bet! And Dave Bowers reveals them here. His style is entertaining, informative, and motivating. . . ."

—Kenneth Bressett, editor of the *Guide Book of United States Coins*

"If there's a single person who could write this book, it's Dave Bowers."

—Bill Fivaz, coauthor of *The Cherrypickers' Guide to Rare Die Varieties*

www.whitmanbooks.com